T0361116

ROUTLEDGE LIBRARY EDITIONS:
BANKING & FINANCE

DOMESTIC AND MULTINATIONAL BANKING

DOMESTIC AND MULTINATIONAL BANKING

BANKING

The Effects of Monetary Policy

RAE WESTON

Volume 33

Routledge
Taylor & Francis Group

LONDON AND NEW YORK

First published in 1980

This edition first published in 2012
by Routledge
2 Park Square, Milton Park, Abingdon, Oxon, OX14 4RN

Simultaneously published in the USA and Canada
by Routledge
711 Third Avenue, New York, NY 10017

Routledge is an imprint of the Taylor & Francis Group, an informa business

British Library Cataloguing in Publication Data
A catalogue record for this book is available from the British Library

ISBN: 978-0-415-52086-7 (Set)
eISBN: 978-0-203-10819-2 (Set)
ISBN: 978-0-415-53853-4 (Volume 33)
eISBN: 978-0-203-10919-9 (Volume 33)

Publisher's Note
The publisher has gone to great lengths to ensure the quality of this reprint but
points out that some imperfections in the original copies may be apparent.

Disclaimer
The publisher has made every effort to trace copyright holders and would
welcome correspondence from those they have been unable to trace.

Printed and bound by CPI Group (UK) Ltd, Croydon, CR0 4YY

Domestic and Multinational Banking

The Effects of Monetary Policy

RAE WESTON

CROOM HELM LIMITED

© 1980 Rae Weston
Croom Helm Ltd, 2-10 St John's Road, London SW11

British Library Cataloguing in Publication Data

Jacket photograph of *The Chase Manhattan Bank,
New York* by Arthur Lavine. Courtesy of The Chase
Manhattan Bank, London

Weston, Rae
    Domestic and multinational banking.
    1. Banks and banking
    I. Title
    332.1   HG1776

    ISBN 0-85664-710-1

Reproduced from copy supplied
printed and bound in Great Britain
by Billing and Sons Limited
Guildford, London, Oxford, Worcester

CONTENTS

To the real world, which is
able to operate without the
assumption of perfect knowledge.

PREFACE

> 'The writer works alone, producing only clusters of words, surely the most whimsical contribution of all to the gross national product.' (Caskie Stinnett, 'Room with a View', *Down East*, June 1978, p.2.)

This writer has not worked quite alone. The model developed in Part 1 and extended in Part 3 is that first provided in a paper presented to the Sixth Conference of Economists, Hobart, Australia in May 1977 entitled 'A Theory of the Banking Firm and the Effects of Regulatory Constraints'. The co-author of that paper, Sheila M. Bonnell, of course should be regarded as co-author of the model, without being held responsible for any inadequacies that remain. Our experience in the production of the model confirms the view that in the case of four-sector diagrams, two sets of eyes are better than one. It is the present author's extreme regret that time and other intervening circumstances have prevented this book from having the same authorship as the paper.

The justification for the 'clusters of words' that follow is primarily that no book yet published begins with the case of a completely unregulated commercial bank and follows the progression of banking through to the multinational banking stage. It is hoped that this contribution will begin to fill that gap. The mystique of banking is such that words in common parlance in banking business like 'merchant banks', 'roll-over credit', 'Eurodollar' and even 'multinational' are the subject of quite imperfect knowledge in the community.

Equally there is a rather nationalistic tendency to regard a national banking system's changing methods of control over the past decade as a national rather than as an international feature. In part this result is due to the tendency within both the UK and the USA to discuss their own domestic banking structures alone in the process of explaining banking operations.

It is hoped to remedy that bias as far as possible within the confines of this book by using a comparatively under-specified model of a bank which is able to be used to analyse the regulatory structures of a wide range of economies and is not dependent on any particular institutional framework for its validity. We further restrict our analysis to commercial banks, the original form of banking in most economies, as well as the base of most of the movement into multinational banking. In the theoretical analysis we explore the operations of an individual or typical bank and even in the empirical parts we are primarily concerned with the influences and factors that relate to a single bank.

More specifically it is intended that this contribution analyse the nature of banking; demonstrate how banking might operate without regulatory constraints; survey the patterns of regulatory constraint in a wide range of economies; analyse the effects of these various forms of constraint on the operation of a previously unregulated bank; examine the move to multinational banking; explore the nature of multinational banking and its particular risks; provide a diagrammatic illustration of certain of the risks of multinational operations; and examine some of the recent proposals to regulate multinational banking.

It is argued, on the basis of this analysis, that while quantitative regulations have the most deleterious effect on purely domestic banks, regulations which affect price will be more critical in the case of multinational banking operations and may have quite disastrous results if imposed without this difference being realised.

Except in the last Part, our concern lies with what might be termed discretionary banking regulation, that is regulations varied as part of monetary policy, rather than with prudential regulation.

INTRODUCTION

With very few exceptions, the textbooks and literature on banking are framed primarily within the context of a particular institutional framework, usually that of the USA or the UK. Those books on comparative banking either deal with central banks or make purely institutional comparisons of national banking systems. There are of course books on the new and fascinating genre, the Eurobank, and some on the multinational banks.

It is the purpose of the present contribution to take a modern view of domestic banking, the effects of regulation on banks, the move to multinational banking and the recent moves to regulate banking operations over a number of countries. At the very beginning we look at the problem of identifying the nature of banking, which is variously regarded as a production process and as an investment portfolio in recent discussions. From an analysis of banking operations it is possible to demonstrate that a more reasonable interpretation of banking, capable of explaining its main operations convincingly, is to analyse banking as a retailing of services.

Since banking has within most of our lifetimes consistently been the subject of regulation, it is conceivable that a number of banking practices may have arisen in response to regulation and would not exist if banking was not regulated. Because of this problem, the most efficient approach to analysing the effects of regulation on the operations of an individual bank is to begin by providing a model of a bank operating in an unregulated environment and to introduce subsequently into that, the various regulatory constraints. Accordingly in Part 1, following a discussion of the nature of banking, a model of a bank in an unregulated environment is introduced. The basis for this model is Fischer Black's world of uncontrolled banking which we amend to provide a model appropriate for our purposes.

The model, which is developed in the latter chapters of Part 1, is summarised in a four-sector diagram which illustrates the critical interdependencies of bank decisions. It is intended that this diagram provide a simplified description of the operations of an individual bank, from which, later in the book, it will be possible to investigate the effects of various types of regulation.

In Part 2, following a brief outline of the main regulatory constraints on banking, banking regulation in nineteen countries is discussed. It is the intention of these chapters to provide, for each of these countries, an outline of the institutional framework within which banks operate, a description of the instruments of regulation used and a discussion of the recent experience of controls (in the seventies in all cases, and in some countries from the date of the last major change in banking regulation in the sixties), and a brief commentary on the effects of recent changes on the operation of individual banks.

There is, of course, much information available about bank regulation in the USA and UK and increasing information about European countries but little on the wide spectrum of systems of banking regulation that exist elsewhere. From this survey it is possible to identify several combinations of constraints which are used depending on the market conditions of particular economies. For example, in a number of countries the influence of external flows of capital and trade is so strong that the major aim of regulation in recent years has been to neutralise these flows, a task complicated in a number of cases by the absence of a money market.

Although it is often said that the main central banking functions derive from that original central bank, the Bank of England, there is no consistent pattern along which domestic banking regulation in these nineteen countries may be seen to be moving in the present decade. For example, while a number of European countries, unimpressed with the efficiency of indirect controls, have returned recently to more direct controls, Australia has moved towards the indirect type of controls and particularly to open market operations. Credit ceilings have proved quite efficient for some small open economies and yet incapable of controlling banking activity in other open economies. West Germany has all but eliminated the ability of its banks to manage their liquidity in the same period as New Zealand has moved from a quite restrictive system of regulation to allowing its banking system wide scope in its liquidity management.

From Part 2 we are able to identify the main individual types of banking regulations used and a number of combinations of controls which have been frequently used, and in Part 3 attention is turned to introducing these regulations to our original model of the unregulated bank. This facilitates the comparisons of the operations of a regulated and an unregulated bank and of the various types and combinations of regulations.

Analysis of the effects of the commonly used regulatory constraints provides some indication of the strategies which banks might employ in reaction to these restrictions. The possibility of price competition between the banks which the unregulated model suggests is not strong, is shown to be further reduced by the impact of regulation, while at the same time the case for non-price competition and product augmentation is strengthened. The tendency of banking towards oligopoly is reinforced, therefore, by regulation. It is possible to find in regulation and its impact a rationale for domestic banks to move into the multinational sphere of operations because of the differing nature of these operations.

In Part 4 the move to multinational banking is examined in more detail. Consortium banks and their growth are analysed and the particular problems of multinational banking in the present decade are discussed. Because the operations of multinational banks differ in many respects from those of purely domestic banks, a detailed examination is made of roll-over credits and interest rate risk, exchange rate risk, information flows and the management problems of multinational banks. A very elementary model of these operations is provided in order to facilitate comparisons with the unregulated and regulated models of banking, and the essential differences which become apparent from these comparisons are analysed.

Part 5 directs attention to the currently controversial question — what kind of regulation or supervision is appropriate for multinational banking operations? — and to the effects of various kinds of regulation on multinational operations and on the operations of the banking firm as a whole. The types of regulation proposed are examined and their various impacts on the model of multinational banking operations analysed. Examination of the costs and risks of these proposed regulations suggests that some of the same effects as result from the regulation of domestic banks may also occur here.

If banks are, as this study suggests, individual enterprises concerned with providing services in order to generate profits and ensure their own long-run survival, care needs to be taken in using regulatory constraints for wider macroeconomic motives, or less desirable results may be produced at this microeconomic level of individual bank operations.

Milton Friedman and the late Harry Johnson have applied standard microeconomic analysis to banking and concluded that, normatively, although minimal official regulation is justified it should be applied so as to maximise competition in banking.

It is argued here that those regulations which affect the quantity of deposits and/or loans may be used on multinational banks with much the same result as on domestic banks, that is, they may limit the extent to which these banks are able to satisfy demand and permit other non-bank institutions to satisfy that demand. On the other hand, the implementation of controls affecting the cost and pricing of loans may be seen to have very serious consequences for the banks and threaten the now only occasionally precarious stability of the multinational banking system.

Part 1

THE NATURE OF BANKING

1 THE ORIGINS OF MODERN BANKING

'Many banking practices are a response to regulation and would not exist if banking were unregulated.' (Fischer Black, 'Bank Funds Management in an Efficient Market', *Journal of Financial Economics*, vol.2 (1975), p.324.)

The antecedents of modern banking appear to be the activities of goldsmiths in seventeenth-century England who, of necessity requiring strongrooms to hold the materials of their trade, found that they were able to rent out the excess space for the safekeeping of money and other valuables. From the provision of this facility there developed the practice of customers depositing money in return for a receipt or certificate of deposit, and gradually not requiring the identical coin they had left but merely coin of equal value. In practical terms the goldsmiths assumed ownership of the coin on deposit and employed it, but they always held sufficient to convert certificates of deposit on demand. From this beginning of deposit-taking, the goldsmiths next began the practice of chequing when they enabled a merchant who wished to pay another merchant to write an order to his goldsmith asking for the transfer of money from his account to that of his creditor without having his deposit certificate converted into coin.

These early embryo commercial banks commenced the issue of notes in small denominations instead of issuing one certificate of deposit to cover a customer's deposit and as these notes became generally acceptable for payment the goldsmiths made them payable to bearer. After their notes began to circulate as a medium of exchange it became possible for goldsmiths to make loans by using the notes not in return for a deposit of coin but for a promissory note given to the goldsmith by the borrower. Provided that not all notes were returned simultaneously for conversion into coin, notes could be issued for a greater value than the goldsmiths held in coin. In most circumstances the goldsmiths were able to predict with considerable accuracy the amounts of coin that were likely to be redeemed from them. However, when depositors as a whole decided to convert their paper money into coin, as happened for example when news of the destruction of the British fleet at Chatham reached the country in 1667, the goldsmiths were unable to satisfy the demand and became bankrupt.

Not only goldsmiths but also merchants issued notes only fractionally secured by holdings of coin, and in England, France and Sweden governments began to grant charters incorporating companies to accept deposits, transfer money and issue notes only fractionally secured by reserves. Probably the first modern bank was the Bank of Sweden begun by John Palmstruck in 1656 which, in spite of early difficulties with fractional reserve banking, including at least one occasion when payment on its notes was suspended, survives to the present day and operates as Sweden's central bank. The Bank of England, also eventually a central bank, was established in 1694 by William Patterson when a charter was granted on condition that £1.2 million was advanced to the government at 8 per cent interest to provide for the financing of the wars with France. The advance was made from the sale of shares in the Bank, but since its capital equalled its loan to the government the Bank began with a cash shortage which by 1696 had forced it to suspend conversion of its notes.

Mints notes that it was not until the 1770s in England and the 1820s in America that it was suggested that bank advances ought to be restricted to short-term commercial purposes because if only real bills were discounted it was argued that the growth in bank money would be in proportion to the needs of trade.[1] While this 'real bills doctrine' has shown considerable durability and in a number of countries the preponderance of bank advances are still short-term in nature, banking in the modern world has reached the much wider scale of operations discussed later.

The nature of central banking was by no means clearly defined until early in the present century, although the Bank of England had assumed what were later agreed to be the main functions of central banking during the nineteenth century. From its original charter the Bank of England retained its right to issue notes and in 1833 legislation provided that only its notes were legal tender. The growth of joint-stock banking increased the ambit of the Bank of England's influence as it acted as the custodian of private banks' cash reserves and this position was further enforced in 1854 when it was agreed that differences between the other banks of clearing would be settled by transfers between their accounts at the Bank.

Hawtrey[2] alleges that the Bank of England only grudgingly assumed the responsibilities of lender of last resort and it was not until the third of the nineteenth-century financial crises, that of 1866, that the Bank 'accepted the responsibility of unstinted lending'[3] and in fact it was only in Walter Bagehot's publication, *Lombard Street*,[4] in 1873 that the expression 'lender of last resort' was first used. Even Bagehot, in recognising the accomplished fact of the Bank's role as lender of last resort, commented that he would have preferred this last resort responsibility to have been spread among a number of equally sized leading banks.

Once accepted as a responsibility by the Bank of England, the lender of last resort function came to be taken as a role of central banks to the extent that the US Federal Reserve Banks automatically assumed this responsibility on their establishment. The discount rate, often referred to as the Bank rate, remained a primary instrument of control into the present century; however, on a number of occasions when liquidity was high, the Bank of England found it very difficult to implement effective discount rate changes. On such occasions the Bank withdrew funds from the discount market by selling Consols (Consolidated Government stock) for cash and buying them back for the period of monthly settlement that was unexpired. Sayers[5] describes the procedures for reducing the available money supply as piecemeal rather than systematic and says that the sheer diversity of techniques employed suggested that the Bank was not satisfied with any of them.

As liquidity became an increasing characteristic of the system, the Bank of England began to use open market operations to facilitate the effectiveness of discount rate policy and the Federal Reserve System, on its establishment in 1913, was authorised to use open-market operations as a supplement to discount rate policy.

Variable reserve requirements appear to have been first used in the United States which in 1933 legislated to provide that commercial banks should maintain minimum credit balances of fixed percentages of their demand and time deposits, and in 1935 legislated to give the Federal Reserve power to vary these reserve requirements from time to time, within limits above the normal minimum reserve ratios. Very many countries now use variable reserve requirements as a major instrument of regulation of banks.

Although the rationing of central bank credit was one of the earliest control instruments used by the Bank of England even in the eighteenth century, its consistent use was a contradiction of the Bank's gradually accepted role as lender of last resort and, accordingly, only in difficult situations was rationing used, on occasions together with direct quantitative control of bank credit. This latter technique has become the more general regulatory instrument although its use is recognised as likely to result in distortions of the structure and efficiency of the banking system if applied as a long-run instrument.

It is difficult to date the commencement of selective credit controls, primarily because these may have been accomplished at times by moral suasion which has been very informally used over the whole history of the Bank of England as a method of influencing the banks. Truptil[6] quotes from the *Financial News* a comment which describes the efficiency of moral suasion as used by the Bank of England: 'A city which for six months on end can obey a sanctionless ordinance to refrain from issuing foreign loans . . . is . . . an organism knit together by bonds of a finer fibre than the common desire to make money' (p.197).

The efficacy of moral suasion, already weakened by proliferation of institutions to control, may be regarded as almost drowned out in the seventies by the huge liquidity flows characteristic of this period. Many central banks, hitherto able to rely on moral suasion without any legislative coercion, found that the directions given were either ignored or evaded.

As the range of controls used by central banks has widened so has the range of operations of the commercial banks. Christians[7] describes the 'continental European-style universal bank' as providing these services: accepting deposits of all sizes for the most varied terms; granting short, medium and long term credits to business and the private sector; buying and selling securities; handling payment transactions; financing imports and exports; and dealing in foreign exchange, notes and coin. Banks in many countries, while not necessarily describing themselves as universal banks, nevertheless either offer this range of services or are moving in that direction.

Notes

1. Lloyd W. Mints, *A History of Banking Theory in Great Britain* (University of Chicago Press, 1945).

2. R.G. Hawtrey, *Art of Central Banking* (Cassell, London, 1932).

3. Ibid.

4. Walter Bagehot, *Lombard Street*, 14th edn (John Murray, London, 1915).

5. R.S. Sayers, *Modern Banking*, 5th edn (Oxford University Press, 1960).

6. R.J. Truptil, *British Banks and the London Money Market* (Jonathan Cape, London, 1976).

7. Dr F.W. Christians, 'Why the Universal Bank Works', *The Banker* (October 1977).

Further Reading

Giuseppi, John, *The Bank of England: A History from Its Foundations in 1694*

(Evans Bros, London, 1966)

Nevin, Edward and E.W. Davis, *The London Clearing Banks* (Elek Books, London, 1970)

2 THE ESSENCE OF BANKING

> 'It is the conglomeration of all the various services and functions that sets the commercial bank off from other financial institutions. Each then is an integral part of the whole, almost every one of which is dependent upon and would not exist but for the other.' (J. Clary in *US.* v. *The Philadelphia National Bank and Girard Trust Corn Exchange*, 201 F. Supp. 348 (1962) 363.)

The many analyses of banking at a microeconomic level that concentrate on the allocation of a bank's funds between competing stocks of assets, regard a bank not as a firm but as a rational investor operating in an environment of uncertainty or as Klein[1] puts the point 'the neoclassical analysis of the firm has yielded to portfolio theory' (p.205). Unfortunately this view appears to do much less than justice to the art of banking. The comment of the celebrated European banker, the late Louis Camu,[2] that 'current usage tends to confuse the image of the banker with that of the financier' appears a quite appropriate description of the debate about banks as firms or investors (p.67).

Camu's definition of the financier accords with that of the rational investor who manages a portfolio of mainly financial assets and may be contrasted with his definition of the banker who is 'primarily a large retailer'. While the essence of the rational investor's activities are those of the portfolio manager who seeks to restrict the range of activities on which there is risk so that the maximum return consistent with the preferred level of risk is obtained, the essence of banking is rather that of the firm which has potential customers of many sizes, all of whom it wishes to serve. Of course, a basic tenet of the rational investor is broken consistently by bankers as their diversification normally exceeds the 'optimal' limits to which the former would restrict his investments.

'The business of lending in tiny amounts', as Camu describes retail banking, is an art rather than a science which depends on dealing with customers and not only with their actual or intended financial resources. For example, it is in the interests of the banker to maintain close contact with those customers who have access to alternative sources of credit and those who have large, long-held and stable deposit balances, and to allow these customers access to credit as continuously over time as possible. This is not necessarily consistent with either minimising risk or generating maximal returns, but it is highly consistent with the basic principles of banking as a retail business.

It would be unexpected if the traditional portfolio paradigm was a reasonable approximation of bank behaviour, given the typical portfolio theory assumptions that a firm has an unlimited and riskless ability to borrow and that there are perfect financial markets. Of course in a perfect market without the transactions and information costs that only occur in imperfect markets, there would be no role for financial intermediaries. Further, portfolio theory classifies earnings and other balance sheet entries as stocks, but as Boris Pesek[3] has noted 'bank money is constantly sliding into an abyss of non-existence' and is not comparable to a stock 'but rather to a river, constantly renewed in the mountains and constantly disappearing down the valley, with the banker controlling the sluice' (pp.360-1).

The necessity for alternative deployments of bank funds to have quantifiable or at least measurable returns which is a basic requirement of portfolio theory is difficult in the case of bank branching. Although it may be reasonable to argue that depositors are responsive to the presence of nearby bank branches in the sense that they are prepared to hold larger deposits in a bank conveniently located to them, it is much more difficult to find a sufficiently high and reliable return from branching to justify the allocation of funds to branching in preference to investment in securities. Nevertheless, it may be argued that without regulation branching may not be regarded as a competitive ploy, and even with regulation restricting other forms of competition, a bank is more likely to find it costly than rewarding to have its deposits spread over a large number of branches. It is interesting that the provision of branches is also difficult to place within the context of the theory of the bank as a producer (as will be seen below), but that it is quite explicable within the theory of the bank as a retailer.

Most telling of the omissions that portfolio theory has as an explanation of the behaviour of banks are those noted most recently in a paper by Sealey and Lindley;[4] the total lack of production and cost constraints and, as a result, the omission of the impact of these constraints on the operations of the bank. In response to these inadequacies, a number of studies have appeared which attempt to describe the operations of a bank in terms of the concepts of the theory of the firm. In particular those studies which have recently pursued this path have concentrated on using the theory of production to develop a theory of the banking firm as a profit-maximising producer.

For example, one view of banking used in the literature is as a 'producer' of specialised financial commodities[5] which are created, in the words of Benston and Smith,[6] 'whenever an intermediary finds that it can sell them for prices which are expected to cover all costs of their production' (p.215). Within this approach, which appears to regard a bank as a form of manufacturer, there is a considerable divergence of opinion. MacKara[7] describes deposits as an input to banks and loans and investments as an output, while Pesek[8] and Towey[9] argue that banks produce money by employing loans as inputs, and Melitz and Pardue[10] prefer the idea that deposits are inputs from which credit is produced. Most recent of the contributions to this approach is that of Sealey and Lindley[11] who describe the production process as a 'multistage production process involving intermediate outputs, where loanable funds, borrowed from depositors and serviced by the firm with the use of capital, labor and material inputs, are used in the production of earning assets' (p.1254).

Ragnar Frisch[12] distinguishes between the technical process of production — which is a process of transformation, directed by human beings, by which outputs are generated by the transformation of inputs which cease to exist in their original form — and production in the economic sense. The latter Frisch defines as 'the attempt to create a product which is *more highly valued* than the original input elements' (p.8) in terms of market prices.

Applied to the operations of banks, however, production in the economic sense does not seem to be particularly applicable. Consumers or borrowers take loans from banks rather than from the ultimate source of the funds, the original lender, because it is cheaper for them to do so. That is, banks allow borrowers access to funds in a divisibility that is convenient to them and without the borrowers undertaking the cost of search for an ultimate lender and without the ultimate lenders facing the risk of loss or bankruptcy. The provision of loans by banks is cheaper than those provided without intermediation because banks possess a comparative advantage over those alternative sources in processing the necessary documents, in acquiring information about the credit-worthiness of borrowers, in the search for sources of funds and in monitoring the progress of the loans.

Further, it may reasonably be argued that a cheque account does not have the essential characteristics of a product, but is rather a service in which a bank provides storage and transfers of funds for its customers. Sealey and Lindley[13] argue that the technical production in which banks are involved, that is, the transformation process in which inputs lose their identity and other goods or services are generated, involves acquiring funds from the surplus spending units and lending them to deficit spending units. Demand deposits do not fit very easily into this approach and neither do investment advisory services or safe deposit services, since no transformation is really involved in these cases.

It may of course be said that credit is created or produced by banks and that the theory of production ought to be applicable to this aspect at least; however, an individual bank is unable to create credit and perhaps more reasonably ought to be regarded as a distributor of funds and a provider of certain ancillary services.

Although it is possible that further advances in the theory of production and in portfolio theory may provide tools more suitable for the analysis of banking operations than the current states of either theory, for present purposes a more consistent interpretation of the variety of banking services may be provided if we regard the banker as a retailer of services. It is to this interpretation that we turn in the next chapter.

Notes

1. Michael A. Klein, 'A Theory of the Banking Firm', *Journal of Money, Credit and Banking*, vol. 3, no. 2, part 1 (1971).
2. Louis Camu, 'The Daily Life of a Banker', *The Banker* (April 1977).
3. Boris Pesek, 'Banks' Supply Function and the Equilibrium Quantity of Money', *Canadian Journal of Economics* (August 1970).
4. C.W. Sealey Jun. and James T. Lindley, 'Inputs, Outputs, and a Theory of Production and Cost at Depository Financial Institutions', *Journal of Finance*, vol. 32, no. 4 (September 1977).
5. W.F. MacKara, 'What Do Banks Produce?', Federal Reserve Bank of Atlanta *Monthly Review* (May 1975); Pesek, 'Banks' Supply Function'; Richard E. Towey 'Money Creation and the Theory of the Banking Firm', *Journal of Finance*, vol. 29, no. 1 (March 1974).
6. G. Benston and Clifford W. Smith Jun., 'A Transactions Cost Approach to the Theory of Financial Intermediation', *Journal of Finance*, vol. 31, no. 2 (1976).
7. MacKara, 'What Do Banks Produce?'
8. Pesek, 'Banks' Supply Function'.
9. Towey, 'Money Creation'.
10. J. Melitz and Morris Pardue, 'The Demand and Supply of Commercial Banks' Loans', *Journal of Money, Credit and Banking*, vol. 5, no. 2 (May 1973).
11. Sealey and Lindley, 'Inputs, Outputs, and a Theory of Production'.
12. R. Frisch, *Theory of Production* (Rand, McNally and Co., Chicago, 1965).
13. Sealey and Lindley, 'Inputs, Outputs, and a Theory of Production'.

Further Reading

Baltensperger, Ernst and Hellmuth Milde, 'Predictability of Reserve Demand, Information Costs and Portfolio Behaviour of Commercial Banks', *Journal of Finance*, vol. 31, no. 3 (1976).

3 THE BANKER AS A RETAILER OF SERVICES

'The Banker, therefore, is primarily a large retailer. His bank
is a great emporium of credit deals and highly diversified
information.' (Louis Camu, 'The Daily Life of a Banker',
The Banker, April 1977, p.70.)

The advantage of analysing banking operations within the format of the
theory of the retail firm rather than of the manufacturing firm or by
means of portfolio theory is that a number of important banking
activities which are only justified uneasily, if at all, by the alternative
theories, are readily explicable on this basis. As will be shown below,
the place of demand deposits in banking operations is the neatest
example. We begin by examining the nature of retailing and then
analyse banking operations within this framework.

Retailing is a sub-set of the marketing sector of the economy. It is
the function of the specialised institutions within this sector to add
economic value to the products or services they handle by the creation
of time, space and possession utility. Retailing is the sale or distribution
of goods and services to final consumers. The description 'final consumers' implies that they do not buy for resale or further manufacture,
but for the satisfaction in use which the products or services will give
them. Time utility is that increment of economic value that is achieved
by storing or holding a commodity until it is most marketable, while
space utility is economic value created by the distribution of goods and
services at places convenient to consumers, and possession utility may
be described as the value created through the provision of information
to the potential purchaser of the good or service about the attributes
and utility of that good or service.

McNair[1] has described the progressive development of distributive
enterprises as involving three stages: in the first stage, their success is
achieved by offering lower prices; in the second stage they improve the
quality of the merchandise they carry; while in the third stage, during
which increasing costs, a rising proportion of fixed capital to total
investment and a decline in the rate of return on capital often occur,
they compete by offering services.

'Retail' in French means to cut again or to sell again in different
quantities to that bought. Gist[2] describes the economic base of retailing
as composed of five elements. The first element is specialisation and

division of labour. Within the marketing sector of the economy, retailing enterprises specialise in selling in detail to consumers, dividing up the market so that groups or communities of consumers are served by sufficient separate enterprises for at least a competitive profit to be earned by each of them. Second of the elements is spatial convenience, that is, a retailer supplies a given set of consumers with the goods or services that they require at places convenient to these consumers. Third, retailing as a form of distribution may correct what Alderson calls 'discrepancies' in distribution generated from economies in manufacturing. Specialisation in manufacturing tends to result in each manufacturer producing a large volume of a few varieties of his product, but these large amounts must be divided up by retailers who will need to display a variety of the product concerned in an attempt to satisfy the preferences of consumers and therefore they are likely to 'break bulk' or sell again in smaller quantities. Both the satisfaction of consumer preferences and breaking bulk are valuable economic functions, as they involve the provision of goods or services of the right kind in the right quantities for consumers.

The fourth element, the retailer's role as a source of information, suggests that consumers are information seekers who acquire from retailers advice on goods and services with which they are not familiar. Smith[3] (pp.16 and 19) suggests that the only way in which information is relevant here is as a demand by the consumer for a wide range of goods and services from which to choose 'including the provision of adequate data concerning items of which specimens are not immediately available' (p.19). As the final element Gist suggests that retailing creates value in offering services such as hours of opening, choice of stock and a variety of ancillary services to consumers.

Henry Smith in a classic study of retailing[4] concluded that 'taking all the facts into account it looks as if there is something queer about competition in the retail trade' (p.7) which may be explained by the application of the theory of monopolistic competition which is based upon the characteristic of retailing that at any moment a consumer wishing to make a retail purchase will not want or be able to find the goods and services at the lowest possible price and so his choice of retail outlet will be based on imperfect knowledge. Hood and Yamey[5] however, argue that the economics of retailing cannot satisfactorily be explained by 'an essentially static and long-run theory of monopolistic competition' (p.136). Changes in retail techniques and the continuous flow of new entrants will continuously unsettle the market in their view and make discussions of long-run equilibrium, in which supply is adjusted to demand and firms earn 'normal' profits, inappropriate. Hood and Yamey also argue that 'the use of an oversimplified theory of oligopoly is equally unrealistic', particularly to the extent that this implies tacit or formal arrangements to set prices.

It is sufficient for our purposes to allow that retailing is likely to be characterised, depending on which sub-group is being discussed, by imperfect competition. Because of the wide range of the sizes and types of operations described as 'retailing' and the restrictions under which some sub-groups operate, it seems quite inappropriate to be more specific about the precise form of competition. Further there is the problem of whether to analyse the retailer himself as the unit concerned or a particular range of the goods and services he provides as the unit, each of which is likely to yield different answers.

The theory of retailing which seems appropriate is that which regards all retailing as characterised by imperfect competition, and the particular sub-groups of retailing as characterised by their special features as monopolistically competitive, oligopolistic, duopolistic or even mono-polistic. For the particular area of retailing with which we are concerned, banking, in an unregulated state there is a tendency to oligopoly which is reinforced by the effects of regulation.

Next, it is necessary to consider the definition of services and the distinction between these and products. Victor Fuchs[6] writing in 1968 noted that Stigler's 1956 comment that 'There exists no authoritative consensus on either the boundaries or the classification of the service industries' could still not be challenged. In contrast, products are tangible goods, which can be invented, processed, manufactured, trans-ported, replicated and often mass produced. The process of production, in the technical sense, requires that certain raw materials or inputs enter into a process in which they cease to exist in their original form and from which output in the form of products is generated.

While products are things, services are not necessarily tangible and are often flows or concepts of value. Services can be developed experi-mentally but cannot be tested in laboratories as can most products and the service will often be independent of any of its tangible trappings. Services require people to render them and their provision is often associated with high fixed costs for staff, buildings and communications.

Shostack[7] demonstrates the distinction between products and services by comparing automobiles with airline travel. Automobiles are physically owned — tangible objects, the exact nature of which may be varied by the addition of other tangible objects in the form of options. Automobiles may be used to provide the service of transportation but are not, of themselves, a service. In contrast airline travel is in essence a service in which the most vital element is transport but which may attract a different clientele according to its flight schedule, the type of aircraft used and the pre-post and in-flight services provided.

Fuchs[8] (p.12) points to a further contrast, in that the consumer often plays an important role as a co-operating agent in the provision of services which does not occur in the production of goods. For example, Fuchs notes that productivity in banking will be affected by whether a bank officer or a customer fills out the deposit slip and, if the customer does so, on his knowledge, experience, honesty and motivation. In addition to being more customer-oriented, many service industries are more labour- than capital-intensive and may have more labour-embodied technical change than capital-embodied change. Services are therefore more consistently capable of being individually tailored to customers' needs than are the majority of goods.

It remains for us to consider the extent to which banking operations may be appropriately analysed within the framework of the theory of retailing. In many countries the bulk of bank deposits are made in the form of current or demand deposits. By the use of cheque accounts which are a characteristic service provided for demand deposits, consumers are able to make consumption decisions across both space and time. Demand deposits offer consumers a more convenient and, for that reason, cheaper means of effecting transactions than by the use of barter or currency. Other advantages which demand deposits provide for holders are their complete divisibility down to the minimum unit of currency and the ancillary provision, by means of cleared cheques and bank statements, of complete records after transactions. In terms of retailing, demand deposits allow the breaking of the bulk of the deposit into completely divisible units for the purchase of assets or the payment of debts at the option of the consumer. The deposit does not change its form, it continues as liquidity, it is merely now able to be more easily divided for the purpose of making payments. Because of their specialisation in the provision of demand deposit facilities banks are able to reduce transactions costs for these below the level of transaction costs which consumers would incur in using either barter or currency. Additionally the demand deposit has time utility since the consumer is able to vary his payments across time as well as across space. Consumers value the services provided by the demand deposit facility sufficiently highly that in a large number of countries not only need no interest be paid by a bank on these deposits but charges are levied on them.

Banks provide their demand deposit and other services to consumers (whether these are businesses or individuals) from a number of branches and agencies located at places spatially convenient to these consumers. Through these branches and agencies banks provide loan facilities to customers. It is comparatively risky and expensive for deficit and surplus spending units to transact directly with each other rather than through the intermediation of a bank. That is, banks by specialisation in the provision of loans are able to obtain economies in the gathering, checking and continuous monitoring of information about classes of borrowers, they can gain access to credit information collected by others and they are able to reduce significantly the costs of search which would be incurred by borrowers and lenders if they had to seek each other out directly. The types and amounts of loans, again a breaking bulk transaction, that a particular bank will offer depends both on the areas in which it has expertise and the clientele which it services. Clients will wish to have banking services available at their spatial convenience and banks will find it worthwhile to establish local branches to specialise in the provision of services, particularly since convenience of location rather than lowest price is the more consistent attraction for clients in an imperfectly informed position. Loans will be individually tailored to the borrower's circumstances which will include the bank's own experience in lending to borrowers of similar characteristics as well as information available about the individual and the collateral he may be able to provide.

In their specialisation over space banks may also specialise in particular clientele, that is, businesses or households. The other services provided by banks in addition to accepting deposits and making loans include the provision of financing services for foreign trade including dealing in foreign exchange and notes and coin, investment advice and facilities for safe deposit. These services are all able to increase the value of the banks to the consumer since once he deposits with them the marginal transportation and inconvenience cost for these will be zero to him. The more extensive the additional services provided, the less likely that a consumer will shift his business to another financial intermediary which provides less services.

The investment in securities by banks is capable of several interpretations that are consistent with the view of banking as a retail service. First, as the alternative means of holding the funds invested in securities may be in the form of reserves, these investments may be regarded as a least-cost means of holding liquidity as a potential inventory from which future loans may be provided. Second, if loans are regarded as a service provided to individuals and businesses for reward, investment in securities may be regarded as a service provided to equity markets and money markets for reward. Third, it may be considered that investment in securities is merely a specialisation in an area in which more complete information is available on which to assess risk and that this provides an investment of stable risk, although not of stable return, to complement investment in personal and business loans of stable return but less stable risk.

The holding of some part of reserves in the form of cash rather than of securities accords with the need to hold sufficient cash to accommodate the demands of customers and this amount may be minimised over time with greater experience of customer requirements.

From this interpretation of banking as the retailing of services it can be seen that the main activities of banks are readily explicable. It is further apparent that Camu's explanation of the nature of banking fits neatly into this interpretation. Viewing banking as a retailing of services does not, of course, move us away from analysing its operations by the use of the theory of the firm, it simply eschews the theory of production and portfolio theory as appropriate vehicles for analysis.

Since a major concern of this study is the identification of the effects of regulation on banking, in order to isolate and identify these effects it is necessary first of all to examine the operation of a banking firm in an unregulated environment. The theory of the banking firm developed in the remainder of this Part uses the diagrammatic approach as the most appropriate way of demonstrating the inherent interdependencies of banking decisions. It is to the development of this model that we now turn.

This does not of course mean that neither the theory of production nor portfolio theory is ever appropriate for the analysis of banking. Portfolio theory in particular is clearly very relevant to the investment decisions of banks, and one major service provided by banks, of course, is the management of an investment portfolio on behalf of depositors who, because of information costs, indivisibilities, and relative time utility, do not wish to hold risky assets directly. All that is alleged here is that the overall operations of a bank fit better into the retailing of services than into the production or portfolio theories.

Notes

1. M.P. McNair, 'Expenses and Profits in the Chain Grocery Business', *Bulletin 84*, Harvard Business School, Division of Research (1971).

2. Ronald R. Gist, *Basic Retailing* (John Wiley, New York, 1971).

3. Henry Smith, *Retail Distribution: A Critical Analysis*, 2nd edn (Oxford University Press, London, 1951).

4. Ibid.

5. J. Hood and B.S. Yamey, 'Imperfect Competition in Retail Trades', *Economica*, n.s., vol. 18, no. 70 (May 1951).

6. Victor Fuchs, *The Service Economy* (National Bureau of Economic Research, No. 87, General Series, New York, 1968).

7. G. Lynn Shostack, 'Banks Sell Services – Not Things', *The Bankers Magazine* (Winter 1977).

8. Fuchs, *The Service Economy*.

4 UNCONTROLLED BANKING: THE FISCHER BLACK MODEL

'It seems likely that without all of these restrictions, a great deal of the banking business would be done by a few large banks that are rational in scope.' (Fischer Black, 'Bank Funds Management in an Efficient Market', *Journal of Financial Economics*, vol.2, no.4 (1975), p.325.)

In this chapter the basis for our model of the bank as a firm, Fischer Black's world of uncontrolled banking, is outlined and in the following chapter we proceed to a modification of this model which we regard as reasonably descriptive of modern banking.

Fischer Black postulates a world without money in which payments are handled by cheque or credit card and in which banks are the major financial institutions. The banks operate one major clearing corporation to capture the economies of scale in cheque clearing. A banking firm in this environment will accept deposits under conditions it alone decides, including paying any rate of interest it wishes to specify. Transfers of credit by cheque will be permitted between two interest-bearing accounts. While it is likely that current account deposits will be paid interest, depositors will also most probably be charged the full cost of transferring credit from one account to another.

On the other side of the balance sheet, a banking firm will lend to individuals, businesses and governments and will probably establish a schedule of interest charges for each borrower, permitting each to write cheques on his account to increase the loan according to need. The interest rate charged, it is suggested, will depend on the borrower's current borrowing outstanding, his wealth, his current and expected future income, and on the extent of the collateral he is able to provide. Repayments of loans will be flexible; provided that the bank is continuously satisfied about the borrower's ability to repay, no consistent payment of principal or interest being required. Besides being participants in an active market for inter-bank funds the banking firms will compete in the setting of interest rates and service charges, but they will pay a common rate of interest on deposits to all depositors.

The banking firm will generate its profits from the administration of loans and the handling of transactions and, because of this, it will want to entice to itself customers with both positive and negative balances.

In this environment depositors will be protected because every bank will find it necessary to hold capital equal to a certain fraction of its loans, because the major banks will be so large that their loan portfolios will be protected by diversification, and because the government may also provide deposit insurance to protect against general unforeseeable losses that may affect a large proportion of loans in all banks' portfolios.

Currency is introduced into this world of uncontrolled banking by allowing the federal government to print it and issue it to the banks on request. As long as a positive interest rate is paid on deposits, individuals and businesses will find it in their interests to minimise their holdings of currency. Bank holdings of currency will be determined by the daily deposit and withdrawal patterns of individuals and businesses and by the cost of making transactions with the government.

There will be no government bonds as the government borrows from the bank as do individuals and businesses. It is also unlikely that businesses will need to issue debt since this may be readily acquired at less cost from banks. Of course, in the case of banks lending to governments rather than to businesses or individuals, it is likely that the interest rate charged will be independent of the size of the loan because of the minimal risk of default.

There are a number of inconsistencies in Fischer Black's interpretation of a world without money. He begins by assuming that the major financial institutions will be banks but then offers them such a universal role in the economy that there is no scope for other financial institutions or even capital markets to operate. Further, he assumes that there will be major banks 'so large that their loan portfolios will be protected by diversification'[1] and also other banks, but does not explain how this size differential began, was created, or had persisted. The behavioural assumptions of individuals are not made explicit and while banks will allow individuals to increase their loans whenever they need the money, it is said to be unlikely that individuals will approach the maximum amount the banks will lend to an individual.

The interest paid by borrowers is to be based on the amounts borrowed, the borrowers' wealth, current income, future income prospects and collateral. This would appear to require that the banks were perfectly informed about the present and expected future position of all of their customers which could presumably be accomplished only at prohibitive cost or alternatively, if the banks must decide on the limits and the interest rates by applying more general rules to individual circumstances, there seems to be scope for other financial institutions to make up any resulting shortfall in finance for individuals and businesses.

Fischer Black notes that in his world without money, the economies of scale in cheque clearing will justify the establishment of only one major clearing corporation, but no other reference is made to any other difference in costs between sizes of banks, an omission which implies that the costs of branch establishment, and of accepting and servicing accounts are constant for all banks. An even more critical omission in the scenario is the specification of any real limiting device to the extension of credit. While it is noted that the government's expansion of borrowing is limited by the necessity of the approval of Congress for each increase, no readily identifiable limits appear to exist to individual or business borrowing in the aggregate, other than that they will wish to have income and borrowing power available for future consumption. The difficulty which this omission raises for Fischer Black's model is that no justification is found in that model for individuals and businesses to pay back their loans from banks.

The limitations of Fischer Black's world without money appear primarily because we wish to use it as a base for a microeconomic theory and not, as he intended it, as a basis for demonstrating in a macroeconomic context the proposition that unregulated banking does not lead to an uncontrolled increase in prices.

Note

1. Fischer Black, 'Banking and Interest Rates in a World without Money', *Journal of Bank Research* (Summer 1970).

5 A MODIFIED UNREGULATED WORLD

'Financial intermediation depends on adequate information. The information obtained in the process of one transaction can be used in another. Given economies of information of this kind, why are not all forms of financial intermediation provided by one single institution?' (C. A. E. Goodhart, *Money, Information and Uncertainty* (Macmillan, London, 1975), p.137.)

Our world of uncontrolled banking, which is essentially a modification of Fischer Black's model, requires a number of assumptions. Money is assumed to exist in the form of currency, but, because of the additional assumption that banks pay interest on their deposits, both individuals and businesses will find it in their interests to minimise the amount of currency held. Banks are the only financial institutions and will remain so for as long as they are able to satisfy the financial demands of the community. We assume that banks may specify the conditions on which they will accept deposits and make loans and that they will hold some portion of their deposits in the form of reserves to minimise uncertainty. In this world uncertainty prevails and the acquisition of the information necessary to reduce or to minimise uncertainty can only be made at a cost. The aim of banks operating in this world is long-run profit maximisation from their business which is assumed to be the retailing of monetary services.

Following Fischer Black we propose that, because of economies of scale in cheque clearing, it is probable that only one major clearing corporation will exist for all the banks. There are, however, other areas which suggest the existence of economies of scale. While the same costs are consistently involved in the opening and servicing of deposit accounts, it is likely that with a large number of depositors a bank may benefit from the imperfect correlation in its customers' flows of payments and the consequent reduction in the variance of funds. The role of banks as financial intermediaries allows them advantages in the acquisition of information about certain classes of borrowers and lenders that enables them to assess risk more realistically for transactions with these classes of customers.

Increasingly as the extent of a bank's business grows, more information about customers is acquired at less cost per unit of deposit.

Baltensperger[1] suggests that, while the costs of acquiring information are reduced when they are spread over a large number of depositors and borrowers, the other method of reducing these costs is the requirement of collateral. If banks are to remain the only financial intermediaries in the uncontrolled world it is necessary that they make loans to those who require them even where they do not have collateral, although clearly a higher scale of interest rates would then be appropriate. Banks may well find it in their best interests to acquire information about this riskier end of the market even if it is expensive to do so and perhaps to compensate at least partially for this expense by requiring as much collateral as possible from those borrowers able to provide it.

The implication of the existence of these economies of scale for the individual bank is that it must attempt to obtain at least a certain minimum scale of operations. One further consideration makes the attainment of a certain size a vital prerequisite for long-run profit maximisation. Let us assume, quite consistently with our previous assumptions, that there is free entry into the banking industry. Fischer Black suggests that there will be several competing major banks and other smaller banks.[2] In our view it is logical for an oligopoly to develop for the following reasons. Unless the minimum size at which economies of scale obtain is reached, the banking firm will be operating at a higher cost level than its competitors. At this early stage it will also need to hold a sufficient part of its deposits in the form of liquid reserves to cope with its inexperience in estimating risk; however, at levels of operation which are too low for economies of scale to be achieved, the more reserves the bank holds, then the less able it is to expand its business by increasing loans. It is here that the bank runs a high risk of being taken over by a larger bank which will be able to economise on its victim's holding of reserves. Because of the attractiveness of small banks as an acquisition by larger banks there will be a very high mortality rate of banks operating at low levels of activity.

The risk of loss of control of its own operations will be sufficiently strong in these circumstances for new entrants to eschew any level of operations below the level at which economies of scale obtain, with the result that the industry is likely to have a preponderance of at least medium-sized banks. Although at very high levels of activity a further constraint (described below) operates, it is unlikely that the medium-sized banks will combine to form one monopoly bank because the size of its operations would invite government control as it would then resemble an uncontrolled central bank.

An advantage gained by medium-sized banks in the industry as a result of the economies of scale would be the opportunity to increase the proportion of reserves held in the form of income-earning investments with the obvious increase of profits. We assume that profits for banks are generated from the interest rate and cost differential between deposits and loans and from the investment of free reserves. In the uncontrolled world we are imagining, it is assumed that government bonds and company debentures exist because of the desire of both government and businesses to have alternative sources of funds or avenues of investment than banks. That is, we depart from Fischer Black because we are not confident that banks will extend credit sufficiently far, or indeed more cheaply, than equity capital could be obtained by firms and government on their own account.

Notes

1. Ernst Baltensperger, 'Cost of Banking Activities: Interactions between Risks and Operating Costs', *Journal of Money, Credit and Banking*, vol.4, no.3 (August 1972).
2. Fischer Black, 'Banking and Interest Rates in a World without Money', *Journal of Bank Research* (Summer 1970).

6 THE LIABILITY SIDE OF A BANK'S BUSINESS: DEPOSITS AND CAPITAL

'By what standards may we judge the adequacy of bank capital? Capital should be sufficient to permit suitable accommodation of borrowers, adequate return for stockholders, and proper security for depositors.' (David R. Kamerschen and Eugene S. Klise, *Money and Banking* (South-Western Publishing, Cincinnati, 1976), p.135.)

A bank in an unregulated world will commence its operations by offering a sufficient rate of interest on deposits to attract at least the minimum level of deposits at which economics of scale are obtained. This minimum level of deposits may be achieved by providing higher interest rates on some longer-term fixed deposits and, as each bank will have its own preferred time structure of deposits, it is unlikely that increasing rates on a particular time-span for fixed deposits will incite much opposition from existing banks. Because more business is done in current accounts, a bank which attempts to put up its rates on these deposits will probably persuade existing banks to raise their rates to keep the new entrant out. If the new bank fails to attract sufficient deposits to reach the minimum level, it is likely to have a higher cost structure than other banks and to find it difficult to obtain a sufficient return on its loans to generate profit. A bank in such a position will find itself very vulnerable to takeover by existing banks. We discuss this possibility in more detail in the chapter on 'Constraints'.

Once a new bank has successfully achieved the minimum operating level at which economies of scale obtain and thus becomes an established competitor, it is very likely that it will agree on a maximum rate of interest on deposits with other banks. There is no reason why banks would not leave some time deposit rates open to competition between themselves. That is to say, the banks will be price-setters in the deposit market, subject to the caveat that if they agree not to pay any interest at all on some deposits, they are allowing other financial intermediaries to come into existence to service that area of business. The supply of deposits by the public to a particular bank will be a function of the interest rate paid on deposits and on the competitive position of the bank. If the bank is very small and new it will need to offer a rate of interest for at least some time-span of deposit above that agreed by the

other banks to attract business and, at the other end of the scale, if it
requires a greater than customary share of deposits to allow it to offer
loans to riskier areas of business for which it can charge higher lending
rates, it may need to raise its rate of interest at least on some part of its
structure of deposits to accomplish this purpose.

Figure 1

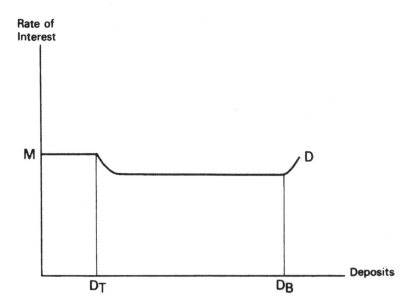

We may represent the pricing and acceptance of deposits by a single
bank by Figure 1, in which we plot deposits along the horizontal axis as
a function of the rate of interest which is measured along the vertical
axis, allowing that the rate of interest here includes the implicit cost
of servicing deposits. The curve MD includes both current and time
deposits, so that any point on that curve will represent a particular
preferred combination of current and time deposits for the bank.

It has been argued that, besides offering rates of interest on deposits,
banks may compete for deposit business on the basis of the strength of
their ratios of capital to deposits. That is, the public will attempt to
minimise the risk of loss on their deposits by shifting deposits away
from banks with low ratios of capital to deposits and into those with
high ratios. This is justified if it is believed that it is the function of
bank capital to absorb short and medium-term losses resulting from

events which reasonable foresight could not be expected to anticipate, so that a bank could maintain its operations without any loss of momentum even if these events occur.

In the unregulated environment with which we are at present concerned, the banks in reaching agreement on rates of interest for at least most deposits will wish to assure themselves of no loss of business to competitors by maintaining consistent ratios of capital to deposits. The appropriate ratio will depend on the volume and liquidity of their loans. For the purposes of our model, therefore, we associate the range of deposits from DT to DB with a stable ratio of capital to deposits which is sufficient to cope with the possibility of unexpected losses.

Moore[1] commented in 1968 that 'the economic function of bank's equity capital is a cupboard which, upon current inspection, appears surprisingly bare'; however, Mingo[2] and Pringle[3] have developed this area more recently. We consider this work in Part 3 since, for present purposes, no growth in the level of business over time is assumed and, also, because capital-adequacy ought more reasonably to be considered together with regulation.

Notes

1. Benjamin J. Moore, *An Introduction to the Theory of Finance* (The Free Press, New York, 1968).

2. John J. Mingo, 'Regulatory Influences on Bank Capital Investment', *Journal of Finance*, vol. 30 (September 1975).

3. John J. Pringle, 'The Capital Decision in Commercial Banks', *Journal of Finance*, vol. 29, no. 3 (1974).

7 LOANS AND THE HOLDING OF RESERVES

'[T] he perpetual apprehension that makes . . . bankers keep a large reserve – the apprehension of discredit.' (Walter Bagehot, *Lombard Street*, 1873 (Irwin, Illinois, 1962), p.20.)

In classifying banks as single-product or service, rather than multi-product, firms we appear to be taking a traditional rather than a realistic view of the ambit of banking operations. But if we refer to the earlier discussion of banking as the retailing of services, it may be reasonable to interpret the services other than lending as only necessarily provided by banks under conditions of regulation. The portfolio or investment operations of banks we classify, following Falkenberg[1] (p.107) as 'an impersonal form of loan' and therefore part of the single service. Diversification into the provision of other services is explained in the context of our model as a response by banks to the restriction of their primary activity as a consequence of regulation.

Banks in our unregulated world will compete in the setting of interest rates on loans with the level of interest charged for any particular borrower depending on the amount of collateral he can provide, the information that the bank has available about that particular class of borrower, and the risks of lending over the particular time period and for the particular purpose required. In a world of perfect certainty and knowledge, the bank would be completely sure of the repayment of its loan and for this reason would not need to hold any cash or other reserves in order to cover the risk of default.

While our world is unregulated, it is also characterised by imperfect knowledge. In these circumstances it is likely that information flows are imperfect, although a bank may use its real resources to improve the information flow about its customers and reduce the degree of uncertainty about loan repayment. Because information flows are not only imperfect but also very costly to improve upon by any means other than experience in lending, different banks will be able to offer different rates for a similar loan to a particular individual. In the interests of reducing uncertainty concerning flows of funds a bank will ask for interest payments on loans to be met at regular intervals. In order to maximise its chances of surviving in the long run and its aim of profit maximisation in an uncertain world, a bank will wish to hold back some part of deposits as a hedge against its own possible errors in the assessment of borrowers and in order to guard against short-run unexpected defaults. Since bank loans are comparatively illiquid some part of the reserves held will be in cash and most, if not all, would need to be quite liquid. A further reason why reserves of some liquidity are necessary is because the bank does not know the pattern of inflows and outflows its deposit accounts will experience and these unexpected variations also need to be covered.

The bank will establish its optimum mix of loans on the basis of the information which it has about various classes of customer and its preferred time pattern of loans which may in part be a function of the time structure of its deposits. We make the bank's loan function a supply function rather than a demand function because it reflects the terms on which the bank is willing to supply loans. Loans are not only illiquid when granted, but the bank may not feel that it is able to reduce seriously the level of loans. It is commonly argued that bank loan portfolios may become increasingly risky as the quantity of loans increases and banks may therefore refuse to meet increased demand for loans in conditions of economic expansion, but Kane and Malkiel[2] suggest that where loans are requested by customers who have access to alternative sources of credit (in this case, other banks) and have maintained large, stable deposits over time and who have previously been given loans by the banks, it will be in the interests of banks to accommodate these requests. In these circumstances the bank is likely to find that it is easier for it to vary the terms on which it accepts deposits in order to increase its funds for lending, than to restrict its provision of loans.

The protection of depositors in this unregulated world will be accomplished primarily by the holding of reserves by banks, although it is also likely that because the banks will usually be medium-sized, the protective attributes of loan diversification may reduce the risk for depositors.

Notes

1. John F. Falkenberg, 'The Sources of Bank Profitability', *Journal of Bank Research* (Summer 1973).
2. Edward J. Kane and Burton J. Malkiel, 'Bank Portfolio Allocation, Deposit Variability and the Availability Doctrine', *Quarterly Journal of Economics*, vol.74, no.2 (May 1965).

Figure 2

Rate of Interest

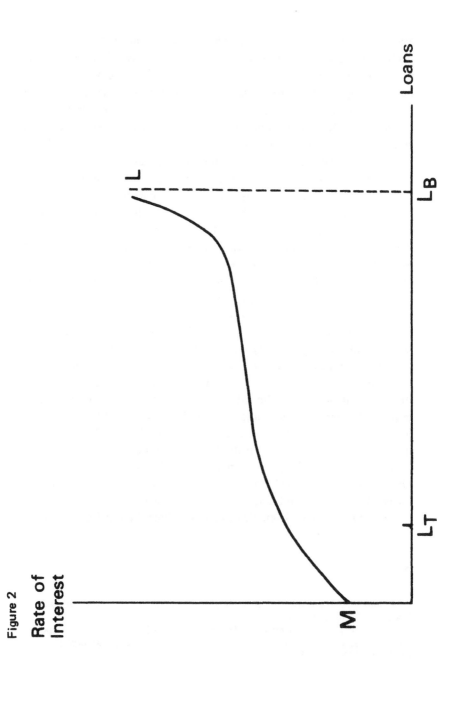

Loans

8 THE COSTS OF BANKING OPERATIONS

'Since it is often impossible to trace the source of funds used by the bank, it is difficult to "cost" them and determine profitability accordingly.' (Ray Shaw, 'An Analysis of Bank Profitability', *The Bankers Magazine*, January 1978, p.45.)

A bank operating in the unregulated environment we have specified will face the fixed costs involved in the operation of the clearing house and in the location and establishment of branches. Here we are concerned with the variable costs of banking operations from which certain of the comparative advantages of banks derive.

In accepting deposits banks must provide documentation and the facilities for the transfer of these deposits through cheque accounts. These operating costs may be assumed to vary directly with the level of deposits and the proportion of these held in chequing and non-chequing accounts. Because the precise inflows and outflows into its deposit accounts are uncertain, the bank is likely to forego earnings on part of its funds and hold these in the form of reserves in order to minimise the effects which fluctuations in deposits might have on other uses of funds such as lending. Part of the cost of deposits therefore ought to be regarded as the earnings foregone on this holding of reserves. Banks must also provide monitoring services for deposits, although these may be minimised by the provision of certain deposit facilities such as negotiable certificates of deposit in which the costs of monitoring may be shifted from the issuing bank to the bearer as holder in due course.

In its lending operations, a bank will find it necessary to collect, collate, check and continuously update information about borrowers. On the basis of its historical records of lending experience to certain groups of borrowers it will be more informed about the likelihood of repayment of these loans. On a larger scale the bank may find it advantageous to use more sophisticated credit scoring and analytic techniques to quantify and summarise its knowledge of lending experience. In cases where collateral is required for loans, once its value has been ascertained it will be necessary for the bank to monitor this value over the life of the loan.

If there are agencies which provide information about the financial position of potential borrowers, the bank will be able to obtain this information at a lower cost than others because of its acknowledged discretion in the use of such information. The more information the bank is able to acquire about potential borrowers, then the less risk and consequently the less cost it faces in its business operations. The acquisition of sufficient information about potential borrowers in order to lower risk may be regarded as the most expensive barrier to entry which a new bank needs to overcome, since, unless it does so, its loans will be made at a higher risk than those by existing banks.

One cost which the portfolio approach disregards is that of raising new capital by equity issue, the retention of earnings or the issuing of new debt. Mingo and Wolkowitz[1] describe the primary function of a bank's capital to be to maintain a bank's soundness. Accordingly, it is reasonable to allow that the bank will find it prudent to raise its capital in order to maintain a constant ratio of capital to deposits. Nevertheless, it is likely to face a less than perfectly elastic supply of capital and must incur an increasing cost of capital on its new funds.

Note

1. John Mingo and Benjamin Wolkowitz, 'The Effects of Regulation on Bank Balance Sheet Decisions', *Journal of Finance*, vol. 32, no. 5 (December 1977).

9 CONSTRAINTS ON THE SCALE OF OPERATIONS

'In effectively competitive markets, firms of less or greater than optimum scale are forced to make scale changes or fail.' (Almarin Phillips, 'Competition, Confusion, and Commercial Banking', in Paul F. Jessup (ed.), *Innovations in Bank Management* (Holt, Rinehart and Winston, New York).)

In our view effective limits to market structure may exist even in an entirely unregulated world. These limits take the form of two constraints, one at the lowest level of activity at which a bank may reasonably operate and the second at low and high levels of activity. These constraints may be termed respectively, the takeover constraint and the bankruptcy constraint.

As has already been mentioned, when a bank fails to reach the minimum size at which economies of scale may be obtained, it will be operating at a higher cost level than its competitors. Further it will find it necessary to hold more of its deposits in the form of liquid resources than other banks in order to cope with its inexperience in risk estimation. Because of both of these characteristics of its operations the bank here runs a high risk of being taken over by a larger bank which will be able to economise on its victim's holding of reserves. The attractiveness of these small banks as acquisitions by larger banks is sufficient to ensure a very high mortality rate for banks operating at low levels of activity.

In the past decade it has been argued in support of bank mergers in the UK, USA and Australia at least, that the introduction of computerised banking has had the effect of raising the level of business at which the economies of scale may be gained from this form of operation beyond the previous levels that were sufficient for existing economies of scale to be obtained. In Australia this was one of the grounds given for the merger of the English, Scottish and Australian Bank with the Australian and New Zealand Bank.

Further, as we shall see in more detail in Part 2, the monetary authorities in Malaysia and Indonesia have been exerting pressure consistently on the small banks to merge together to form more viable units. With pressure against mergers being equally strong in more developed economies, mergers have nevertheless been a consistent feature of banking in the past two decades. In consequence, although studies such as Murphy's[1] support the view that few economies of scale exist above

100 million dollars in deposits, it is apparent that the banks themselves, at least in the developed economies, believe that advantages attend greater size. It is possible that, as with other businesses, one means of diversification is to take over a company in the same business which operates in another area or serves a different clientele, and there is no reason to expect that this rationale applies any less to banks than to other businesses.

In the context of our model of banking in an unregulated world it is argued that the main operation of the takeover mechanism will be in the elimination of the small banks which potentially threaten disruption to the oligopoly to the extent that they may find it necessary to raise interest rates on demand deposits above the established level in order to attract sufficient business to obtain a viable level of operations. Within the context of the model and without incorporating the additional detail of computerisation, justification for takeovers at other levels of activity is difficult to find. It is thought that combining into a very large unit or units would result in operations of such magnitude that government control would be invited by the threat that the size of these operations would otherwise resemble an uncontrolled central bank.

Where established banks do not see any advantages in taking over the banks operating below the minimum viable level, these small banks are likely to become insolvent or wind their businesses up, unless they are able to survive in certain specialised areas where their local knowledge may be sufficient to enable them to minimise the costs of acquiring information about potential borrowers.

An upper constraint on the size of any bank's operations will be determined by two factors in our model; first, by the achievement of a level of loan business which may only be raised by accepting very much riskier business and, second, by the equivalent achievement of as high a level of depositors as may be obtained without reducing the ratio of capital to deposits below the level of other banks. Depositors would require higher rates of interest to deposit with a 'riskier' bank. Alternatively, it could be argued that the increasing cost of new capital will require the bank to raise the charges on its new loans.

Since these factors imply an expansion of activity only at increasing cost, this appears to be an unlikely strategy for a bank to follow, but if it is assumed that a bank is sufficiently risk-loving to expand operations and incur these costs, the move into riskier loan business invites bankruptcy if these risks are underestimated.

While an upper constraint of this type may be considered unnecessary as banks are unlikely to move past their point of maximum profit, satisfaction with this maximum profit and sufficient risk aversion to deter them from exploring the riskier areas of loans will impose a restriction on the size of banks to medium-sized, rather than very large. Of course, in the area of riskier loans, there will be sufficient business for non-bank financial intermediaries to emerge, but on the information available these are likely to be too high cost enterprises to provide serious competition for the banks.

Note

1. Neil B. Murphy, 'A Re-estimation of the Benston-Bell-Murphy Cost Function for a Larger Sample with Greater Size and Geographic Dispersion', *Journal of Financial and Quantitative Analysis* (December 1972).

10 THE DIAGRAMMATIC MODEL

'The work of art is the exaggeration of an idea.' (André Gide, *Journals*, translated by Justin O'Brien, p.896.)

In this chapter we proceed to the diagrammatic illustration of the interdependence of the decisions made by a banking firm operating in the banking industry in the unregulated environment which has been described in the earlier chapters. While the presentation is, of course, a simplification of the real world, in our view the essential decisions and critical interdependencies are highlighted rather than obscured by this approach. The four quadrants of Figure 3 represent the pricing and acceptance of deposits (quadrant I), the pricing and offering of loans (quadrant II), the cost of loans and derivation of profit (quadrant III), and earnings on reserves (quadrant IV).

Beginning in quadrant I we plot deposits along the horizontal axis as a function of the rate of interest, which is measured along the vertical axis, allowing that the rate of interest includes the implicit cost of servicing deposits. The curve MD includes both current (demand) and fixed (time) deposits so that any point on that curve represents a particular preferred combination of current and fixed deposits for the bank. On the basis of the arguments made earlier, a bank will find it too costly and too risky and will be too vulnerable to takeover if it operates with a level of deposits of less than D_T. Because of the oligopolistic nature of an industry with medium-sized units it is likely that the banks will co-operate in not offering more than an agreed maximum rate on deposits. The exceptions to this agreement, implied by the slope of the curve DM to the left of D, and to the right of D_B, relate in the first case to new entrants attempting to reach the minimum efficient level of operation and, in the second, to an attempt to bid business away from other banks by increasing interest rates to attract more deposits in order to cope with a rise in the riskiness of loans.

Consistent with the earlier argument that banks will find it prudent to hold some part of deposits in the form of reserves, we assume fractional reserve banking and take the level of loans appropriate to each level of deposits to be 80 per cent of the level of deposits. In quadrant II, loans are plotted on the horizontal axis and a loan function, LM, is defined. Maximum and minimum constraints determine the slope of the function above L_3 and below L_T. The minimum level of loans is

Figure 3

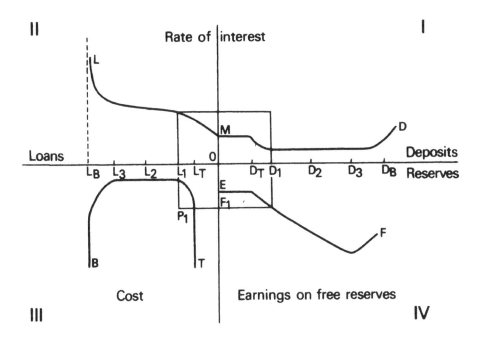

associated with the threat of takeover (or insolvency) as is the minimum level of deposits in quadrant I. Between L_T and L_3 the rate of interest charged on loans will tend to reflect the levels general in the industry and we assume that the bank has already estimated its optimum time structure of loans on a preference function so that any point between L_T and L_3 will represent a preferred structure of loans. Once the volume of loans exceeds L_3 the bank is undertaking a higher proportion of risky loans than previously and the threat of bankruptcy exists if these risks are underestimated.

The differential between the rate of interest paid on deposits which includes the implicit cost of servicing deposits, and the rate of interest charged on loans, is the first of the bank's sources of revenue.

In quadrant III we represent the cost of loans as a U-shaped cost curve reflecting both the transactions costs and the normal fixed costs associated with banking operations. Implicit in the positioning of the two constraints on this curve is the risk of loss of control of the business which at the L_T level may occur through either takeover or bankruptcy and at L_B and beyond may occur through insolvency. It can be seen from quadrant III that costs rapidly approach a minimum level after a sufficient level of loans to minimise the risk of takeover is reached because, consistently with the loan function in quadrant II, there is a large area of optimal lending reached once business is expanded. To the left of L_3 costs rise more slowly than they fell between L_T and L_1, because these costs are initially only compensation for increasing risk and only gradually does the assumption of more and more risk threaten bankruptcy or infinite costs.

From the assumption of fractional reserve banking, it is necessary that the bank holds a proportion of its deposits as reserves. We define reserves as a proportion of deposits on the horizontal axis and earnings on those reserves on the vertical axis. At low levels of business the bank's inexperience in loans will make the risk of loss high and, for this reason, reserves held at these levels will be almost completely liquid. Another way of explaining this is that the reserves held must initially be held in the most liquid form to compensate for the bank's lack of information, but that as more and more customers are acquired so too is more information. This increased flow of information at lessening cost allows a more accurate assessment of risk to be made and a lower level of purely liquid reserves is required than previously.

This reduction in the cost of information which can be seen to be reflected in the rise in earnings between D_T and D_3 is reversed at D_3 as the bank moves into the area of increasing risk. Beyond D_3 information about the riskier loans will be more expensive to acquire and a new level of liquid reserves will need to be held to compensate for this risk.

Sealey[1] suggests that a bank in fact has three alternative sources of liquid funds, borrowing, selling securities or using reserves to compensate for, say, an unexpected outflow of deposits. In the context of the model used here securities will be held as part of reserves, which leaves the bank two alternatives, borrowing or use of reserves. Pierce[2] has shown that liquidity may be measured as the amount acquired either through borrowing or the sale of an asset in a particular time period and in a given state of the economy, relative to the maximum amount that would be realisable from the sale of the asset if time were not a factor. In these terms currency held as reserves will be more liquid and therefore more completely realisable than borrowing, which in imperfect markets is likely to be at increasing cost. It is therefore argued that because the existence of uncertainty will require the bank to hold some proportion of reserves as liquidity, the least-cost source of funds in the event of an unexpected outflow of deposits ought to be these liquid reserves, the cost of holding which is already undertaken, rather than borrowing at further cost while continuing to hold liquid reserves.

In Figure 4 the profit function is derived from the results of the interdependent decisions displayed in the four quadrants. If we take the initial level of deposits in the bank as equal to D_1, then on the basis of holding a 20 per cent level of reserves, the bank will lend out L_1 in loans. The revenue from this process which is equal to $i_{L_1} - i_{D_1}$ (the difference between the interest on loans and the interest on deposits), is added to by OF_1 which comprises the earnings on reserves. Offset against this total is the cost of loans C_{L_1} which will leave the bank with P_1 as profit. If the bank's level of deposits was D_2, the interest rate i_{D_2} would be paid and loans would be made at interest rate i_{L_2} producing $i_{L_2} - i_{D_2}$ revenue to which may be added OF_2 of earnings on reserves. Deducting the cost of loans C_{L_2}, a profit of P_2 is found.

Finally we may identify the maximum profit as associated with a level of deposits, D_3, from which L_3 is loaned, generating $i_{L_3} - i_{D_3}$ as revenue to which may be added OF_3 in earnings on reserves. From this revenue the deduction of C_{L_3} will leave P_3 profit. This is the maximum profit because here the highest rate of return may be achieved on the portfolio of loans without increasing the risk of loss and, here also, the proportion of free reserves held in income-earning assets reaches its maximum.

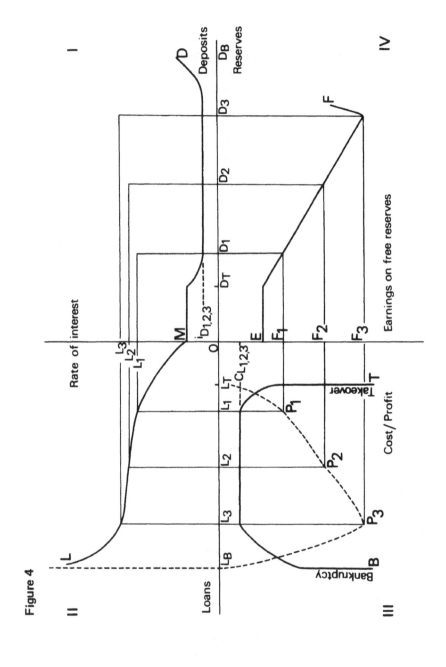

Figure 4

Notes

1. C. W. Sealey Jun., 'A Further Reconsideration of the Optimal Reserve Management at Commercial Banks', *Southern Economic Journal* (July 1977).

2. James L. Pierce, 'The Theory and Measurement of Bank Portfolio Selection' in G. P. Szego and K. Shell (eds.), *Mathematical Methods in Investment and Finance* (North-Holland, 1972).

11 CONCLUSION

To this stage we have analysed the nature of banking and suggested that it is most appropriately treated as the retailing of services, contrary to the more popular views that banking is either an application of the theory of production or of the theory of portfolio selection. It is by no means denied that these latter two theories may provide insights into certain aspects of banking operations, but there are a number of common characteristics of bank operations that fit very insecurely within either of those frameworks and it is felt that this justifies investigating alternative descriptions of banking.

From a modified version of Fischer Black's unregulated world we investigate the actions of a banking firm and suggest that it is likely to be an oligopolistic enterprise making a series of interdependent decisions aimed at the maximisation of long-run profits. It can be seen that the major difficulties faced by the banking firm in an unregulated world are the existence of uncertainty about the inflow and outflow of funds, the appropriate assessment of risk in relation to loans and the maintenance of a viable level of liquidity in reserves.

To some extent the introduction of regulatory constraints may modify part of these difficulties, but the offsetting disadvantage appears as a loss of control because it may be that the effect of the constraints is to put the bank's operations under central bank control.

In the following Part we look at the impact of regulatory constraints in nineteen countries as a prelude to introducing the more common forms of regulation into our model.

Part 2

THE IMPACT OF REGULATION ON DOMESTIC BANKS

'One convincing talk in confidence to top bankers could achieve more in one congenial after-dinner hour than an array of decrees could in a year if forced upon recalcitrant institutions.' (D. J. J. Botha, 'Dr. M. H. de Kock on Central Banking', *South African Journal of Economics*, vol.43, no.1 (1975), p.73.)

1 INTRODUCTION

While there are numerous texts on comparative banking and excellent studies such as de Kock's on central banking, only recently with the interest taken by the EEC in the harmonisation of banking regulation within the Community has attention been given to the use of various regulatory constraints on banking in different economies. One of the limitations to the general use of a number of excellent textbooks on money and banking is that they place their analysis entirely within the context of a particular country's institutional framework.

It is the intention in this Part to examine the regulation of banking in nineteen economies and within a united Europe. The banking regulations with which we are concerned are not the prudential controls but rather those regulatory constraints that are imposed and varied as part of the implementation of monetary policy. Further, we are no more than peripherally interested in the macroeconomic effects of this regulation; our main concern is with the impact of these constraints and of changes in the constraints on the operation of an individual commercial bank within each economy.

From this survey it is expected that we shall be able to identify the main types of regulation used which we may then introduce into our unregulated model in Part 3. We survey here, for each of the nineteen economies, the institutional framework within which the banks operate and the menu of regulatory instruments available, and we outline the experience of these controls in the seventies and in some cases from the last major change in banking regulation in the sixties. Finally, for each economy, a brief commentary is given on the effects of recent changes on the operation of individual banks.

The nineteen economies with which we are concerned in this Part are the UK, France, Germany, Belgium, the Netherlands, Ireland, Italy, Denmark and Norway in Europe, and the USA, Canada, Japan, South Africa, Australia, Papua New Guinea, New Zealand, Malaysia, Indonesia and Egypt. Although it is often suggested that the Bank of England has been the source of the main central banking functions, the relationship between government and the monetary authorities in most economies derives from the legislation under which the central bank was established. This legislation reflects the administrative structure of government as much as the necessary features of central banking and a number of central banks have found that they are unable to accomplish their objectives because insufficient power is given to them in the enforcement of banking regulations. For some central banks, however, the conditions in the economy itself inhibit the full exercise of powers, for example, as is noted at the beginning of the chapter on 'Banking Regulation in Belgium', the situation of the Belgian Treasury and the capital flows between Belgium and other countries may prevent the application of monetary policy instruments by the Belgian central bank.

Most of the published work on the use of regulatory constraints on banks published in English refer to the US or UK situations. Unfortunately for those who would wish to infer that either or both of these represent situations replicated in other countries, the USA and the UK appear to have a much wider menu of regulatory constraints available to them than the other economies which are surveyed in this Part. The inadequate size of government securities' markets in many cases proved to be a very limiting factor when, in circumstances of substantial capital flows, more direct controls were unable to cope.

We begin our survey with the UK and European economies and look at banking regulation in a united Europe in order to provide a more complete picture, before moving to the other main economies, the United States, Japan, and several past and present Commonwealth countries, and finally we consider Indonesia, Papua New Guinea, Malaysia and Egypt, whose banking regulatory structures are of quite recent origin.

2 THE REGULATION OF BANKING

'The role of banker, in life as in certain games of chance, is often thought to confer a special advantage on those who play it, which therefore requires to be carefully circumscribed.' (Sir Jeremy Morse, 'Control of Multinational Banking Operations', *The Banker*, August 1977, p.101.)

In essence banking has been the subject of regulation in order that depositors might be protected against loss, that the volume of money and credit should be controlled, and that the formation of monopolies or cartels should be prevented.

Traditionally it has been argued that because the banking system as a whole can create money, if this power is left unchecked rampant inflation will ensue. Although Friedman and Schwartz,[1] Pesek and Saving,[2] and Pesek[3] agree that unregulated banking would lead to an uncontrolled increase in prices, Fischer Black, in the paper on which our model is based, demonstrates the inadequacy of this position. In addition it may be argued that through its monopoly control of the monetary base, it is the central bank and not the banking industry that is the primary determinant of the money supply and that this control is sufficient to check any attempt to expand credit continuously. Nevertheless, on the basis of the argument that banks alone can expand credit, controls have been implemented in the form of absolute quantitative limits and restrictions on the composition of bank asset portfolios.

Arrangements for control, inspection or supervision (or all three) of banks have been justified by the need to protect depositors against the risk of losses. Requiring banks to hold a certain proportion of their deposits in the form of highly, if not totally, liquid reserves will probably cover the risk of unexpected losses on loans, and inspection of balance sheets and accounts should minimise the risks of incompetence in management, but a wider form of insurance is often required to protect against unexpected events which might threaten catastrophic losses on a large proportion of all banks' loans. In exchange for providing 'lender of last resort' facilities to the banks, a central bank will require that certain conditions be met by banks. As an alternative, perhaps the most efficient means of protection for investors would be a voluntary deposit insurance scheme in which the premium would vary between banks according to an actuarial calculation of the degree of risk in each bank's portfolio. In some countries forms of deposit insurance have been implemented.

The argument for regulating banking, that it is an industry characterised by economies of scale which lead to concentration and hence to monopoly cannot, as Meltzer[4] has noted, be applied to banking without major qualifications, the most substantial of which is that the government through the central bank has a stronger power of monopoly in the issue of currency. Curiously, while this monopoly argument has been made for banking control, so has the opposite argument – the absence of monopoly. This latter argument suggests that ease of entry and the prevalence of competition leads bankers to take excessive risks which increase bank failures. Meltzer has pointed out that this argument assumes that the quality of bank credit is independent of monetary policy and further, that it seeks to shift responsibility for the errors and inadequacies of public policy on to banks.

Restrictions on interest rates in banking and qualitative constraints on the direction of lending are implemented, it is argued, in order to allow the less affluent greater access to banking services. However, the restricting of nominal interest rates to low levels will be destabilising in inflationary periods, and directing the distribution of lending is an inefficient procedure which fails to distinguish adequately between those potential borrowers who badly require funds from those who would be able to obtain credit in a perfectly competitive money market, and which may force banks into dependence on economic conditions in the sectors to which they supply credit because they are unable to hedge their risks by lending to a wide enough spectrum.

A substantial argument often made in favour of all of those controls which interfere in a bank's decisions on its asset portfolio composition is that they permit monetary policy action to be effective in controlling bank lending in particular. This argument, however, which remains the most serious justification for the continuation of banking regulation, depends on banks being the major source of borrowing by consumers to the extent that other financial intermediaries have come into existence to make up these shortfalls in supply.

It cannot be argued that the regulatory controls imposed on banking distinguish between those imposed for prudential reasons and those imposed as part of monetary policy, and there has been a tendency to use the former for the purposes of the latter. The complex of regulatory constraints imposed on banking prevent the banking system from operating at optimum efficiency, and although it could be argued that this is a reasonable trade-off for a greater efficiency in monetary policy, this latter result is not by any means always achieved.

From the point of view of the individual bank which is the focus of interest of this study, all of the forms of control affect the preferred operational pattern of the business, some of them only marginally, others more seriously. Because the nature of regulatory constraints and their methods of implementation vary so widely between countries, we provide in the remainder of this Part, following a preliminary outline of the main instruments used, a discussion for each of nineteen countries of their institutional structure, the instruments of banking regulation, changes in and use of regulatory instruments in the 1970s and a brief commentary on their impact on individual banking operations.

The constraints on banking operations in which we are most interested are those which are used as part of monetary policy rather than those which are merely prudential regulation. Probably a better way of distinguishing between these two types of control is to regard prudential regulation as usually comprising fixed or invariant requirements, while the remaining regulations may be regarded as capable of being varied almost continuously over time in response to monetary authorities' policy movements. In general terms the variable banking regulations may be grouped under four headings – reserve requirements, qualitative controls including moral suasion, quantitative controls and indirect controls.

Notes

1. M. Friedman and Anna J. Schwartz, 'The Definition of Money: Net Wealth and Neutrality as Criteria', *Journal of Money Credit and Banking* (1969).

2. Boris Pesek and T. R. Saving, *Money, Wealth and Economic Theory* (Macmillan, New York, 1967).

3. Boris Pesek, 'Comment', *Journal of Political Economy* (1968).

4. Allan H. Meltzer, 'Controlling Money', *Federal Reserve Bank of St Louis Review* (May 1969).

3 CONTROLS ON BANKING IN THE UNITED KINGDOM

'The Bank [is] generally accepted as the organisation mainly responsible for bank supervision in this country . . . Unlike the central banks or other supervisory authorities in – I think – all other countries, we have never had that role formally entrusted to us . . . So we cannot point to any specific basis in legislation on which our authority in this sphere rests.' (George Blunden, 'The Supervision of the UK Banking System', *Bank of England Quarterly Bulletin*.)

Introduction

In a country in which a major part of law derives from the custom of the people and the decisions of judges, it should perhaps not be surprising that British banking has not been based historically on legislation and that until very recently indeed there has not even been a statutory definition of the term 'bank'. It has been customary to regard a bank as such if it is accepted as a bank by the general public, which implies that it will accept money on current account, pay cheques drawn by its customers and collect cheques for them. Those accorded by custom the status of 'bank', however, required the permission of the Department of Trade and Industry to advertise for deposits and to describe themselves as banks.

Although the Bank of England Act, 1946, authorised the Bank to 'request information from and make recommendations to bankers' and, with Treasury approval, to direct 'any banker for the purpose of securing that effect is given to any such request or recommendation', supervision has rather been based on custom and convention and these legislative powers have remained unused. The Bank of England's view has been that this rather informal system made allowance for its belief that 'each bank is a unique institution which must be judged individually', and facilitated the exercise of personal judgement in assessing 'the quality and reputation of management and, where appropriate, of ownership'.

While there are considerable advantages to this system as an effective means for the day-to-day operation of supervision, there is the obvious result that little measurement of the efficiency of the control of the banks may be undertaken because of the paucity of public knowledge about the timing and the detail of controls. Not that the danger of being misunderstood is confined to banking and monetary policy; an excellent example of imperfect information flows was the 1968 US tax cut which, according to the University of Michigan Survey Research Centre, failed to result in the expected consumer reaction of increasing expenditure because a majority of consumers surveyed thought there had in fact been a rise in tax.

Despite the lack of modification of the system under which it operates, the domestic banking industry is highly concentrated with the clearing banks – Barclays Bank, National Westminster Bank, Midland Bank and Lloyds Bank in England, and the National and Commercial Banking Group and the Bank of Scotland in Scotland – accounting for some three-quarters of bank deposits by domestic residents. All of these are private banks, the only state bank being the central bank, the Bank of England. In general these banks have until recently been short-term, rather than medium- or long-term lenders.

The description 'retail' is given to the deposit banks, that is the London and Scottish banks mentioned above and a few other banks (the Cooperative Bank, C. Hoare and Co., Isle of Man Bank, Lewis's Bank, the Scottish Cooperative Wholesale Society Ltd Bankers, and Yorkshire Bank), while the merchants, overseas and foreign banks are described as 'wholesale' banks.

From Radcliffe to Reform

The Bank of England in a 1969 paper, 'The Operation of Monetary Policy since the Radcliffe Report', confirms that the main concentration of monetary policy over this period was on influencing bank lending. Because of the importance attached to maintaining a continuous and effective market in government securities, neither open-market operations nor interest rate policy were favoured as means for the implementation of short-run policy changes. Accordingly direct controls on banks, in particular requests to restrain their lending, were often used. The pressure of direct requests was reinforced by the use of the scheme of Special Deposits which was first employed in April 1960. This scheme provided for calls for deposits by the Bank of England (to the extent the Bank felt necessary for credit control purposes) and for the payment of an interest rate close to the Treasury bill rate on these deposits. Reaction by the banks to a call for deposits tended to be to replace any reductions in their holdings of Treasury bills by expansion of their loans to discount houses which also counted as liquid assets.

The distinction which the Bank of England wished to make between special deposits and a variable liquidity ratio was that a call for special deposits was assumed to have an announcement effect sufficient to affect business expectations and spending, but there has been no evidence that this result was ever achieved.

Accordingly the brunt of monetary policy with respect to banks was borne by credit ceilings. The disadvantage of this technique as a means of control was that it tended to become ineffective if implemented for extensive periods. Further, the application of ceilings tended to increase the loss of bank business to other financial institutions whose activities were uncontrolled.

Apart from the difficulties encountered in the application of credit ceilings, it also became apparent as the sixties drew to a close that the other main arm of monetary policy, the Bank of England's operations in the gilt-edged market, not only was failing to achieve the desired efficiency and smoothness of operation in that market, but also was affecting the banking sector. The Bank of England's dealings in the gilt-edged market, as banker and issuing house to the government, began with the selling of new securities and the buying in of those approaching maturity, but widened as dealing in other maturities seemed to improve the efficiency of the Bank's operations and as the smoothing out of the fluctuations in interest rates caused by market forces appeared a useful objective. The result of this widening of the Bank's interest in the market was that the Bank became prepared to deal in the whole range of British government securities in the market. It was the impact on the gilt-edged market of the Bank as a dealer with limitless resources which created difficulties. Market-making by private securities dealers was discouraged and, as an unintended result, the operations of the Bank of England in the market often facilitated movements out of gilt-edged securities by banks even if this was a reverse of the intention of monetary policy at the time.

Apart from doubts created by the use of credit ceilings and the gilt-edged market operations in achieving an efficient monetary policy, various committees of inquiry, since the Radcliffe Committee's recommendations for a flexible interest rate policy and the concentration of policy on general liquidity, had advocated changes. In its 1967 *Report on Bank Charges*,[1] the National Board for Prices and Incomes recommended the elimination of the London clearing bank interest rate cartel as well as the abandonment of official ceilings on bank advances. The 1968 Monopolies Commission *Report on the Proposed Merger*[2] of Barclays Bank, Lloyds Bank and Martins Bank commented that the ceilings and the interest rate agreement produced inefficient financial intermediation as well as monopoly profits.

The Bank of England itself had noted in June 1969 that —

Direct controls, unlike calls to Special Deposits, leave the banks free to manage their holdings of government debt as they see fit. In the longer run, however, it is recognised that distortions of the structure and efficiency of the banking sector may result.

Goodhart,[3] writing of the period from the Radcliffe Committee to the end of the 1960s, noted that the authorities had absolute control over the Bank rate and, through this, other rates on bank deposits and advances, but that they were unable through open market operations, even supplemented by calls to special deposits, to control the money supply. The banking system was able to escape from the effects of the last two measures by substituting, after only a minimal lag, private sector liquidity for the withdrawn Treasury bills. Goodhart argues that this failure to control the money supply led the monetary authorities to expand the use of direct controls.

Goodhart dates the change in policy enshrined in the 1971 reforms from the 1968 withdrawal of the Bank of England's previously automatic support in the gilt-edged market. Between 1968 and 1971 there were substantial mergers which reduced the number of the London clearing banks to five, and the annual accounts of these banks were published revealing for the first time their true profits.

The Bank of England in a recent submission to the Committee to Review the Functioning of Financial Institutions, which is chaired by Sir Harold Wilson, noted that these last two changes and the reforms which are described below were 'to encourage a more competitive and innovatory attitude within this dominant part of our banking system and to encourage also a more efficient use of the considerable real resources used in it' (1977, p.311).

1971: Reform

The Governor of the Bank of England in a speech made in Munich in May 1971 commented that the new approach implicit in the proposals reflected changes in the authorities' attitude towards two questions: first, what monetary variable should policy attempt to influence; second, by what means should it be influenced? In the first case, the shift in area of influence was towards what the Bank of England referred to as 'broader monetary aggregates', and in the second case, these should be influenced primarily by open market operations reinforced, where necessary, by calls for special deposits.

These attitudes were reflected in the three main aspects of the new monetary control arrangements; the abandoning of the interest rate agreements, the setting up of new reserve requirements and the preference for open market operations.

It was a feature of the interest rate agreements between the London and Scottish clearing banks that their effect had been to keep interest rates down rather than up, a view confirmed not only by the banks' evidence to the Monopolies Commission in 1968 but by the Governor of the Bank of England and the Treasury in evidence at the same inquiry. The 1971 reform discontinued this agreement as well as the agreed market tender for Treasury bills, and each bank was setting its own rates for fixed deposits and for lending.

The banks' new minimum reserve assets were defined to include at least 1.5 per cent in non-interest-bearing deposits at the Bank of England; government securities within a year of maturity, money at call with the discount houses and a limited quantity of other bills including local authority bills eligible for rediscount at the Bank of England. These minimum reserve assets had to total at least 12.5 per cent of eligible liabilities, which were defined as sterling deposits of less than two years maturity and sterling assets obtained by switching foreign currencies.

It was intended that the minimum reserve assets ratio would 'provide the authorities with a known firm base for the operation of monetary policy', and this was supplemented by a provision for calls to special deposits which were to consist entirely of deposits at the Bank of England which would bear interest at close to the going Treasury bill rate.

It was the intention of the reforms that the main method of controlling the cash base of the banks and their reserve assets was to be open market operations. To this end the Bank of England, in the words of its Governor, would 'not normally be prepared to facilitate movements out of gilt-edged by the banks, even if their sales should cause the market to weaken quite sharply'. Open market operations would change the returns on the various assets held by banks, thus inducing them to adjust to accommodate the effects of these changes.

Nevertheless, although primary control was from 1971 on to be by means of indirect market-oriented controls, there have been occasions on which direct controls have been required, for example in August 1972 and in September 1973 when the Governor of the Bank of England asked that the banks 'make credit less readily available to property companies and for financial transactions not associated with the maintenance and expansion of industry'.

Since 1971 the major change has been to intensify and now to provide regulation for the Bank of England's supervision of the banking system. Mr George Blunden of the Bank of England, in an address on 17 March 1975 to an Institute of European Finance Seminar, noted a number of factors which had led to the recognition of the need for intensified supervision. First, the rapid expansion in the number of banks in London, both from the move by foreign banks to open branches or subsidiaries there and from the growth of domestic secondary banks, allowed many institutions to obtain more substantial funds for onward lending than had hitherto been possible for them, and this raised the risk that the collapse of one could affect a whole range of banks. Second, these potential difficulties took a new form in late 1973 and 1974 with the collapse of the property market which rendered some institutional lending books in sterling very illiquid, and in the face of the resulting problems the Bank reviewed its methods for the support and supervision of the banking system and took more interest in institutions in the secondary banking area.

Third, in 1974 again losses on foreign exchange movements by a number of banks and the failure of a few small banks within Europe created some potential dangers and the Bank of England considered it 'prudent to clarify the responsibilities of parent banks in respect of their subsidiaries or affiliates operating internationally, and to extend international co-operation in supervision' and obtained, by early 1975, an acknowledgement that the parent banks would support those banks in difficulties. All authorised banks in London were written to by the Bank in a letter which suggested measures to prevent unsatisfactory control of foreign exchange dealings.

Following the move taken by the EEC towards harmonising the existing national banking systems within Europe, and under the aegis of the Governors of the Central Banks of the Group of Ten, a Committee on Banking Regulations and Supervisory Practices was set up in Basle in late 1974 in order 'to foster cooperation, mutual confidence, understanding, and some harmonisation of practices among supervisory authorities in the member countries'. George Blunden commented in his 1974 address that differences in the legislative backgrounds of the banking systems and in the political structures were so great that no unified system could be operated. Nevertheless periodic discussion and consultation is occurring continuously.

The Bank of England increased its collection of information from the individual banks and required the information at least quarterly rather than annually as had been done in the past. Separate arrangements were made for the London and Scottish clearing banks in 1975 on the basis of arrangements and principles worked out with those banks, and these are set out in 'The Capital and Liquidity Adequacy of Banks' in the *Bank of England Quarterly Bulletin*, September 1975, in which it was emphasised that not only parent banks but also their subsidiary companies should possess appropriate capital and liquidity for their business operations.

The White Paper, *The Licensing and Supervision of Deposit-Taking Institutions* (Cmnd. 6584, August 1976), presented to the House of Commons on 3 August 1976 appeared to have been predicated by the earlier problems of the secondary banking system, by the need to harmonise EEC banking law, and by the government's desire to provide greater protection for depositors than previously. Under the system proposed in that Paper, institutions would only be permitted to carry on the business of accepting deposits if they held a licence granted by the Bank of England, although those enterprises granted a statutory recognition as a 'bank' would be exempt from this requirement. Where such exemption is granted, exacting criteria for minimum capital and reserves, the type and range of banking services to be provided, and reputation and status must be met.

The White Paper also provides for a mandatory deposit protection fund along the lines of the US Federal Deposit Insurance Corporation which the Bank of England will administer. Justification for this type of protection can be seen in its prevention of the 'lifeboat' operations in which the banking system became involved when secondary banks faced difficulties in 1974 and 1975, because with this insurance of deposits confidence in the solvency of banks is secure and there is no incentive for a 'run on a bank' to occur.

Operation of Banking Regulation in the 1970s

The new regime of banking controls introduced in 1971 came into effect when the economy was operating at a reduced level of activity. Initial reaction to the abandonment of the clearing banks' agreements on interest rates was to lower the base lending rates of the banks below the Bank rate and for the banks to provide loans on a medium-term basis to expand their interests in personal loans and consumer credit, and to offer a wider range of deposit terms, including for some the issuance of negotiable sterling certificates of deposit.

Bank lending ceilings were eased by the Bank during 1970 and 1971 but it was not until the September quarter of 1971 that bank lending was moving close to the ceiling, and this could be attributed almost entirely to personal lending. Ceiling restraints were removed in September, but industrial activity was recovering too slowly for this to be reflected in the productive sector and the main increases in lending were to the personal sector, property, finance, retail and other distribution.

By 1972 bank lending was increasing rapidly. A large volume of new deposits had been generated and the money supply was growing at a sufficiently strong rate to fuel growing inflation. While banks were asked to restrict lending to some areas and calls were made to special deposits, interest rate policy remained the main instrument for the restraining of the money supply. Towards June interest rates moved up as a consequence of balance of payments factors, and the Treasury bill discount rate was pushed above Bank rate. The authorities raised the Bank rate in response and the banks were faced with an outflow of funds which seemed to leave them with only sales of gilt-edged securities as a source of funds with which to meet their reserve requirements. In order to prevent the obvious interest rate impact on a weak gilt-edged market, the Bank provided temporary assistance in the form of a special loan against the security of short-dated gilt-edged securities, for two weeks.

Later in the year, in early autumn, once again the Treasury bill rate rose above Bank rate and the authorities found it necessary in mid-October to replace the Bank rate with a minimum lending rate which was to be equal to the average tender Treasury bill rate plus 0.5 per cent, rounded up to the nearest 0.25 per cent. This new rate was used by the Bank to lead rather than follow the market, so that the Treasury bill rate could be levered up. As the money supply continued to expand and the Exchequer had a large deficit to finance, a call was made for special deposits of 1 per cent of eligible liabilities in November and of 2 per cent in December from all banks and finance houses, in an endeavour to control rather than to restrict the rate of expansion of bank lending. The December call, in particular, led to a strong rise in short-term interest rates, including lending rates.

In 1973 the substantial rate of expansion of the economy was showing signs of strain but it was not until later in the year that the Government began to direct restraint. The substantial increase in the public sector borrowing requirement was met to a major degree by the banks whose assets and deposits rose accordingly, although by the start of 1974 calls for increased special deposits had absorbed almost all of this increase. The private sector borrowed from the banks quite heavily and the growth of deposits and advances was a major component in the high rate of money expansion. During the second half of 1973 the implementation of monetary measures forced interest rates up again. In July a further 1 per cent call was made to special deposits and the Bank of England's minimum lending rate rose from 7.5 per cent to 11.5 per cent and the banks were forced to adjust their base rates upward in August. Although the minimum lending rate fell slightly in October, in November the Bank temporarily suspended the formula for calculating it and raised it administratively to 13 per cent and announced a 2 per cent call for special deposits, although only 1 per cent was in fact accepted.

Because of the volatility of interest rates within the sterling money markets, it was often profitable over this period for borrowers to borrow from the banks on overdraft and deposit the funds elsewhere, as well as to switch between bank overdrafts and other sources of borrowing according to relative rates of interest. The November measures, described by the Chancellor of the Exchequer as a 'tough credit squeeze', were intended to moderate the growth of the money supply. In the same month it became apparent that certain secondary banks which had failed to hold an adequate liquid reserve were unable to cope with the combination of quickly rising interest rates and the declining capital values of some assets. After one secondary bank had its shares suspended by the Stock Exchange, widespread uncertainty was felt about the viability of similar banks, and when this led to the withdrawal of short-term funds from those institutions some of them were also forced into difficulties.

In order to limit the risk that these problems would spread more widely the Bank of England established a standing committee on which the Bank and the London and Scottish clearing banks were represented and which provided advice and support. During December the Bank moved to introduce arrangements which would discourage the arbitraging activities of borrowers. The Bank of England was to be able to specify a maximum rate of growth for the interest-bearing eligible liabilities of every bank and deposit-accepting financier. Growth of these liabilities above the rate specified would mean that the bank concerned would have to place non-interest-bearing special deposits with the Bank of England. The rate of call to special deposits would be progressive in relation to the excess liabilities. At the introduction of these arrangements the banks were told that their interest-bearing eligible liabilities were to be limited to 8 per cent growth over the first six months based on the average for April, May and June 1974 over that for October, November and December 1973. At the end of April the Bank announced that these liabilities could grow at the rate of 1.5 per cent of the base figure per month, calculated on a three-month moving average. Excess growth of 1 per cent would require special deposits of 5 per cent, while excess growth of over 1 per cent but less than 3 per cent would attract special deposits of 25 per cent, and excess growth above 3 per cent would attract 50 per cent in special deposits.

The March 1974 Budget was accompanied by the announcement by the Chancellor of his intentions to reduce interest rates as soon as possible, and this, together with an easing in the banks' reserve position, pushed the minimum lending rate down. Expansion of bank deposits was again the main contributor to the growth of the money supply during 1974, but because the public sector converted its deficit by sales of securities mainly to the private sector and the slower growth of the private sector lowered its financial needs, the expansion was only half that of the previous year. During the year the inflationary influences on costs and the financial difficulties of the industrial sector encouraged the banks to raise their provisions for bad and doubtful debts and to direct attention to maintaining a prudent ratio of capital and reserve to deposits. The Bank of England resumed the interest payments on the special deposits of banks against eligible liabilities which was suspended in 1973, and there was some repayment of special deposits in the first half of the year.

From September 1973 until January 1975 the banks, at the request of the Bank of England, held the rate paid on interest-bearing deposits of less than 10,000 pounds to 9.5 per cent. In February 1975 this request was removed and the interest-bearing eligible liabilities scheme was suspended as no longer necessary. Because the rise in deposits was very much less than had been anticipated in 1974 the growth of the money supply eased and no restrictive action was warranted, while in 1975 the private sector's demand for bank advances virtually did not grow at all, so that though the public sector's finance needs were high and rising the banks were left with higher holdings of reserve assets. No need arose for increased special deposits to mop up the reserves but banks were directed to channel any expansion in lending to manufacturing industry's requirements for working capital, increasing exports, or raising industrial investment, and away from lending to property companies or for financial transactions. Owing to the lack of demand, the minimum lending rate and base rates fell, then rose in July and October, and after that continued their downward trend.

After the 1976 Budget the money supply moved moderately and without influence by the public sector borrowing requirement. Then, however, apparently partly because of exchange rate expectations, bank lending to the private sector rose very strongly and this continued, except for some hesitation in August, right through to November. Rises in the minimum lending rate occurred in May, September and October and in September calls for special deposits, which had been at 3 per cent of eligible liabilities since February, were made for 1 per cent. A 2 per cent call early in October was only half paid, the rest being deferred until January 1977 when, in fact, special deposits were reduced to 3 per cent again.

In November 1976 the special supplementary deposits scheme was introduced with the basis for measuring growth in eligible liabilities taken to be the average of the amounts outstanding for the three months to October and the maximum growth allowed, before penalties were incurred, was 3 per cent for the first six months. At first sight given the growth of eligible liabilities this promised to be a substantial constraint, particularly as it was announced in November, but the growth of lending to the private sector dropped significantly and eligible liabilities fell each month after November.

The Bank of England restated its lending directions in July, asking the banks to provide funds for manufacturing industry's working capital and fixed investment as well as for the expansion of exports and import savings, while limiting lending to individuals, property companies and for financial transactions. When the market believed the record coupon rate of 15.5 per cent reached in December would be the peak, money flowed out of short-term holdings and into gilt-edged securities. The Bank moved to relieve the shortage of funds in the short-term markets and from November attempted to moderate the decline of the minimum lending rate, which by April 1977 was down to 8.25 per cent. Base rates which had reached a peak of 14 per cent in 1976 declined to 9 per cent by April.

A limit for domestic credit expansion stated in the letter of intent sent to the IMF in December 1976 reflected no shift in monetary policy, but this limit was interpreted in the market as implying further restraint with the result that large inflows of capital were generated and the government was easily able to fund the public sector borrowing requirement by sales of gilt-edged securities. This flurry had eased by the second quarter of 1977 and the minimum lending rate was lowered on twenty occasions during the year, falling to 5 per cent in November. The 'corset' or supplementary special deposit scheme was suspended in August. A sharp rise in bank lending to the private sector early in the fourth quarter was met by a rise in the minimum lending rate from 5 per cent to 7 per cent at the end of November.

The first British law on the supervision of banking is now at the draft bill stage with the publication of the Banking and Credit Unions Bills (Cmnd. 7303) and, although it may be argued that the proposed Act will only provide the Bank of England with statutory power to pursue its already well-trodden path, there seem to be several controversial elements in the proposed legislation. Final impetus to formal legislation was given by the EEC banking directive that all members should have a system of authorising banks by mid-December 1979.

In the first of the Bill's three parts, the procedures for the licensing and recognition of banks are set out which provide for a first and second division of banks. To be a recognised bank, an institution must have enjoyed for a reasonable period of time a high reputation and standing in the financial community; it must provide either a wide range of banking services or a very specialised banking service; it must pursue its business with integrity, prudence and professional skill under the direction of at least two individuals; it must (except for deposit-taking institutions as at 25 July 1978) have net assets of 5 million pounds sterling to provide a wide range of banking services and of 250,000 pounds sterling to provide a highly specialised banking service; and it must maintain its net assets at a level commensurate with its scale of operations.

To be a licensed institution, that is, within the second division, it is necessary that every director, controller or manager be a fit and proper person to hold that position; that at least two individuals direct the business; that net assets be at least 250,000 pounds sterling (except for those already taking deposits as at 25 July 1978); and that the institution conduct its business prudently, maintaining adequate net assets, liquidity and provision for contingencies and for bad and doubtful debts.

Provision is made within the licensing and recognition part for the Bank to be able under certain circumstances to revoke a licence or recognition or to demote a recognised institution to a licensed institution, and it is made an offence for an institution to take deposits unless it either has a licence to do so from the Bank or Bank recognition as a bank. The Bank may grant a conditional licence dependent on the institution fulfilling conditions imposed by the Bank.

Licensed institutions are required to provide information and documents to the Bank which may instigate investigations of licensed institutions at its option and which may petition to wind up a licensed institution. The information to be provided will have its confidentiality protected.

A deposit protection scheme is set out in the second part of the Bill, to apply to all recognised banks and licensed institutions except for the National Girobank, the National Savings Bank, and building societies (the latter will have their own scheme). A Deposit Protection Board is to be appointed to levy and manage monies of the Fund. Its membership will include three *ex officio* members in the Governor of the Bank (who is to be Chairman), the Deputy Governor and the Chief Cashier, and ordinary members appointed from the Bank by the Treasury, and including not more than three other members who are controllers, directors or managers of contributory institutions.

Initial contributions by an individual institution are to be calculated as a percentage of its deposit base, which is defined as the total amount of sterling deposits with the UK offices of that institution other than secured deposits, deposits originally of over five years to maturity, and deposits in respect of which the institution has issued a sterling certificate of deposit within the United Kingdom. The minimum initial payment is to be 5,000 pounds sterling and the maximum 300,000 pounds sterling. If at the end of any financial year the Fund has less than 3 million pounds the Board may levy further contributions to restore the Fund to within its proposed initial range of between 5 and 6 million pounds, and if it appears that the Fund may be exhausted by payments, the Board is able to levy special contributions to be repaid *pro rata* at the end of the year if unused. Any one institution's contributions, including further or special contributions, are not to exceed 0.3 per cent of its deposit base although power is given to the Treasury to raise that to 0.6 per cent. It is intended that the Fund's monies be invested in Treasury bills.

Payments from the Fund to be made after a contributing institution becomes insolvent are limited to three-quarters of each individual deposit to a maximum deposit of 10,000 pounds. On these payments being made the insolvent institution then becomes liable to the Board for that amount and its liquidator may make no further payments to depositors until the insolvency payment has been repaid to the Board.

The third part of the Bill provides the Treasury, after consultation with the Bank, with power to regulate the issue, form and content of advertisements inviting the making of deposits and set out those institutions that may use the name 'bank'. In addition to the recognised banks, included in the list are the Bank, trustee savings banks, the Central Trustee Savings Bank and the Post Office in the provision of its banking services, and savings and municipal banks (providing here that 'savings' or 'municipal' is also indicated). In the case of licensed institutions formed outside the United Kingdom, permission is given to use the name under which they transact in their country of origin if it is accompanied by an indication that the institution is formed under the law of that country.

Although the Bill generally formalises existing arrangements there are some elements of controversy in the second part which sets up the deposit protection scheme. Tim Hindle,[4] in a commentary on the Bill, argues that the Bill appears confused between proposing an insurance fund and providing for a lifeboat operation. In the original proposal a small cash fund of roughly the level of initial contributions set out in the Bill was to be backed by a standby guarantee. The Bill substitutes for the standby guarantee the ability of the Fund to demand up to 0.3 per cent of the deposit base of institutions, an amount equivalent to the cost of lifeboat arrangements. In its background paper for the Wilson Committee[5] the Bank of England concludes by stating its belief that proposed arrangements 'will go far to reduce the risks of major difficulties arising and will provide a satisfactory basis for dealing with any which do occur' (p.236).

Commentary

Perhaps the clearing banks could be forgiven for thinking that in the 1970s the sins of others were visited upon them instead. Botha's[6] comment that 'One convincing talk in confidence to top bankers could achieve more in one congenial after-dinner hour than an array of decrees could in a year if forced upon recalcitrant institutions' in many respects represents the informal arrangement for the control of banking which in the 1970s has been successively eroded by increasing attempts, not only to formalise the relationship between the Bank and the industry, but also to extend the ambit of that relationship to encompass a ball-room-full rather than a dinner-table-full of the representatives of financial institutions.

Of course it may be argued that the secondary banking crisis and the 'lifeboat' provisions were exceptional events in which the traditional banking sector was only minimally involved, yet the Bank appears to have entered the 1970s with the intention of providing a firmer base than previously for the operation of monetary policy. Although the main means of influence was to be open-market operations, the 'corset' or supplementary deposit scheme recurs in the operation of banking regulation throughout the 1970s and interest rates often moved perversely and forced changes in policy.

From the point of view of an individual bank, the problems of swings in interest rates and the financial difficulties of the industrial sector created pressures to maintain prudent ratios of capital and reserves to deposits, while the increased concentration of the industry and the additional information required in their public accounts, in the Bank of England's view, increased competitive and innovatory forces within the industry. Any belief that reliance on open-market operations would allow the banks their traditional manoeuvrability with respect to changes in policy appears to be limited by the recourse to more direct controls on credit which have occurred in recent years.

Notes

1. National Board for Prices and Income (UK), *Report on Bank Charges* (HMSO, London, 1967).

2. Monopolies Commission, *Report on the Proposed Merger of Barclay's Bank, Lloyd's Bank and Martin's Bank* (HMSO, London, 1968).

3. Charles Goodhart, 'Monetary Relationships: A View from Threadneedle Street', Reserve Bank of Australia *Economics Conference* (July 1975).

4. T. Hindle, 'Britain's Banking Bill — Umbrella or Safety Net?', *The Banker* (August 1978).

5. Bank of England, 'The Secondary Banking Crisis and the Bank of England's Support Operations', *Quarterly Bulletin* (June 1978).

6. D. J. J. Botha, Review of 'Dr. M. H. de Kock on Central Banking', *South African Journal of Economics*, vol.43, no.1 (1975).

Further Reading

Bagehot, Walter, *Lombard Street*, 14th edn (John Murray, London, 1915)
Bank for International Settlements. *Eight European Central Banks* (Allen and Unwin, London, 1963)
Dean, J.W., 'The Secondary Reserve Requirement', *Manchester School* (March 1975)
De Kock, M.H., *Central Banking*, 4th edn (Crosby Lockwood Staples, London, 1974)
Economist Intelligence Unit. 'Special Report 2: The Banking System and Industrial Finance in the EEC', *European Trends*, no.49 (November 1976)
Goodhart, Charles, 'Monetary Policy in the U.K.' in K. Holbik (ed.), *Monetary Policy in Twelve Industrial Countries* (Federal Reserve Bank of Boston, 1973)
Harrod, D., 'Bank Regulation', *Journal of the Institute of Bankers* (October 1976)
Morgan, E. Victor, Richard Harrington and George Zis, *Banking Systems and Monetary Policy in the EEC* (Financial Times Ltd, London, 1974)
Wilson, J.S.G., 'The Wilson Committee on "Financing Industry and Trade"', *The Three Banks Review* (June 1978)

4 THE REGULATION OF BANKING IN FRANCE

'Disciplines and codes imposed by legislation must always be so detailed that they are inevitably rigid and inflexible.' (The President of the British Bankers' Association, quoted by M. P. Debono, 'Squeeze the French Way', *The Bankers' Magazine*, July 1973, p.11.)

Institutional Framework

The law of 2 December 1945 nationalised the recognised central bank, the Banque de France, and the largest deposit banks, Banque Nationale de Paris, Crédit Lyonnais and Société Générale, who account for approximately half of all French bank loans. Three main categories of banks were recognised at that time; *banques de dépôts, banques d'affaires* and *banques de crédit à long et moyen terme*. The main distinction then made between the first two groups – that the former could not take deposits of longer than two years' duration while the latter could only take deposits of less than two years' duration from companies with whom they did other business – was eliminated on 26 January 1966. Nevertheless some distinctions between the deposit banks and the merchant banks have persisted. Our particular concern is the deposit banks.

While the Governor of the Banque de France alone determines the interest rate and has the power of veto over the governing body of the Bank, the Ministry of Finance is the final arbiter of policy. It was intended that the National Credit Council (Conseil National de Crédit), which comprises representatives of labour, business, agriculture and government, become an important instrument in the formation and implementation of monetary policy, but it has tended to become merely a formal institution.

The Treasury and the national agricultural fund, the Caisse Nationale de Crédit Agricole, are important in the provision of finance. The Treasury makes use of the money placed in postal cheque accounts, grants credit for medium and long-term projects through its Economic and Social Development Fund, and can affect the liquidity of the banking system by selling or buying Treasury bills or by encouraging deposits in postal cheque accounts. When the requirement that commercial banks hold a percentage of their assets in Treasury bills was abolished in 1967, the importance of the Treasury in monetary affairs declined.

There is what has been called a 'parallel banking system' in France which is composed of semi-public credit institutions like the state deposit fund (CDC) which finances local authorities and housing, the mortgage fund, the industrial fund, and the national agricultural fund, the regulation of which is mainly in the hands of the Minister of Finance. These institutions may affect central bank policy as the CDC operates in the call money market and the mortgage and industrial funds receive most of their funds from the bond market. Until the middle of the sixties, flows of funds into this parallel system were encouraged in order to finance state projects and to aid small savers.

Dieterlen and Durand[1] comment on the French banking system before 1963 that 'changes in the discount rate were insufficient, open market policy was seldom used and a required reserve system was non-existent' (p.127).

Prior to 1967 banks had to maintain a *coefficient de trésorie* or treasury ratio, which was a minimum ratio between the total of their Treasury bills and rediscountable medium-term credits and the total of their current and term liabilities. The liquidity ratio, established in March 1948, required the banks to maintain a ratio between their short-term assets (*avoirs liquides et mobilisables*) and liabilities (*engagements à court terme*) in domestic and foreign currency of 60 per cent. A 1946 decree gave the Commission de Contrôle des Banques the power to introduce two other ratios; a solvency ratio fixing the relationship between capital plus reserve and total lending to third parties, and a division of risks ratio relating capital plus reserves to total loans granted to any one non-public sector customer. Neither of these decrees has been enforced.

Banks were able to rediscount short-term bills representing loans granted within an individual ceiling fixed by the Governor of the Banque de France. Because the discount rate was low, in the absence of ceilings the banks would have had incentive to increase their borrowing without limit.

There is a Service Centrale des Risques set up in 1946 and controlled by the Banque de France which collects the names of the clients of individual banks who have used credits of 100,000 francs or more and advises the banks of the global amounts granted to each of its customers. This service assists the authorities' supervision of the banking system and of the division of credit.

A basic instrument of control has been the *encadrement de crédit* or general quantitative credit restriction which has been used to restrict bank lending. Before 1967 any bank which raised its lending beyond the restricted amount faced a gradual reduction in its discount ceiling.

Because it affects small customers and discriminates against those who primarily finance through banks, it is regarded as a disadvantageous policy tool for banks; however, it may be argued that it has a sufficiently broad effect on the whole banking system to be a necessary mechanism of control.

1967

The system of fractional reserve requirements for banking was introduced into France by the Conseil National de Crédit decree of 9 January 1967. The Banque de France was empowered to set the reserve ratio at any point under the maximum which was first set at 10 per cent and later raised to 25 per cent. Different ratios were set for demand and savings deposits. The amounts held by the Banque de France were not to return any interest, and any bank failing to comply with the ratio would be subject to an interest claim from the Banque de France up to a maximum of the discount rate plus 3 per cent. The obligation imposed by the decree was that the monthly mean of their account calculated from the 21st of one month to the 20th of the next complies with the regulations.

In the same month (January 1967) the *coefficient de trésorie* was abandoned but the banks were still required to maintain a minimum portfolio of rediscountable medium-term bills, which was originally set at 20 per cent of total lodgements.

1969

From September 1969 banks were required to maintain three ratios fixed by the Commission de Contrôle des Banques. The first ratio requires that the amount of a bank's non-rediscountable medium and long-term lending should not exceed by more than three times the total of its resources – that is, capital reserves, time deposits of three months or longer, and loans of three months or more from non-banking establishments in the money market. For banks which lack the medium-term resources to comply consistently with this requirement, it is sufficient that the total of their resources and their loans or refinancing at more than two years should cover by at least 80 per cent their non-rediscountable lending of over two years.

Secondly, banks had to restrict the total of their non-rediscountable medium and long-term lending, real estate investments and participations to not exceed the total of their capital, reserves, savings accounts and time deposits of over three months received from clients and banks.

Thirdly, total investments in real property, equities and bad and doubtful debts were not to exceed capital plus reserves.

Regulation in the 1970s

The Wormser Report on the money market and credit conditions published in 1969 argued that the multiplicity of rates at which the Banque
de France could intervene in the market was inefficient and that the
day-to-day open-market rate persisted above the discount rate with the
consequence that banks could refinance by presenting mobilisable bills
to the Banque de France for rediscount. The Report recommended the
replacement of administrative decisions by market decisions, in particular
by ending the system of preferential discount rates and by replacing rediscounting with open-market operations.

In the years following the publication of the Wormser Report, the
Banque de France modified the system in the general direction recommended by the Report. From 1 April 1971, French banks were required
to hold minimum obligatory cash reserves as a percentage of their credits
as well as of their deposits, in order to allow the authorities more direct
influence on credit expansion.

Also in 1971 the money market rates were allowed to fall below
the discount rate so that the latter became a penalty rate. The Banque
de France moved from fixed-rate lending to the banks to variable-
rate lending which led to the abolition of discount ceilings in early
1972. Day-to-day interventions in the money market continued with
the result that banks were able to meet their cash requirements regularly.

From the latter half of 1972 monetary policy became increasingly
restrictive and the favourite instrument of special deposits was used. In
December 1972 the authorities announced that bank lending on 3 April
1973 should not exceed by over 19 per cent the lending on 5 April 1972
and that lending on 3 July 1973 should not exceed lending on 30 June
1972 by more than 17 per cent. Lending within the 19 per cent and 17
per cent limits was to be the subject of special deposits of 33 per cent
and any excesses would be penalised on an escalating scale, calculated
by taking one-tenth of excess lending plus 0.3 per cent multiplied by the
excess lending. The most serious effect of these restrictions was on the
commercial banks which had increased medium-term lending.

In March 1973 French banks were asked to add to their normal 12
per cent special deposit on non-resident bank and client current accounts
an amount equal to the difference between the balance of non-resident
accounts in French francs on their monthly returns and the balance
they held on 4 January 1973. Although these quantitative restrictions

were continued into 1973, several changes over that period increased their flexibility.

From June 1973 the Banque de France changed its method of intervention in the money market in an attempt to force the banks to anticipate their cash requirements over a longer time horizon and to encourage them to adopt a more cautious credit policy. As its main means of intervention the Banque made periodic auctions, offering to buy outright private short-term paper from the discount houses or to purchase medium-term paper with long-term resale agreements (*pension à terme*) through the specialised institutions. An ancillary process to provide the market with extra liquidity where necessary was the purchase of the more traditional one, three or six-month Treasury bills or medium-term bonds. In July 1973 the Banque de France extended its dealings to one-month promissory notes by the banks either for first-category paper in the process of renewal after maturing at the end of a month or for discountable commercial paper.

In June 1974 the holdings of ordinary compulsory reserves were becoming of increasing size coincidentally with rising refinancing costs, but the formula used as a basis for calculating the supplementary reserves which were used as a penalty for exceeding the normal credit levels was tightened. Further new regulations which operated from December 1974 made the supplementary reserve requirement apply for any increase in credit over 5 per cent between the average of the last quarter of 1974 and that in the period ending June 1975. Nevertheless, bank liquidity increased throughout 1975, since the progressively scaled supplementary reserve requirements were set rather high in relation to the demand for credit and there were exemptions allowed for credits made to the export and energy-saving areas. The generally easier conditions lasted into mid-1976 but, although liquidity growth slowed during 1976, the authorities felt that inflation was again becoming a problem and more restrictive limits for bank credit growth were set in the second half of 1976, and in October the ordinary reserves requirement was set at 0.5 per cent of all bank credit outstanding.

From 1 January 1977 the rules governing the obligatory bank reserves were changed to enlarge the base for calculating the reserves, while from the end of August the official discount rate and the Banque de France's rate for ordinary advances were lowered.

Commentary

M. P. Debono[2] writing in 1973 referred to the escalation of the special deposit provisions as 'complicated and, for some, very costly exercises', although from 1974 onwards it may be argued that the controls implemented left the banks quite considerable scope for management. Although attempts to use money market intervention to influence bank management of funds were made in 1973, this has only been a supplementary rather than a main regulatory control, though the money market itself is increasing in importance.

Those changes in policy preference in the late sixties which promised to remove direct credit ceilings from the range of controls were, as in many other countries, unable to survive the problems created by inflation and, in France as in other countries, ceilings returned as a major weapon. The even application of this tool to all banks, particularly to those banks which had followed fully an earlier Banque de France direction to switch foreign currency loans into domestic currency, created hardship for the latter banks. At the same time, as Debono points out, banks responding immediately to early official warnings would not have had difficulty. Of course, one implication of the use of selective credit controls requiring substantial changes is that banks might reasonably attempt to minimise their involvement in medium or long-term commitments, in order to be able to change their lending commitments quickly if necessary.

Notes

1. Pierre Dieterlen and Huguette Durand, 'Monetary Policy in France' in Karel Holbik, *Monetary Policy in Twelve Industrial Countries* (Federal Reserve Bank of Boston, 1973).
2. M. P. Debono, 'Squeeze the French Way', *The Bankers Magazine* (July 1973).

Further Reading

Banque Worms et Cie, Paris, 'The Evolution of the French Banking System', *Bank of London and South America Review* (November 1967)
Bingham, T. R. G., 'Monetary Policy in France: Price Incentives and Quantitative Controls', *Banca Nazionale del Lavoro Quarterly Review*, no.115 (December 1975), pp.387-403
Brunsden, Peter, 'Controls over Banking in France', 2 parts, *The Banker* (September and October 1972)
Economist Intelligence Unit, 'The Banking System and Industrial Finance in the EEC', *European Trends* (November 1976), pp.29-42
European Communities Monetary Committee. *Monetary Policy in the Countries of the EEC* (Luxembourg, 1972)
Hodgman, Donald R., 'The French System of Monetary and Credit Controls', *Banca Nazionale del Lavoro Quarterly Review*, no.99 (December 1971)

Marjolin, Robert, Jean Sadrin and Olivier Wormser, *Rapport sur le marche moné-taire et les conditions du crédit* (Ministère de l'économie et des finances, Paris, June 1969)
Melitz, Jacques, 'Inflationary Expectations and the French Demand for Money', *Manchester School* (March 1976)
Organization for Economic Cooperation and Development, *Monetary Policy in France*, Monetary Studies Series (Paris, 1974)

5 BANKING REGULATION IN THE FEDERAL REPUBLIC OF GERMANY

> 'In many ways, the Bundesbank is in a better position than any other EEC central bank to carry out an effective monetary policy. It has . . . a large measure of autonomy by statute . . . a wide range of policy instruments under its control . . . a fairly well developed money market . . . and it need worry very little about providing for the public sector . . .' (E. Victor Morgan, Richard Harrington and George Zis, *Banking Systems and Monetary Policy in the EEC* (Financial Times Ltd, 1974), p.44.)

Institutional Structure

In the German banking system there are a few very large banks like Deutsche Bank, Dresdner Bank and Commerz Bank which between them account for about 41 per cent of commercial banking business, many medium-sized banks, and some very small ones, including sole proprietorships. Private, publicly owned and co-operative banks coexist and even within each of these three categories there is a considerable range of enterprises. For example, the publicly owned group includes municipal savings banks, banks owned by the Länder and financial institutions owned by the Federal Government.

There are more than 700 savings banks with over 16,000 branches, and more than 2,000 credit co-operative banks with more than 19,000 branches and over 40 mortgage banks.

Although most commercial banks offer their customers short, medium and long-term facilities as well as all the other services and are referred to as 'universal banks', they are comparatively more important in the supply of short-term lending yet, unusually among the commercial banks of most of the countries surveyed in this Part, more than a third of their lending is long-term. Among the activities of the German banks the acquisition of securities is of much more importance than in most countries and the securities market is to some extent an inter-bank market with the function of converting funds placed with banks for short and medium terms into long-term loans.

The central bank, the Deutsche Bundesbank, was created on 1 August 1957 through the amalgamation of the Land Central Banks and the Berlin Central Bank with the Bank Deutscher Länder. Under German law the Bundesbank is a legal person whose functions are defined by legislation as 'regulating the money circulation and the supply of credit to the economy with the aim of safeguarding the currency'. While the Bundesbank's capital is owned by the government, its officers are appointed by the President of the Republic on the government's recommendation and it has a general obligation to support government policy, the Bundesbank Law allows autonomy to the Bundesbank within its own area and the government may not issue instructions to the Bundesbank.

Instruments for Banking Regulation

Deutsche Bundesbank has certain statutory autonomy, a well-developed money market, minimal lending to the public sector and a wide range of regulatory instruments under its control.

Under Article 16 of the Bundesbank Law, it may require the banks to maintain with it minimum credit balances, calculated as a percentage fixed by the Bundesbank of those liabilities stated to be subject to minimum reserves. This reserve requirement may be dependent on location, size, and type of deposits and whether they are domestic or foreign, or on the rate of increase of liabilities. Ratios are in general high in 'Bank places' or *Bankplätze*, which are places where the Bundesbank has an office or branch. Banks are divided into four categories according to the amount of their liabilities with ratios usually lower for the smaller banks. Different ratios are set for sight, time and savings deposits with the highest minimum requirement for sight and the lowest for savings deposits. Because of the Bundesbank's wish to minimise capital inflows, ratios for non-resident deposits have been higher than for resident deposits. On some occasions the Bundesbank has fixed minimum reserve ratios for increases in some liabilities, more often for non-resident deposits and only rarely on increases in domestic liabilities.

To the extent that a bank fails to maintain the minimum required reserves, interest is charged at a penal rate on the shortage. Because the Bundesbank does not pay interest on these reserve balances, minimum reserve policy influences interest rates as well as liquidity. It is the practice to apply the particular ratios fixed to the average of a bank's liabilities over a four-week assessment time between calendar months and a bank may, at its option, calculate this average on the basis of only four daily positions spread evenly over the period.

Banks are able to rediscount bills with the Bundesbank as a matter of automatic recourse provided both that the amount lies within the quota set in relation to the size of each bank's capital and that the paper be eligible, that is, bear the signatures of three solvent parties and have less than three months to maturity. This process should be distinguished from discount-rate policy which determines the rate or price at which such funds are available from the Bundesbank. There is a discount rate which is that rate at which the Bundesbank will discount eligible commercial bills and an advances rate, usually referred to as the lombard rate, which is normally one to two per cent above the discount rate. This latter lombard rate is the rate at which the Bundesbank extends credit to the banks outside the rediscount quotas in order to allow them to satisfy short-term demands for liquidity. It is usual for this rate to be the most closely correlated, among the officially set rates, to those on the money market.

Before 1967 cartel arrangements within the banking sector ensured that changes in the discount rate were quickly reflected in bank rates, but from that year competition in the setting of bank interest rates was encouraged in the expectation that this would improve efficiency.

Lombard credits are granted against the pledge of specific securities, usually domestic bills of exchange, Treasury bills, non-interest-bearing Treasury bonds, fixed interest debentures or equalisation claims. The last securities are those issued to financial institutions in compensation for losses incurred in the course of currency reform. When equalisation claims are converted by the Bundesbank into Treasury bills, they are referred to as 'mobilisation paper'.

Two aspects of the money market are relevant for open-market operations; first, credit institutions in the market make surplus Bundesbank funds available to other banks, and second, dealings in money market paper take place between the Bundesbank and either credit institutions or public authorities. Because of this latter aspect the interest rates on this paper are determined by the Bundesbank in fixing the terms on which it buys or sells the paper. Section 21 of the Bundesbank Law allows the Bank to deal in long-term securities, if necessary, in order to regulate the money market.

During the period 1957 to 1970 the use of minimum reserve policy was the dominant feature of monetary policy with an increasing tendency towards the end of this period to enforce the attainment of quantitative intentions such as a particular rate of expansion of the credit supply by this means. Further during this period there was no significant Bundesbank holding of long-term securities and no dealings, even in money market paper, between it and the non-banks. Application of discount rate and lombard rate policy was rarely disassociated from minimum reserve requirement changes and few, if any, attempts had been made over the 1957-70 period to make any direct restriction of bank lending.

Banking Regulation in the Seventies

At the beginning of 1970 the Bundesbank was maintaining a sharp liquidity squeeze on the banks and allowing interest rates to rise in order to restrict the strong economic upswing. In March the discount rate was pushed up to 7.5 per cent, its highest postwar rate, and corresponding changes were made in the other rates. By this time the banks had exhausted their rediscount quotas and attempted to obtain funds from abroad, but they were thwarted in this move by the imposition, from April, of a 30 per cent reserve on the growth of external liabilities and the subsequent reduction of rediscount quotas by an amount equal to the growth in liabilities from security transactions with non-residents.

By mid-1970 interest rates were falling overseas and the Bundesbank was faced with the difficulties of moving interest rates so as to minimise the interest rate differential between Germany and other countries while still reducing liquidity. In July all minimum reserve ratios were raised by 15 per cent and from September, while special ratios on foreign liabilities were abolished, supplementary ratios of 40 per cent on sight and time deposits and 20 per cent on savings deposits were imposed on increases to liabilities above the April-June average. A number of banks found it difficult to meet these requirements which were uniformly applied to all banks, and, after making some modifications due to hardship, the supplementary ratio was abolished in November on the increase in domestic liabilities. At the same time the basic reserves on all liabilities were raised by 15 per cent and a supplementary 30 per cent reserve was imposed on external liabilities above the average for the last two weeks of October and the first two weeks of November. Both the discount rate and the lombard rate, as well as the Bundesbank's selling rates for money market paper, were lowered from mid-year on and open-market operations with the general public, begun in mid-1971, strengthened the Bundesbank's leverage on bank liquidity.

Between October 1971 and February 1972 there was an easing of monetary policy with three reductions in the discount and lombard rates and two reductions in the minimum reserve ratio, but by May 1972 the pace of inflation had become a matter of concern and the Bundesbank then announced reductions in rediscount quotas and, from July, a rise in reserve requirements against domestic liabilities. From that month until October 1973 increasingly severe credit restrictions were imposed. Rediscount quotas were reduced by 10 per cent in July 1972 and again by the same amount in August, and in February 1973 not only were they cut by a further 10 per cent but their use was limited to 60 per cent of the new total. The minimum reserve ratios were raised in July 1972 (by 20 per cent), August 1972 (by 10 per cent), and March 1973 (by 15 per cent) on domestic liabilities, and the ratios on non-resident liabilities were raised to 40 per cent, 35 per cent, and 30 per cent against sight, time and savings deposits respectively in July 1972, when the incremental requirement on non-resident deposits was raised from 40 per cent to 60 per cent. In February 1973 the Bundesbank was authorised to freeze up to 100 per cent of the growth in foreign liabilities. Further pressure on bank reserves was exerted by increasing public bond issues such as the issue of 8.5 per cent eight-year non-callable stabilisation bonds in March 1973, the proceeds of which were frozen at the Bundesbank. In line with previous restrictions the discount rate and the lombard rate were lifted in a series of moves from 3 per cent and 4 per cent respectively in October 1972 to 6 per cent and 8 per cent in May 1973.

Traditionally the banks had 'free liquid reserves' at their disposal which allowed them to satisfy the Bundesbank's requirements without any real difficulty, while the Bundesbank was able to attain its policy targets indirectly by influencing the amount of these free liquid reserves. It became clear to the Bundesbank, particularly during the floating exchange rate period of May to December 1971, that even when it was able to reduce free liquid reserves to what should have been a critical level, credit expansion did not even show signs of easing. This meant that the Bundesbank was unable by its usual techniques to control the monetary trend.

A change in the techniques of monetary control was clearly warranted and this occurred in March 1973 when the Bundesbank reduced the free liquid reserves to an insignificant minimum and withdrew from the money market, in which it had hitherto been the main operator. This withdrawal from the money market caused sharply rising interest rates which the Bundesbank did not permit its discount rate to follow, and as this latter rate was the indicator for lending rates, these tended to stay low while the cost of borrowing reached unprecedented levels. Under this policy if the banks moved beyond the rate of expansion of lending which the Bundesbank thought to be appropriate, they would quickly be faced with a strong increase in the cost of obtaining funds on the money market which would force them to limit their expansion as the potential for profit would be seriously reduced.

In fact this was the scenario after March 1973 with the reduction of free liquid reserves to near zero, a growth rate for 'central bank money' of 5 per cent per annum, a halving of the growth rate of the money stock and the curbing of both bank lending and non-bank demand for credit.

'Central bank money', which became the new target variable in place of free liquid reserves, comprises currency in circulation including the cash holdings of banks and the reserves required for domestic liabilities. If there was a slow-down in the expansion of central bank money, the banks would attempt to replace the loss of deposits by attracting new business and by persuading their customers to shift from sight deposits into time deposits, which have lower reserve requirements. The banking sector *in toto* would be unable to maintain the expansion of deposits and would be forced to reduce lending. In order to be able to make the loans to which they were already committed they would reduce their securities investments, raise their loan interest rates and tighten their lending conditions to reduce new business. In combination the effect would be to lower prices and raise interest rates on securities, money and capital markets, with subsequent effects in reducing total demand for goods and services, output and employment.

Central bank money is created when the Bundesbank extends credit to the banks or accepts money market paper; or the Bundesbank's currency reserves rise; or government agencies either reduce their Bundesbank deposits or borrow from the Bundesbank; or the Bundesbank buys open-market paper; or if there is a reduction in the non-banks' special deposits and the additional reserve requirement on banks' foreign liabilities.

As a consequence of this change in technique the tight money policy of 1973 was able to restrict very substantially the expansion of central bank money, with the result that interest rates rose and the increase in liabilities subject to minimum reserve requirements, and the loans and investments based on them, were heavily reduced in housing and in industry.

In 1974 the Bundesbank faced a more complex task in minimising the effects of the oil crisis, of the continued falls in exports, and of the crisis of confidence after the closing of the Herstatt Bank. Low monetary growth occurred in the first quarter of 1974 and the Bundesbank in an early response to signs of a recession lowered the special rates for Bundesbank credit with the result that the interest rate level dropped in the second quarter. In reaction to the crisis of confidence caused in June by the collapse of the Herstatt Bank (discussed below in conjunction with the 'Lex Herstatt') which threatened other banks with liquidity difficulties caused by large withdrawals of deposits, the Bundesbank allowed fuller utilisation of rediscount quotas and granted lombard loans at the lombard rate. On 12 September the Bundesbank, the Federal

Association of German Banks and other bank associations agreed to establish a Liquidity Consortium Bank as a private limited company with the object of conducting bank transactions with banks to ensure the latters' liquidity and guaranteeing banking arrangements. Paid-up capital was 250 million Deutsche marks in which the Bundesbank had a 30 per cent share, with provision made for further obligatory payments of capital up to a total of 750 million Deutsche marks.

There were reductions in the cost of money to banks in 1974 which were reflected in reduced interest rates on deposits, but there was considerable slack in industry's demand for loans while those firms which were anxious for loans were often those in difficulty and with poor credit ratings, and accordingly lending rates were not reduced to the same extent. Subdued monetary expansion characterised much of 1974 until October, when the Bundesbank changed the course of its monetary policy to stimulate monetary conditions more strongly. Both the discount rate and the lombard rate were reduced and the banks' rediscount quotas were raised in order to allow them some liquidity margin. Further reductions in the discount and lombard rates were made in December 1974, and in February and March 1975 the Bundesbank sold mobilisation and liquidity paper to the banks in order to smooth out interest rate fluctuations on the money market.

Throughout 1975 the Bundesbank continued its moderate expansion of the money supply which led to a decline in the interest rate structure and a fall in the cost of money market funds. As there was still a declining demand for funds from the industrial sector, the banks found it necessary to vary their lending policies, in particular to encourage long-term borrowing and instalment finance which rose by 30 per cent over the previous year's figure. More funds than previously were also directed to investment credits at fixed terms, refinanced through quoted bonds, and lending to public authorities and central and state governments more than doubled.

From July the Bundesbank began buying public authority bonds on the open market, a process which supplied some 7.5 billion Deutsche marks to the banking system by October and in the latter month it discontinued its intervention policy on the bond market. In November by agreement with the Bundesbank, temporarily free balances of the Federal Government were transferred to the banking system to smooth out money market interest rate fluctuations.

Early in 1976 the public authorities, which had raised substantial loans at the end of 1975, reduced their borrowing, and while there was an increase in the extent of private borrowing this was insufficient to fill the shortfall. Compared to their borrowing from banks of 48 million Deutsche marks in 1975, the public authorities borrowed 30 billion Deutsche marks from them in 1976. Further substantial Federal cash balances were again placed with the banks in January and February. However, speculative inflows of foreign exchange in February and March led the Bundesbank to try to prevent a tendency to excess liquidity by raising the minimum reserve ratios for bank liabilities by 5 per cent from 1 May and a further 5 per cent from 1 June, which tied up about 4 billion Deutsche marks in liquidity.

From July there was an acceleration in monetary expansion due to new inflows of foreign exchange and increased demand for credit, and in order to hold bank liquidity at a reasonable level the Bundesbank used open-market operations in fixed interest securities to the extent that the Bundesbank's holding of securities fell from more than 6 billion Deutsche marks in August to 1.5 billion Deutsche marks by the end of November. By the end of the year the banks were making a record recourse to lombard loans, but not, surprisingly, to the cheaper rediscount facilities, to cover the seasonal expansion of central bank money.

Revision of the legislative provisions under which the German banking system operated was made in 1976, primarily in response to the events surrounding the Herstatt failure, although it should be noted that this was merely the most spectacular of a series of bankruptcies and difficulties which included the insolvency of the Dusseldorf joint-venture Bank-Kredit Bank, the over 1,000 million Deutsche marks loss of Hessische Landesbank in credit commitments, and a large uncovered foreign exchange position held by the Westdeutsche Landesbank. Although Herstatt, a partnership limited by shares, was not a private bank, the private bank group lost 13.1 per cent of its volume of business in the third quarter of 1974.

The New German Bank Act of 1 May 1976, known as the 'Lex Herstatt', was based on earlier proposals for revision by both the Federal Banking Supervisory Office and the Deutsche Bundesbank, but the events culminating in the closure of Bankhaus I. D. Herstatt KG required an improvement in bank supervision. Deutsche Bundesbank in announcing the Lex Herstatt noted that there was a commission appointed by the Minister of Finance studying basic banking questions and foresaw a more complete revision of the Act when that commission reported. Three particular aspects were the subject of the 1976 Act: the limitation of risks arising from bank lending; a widening of the scope within which the Federal Supervisory Office and the Bundesbank could take action and acquire information; and additional provisions to safeguard deposits.

Herstatt was a major German commercial bank based in Cologne, with assets prior to 1973 of over two billion Deutsche marks. During 1973 and 1974 the bank's forward foreign exchange deals resulted in huge losses said to be of the order of 400 million Deutsche marks. On 26 June 1974 the Federal Supervisory Office under its authority to order liquidation when the safety of deposits is endangered and other alternatives are lacking, withdrew Herstatt's licence to conduct a banking business and ordered its liquidation.

The first aspect of the 1976 Act attempted to reduce the possibility of a further Herstatt-type failure by limiting the risks incurred by banks. Large loans were considered to be the central problem, as the Deutsche Bundesbank itself said (July 1976, pp.17-18), 'it is known that the great majority of bank insolvencies since 1962 has been connected with irrecoverable large loans'. To cope with this difficulty, an individual large loan including loans promised must not exceed 75 per cent of the bank's liable capital, the five largest loans including loans promised must not exceed three times the bank's liable capital, and all large loans actually taken up combined must not exceed eight times the bank's liable capital. The term 'loan' was widened by incorporating in its definition the words 'financial assets acquired against payment' which included assets acquired in the course of factoring and under repurchase agreements. With regard to the term 'borrower' a 'man of straw' clause was added which provided that persons and enterprises for whose account a loan is raised together with the person or enterprise raising the loan in his name are considered as one borrower. Further in granting loans of over 50,000 Deutsche marks, banks were obliged to require the borrower to disclose his financial circumstances in the form of his annual accounts unless collateral is provided.

In widening the supervisory authorities' scope for taking action and obtaining information, banks were now required to have at least two managers working for the responsible management of a bank, and the licensing of sole proprietorships to conduct a banking business was not to be permitted. Reporting requirements now included any change in participation in another enterprise exceeding 5 per cent of the capital; any changes in the firm's name, the articles of association or the by-laws; the beginning or termination of any business other than banking; and the establishment, relocation or closing of the representative office of a foreign enterprise conducting banking business. Previously there had not been an obligation on banks to produce their annual accounts within a specified period, but banks were now required to provide their annual accounts within three months of the end of the accounting year and auditors had to supply the Supervisory Office with much more information than before.

Apart from violations of the two-manager principle and the prohibition of sole bankers, the Act specified in more detail the conditions under which a bank's licence may be revoked because the fulfilment of its obligations to its creditors is endangered. The loss of half of the liable capital or of over 10 per cent of the liable capital in each of three successive accounting years is set as criteria for this by Section 35(2)5.

The difference in structure between the various groups in German banking made the statutory regulation of deposit protection inapplicable and, for this reason, only supporting provisions supplementing existing deposit guarantee schemes were enacted. The Federal Association of German Banks set up a new deposit guarantee fund to protect all deposits of non-banks, per depositor up to 30 per cent of the liable capital of the bank. The Supervisory Office was given authority to call a moratorium for banks in difficulties and that Office alone may file the petition in bankruptcy.

Until 1977 the reserve requirements system was very complex with the reserve required dependent on location (higher where the Deutsche Bundesbank had an office), on size, on type of deposits, on whether the deposits were domestic or foreign and on the rate of increase in liabilities. On 1 March 1977 this system was superseded by a progressive scale procedure and the curtailing of the privilege previously granted to banks located in places without a Bundesbank office. It was the purpose of these changes to avoid the abrupt rises in required reserves that resulted under the old system. The new procedure set the applicable minimum reserve ratios according to the amount of individual types of liabilities, divided into reserve stages. Sight liabilities, time liabilities and savings deposits each have three stages: 10 million Deutsche marks and less; from 10 million Deutsche marks to 100 million Deutsche marks; and over 100 million Deutsche marks, with minimum reserve ratios applicable to each stage. Compared to the old system the size of the stages has increased three-fold and the average reserve ratios now rise steadily in line with the rise in liabilities and are on a generally lower scale.

In February 1977 the differences in reserve ratios in 'Bank places' (that is places where the Deutsche Bundesbank has an office) and elsewhere was 3.45 per cent for sight liabilities and 1.15 per cent for savings deposits. The 1 March revision introduced a discount of constant size of 1 per cent for sight liabilities and 0.5 per cent for savings deposits for banks located in places without a Bundesbank office.

Originally the application of different reserve ratios to 'Bank places' and other places had been justified by the assumption that those banks located in places without a Bundesbank office would find it more difficult and time-consuming to procure cash. Now not only was this not necessarily true but in general banks required relatively less cash balance to maintain their solvency.

In the first four months of 1977 monetary expansion slowed, even though money market conditions remained rather easy with the boost of 1 billion Deutsche marks in free reserves due to the technical change in the minimum reserve system and an increase in banks' rediscount quotas. Further measures to boost liquidity were announced on the 18 May to be effective from 1 June, with reserve requirements reduced by 5 per cent and rediscount quotas raised by 2.5 billion Deutsche marks, while the lombard rate was lowered from 4.5 per cent to 4 per cent on 15 July and the discount rate was lowered 0.25 percentage points on 25 August.

By the end of the year, although there had been some increase in bank lending, there was not sufficient demand for credit, particularly from the private sector, to counter the downward pressure on bank lending rates. Both short and long-term interest rates declined during the year and by October long-term interest rates were at their lowest level since 1962.

On 15 December 1977 the Bundesbank announced a number of new measures to minimise the effects of acute foreign exchange disturbances on domestic economic conditions. From 16 December the discount rate was lowered from 3.5 per cent to 3 per cent and the lombard rate from 4 per cent to 3.5 per cent, moves that were expected to increase the tendency to reduction in the interest rates charged for bank loans and paid on bank deposits. The Bundesbank also raised from 1 January 1978 the reserve ratios on liabilities to non-residents to 20 per cent on sight liabilities (previously 12.75 per cent), to 15 per cent on time liabilities (previously 8.95 per cent), and to 10 per cent on savings deposits (previously 5.65 per cent). The growth of a bank's liabilities to non-residents was to be subjected to an additional minimum reserve of 80 per cent in order to reduce the banks' interest in the growth of shorter-term financial investments by non-residents.

Commentary

By comparison with their position in 1970, the banks at the end of 1977 found their activities much more constrained by the Bundesbank. During this period the banks' ability to manoeuvre their liquid reserves so as to satisfy the Bundesbank's requirements without seriously affecting their activities was almost entirely removed by the change in policy technique, under which not only were their free liquid reserves reduced to an inoperable minimum but the accompanying withdrawal of the Bundesbank from the money market made access to other funds through the money market prohibitively expensive.

There were signs of liquidity difficulties for some banks as a result of the application of other policy instruments. For instance, in July 1970 the imposition of supplementary ratios on increases in liabilities caused hardship for some banks and were modified and then abolished, and in 1974 heavy deposit withdrawals consequent on the failure of the Herstatt bank threatened banks with liquidity difficulties and some relaxation of Bundesbank controls was made in response. In the 'Lex Herstatt' of 1976, attempts to reduce the likelihood of similar failures were concentrated primarily on restricting banks' abilities to provide large loans, though the requirements could not be regarded as any greater than a prudent banker might adopt.

The 1977 changes in the reserve requirements system were in the direction of simplification and produced a lower level of ratios; however, the Bundesbank continued to apply these requirements to the banks together with its other controls.

Although there is no doubt that the 'Lex Herstatt' performed the very useful function of limiting the risks which banks could incur, it also provided the basis for much more effective central bank control of the banking system with its requirements of increased information and greater supervision. Of course these latter requirements may also be justified as a means of minimising the possibility of further bank failures but they do seem to imply greater central bank direction for banking activities. However, given the comparatively slow response of monetary policy moves to changes in economic circumstances, together with a banking system which is of most importance in short-term lending, the possibility of increased central bank direction suggests that the banks in the future may find it less easy to respond to changes in the short-run demand for funds.

Further Reading

Bank for International Settlements, *Eight European Central Banks* (London, 1963)

De Kock, M. H., *Central Banking*, 4th edn (Crosby Lockwood Staples, London, 1974)

European Communities Monetary Committee, *Monetary Policy in the Countries of the European Economic Community* (Institutions and Instruments, 1972)

Holbik, Karel, *Monetary Policy in Twelve Industrial Countries* (Federal Reserve Bank of Boston, 1973)

Morgan, E. Victor, Richard Harrington and George Zis, *Banking Systems and Monetary Policy in the EEC* (Financial Times Ltd, London, 1974)

Nadelmann, Kurt H., 'Rehabilitating International Bankruptcy Law: Lessons Taught by Herstatt and Company', *New York University Law Review*, vol.52, no.1 (April 1977)

Orsingher, Roger, *Banks of the World*, English translation (Macmillan, London, 1967)

OECD, *Monetary Policy in Germany*, Monetary Studies Series (1973)

6 THE BANKING SYSTEM IN THE NETHERLANDS

'Dutch banking practice, like British, has traditionally been to look after the customer well, but to let him make the pace.'
(T. C. D. Gadsby, 'The Impact of Foreign Banks', *The Banker*, July 1972, p.963.)

Institutional Structure

The commercial banking system of the Netherlands is dominated by two large, private, Dutch-owned banks with substantial branch networks; the Amsterdam-Rotterdam Bank (AMRO) and the Algemene Bank Nederland (ABN) who, between them, account for about 60 per cent of the commercial banking system's business. However, the commercial banks only account for 55 per cent of the resources of the Dutch financial sector. Other institutions of importance in the financial sector are the private savings banks, the Post Office Giro, the Post Office Savings Bank and the agricultural co-operative banks. This last group formed in 1972 the Cooperatieve Centrale Raiffeisen Boerenleenbank (Rabobank), the biggest banking group in the country.

Commercial banks accept deposits on current account and deposit account and have been attempting to increase their savings deposits since the early 1970s. Their lending is by overdraft, term loan and revolving credits, with the duration of term loans moving towards the medium term, in contrast to the banks' more traditional role as providers of short-term funds.

A distinctive feature of banking in the Netherlands is the combination of stockbroking and banking functions in the commercial banks and their further participation in the securities markets as managers and underwriters of new issues. Although the commercial banks were not very concerned originally with small clients – their interests were traditionally served by the savings and agricultural co-operative banks – they have tended more recently to widen their business beyond industry and commerce in line with the breakdown of the specialisation between the financial institutions within the Netherlands.

Legally, the central bank, the Nederlandsche Bank, is a joint-stock company whose capital since 1948 has been owned entirely by the state. In principle the Bank has complete jurisdiction over monetary policy, subject to direction in some cases by the Minister of Finance. While the governing board of the Bank, comprising five members appointed by the Crown for a seven-year term, is responsible for monetary policy and, in particular, for the control of the banking system, the Bank Act 1948 does provide for the Minister of Finance to issue directives to the Board for the purpose of co-ordinating the monetary and financial policy of the government. However, this power is subject to a right of appeal by the Board to the Crown which is then to decide if the directives should be followed. It is thought by many commentators that the effect of this is to make the Bank the equal rather than the subordinate of the Minister of Finance with regard to monetary policy.

The Bank Act of 1948 further provides that the Nederlandsche Bank shall give free banking services to the government and to the Postal Savings Bank as well as to any other public institutions specified by the Minister of Finance.

Short-term money markets in the Netherlands include markets in Treasury bills, inter-bank loans, Eurocurrency and in inter-company deposits and these are quite active and sizeable markets.

Instruments of Banking Control

Discount policy, money market intervention, reserve requirements, quantitative and qualitative restrictions and moral suasion have been used for credit control by the Bank. In the 1950s the banking system was very liquid and for this reason although discount policy was used it had to be backed up by open market operations and changes in reserve requirements.

Banks have recourse to the Nederlandsche Bank by discounting short-term money market securities such as Treasury paper and commercial bills of exchange, although the Bank is free to decide whether or not to discount suitable paper or to accept it as security for an advance. There has never been a clearly defined limit to any bank's recourse to the central bank, although the Bank regards this recourse as a privilege only exercisable to tide a bank over temporary problems. Under a Royal Decree of 25 June 1968 the Bank was authorised to provide advances against the collateral of debt certificates, a power intended to be used when a bank ought to have its liquidity increased but lacks sufficient eligible collateral.

A change in the discount rate generally influences interest rates fixed by the banks, but it is not necessarily influential on the money market interest rate level which is more usually determined by international interest rates. It is as an indication of a potential lightening or easing of monetary policy that the discount rate has most significance.

In 1954 the Nederlandsche Bank concluded a gentlemen's agreement with the main commercial banks and the agricultural credit banks under which the banks agreed to maintain minimum non-interest-earning balances at a level determined by the Bank, with the Bank. A ceiling of 15 per cent was laid down in the agreement but the Bank announced that it would only raise this ratio above 10 per cent if it first sold most of its open-market holdings and also consulted the banks. In practice 10 per cent was never exceeded. Owing to the high liquidity of the banks the minimum reserve requirement policy was only very limited in its influence in the 1950s and moral suasion was additionally required to limit either the direction or the extent of bank lending. The main purpose of the minimum reserve requirement appears to have been as a means of limiting the influence of the external sector on the domestic money supply which was done by varying it in response to changes in foreign exchange reserves. When the period of large balance of payments surpluses ended in mid-1961 the minimum reserve was lowered down to zero in September 1963 and no similar technique was applied until the mid-1970s.

The Bank was able to conduct open-market operations from 1948 when the Bank Law of that year authorised it to buy and sell bills accepted by banks, Treasury paper and Dutch government or government-guaranteed bonds officially quoted on the Amsterdam stock exchange. Between 1952 and 1964 the Bank used open-market operations to assist discount rate and minimum reserve requirement policy. As with the latter policy, open-market operations in the 1950s were often used to cope with external flows, and also to alleviate in the late 1950s short-run liquidity difficulties in the money market. Into the 1960s open-market policy continued to cushion short-term fluctuations in the market especially to hold interest rates to a comparatively low level internationally. Between 1963 and 1970 the Bank intervened in the forward foreign exchange market rather than in the domestic money market and it was not until 1971 that the Bank again sold Treasury paper in the domestic market.

In May 1960 the Bank agreed with the commercial banks on a system of quantitative restrictions for short-term lending to the private sector which came into force in 1961. The 1965 law on the supervision of the credit system under which this agreement had been concluded allows that the Bank may issue instructions only with respect to major categories or forms of credit. The ceilings on loans to the private sector were revised in a generally upward direction during the 1960s with brief periods in 1963 and from mid-1967 to the end of 1968 in which ceilings were abolished. It was provided that any bank in excess of its lending limit could be required to place non-interest-bearing deposits with the Bank up to the level of the excess. Short-term lending for the purposes of the ceiling agreement comprises loans with an average initial term of less than two years. Some regulation of long-term lending has been accomplished by informal directions.

Control by means of continuous ceilings on credit was not regarded as entirely satisfactory nor even of uniform effect since the established banks usually had higher ceilings than more recently established banks. In 1968 discussions were held between the Nederlandsche Bank and the banks concerning a more flexible system of control and from renewed discussions in 1972 and 1973 ceilings were removed in 1972 and replaced by a new liquid assets ratio.

Recognition of moral suasion as an instrument of control occurs in the 1965 Act on the supervision of the credit system where it is provided that the Bank should first attempt to reach agreement directly with representatives of the banks on the course they wish to be adopted and that only if agreement is impossible may the Bank issue general directives. These directives must have the approval of the Minister of Finance, be presented to Parliament for ratification within three months and have a maximum validity of one year with provision for one extension by the Bank for the same period.

These instruments of monetary policy have been developed in relation to the method used by the Bank to calculate the admissible liquidity supply of the economy. Monetary policy is directed primarily to maintaining liquidity supply, which is defined as currency, demand, time and liquid savings deposits and short-term claims on public authorities held by financial non-bank institutions, as a fairly constant proportion of gross national product.

Regulation in the 1970s

During 1969 credit restrictions had become progressively tighter and commercial bank credit contracted accordingly. These restrictive measures, increases in the discount rate, and quantitative restrictions in the form of credit ceilings and guidelines, continued into 1970 with only slight variations. The credit ceilings were extended until April 1970 with a 5 per cent increase in the ceiling, and although the ceilings on net foreign assets of authorised banks were suspended in April, the ceiling on short-term credit was further extended, first until August with a 1 per cent increase, and then until December with a 3.5 per cent increase. More informal agreements limiting short-term lending by banks to local authorities and restricting the increase in banks' medium and long-term assets to the rate of growth of their medium and long-term liabilities continued into 1971. Personal loans by commercial banks were limited to a growth of 8 per cent in 1971, but credit ceilings were raised twice more and two cuts were made in Bank rate. The latter moves were more in response to exchange market uncertainties than to any domestic influences.

While the overall liquidity ratio was reduced from 33.1 per cent in 1971 to 32.5 per cent in 1972, its lowest level for more than six years, there were some signs of an easing in monetary restrictions. Bank rate was reduced from 5 per cent at the beginning of January 1972 to 3 per cent in September, but in November movements in international interest rates forced the authorities to move it to 4 per cent again. Expansion of personal loans was again restricted but in March the lending arrangements concerning the relationship between banks' long-term assets and long-term liabilities were discontinued and both the global restrictions on bank credit expansion and the obligation on banks to maintain non-interest-bearing penalty deposits with the Bank were suspended and, in July, abolished.

Discussions between the Nederlandsche Bank and the other banks on creating a more flexible system of credit control, which had foundered in 1968 on aspects of a proposed liquid assets ratio, were resumed during 1972 and 1973 with the object of establishing a system of indirect credit controls to replace the more direct system of credit ceilings. Under the new system of controls introduced in the middle of 1973, focus was directed to bank holdings of cash and other liquid assets in relation to deposit liabilities. Nederlandsche Bank was able to use open-market operations and alterations to its facilities as lender of last resort to vary the proportions of cash and other liquid assets held against deposits and by that procedure affect the size and composition of liquid assets. The significant difference between this new system and a straight cash reserve system is that the new system does not enable banks to replenish cash holdings from other liquid assets. Liquidity requirements when operated in a 'mild phase' allow the banks to maintain a margin of free liquidity. In a 'severe phase' liquidity requirements are adjusted by the Bank in order to force the banks to depend on recourse to the Bank for the required liquidity and operational purposes.

Liquidity reserve requirements for the commercial banks were introduced in July 1973 with a reserve ratio of 8 per cent against short-term deposit liabilities set for the initial period with provision to raise this to 14 per cent if it was thought necessary. In August quotas were introduced for banks borrowing from the Bank at the official discount rate, with the provision that those banks which exceeded their quota were to be charged an interest surcharge at a rate of 3 per cent per annum on the excess, subsequently reduced to 2 per cent on an annual basis in October. In December 1973 this provision was varied so that banks exceeding their quota for Bank credit by more than 75 per cent pay an interest surcharge of 4 per cent per annum on the amounts over and above 75 per cent.

As a consequence of the oil crisis in late 1973 domestic money market conditions tightened considerably with Bank rate doubling from 4 per cent to 8 per cent between June and December. Nevertheless since money market rates reached historical highs there was some distortion in the interest rate structure and funds shifted from savings to time deposits. Some adjustments were made to the system in January 1974, with new quotas set for all institutions combined of 725 million guilders of Bank credit for the period 1 March to 19 June (compared to a quota of 550 million guilders during the previous six months), and a change in the surcharge arrangements with a 2 per cent surcharge to be charged on amounts exceeding the ceiling by up to 50 per cent and a surcharge of at least 2 per cent on excesses above this level. In February the interest surcharge on banks exceeding their quota for credit was reduced from 2 per cent to 1 per cent. Comparatively high interest rates were maintained throughout 1974 in order to maintain parity with international rates. Although it had been intended to move into a severe phase of indirect credit controls in the latter half of the year demand weakened and monetary policy was merely maintained rather than strengthened. In consequence bank credit provided to the private sector expanded by 29 per cent, though part of this was in the form of special credit facilities covered by a state guarantee for businesses in liquidity difficulties owing to the oil crisis.

The recession which had begun in the latter part of 1974 deepened in 1975 and as a result demand for bank credit from the private sector dropped away. When the distortion in the domestic interest rate structure was removed in April funds moved back from savings deposits to time deposits. With a large government deficit to be financed, the Bank used open-market operations and an increase from zero to 1 per cent in that part of bank cash reserves to be held at the bank to absorb liquidity. In June the 1965 requirement that local governments only borrow centrally under government direction to avoid overstraining the capital market was removed and local authorities were able to operate in the bond market. At the same time foreign governments and private traders were allowed to operate in the capital market.

During 1976 the main domestic difficulty threatened to be a strong growth in the private sector demand for credit, with a rapid increase in short-term money market interest rates encouraging customers to move their funds from savings to time deposits and expanding the growth of the money supply. Five increases in the discount rate were made, raising it to 7 per cent, and the free liquidity margin of the banks was tightened, but in October the penalty rates on above-quota borrowing by the banks were reduced to 1 per cent for excess borrowing up to 50 per cent and to 2 per cent for any borrowing over and above the first 50 per cent excess.

In early 1975 an agreement had been reached between the Bank and representatives of the banks about revised solvency and liquidity directives. The solvency requirements vary according to the degree of risk of the assets concerned and it is the objective of the liquidity directives to ensure that credit institutions maintain a large enough margin of liquid assets against their liabilities to enable them to bridge any gap occurring in the ordinary course of business when repayments to creditors may exceed repayments by debtors. An additional directive is the fixed asset rule under which the total value of a credit institution's fixed assets may not exceed its own resources. While none of these provisions are the subject of variation as part of monetary policy, their impending implementation forced the banks to increase their guarantee capital, which comprises capital, reserves and subordinated bonds, by means of public or private issues of stock or subordinated bonds during 1975 and 1976. The reason for this lies in the expansion of business in the seventies which had not been matched by any growth in capital.

In March 1977 the Nederlandsche Bank began discussions with representatives of the banks on a possible re-introduction of credit restrictions because of the strong growth in 1976 and into 1977 of short-term and long-term lending to the private sector. The Bank indicated during these discussions that credit expansion in 1977 would have to be restricted to 12 per cent. On 16 May the Nederlandsche Bank announced that it had reached agreement with the banks on restrictions that limited the growth of short-term credit to the private sector and of long-term assets, to the extent that these were not financed by capital market funds, to 12.5 per cent in 1977. If the combined credit institutions exceed this ceiling, the individual banks responsible would have to hold a non-interest-bearing deposit with the Bank of 50 per cent of the excess, although the Bank reserved the right to instruct those banks which go above their ceiling to eliminate their excess. The Bank also announced that it was aiming for a 2 per cent margin of free liquidity for the banks for the 19 May to 15 June period and, in consequence, reduced the liquidity requirement by 0.5 percentage points to 10.5 per cent. Since direct restrictions had been implemented the Bank saw no reason to maintain the existing margin. The upward trend in interest rates was confirmed in November when Nederlandsche Bank increased its discount rates by one percentage point.

Commentary

During the 1950s a combination of discount policy, open-market operations and reserve requirement changes was used but after 1961 monetary policy was implemented through quantitative restrictions. However, control by means of credit ceilings was not looked on any more favourably within the Netherlands than elsewhere and late in the 1960s discussions began between Nederlandsche Bank and the banking system in an endeavour to develop a more flexible control system. Under the new system which operated from the middle of 1973 much tighter central bank control over bank liquidity was possible because the new system did not incorporate any mechanism by which the banks might replace cash holdings from other liquid assets. Nevertheless the strong growth in the demand for credit in 1976 and into 1977 led the Nederlandsche Bank to move back to the use of credit ceilings. Under the more flexible control system it appeared to be possible for the central bank to manipulate liquidity in periods of reduced and weak demand for credit, but when demand became strong it appeared that the central bank required ceilings to modify this demand to its own requirements. The implication of this shift back to direct controls may be that the more flexible control system depended more on its ability to signal the changing direction of policy than the direct system and reactions to such signals had been overwhelmed by the sheer volume of the demand for credit. Alternatively, though less convincingly, it could be argued that the apparent early effectiveness of the indirect controls was due rather to the effects of the distortions in interest rate structure, since the removal of these distortions appears to coincide with the recovery of the private sector's demand for credit.

The range of controls over bank liquidity in the Netherlands appears to be very extensive by comparison with those possessed by central banks in other economies, and money market intervention has been traditional rather than a recent innovation, yet in times of strong demand for credit only the ceiling constraints appear to be effective controls. The argument that distortions in both the structure and efficiency of the banking sector are the longer-run consequences of the application of ceiling constraints could perhaps be tested in the Netherlands, because the older established banks, at least, have had long experience in coping with these constraints.

The Netherlands does not seem to have been much better placed to respond to the large inflows of capital which have been characteristic of the 1970s than those European countries without the policy of open-market operations. For an individual bank operating within the Netherlands' system of regulatory constraints some evasion of the controls may be possible, but it would be very difficult for a bank to manage its own liquidity effectively in the face of the range of controls used by the central bank.

Further Reading

Bank for International Settlements, *Eight European Central Banks* (Allen and Unwin, London, 1963)

Banker, Annual Surveys of Banking, 1972-7

De Kock, M. H., *Central Banking*, 4th edn (Crosby Lockwood Staples, London, 1974)

Economist Intelligence Unit, 'Special Report 2: The Banking System and Industrial Finance in the EEC', *European Trends*, no.49, November 1976

European Communities Monetary Committee, *Monetary Policy in the Countries of the European Economic Community*, Institutions and Instruments, 1972

Holbik, Karel, *Monetary Policy in Twelve Industrial Countries* (Federal Reserve Bank of Boston, 1973)

Karsten, C. F., 'Banking in the Netherlands' in H. W. Auburn (ed.), *Comparative Banking*, 3rd edn (Waterlow, England, 1966)

Morgan, E. Victor, Richard Harrington and George Zis, *Banking Systems and Monetary Policy in the EEC* (Financial Times Ltd, London, 1974)

Orsingher, Roger, *Banks of the World*, English translation (Macmillan, London, 1967)

7 BANKING REGULATION IN BELGIUM

'The policy measures taken by the Banque Nationale de
Belgique leave no doubt that cooperation and goodwill of all
interested institutions are necessary for a successful monetary
policy. Classic instruments of monetary policy are often not
applicable because of the Treasury's situation or because of
capital flows between Belgium and other countries.' (Jacques
Finet, 'Monetary Policy in Belgium' in K. Holbik (ed.),
Monetary Policy in Twelve Industrial Countries (Federal
Reserve Bank of Boston, 1973), p.67.)

Institutional Framework

The main credit institutions in Belgium are commercial banks, the Caisse
Générale d'Epargne et de Retraite (the National Savings Bank), *caisses
d'épargne privées* or private savings banks, the Post Office Giro and some
public and semi-public agencies. Prior to 1935 there was no banking
legislation in Belgium and the traditional banks were mixed banks which
granted all forms of credit and purchased shares in industrial and commercial companies. In the 1930s the equity interests of the banks
encountered serious losses and a Royal Decree of 22 August 1934
separated the mixed banks into holding companies which could hold
industrial portfolios and finance themselves by share capital and bond
issues and deposit banks whose role was limited to the collection of
deposits and the granting of short-term credit. The holding companies
or *sociétés financières* have substantial share holdings in various industries, in particular the Société Générale de Belgique linked with the
Société Générale de Banque and the Société de Bruxelles.

Of the commercial banks, all of which are privately owned, three
dominate, the Société Générale de Banque, Banque de Bruxelles and
Kredietbank, but the total of all commercial bank liabilities comprises
only about a third of the liabilities of financial intermediaries. Commercial bank deposits may be either current or fixed term and the banks
issue bearer bonds or *bons de caisse* of various terms to maturity but
usually of three or five years. Further the banks have been able to raise
their capital by issuing stock and since 1967 have been authorised to
purchase company bonds. These longer-term sources have facilitated
the extension of medium and long-term credit by the banks. A special
facility, Creditexport, operates through a syndicate of the main banks

and four public sector intermediaries to provide finance for exports of capital goods and investment. Member banks are responsible for arranging the terms of loans with their customers and then they discount the export paper with the Société Nationale de Crédit à l'Industrie (SNCI) which distributes shares of the loan to the other banks and public sector intermediaries according to their pre-arranged quotas up to a maximum absolute figure.

The largest bank in the country is the National Savings Bank which accepts current account as well as savings deposits for fixed periods of six months to five years or under a scheme which allows withdrawal without notice only in the first week of each quarter and uses its resources in industry and housing loans as well as in the purchase of government bonds and debentures. Private savings banks operate similarly to the National Savings Bank except that the bulk of their deposits are at less than two years' notice. Largest of the public and semi-public agencies is the SNCI which, during the 1930s, took over many assets from the loss-ridden banking system and subsequently acted as an investment bank borrowing with bond issues and making medium and long-term loans to industry. Owned half by the state and half by private shareholders, the interest on its bonds is tax-free and the principal is state-guaranteed. It ranks as the fifth largest bank after the National Savings Bank and the big three commercial banks.

Recently the Crédit Communal de Belgique, the bank for local authorities, has made moves to diversify into other areas. Other agencies of note are the Caisse Nationale de Crédit Professionnel which provides funds for small firms and the Institut National de Crédit Agricole which provides funds for agriculture. The Post Office Giro system also functions as a deposit bank.

Banque Nationale de Belgique, the central bank, is a public company in which the state owns half the shares. Until December 1973 the BNB did not have sufficient statutory power to enforce specifically those instruments of monetary policy which it had been its traditional role to use. While the BNB is an autonomous, private institution directed by a council, half of whose members represent the country's different economic interests, a government commissioner appointed by the Ministry of Finance as permanent government representative does have a power of veto over all decisions. Supervision of the monetary system is by no means the sole prerogative of the BNB; the Commission Bancaire, the Institut de Réescompte et de Garantie (IRG) and the Fonds des Rentes also have important tasks. The Commission Bancaire has supervisory powers over both the commercial banks and the *sociétés financières*, sets solvency rules for capital and reserves, sets the liquidity ratios and collects information on a regular basis from the banks. Although the Commission is administered by a full-time chairman and six part-time members all of whom are government appointees the six part-time members are chosen equally from those proposed by the BNB, the Belgian Bankers' Association and the IRG.

The IRG, established in 1935 to assist in providing bank liquidity, is active as a discount house in the money market, is able to refinance itself by rediscounting assets with the BNB, and discounts bills held by the banks and, if acceptable, those held by companies and individuals. The institution responsible for open-market operations is the Fonds des Rentes which was established in 1945 specifically to manage the government securities market. Its management committee of six has half its members appointed by the Ministry of Finance and half by the BNB. Finance for its operations comes from the issue of *certificats de fonds des rentes* or four-month bills, from money market borrowings, or from borrowings from the BNB.

Such a proliferation of regulatory institutions raises the spectre of lack of co-ordination in control; however, Jacques Finet writing on Belgium's monetary policy in 1973 emphasised the close contact existing between the authorities and both the public and private financial institutions. He argued that the BNB's lack of statutory base for its powers was not a serious omission as the BNB was able to convince the monetary sector of the correctness of policy moves and accordingly to rely on their support. It appears that the special problems which high inflows of capital into the country created in the early seventies (discussed below) made the application of controls by a series of gentlemen's agreements sufficiently difficult that in December 1973 the powers of the BNB were finally clarified by legislation which expressly gave the Bank power to impose balance sheet ratios on the banks, to call for special deposits to be made with it and to fix maximum interest rates on the various forms of bank liabilities. These powers, which extend to both public and private financial institutions, may only be exercised with the authority of the Ministry of Finance.

Instruments of Control

The instruments used by the BNB are the result of tradition rather than original legislative assignment. Although the BNB numbers among its methods of control discount rate policy, intervention on the money market, a monetary reserve ratio and qualitative and quantitative controls as well as operations in the foreign exchange market, credit control in the sense in which it is seen in most other countries in this survey appears to have been only generally used since 1969.

Until 1969, reserve ratios, the discount rate and rediscount quotas were the main methods of control. Under the banking law of 1935 the Commission Bancaire was empowered to set required reserve ratios for banks in consultation with the BNB but it was not until 1946 that three ratios were introduced: a cash ratio which was intended to safeguard the liquidity of the banks; a solvency ratio set between own funds and funds borrowed or deposited; and a cover ratio for short-term Belgian franc liabilities. Both the cash and the cover ratios were discontinued in 1962 and the solvency ratio was replaced in 1965 by an own funds ratio or *coefficient de fonds propres* which is not used for policy purposes.

A reserve ratio system was introduced by the Commission Bancaire's decree of 21 December 1961 which authorised the fixing, on the BNB's proposal, of the proportion of the banks' various categories of monetary and quasi-monetary liabilities that must be held as special sight deposits at the BNB, sight balances with the Fonds des Rentes or government securities of special type deposited with the BNB. This ratio may not exceed 20 per cent for liabilities on demand or less than thirty days, and 7 per cent for liabilities at more than one month and for deposit books and it may not be raised by more than three percentage points in any thirty-day period without the approval of both the Minister of Finance and the Minister for Economic Affairs.

The BNB exercises a qualitative control through its discount policy. Bills presented by the banks for discount must mature in 120 days or less and must either bear three signatures or two signatures and a guarantee. The European Communities' Monetary Committee[1] remarked in 1972 that 'the efficacy of the instrument largely depends on the elasticity of credit demand in relation to its cost' (pp.365-6) and it would appear that certainly in inflationary situations its greatest effect lies in its psychological influence rather than in any limiting of credit.

In 1969 a new system of certification and rediscount ceilings for the banks was introduced under which each bank has a ceiling fixed in relation to its average amount in the preceding year of deposits in Belgian francs, bonds, medium-term notes and its own funds. When that ceiling is reached, a bank is unable to submit bills to the BNB for either discounting or certification. Certification or visa is a preferential rediscounting procedure applied to bills drawn in connection with the foreign trade of the Benelux Economic Union, under which the BNB makes a formal commitment to discount the bill as soon as it is within 120 days of maturity.

Since its creation in 1945 the Fonds des Rentes, an autonomous body whose commitments are guaranteed by the government, has been allocated the task of regulating the market for medium and long-term government paper and by the law of 19 June 1959 it was authorised to carry out open-market operations and its task was extended to the short end of the market. Nevertheless, the scope for open-market operations is seriously limited, in the case of the short-term end of the market by the fact that the public does not have access to short-term government securities, and in the case of the longer-term end by the obligation of the Fonds des Rentes to facilitate the covering of Treasury needs, which is a continuing requirement.

Rates of interest paid on fixed deposits and on bearer bonds by the commercial banks and other financial institutions are fixed collectively by the Comité de concertation des taux d'intérêts or committee on creditor interest rates. The governor of the BNB is chairman of this committee whose determinations are binding and reinforced by the powers of the BNB.

Direct action on bank lending may be quantitative or qualitative, general or specific. From January 1964 to July 1965 the BNB applied quantitative restrictions to the banks and in 1966 the BNB requested that the banks continue to lend for productive investment or modernisation projects but that they should restrict loans to firms having long-run profit problems. In April 1969 the BNB introduced quantitative restrictions on credit granted by banks to firms and individuals who were making speculative investments abroad.

Application and Variation of Controls in the 1970s

In 1970, as a necessary response to the easing of monetary conditions abroad, the monetary authorities lowered the Bank rate and removed the ceilings set in 1969 on bank credit for investment and export finance, although new general credit ceilings were set for September. From 1973 into 1975 the policy stance became increasingly restrictive. An agreement was concluded on 26 July 1973 between the BNB, the Commission Bancaire and the commercial banks for the establishment of a monetary reserve by the deposit of part of bank deposits in convertible Belgian francs in non-interest-bearing blocked accounts at the BNB. Primarily this agreement was aimed at discouraging the speculative inflows of foreign capital and it was applied into 1974. Part of the obligation imposed was the placing of a specified percentage of the increase in deposits into government paper. Also in 1972 and into 1973 the banks' rediscount and visa ceilings were reduced.

In March 1974 the BNB asked the commercial banks to hold their increase in credit to households and firms down to about 14 per cent in 1974. By the beginning of 1974 the discount rate had risen in a year from 5 per cent to 8.75 per cent and the BNB had additionally introduced a special penalty rate, adjustable daily, for the refinancing of those categories of paper not entered under the rediscount and visa ceilings. In combination these measures pushed up money market rates and influenced the banks to raise their lending and borrowing rates, but inflationary pressure was not significantly reduced due to the strength of the growth in foreign exchange reserves.

Early in 1975 the tight monetary arrangements of 1974 were eased with the lowering of the reserve ratio against sight liabilities and the abolition of the reserve requirement against deposits beyond two years, the releasing of direct controls on credit, the increasing of bank liquidity by refunding part of the blocked account funds and the lowering of the discount rate. From 10 March commercial and savings banks decided to reduce their interest rates on savings deposits by between 0.25 per cent and 0.75 per cent; from 13 March the basic discount rate was reduced by 0.75 per cent and the BNB's other interest rates by 1 per cent; and from 24 April the official rediscount rate, other BNB rates and bank interest on time deposits and bonds were reduced by 0.5 per cent.

From these conditions of comparative monetary ease in 1975, the operation of the two-tier exchange market in late 1975 and early 1976 presented the authorities with the necessity of minimising the potential for speculative outflows of capital. Their methods of accomplishing this were to raise short-term interest rates, lower the rediscount ceiling (including reintroducing the double rediscounting ceiling system) and direct the banks to restrict their lending.

These restrictive actions were relaxed at the end of 1976 and the beginning of 1977 when the official discount rate, the Bank's special rates and its rate of interest on current account advances were lowered. More reductions were made in June and the ceiling on direct lending to the Belgian Treasury was raised in July.

Commentary

Surprisingly, in view of the proliferation of regulatory institutions concerned with the Belgian financial sector, the regulatory constraints used by the Banque Nationale de Belgique have developed by custom rather than by legislative endowment. The concentration on reserve ratios, the discount rate and rediscount quotas as controls proved sufficient until the experience of high levels of liquidity generated primarily by large capital flows in the late sixties and early seventies necessitated the employment of controls which had not been successfully accomplished by means of voluntary agreements with the banks. Of course in a market in which the public does not have access to short-term government securities, it is extremely difficult for effective open market operations to be carried out. Because of the government's consistent requirement of long-term funds, provision of which it is the task of the Fonds des Rentes to facilitate, no more success is likely to be accorded attempts to operate in the long-term end of the market.

The 1972-3 changes in policy controls should be seen as an attempt on the part of the authorities to provide more flexible controls which would be more readily able to cope with the strong currency flows which have been a feature of the Belgian economy, even with the operation of a two-tier foreign exchange market. A major aim of the more recent use of banking controls has been to discourage capital inflows as far as possible and to neutralise the effects of those flows which are not deterred. Although it can be argued as easily in the case of Belgium as elsewhere that direct controls may inhibit efficiency in the banking sector, it is quite clear from the Belgian experience that the size of the capital flows with which it has been faced could have been more disruptive had indirect controls with their tendency to lagged effects been used.

From the viewpoint of an individual bank the move towards legislated controls in 1973 could have been viewed with concern. This change was necessitated by the difficulties which the BNB had found in using the gentlemen's agreements for control. It is hard to find other means which could have been used to cope with the strong liquidity inflows with which the economy has been faced in the seventies.

Notes

1. European Communities Monetary Committee, *Monetary Policy in the Countries of the European Economic Community* (Institutions and Instruments, 1972).

Further Reading

Bank for International Settlements, *Eight European Central Banks* (Allen and Unwin, London, 1963)
De Kock, M. H., *Central Banking*, 4th edn (Crosby Lockwood Staples, London, 1974)

Fierens, D. L., 'Banking in Belgium' in H. W. Auburn (ed.), *Comparative Banking*, 3rd edn (Waterlow, England, 1966)

Morgan, E. Victor, Richard Harrington and George Zis, *Banking Systems and Monetary Policy in the EEC* (Financial Times Ltd, London, 1974)

Orsingher, Roger, *Banks of the World*, English translation (Macmillan, London, 1967)

8 BANKING IN IRELAND

'Banking in the Republic of Ireland has changed more in the
past ten years than in the previous fifty. The restructuring of
older banks, the establishment of a large number of new banks,
the emergence of financial markets and the developing role of
the central bank are the main elements in the story.' (Governor
of the Central Bank of Ireland, Dr T. K. Whitaker at the
Manchester Statistical Society 30 November 1971, speech
reprinted in the Central Bank of Ireland *Quarterly Bulletin*,
Spring 1972, p.62.)

Institutional Framework

Although Ireland has had a commercial banking system for centuries with
the Bank of Ireland founded by charter in 1783, even in the Currency
Act of 1927, which was based mainly on the recommendations made by
a Banking Commission in 1926, no provision was made for the establishment of a central bank. At the time the justification for this absence
was that there was very limited scope for monetary policy because there
was no money market in Ireland.

A later Banking Commission established in 1934 strongly suggested
the establishment of a central bank in its 1938 report. However, the
enabling Act was not passed until 1942 and the Central Bank of Ireland
only came into existence in 1943. The Central Bank assumed the responsibilities of the Currency Commission which had, under the 1922
Act, administered functions concerning the provision and redemption
of currency. In addition, the 1942 Act provided the Central Bank with
powers to act as a lender of last resort and to control credit, but it was
not until the 1950s that the functions of the Central Bank were significantly extended beyond those of the Currency Commission.

Under the Act the responsibility for licensing banks was moved from
the Revenue Commission to the Reserve Bank and this shift enabled a
review to be made of the conditions under which bank licences were
granted. Minimum capital requirements were raised and limits were set
for the share of total lending to any single area, and for the proportion
of total share capital that could be held by an individual. A potential
new entrant had to provide a minimum capital of 1 million pounds,
evidence of a sound structure and reputable management, and it had to
show that there was an economic need for its services.

In 1972 the Central Bank moved away from quantitative ceilings as the primary constraint and imposed liquidity ratios instead. Both primary and secondary liquidity ratios were set for the Associated Banks. Primary liquidity consists of cash and deposits at the Central Bank while secondary liquidity is government paper, with each of these expressed as a proportion of the banks' domestic deposits from the non-bank private sector plus net inter-bank borrowing and net external liabilities. In February 1973, the primary ratio was a minimum of 13 per cent and the secondary ratio a minimum of 30 per cent for the Associated Banks. Although these ratios forced the banks to hold 43 per cent in these forms of liquidity, this did not provide the Central Bank with sufficient control over credit creation and the restrictive ratios were reinforced by broad guidelines on new lending as well as by provisions to freeze half of any net capital inflows.

The main category of Irish banks are referred to as Associated Banks, a term which derives from the 1942 Act which gave them a special relationship with the Central Bank. Apart from the Bank of Ireland, most other Associated Banks were founded as joint-stock banks during the 1824-62 period and all of them had extensive branch networks by the end of the nineteenth century.

There were eight Associated Banks in 1965: the Bank of Ireland, the Hibernian Bank (although this had been owned by the Bank of Ireland since 1958), Munster and Leinster Bank, the National Bank of Ireland, the Provincial Bank of Ireland, and the Royal Bank of Ireland, all of which had their headquarters in Ireland; and the Northern Bank and the Ulster Bank which had their headquarters in Northern Ireland.

As a result of a series of bank amalgamations in 1965 and 1966 those banks with headquarters in Ireland formed two groups: the Bank of Ireland, the Hibernian Bank and the National Bank of Ireland formed the Bank of Ireland group; and the Munster and Leinster Bank, the Provincial Bank of Ireland and the Royal Bank of Ireland formed the Allied Irish Banks Group. Of the Northern Ireland-based banks, the Northern Bank, after being acquired by the Midland Bank in 1965, merged in 1970 with the Belfast Banking Company, which was Midland's other Northern Ireland subsidiary, while the Ulster Bank was a subsidiary of the National Westminster Bank. The Ireland-owned banks account for most of the business of the Associated Banks.

From their 670 branches, the Associated Banks offer current and deposit accounts and provide credit by means of an overdraft system which makes funds available for long and short terms. The majority of Associated Bank deposits are small deposits at seven days' notice. In

1972 the overdraft system was augmented by a system of term loans which are granted for specified purposes and are repayable by negotiated amounts within a fixed period. Borrowers are divided into three categories: AAA, government, government-guaranteed borrowers and large companies; AA, customers in the primary, agricultural, manufacturing, construction and services sectors; and A, all other borrowers, including personal accounts. With the introduction of term loans, overdrafts became mainly seasonal working accounts, with the amounts used repaid within a year.

At least partly as a response to increased competition from the non-Associated Banks, the Associated Banks have moved into the instalment credit and merchant banking fields, and increased their participation in the housing finance field.

A uniform structure of lending and borrowing rates agreed to among the Associated Banks is applied in Ireland.

The non-Associated Banks, which are mostly located in Dublin and do not have branch networks, comprise four main groups. The first group in terms of size comprises seven merchant banks, including four subsidiaries of Associated Banks, which operate as wholesale bankers taking deposits of 50,000 pounds and above. Second of the groups comprises branches of the North American banks, the Bank of America, First National Bank of Chicago, the First National City Bank and the Bank of Nova Scotia and a joint venture, the Chase and Bank of Ireland (International). This group's activities only date from about 1965 and are almost entirely concerned with servicing US corporations which have operations in Ireland. Eleven industrial banks, mainly providing instalment credit, make up the third group. Some sixteen miscellaneous banks in the fourth group include the subsidiaries of a French bank and of a Dutch bank.

Other private sector financial institutions are hire-purchase finance companies, twenty-six building societies, which provide almost three-quarters of mortgage finance for housing, fifteen insurance companies and a number of credit unions.

There are also public sector financial institutions, of which the most numerous are the Savings Banks (the Post Office Savings Bank and the five Trustee Savings Banks) with 1,400 branches providing time-deposit facilities and some demand deposit services (the latter mainly provided by the Trustee Savings Banks). The Agriculture Credit Corporation Ltd and the Industrial Credit Corporation Ltd were both established by the state to provide capital for agricultural development and for industry, respectively.

Banking Supervision

Until the middle fifties the level of commercial bank liquidity was so high that central bank assistance was unnecessary, and it was only a long series of external deficits that created an environment in which the central bank could play a role. From 1955 the Central Bank of Ireland began to act as a lender of last resort by rediscounting commercial bills of exchange and Irish Government Exchequer bills and from 1958 the banks began to maintain clearing balances with the Central Bank for the purpose of inter-bank settlements.

The Central Bank of Ireland issued to the Associated Banks in 1965 the first of a series of letters of advice specifying guidelines for the expansion of credit at a time when bank credit appeared to be growing too quickly and the balance of payments position was also causing concern. These letters usually referred to a year in their specification of the exact expansion of credit allowed to Associated Banks, but they were subject to review when the economic conditions or banking circumstances changed. From 1969 the Central Bank extended its advice to the non-Associated Banks and in 1971 these banks were also subject to quantitative limitations on their lending.

As already noted, the absence of an Irish money market was one of the reasons that the Central Bank of Ireland was not established until 1942 and even in the fifties and sixties the Associated Banks continued their traditional placing of money at call and short notice in London, and any excess liquidity of the non-Associated Banks also found its way into short-term deposits in London.

In 1969 the Central Bank of Ireland began to develop a more extensive market for short-term deposits in Dublin, following the report of a committee appointed in 1967 to investigate the ways of developing a money market. The Central Bank agreed to accept a wide range of deposits from Associated and non-Associated Banks, at call and at various periods of notice. It took over from the government the monthly issue of Exchequer bills to the banks and to the public, and it expanded its portfolio of short-dated government stock, in which it made a market for transactions in large amounts at current prices.

At about the same time a Dublin Inter-Bank Market for short-term lending developed with the North American bank group as the main borrowers and the merchant banks as the main lenders. Although the Governor of the Central Bank of Ireland commented in 1972 that 'The centralisation of reserves and the growth of a domestic money market have gone a long way towards establishing a domestic liquidity base for the banking system' Morgan, Harrington and Zis noted in 1974 (p.53) that although the emergence of a domestic money market had resulted in the retention of funds in Dublin, the Associated Banks still held up to 60 per cent of their liquid assets outside the Republic.

The main instrument for control of the banks until the Central Bank Act of 1971 was quantitative limits on credit which were limited in their effectiveness by the dominance of the overdraft form of lending under which official credit limits could be frustrated by the drawing down of already authorised but previously unused overdraft limits. With the passing of the Central Bank Act of 1971 the Central Bank of Ireland assumed the complete range of normal central banking functions.

The close links that exist between the Dublin and London money markets and the free transfer of capital abroad available for Irish residents has had the effect of holding Irish interest rates close to those prevailing in London with Irish rates at about one and a half percentage points below the London rates, possibly the largest differential sustainable without reactions in terms of capital flows.

Recent Use of Controls

The increase in liquidity ratios (the primary to 13 per cent and the secondary to 31 per cent) as part of a more restrictive monetary policy stance in February 1973 was reinforced by the issuing of broad guidelines on the direction of new bank lending, and until August it appeared that these moves were successful. However, between then and November capital inflows raised bank liquidity. The distribution of credit did reflect the Central Bank's directives, with more credit now being extended to industry and less to property companies and the personal sector.

A strong increase in private sector lending in early 1974 prompted the Central Bank to raise the liquidity ratios of the non-Associated Banks and to require the Associated Banks to freeze their lending for other than productive purposes. Lending slowed down markedly in the second half of the year and credit restrictions were eased in March and removed in July of 1975. Interest rates fell towards the end of 1974 and in the first half of 1975, in line with London rates, the Associated Banks' interest rates and the Central Bank's minimum discount rate were reduced.

Further Reading

'Banking in the Republic of Ireland', *Midland Bank Review* (November 1973)

Committee on the Functions, Operation and Development of a Money Market in Ireland (the Ryand Committee), *Report* (Central Bank of Ireland, May 1969)

'Common Market Survey VI: Republic of Ireland', *The Banker* (January 1975)

Fitzpatrick, James, 'Portrait of an Economy', *The Bankers' Magazine* (March 1978)

Kennedy, Kieran A. and R. Burton, *The Irish Economy*, The Economic and Social Research Institute Studies, Economic and Financial Series No.10 (Brussels, March 1975)

Morgan, E. Victor, Richard Harrington and G. Zis, *Banking Systems and Monetary Policy in the EEC* (Financial Times Ltd, London, 1974)

OECD Economic Surveys, *Ireland* (annual 1969 to 1977)

Thorn, Philip and J. M. Lack (eds.), *Banking and Sources of Finance in the European Community* (Banker Research Unit, London, 1977)

9 THE CONTROL OF BANKING IN ITALY

'If we examine the history of finance in Italy in the last one
or two decades, we cannot but be astounded at the singular
contrast between the relative stability of the institutional
structure . . . and the far-reaching changes in the instruments
of monetary policy.' (C. Conigliani and T. Padoa-Schioppa,
'Recent Developments in the Italian Banking System', *Banca
Nazionale del Lavoro Quarterly Review*, vol.29 (1976), p.349.)

The Institutional Framework

The monetary system in Italy is generally overseen by the Interminis-
terial Committee for Credit and Savings (*Comitato Interministeriale per
il Credito e il Risparmio*), CICR. The Bank D'Italia provides fact finding
and implementation of CICR decisions and is an authoritative adviser
to the Government. The Treasury undertakes all cash transactions in
relation to the national budget and participates in money creation by
issuing coins. It is usual for the government's large cash deficits to be
financed by the issue of fixed-income securities in the capital market or
by short-term advances from the Bank of Italy.

Central banking functions are jointly exercised by the Bank of Italy
and the Italian Exchange Office. While the Bank of Italy has a monopoly
on the issue of bank notes and holds the compulsory and free reserves
of the commercial banks, both institutions extend short-term credit to
banks, to the Treasury and to foreign countries.

Italy's Banking Law, which dates from 1936, distinguishes between
short, medium and long-term credit transactions. Banks are able to
operate only in the short-term money market. Short-term deposits are
defined as current deposits and fixed deposits up to eighteen months,
while on the lending side, banks provide finance for a maximum of
twelve months, although fixed investments can be financed by 'rolling
over' a loan through special credit institutions (the medium-term institutions) which are fully or partly owned by the banks. Some of the larger
banks have special departments for long-term lending.

There are two main groups of banks, the public law or public charter
banks of which the Banca Nazionale del Lavoro is the largest, and the
three banks of national interest — Banca Commerciale Italiana, Credito
Italiano and Banca di Roma — which are almost completely controlled
by the state's Instituto per la Riconstruzione Industriale (IRI). In 1972

formal recognition was finally given to the operations of banks in the medium-term sector and they were officially permitted to grant credits of up to sixty months with a ceiling of 8 per cent to 10 per cent of their deposits.

The Operation of Controls

Until 1973 Italian monetary policy tended to use indirect instruments aimed at regulating the process of money creation. Four main instruments may be distinguished — open-market operations; changes in the volume and, after 1969, in the cost of credit to the commercial banks; variations in reserve requirements; and changes in regulations concerning the banks' net foreign positions.

Open market operations were used mostly after 1966 when the government elected to follow a more explicit policy of stabilising long-term interest rates and, almost simultaneously, the Bank of Italy began to buy large amounts of government long-term bonds at issue to facilitate the financing of increasing government deficits. The Bank of Italy has five main ways of financing government debt — the sale of long-term securities to the public; sale of Treasury bills; absorption of Treasury bills in commercial bank compulsory reserves; inflow of postal deposits; and bond subscriptions or overdrafts from the Bank itself. If neither of the first two ways is possible, higher interest rates and increased creation of liquidity must result.

Regulation of the volume of credit to commercial banks has tended to be accomplished by quantitative rationing rather than by means of changes in the discount rate. The Bank of Italy has usually lent to commercial banks by advances on collateral. In 1967 it introduced a supplement to this in the form of advances on collateral with a fixed maturity of 8, 15 or 22 days, which had to be drawn in full when granted, and from 1969 penalty rates were charged on lending above a stated level.

As is well known, the cost of borrowing in any form from the Bank of Italy stayed at 3.5 per cent from 1958 to 1969, during which period policy was directed to restricting the availability of bank credit. Between 1954 and 1969 minimum lending rates (tied to the discount rate) and maximum deposit rates were set by inter-bank agreement, but this agreement was not continuously adhered to by the banks and in December 1969 the cartel was abandoned. A new cartel which set maximum deposit rates was formed in September 1970.

In March 1969 penalty rates were set for fixed term advances made to banks more than once in each six-month period and in July 1969 a

1.5 per cent surcharge over the basic rate was established on ordinary rediscount operations when a bank had outstanding rediscounts of over 5 per cent of its required assets during the preceding calendar semester. The basic discount rate was raised from 3.5 per cent to 4 per cent in August 1969 and to 5.5 per cent in May 1970.

The OECD study of *Monetary Policy in Italy* in reviewing the major instruments of Italian monetary policy prior to 1973 described the compulsory reserve requirements as 'the fulcrum on which the system operates' (p.67). Although all banks must hold minimum reserves against all deposits of non-bank residents and the lire (but not the foreign currency deposits) of non-residents, the ratios and the assets to which they apply vary with the type of deposit and the type of institution. For the commercial banks, deposits are subject to progressively larger requirements depending on the ratio of the individual bank's deposit liabilities to its capital plus reserves. The maximum ratio for an individual bank is 22.5 per cent. From 1953 to 1962 commercial banks could hold their reserves in any combination of cash deposits or Treasury bills with the Bank of Italy. Cash deposits returned 3.75 per cent and Treasury bills 3.88 per cent. After 1 December 1962 commercial banks had to maintain a minimum cash balance with the Bank of Italy equal to 10 per cent of the excess of deposit liabilities over capital plus reserves, and the rest of reserves could still be held in cash deposits or Treasury bills. The return on deposits was raised to 5.5 per cent and that on Treasury bills to 5.82 per cent in October 1970. From 30 September 1965 reserves against increases in fixed and savings deposits of commercial banks could be held in a wide range of long-term securities provided that a minimum of 10 per cent of total deposits was held in cash at the Bank of Italy. The definition of reserves was expanded further in 1967 and 1968 to include school building bonds and bonds of the institution distributing credit for public works (CREDIOP), and also in late 1970 when commercial banks were allowed to substitute certain long-term bonds for cash or Treasury bills. The main purpose of these variations has been to enlarge and improve the operation of the bond market rather than to change short-term monetary management.

While the regulation of banks' net foreign position is also a weapon of monetary management it does not directly relate to the domestic activities of the commercial banks and accordingly is not considered here.

1973/4: The Move to Selective Credit Policy

The introduction of a selective credit policy in Italy was achieved by two provisions, one establishing floors on securities investments by

banks, and the second setting growth ceilings on bank loans. Before discussing their impact, the contents of these provisions will be outlined.

From 18 June 1973 the commercial banks were required to raise
their portfolios of fixed-interest securities during the year by an amount
(net of investments for compulsory reserve and liquidity requirements)
equal to at least 6 per cent of their savings and demand deposits on 31
December 1972. This 6 per cent was to be composed of 5 per cent in
the bonds of the industrial credit institutions and private companies,
and of 1 per cent in government paper (other than Treasury bills) and
securities issued by the autonomous government agencies and by the
CREDIOP on behalf of the Treasury. On 15 December 1973 the required
rate of increase was raised to 9 per cent, the distinction between the
different types of bond issue was abolished and bonds for agricultural
improvement credit were included. And on 18 July 1974 it was required
that the amount due at 30 June 1974 be increased before 31 December
1974 by 3 per cent of the total deposits held on 31 December 1973.

With regard to the ceilings on bank loans, a regulation imposed from
26 July 1973 required that for the period from 31 March 1973 to 31
March 1974 a 12 per cent ceiling should be set for increases in loans to
financial and commercial enterprises and non-profit-making institutions
reaching amounts of 500 million lire or more within that period. The
12 per cent ceiling was also placed on the rest of loans to the same borrowers and on loans to other borrowers reaching amounts of 500 million
lire in the same period. Prefinancing on long-term loans arranged with
the special credit institutions was exempt from these limits. These provisions applied to each individual bank for the total of its customers
within the various categories, but left the expansion of individual loans
unrestricted.

The financing operations of public works contractors, lending to
non-residents and foreign currency loans to residents were exempted
from the growth ceilings (August-September 1973).

On 6 April 1974 these ceilings were renewed for the period of 31
March 1974 to 31 March 1975 with some modifications. The distinction
between loans below and above 500 million lire was abolished and loans
below 30 million lire were exempt altogether. A 15 per cent ceiling was
imposed on the growth of loans of 30 million lire or above to local
authorities and their agencies and on those of 500 million lire or more
to other clients. An overall ceiling was introduced on total loans of
30 million lire or more of 8 per cent for the April to September 1974
period and of 15 per cent for the year April 1974 to March 1975. Loans
to the electricity industry, health services, railways and for agricultural

production were exempted from any ceiling.

With a down-turn in economic activity, little external impact on the money supply and the moderate impact of government financing in 1975, the monetary authorities were able to repeal the exceptional arrangements for liquidity control which were imposed in 1974. Abolition of the import deposit scheme released funds, but it was not until the second half of 1975 that there was any real increase in the money supply. In September an automatic rediscounting system was established between the banks and the Italian Exchange Office to refinance export credits at a preferential rate.

For the latter half of 1975 the minimum amount of fixed-income securities to be held by banks was reduced from 40 per cent of their increase in deposits to 30 per cent, although as the securities were valued at their nominal worth only 25 per cent of new deposit funds were necessary to purchase the securities. The Bank of Italy also moved to create a primary market for Treasury bonds by allowing the Bank, banks and non-bank transactors to take up Treasury bonds.

The ceiling of 15 per cent imposed for the March 1974 to March 1975 period was not reached owing to the down-turn in credit demand and while bank deposits maintained their late 1974 rate of increase into 1975 there was a stronger switch from current account to time deposits. The discount rate was lowered from 9 per cent at the end of 1974 to 6 per cent in September 1975 and the Bank announced that it would provide preferential rediscounting facilities to those banks which lowered their interest rates on lending. It was the intention of the qualitative application of ceilings to limit loans to individuals and governments first, and even when these restrictions were extended to loans to commerce and industry, care was taken to maintain funding for productive investment.

In 1975 these exceptional arrangements for liquidity control were allowed to lapse, although the requirement that the banks hold a minimum amount of fixed-income securities was retained, but with a new base, the increase in deposits. During the year the demand for credit rose quite substantially and monetary policy in the subsequent year, 1976, was used to soak up the excess liquidity created. The discount rate was raised from 15 per cent to 15.75 per cent in February; in February and March the banks were required to hold an additional 0.75 per cent of total deposits at the end of 1975, and then in October to hold a further 0.5 per cent of total deposits at the end of June. Also in October a ceiling on increases in bank credit during the period of November 1976 to March 1977 was set in line with the EEC agreement for credit to the economy for 1976.

Commentary

Seen in the context of Italy's difficult economic conditions, the strong controls used in monetary policy do not appear unreasonable. However, examination of the implementation of the controls from the point of view of an individual bank suggests that the switch to selective credit policy, more directly applied than the indirect instruments used before 1973, lowered the ability of the banks to manage their own funding. Because of the large swings in liquidity and several dramatic rises in the demand for credit the closer controls of selective credit policy are clearly preferable from a macroeconomic policy point of view, but the fall-off in demand on several occasions minimised the effects of easing policy on the banks.

Further Reading

Economist Intelligence Unit, 'Special Report 2: The Banking System and Industrial Finance in the EEC', *European Trends*, no.49 (November 1976)

European Communities Monetary Committee, *Monetary Policy in the Countries of the European Economic Community* (Institutions and Instruments, 1972)

Fazio, Antonio, 'Monetary Base and the Control of Credit in Italy', *Banca Nazionale del Lavoro Quarterly Review*, no.89 (June 1969)

Ferrari, Alberto, 'Monetary Policy in Italy' in Karel Holbik (ed.), *Monetary Policy in Twelve Industrial Countries* (Federal Reserve Bank of Boston, 1973)

OECD, *Monetary Policy in Italy*, Monetary Studies Series (May 1973)

Morgan, E. Victor, Richard Harrington and George Zis, *Banking Systems and Monetary Policy in the EEC* (Financial Times Ltd, London, 1974), ch.6

Robertson, Martin, 'The Short-term Management of the Economy' in Kevin Allen and Andrew Stevenson, *An Introduction to the Italian Economy*, Glasgow Social and Economic Research Studies 1 (London, 1974)

10 BANKING REGULATION IN DENMARK

'Throughout the 1960s, and even more distinctly in the 1970s, the necessity to borrow considerable amounts abroad has had a decisive influence on Danish monetary policy.' (P. Nyboe Anderson, 'External Constraints on Denmark's Monetary Policy', *The Banker*, July 1978, p.80.)

Institutional Framework

Apart from the mortgage societies, which are very important in the financing of real estate, the Danish credit system is dominated by the commercial banks and savings banks. Commercial banks, whose deposits come from business firms and households, may be divided into three categories. First are the three major banks — Kjøbenhavns Handelsbank, Den Danske Landmandsbank and Privatbanken — who account for over half of the combined assets of the commercial banks. Second are a group of medium-sized banks, including Den Danske Rovinsbank and Andelsbankers, which are mainly domiciled in Copenhagen. Third are a group of comparatively small local banks which are based in the provinces. All of the over 100 commercial banks in Denmark are members of the Federation of Danish Banks or Danske Bankers Faellesrepraesentation which negotiates with the National Bank in the formulation of monetary policy. While the commercial banks are joint-stock companies, the savings banks must be non-profit-making institutions. Both types of banks have been the subject of mergers within their respective groups since 1960 as the original tendency for purely local banks is gradually being replaced by larger banks with well-developed branch networks. The two largest savings banks, Sparekassen Kobenhavin-Sjelland and Bikuben, hold over a third of all savings bank deposits. Commercial banks do twice the business of savings banks.

Danish banks pay interest on current accounts, make approximately two-thirds of their mainly short-term lending by overdraft and hold a large proportion of their funds in national and local government bonds, mortgage society securities and National Bank deposit certificates, all of which are readily realisable. In 1958 the Finansieringsinstituttet for Industri og Handvaerk A/S was established to provide medium-term loans for industry where these cannot be obtained from other financial institutions. Share capital for this new institution was subscribed by the National Bank, commercial and savings banks, insurance companies and some trade organisations and it primarily raises further capital by the issue of debentures.

The central bank, the National Bank of Denmark, set up by the Act of 7 April 1936, is managed by a board of directors of twenty-five members, a committee of directors of seven members and a three-member board of governors.

Instruments of Banking Control

Since Denmark lacks not only a domestic money market but also a system of reserve requirements, the instruments of the National Bank are restricted to rediscounting, a system of special deposits and credit ceilings. A wide range of assets including company equities are eligible for rediscount at the Bank. Deposit certificates issued by the National Bank as negotiable short-term securities have a term of ninety-one days and are sold to commercial banks, savings banks and stockbrokers who may freely negotiate them and who may borrow on them at the discount rate from the National Bank. Commercial and savings banks adjust their interest rates to changes in bank rate. Discount rate, bank rate and other rates of interest charged by the National Bank are set by the board of governors.

There are liquidity and solvency requirements but these cannot be modified and, accordingly, have no monetary policy objective. However, credit ceilings have been a major means of monetary restraint in recent years.

Under agreements between the National Bank and the commercial and savings banks concluded in February and March 1965 a new tool for influencing bank lending capacity was established which provided that 20 per cent of the increased deposits in both commercial and savings banks should be deposited in the National Bank, or, for commercial banks, should be applied to increasing their net foreign exchange reserves. Further, the agreements provided that negotiations must take place between the Bank and the banking associations every six months.

The National Bank may also take funds from the banks in the form of deposit certificates originally issued for three months, but supplemented since May 1972 by six and nine-month certificates, issued at a discount fixed by the Bank, which can only be held or traded between banks and savings banks. These certificates will be repurchased on demand by the Bank at a price dependent on the original discount and the unexpired period.

Credit ceilings have been a major tool of restrictive policy in recent years. Banks are allowed to deviate from the normal ceiling within narrow limits but the Bank has complained about the persistence with which some banks have exceeded their ceilings and it announced in December 1972 that it was considering a new rule to oblige banks to make an interest-free deposit at the Bank equal to 100 per cent of any such excess.

The most important interest rates allowed on deposits in banks have been regulated since 1933 and by the Inter-Bank Interest Rates Agreement of 1935 the organisation of commercial banks and savings banks established binding maximum interest rates for demand and time deposits which were in general tied to movements in the official discount rate. Bank lending rates were also moved in line with the official discount rate.

Banking Regulation in the 1970s

A large and continuing balance of payments deficit forced the Bank to impose heavy restraints on bank lending in 1970 and 1971, but as bank liquidity threatened to be very scarce with their lending operations limited by the credit ceiling, certain relaxations in policy were agreed upon in April 1971. The rule under which banks had to tie 20 per cent of increases in deposits was suspended in April and was retrospective to November 1970. In addition the Bank agreed to begin to release tied deposits and to ease the terms governing bank borrowing from the Bank including raising the credit ceiling by 30 per cent.

Bank liquidity improved as a result of these measures but the Budget required a 6 billion Krone liquidity contraction during the first quarter of 1972 and as this would seriously restrict lending the Bank agreed in December 1971 to make additional credit facilities available to the banks. The discountable values of bonds and shares were raised and the Bank made credit lines available to every bank without collateral security during the February-April 1972 period for up to 25 per cent of its total capital and reserves.

Changes in the official discount rate were made several times during 1971 in order to match the international interest rate level. In December 1971 negotiations between the National Bank and the banks established that there would be a general rise in the credit ceiling of 3 per cent for the first half of the year, and a further 3 per cent rise was agreed upon in May for the second half of the year. In order to allow increased credit for business and industry from October a further 2 per cent rise was allowed for that purpose and in December a further 4 per cent rise was agreed for the first half of 1973. Further, the banks were permitted to apply for individual increases within quite narrow limits.

In 1972 as in 1971 changes were made in the official discount rate in response to international interest rate changes and, also as in 1971, the Inter-Bank Interest Rates Agreement was amended to change interest on deposits in line and the banks also changed their lending rates.

The main instrument employed in credit policy in the early seventies was the voluntary agreement between the Bank and financial institutions establishing a ceiling on credit commitments, but in 1973 the Bank requested legislation that would enable binding rules on lending to strengthen the force of the voluntary agreements. During parliamentary debates concerning this legislation the Minister of Finance agreed not to use the legislative powers if the Bank was able to reach suitable voluntary agreement with the banks.

The Credit Regulation Act, which came into operation in October 1973, was intended to strengthen existing credit policy and to facilitate selective management of credit by authorising the Minister of Economic Affairs, after consultation with the National Bank, to promulgate rules on credit ceilings, cash reserve ratios and selective credit policies. It was provided, however, that these powers were to give way, as far as possible to voluntary agreements between the central bank and the commercial banks.

By the Lending Agreements of 2 November 1973 the banks agreed to restrain loans for consumer spending, to use the funds thus released for business and industry and, when they exceeded the credit ceiling, to deposit amounts equal to this excess in non-interest-bearing accounts with the National Bank.

Also in 1973 the Inter-Bank Interest Rates Agreement, which had for forty years regulated the interest rates allowed on deposits, was abolished in January. However, for the rest of 1973 both commercial banks and savings banks continued in general to tie their interest rates on deposits to the official discount rate.

The credit ceiling was raised by 6 per cent in 1973 and by 5 per cent in 1974 but the latter year saw a much slower growth in lending commitments than in 1973. Though the discount rate moved from 7 per cent at the beginning of 1973 to 10 per cent in January 1974 and then fell to 9 per cent, both lending rates and the interest rates allowed on large deposits tended to move independently of this rate.

On 1 January 1975 the Commercial Banks and Savings Banks Act of April 1974 came into force. This Act applied equally to both commercial and savings banks and consolidated previous legislation for both groups, except for the requirement that commercial banks must be incorporated as joint-stock companies, while savings banks must be independent, non-profit-making, self-governing entities. This legislation allowed the

banks for the first time to accept risk-bearing deposits which, subject to
some limits, are the equivalent of net capital for the purposes of the
statutory requirements for solvency. For the commercial banks the Act
requires that cash in hand, plus the value of safe, easily realisable and
uncommitted securities and instruments of credit, must represent not
less than 15 per cent of liabilities payable in less than one month and
not less than 10 per cent of total debt and guarantee commitments.

From 1 May 1975 the previous regulations which allowed large-scale
credit facilities to the banks against collateral security were replaced
by narrow borrowing limits fixed for each bank in relation to equity
capital. These limits represented a very substantial curtailment of credit
facilities and were necessitated by the very large growth of liquidity consequent on the government's financing its large current account deficit
by the sale of Treasury bonds

After negotiations with the government and the banks, in October
1975 the National Bank introduced Special Deposits of either 3 per cent
of deposits held at the end of September 1975 or 24 per cent of the
increase in deposits between the end of March and the end of September
1975 plus 12 per cent of the succeeding monthly increases in deposits.
These deposits, which were to remain tied in the Bank indefinitely,
returned 4.5 per cent per annum with variations according to changes in
the official discount rate between a minimum of 2 per cent per annum
and a maximum of 6 per cent. A further addition to blocked accounts
was 12 per cent of the rise in private bank deposits between October
1975 and March 1976. As a further means of absorbing liquidity deposit
certificates with ninety-one days maturity were offered for weekly
tenders.

Large central government borrowing in both 1975 and 1976 coincid-
ing with a difficult foreign exchange position required a neutralisation
of much of the liquidity increase with minimal effects on the long-term
bond rate. The loan commitment ceiling was maintained and this, together with the special deposit scheme, absorbed considerable liquidity.
Large changes were made in the discount rate. However, credit demand
rose in 1976 but the banks were able to meet this to some extent by
raising their utilisation of credit ceilings. In February 1976 the ceiling
was raised by 3 per cent. A further 2 per cent increase was made in
August and a further 2 per cent in November. The National Bank raised
the official discount rate by 1 per cent to 8.5 per cent in March and by
2.5 per cent to the highest level ever recorded, 11 per cent, in October.
In announcing these changes in discount rates the Bank pointed to
unrest on the international currency markets which had increased

pressure on the Danish krone. The banks drew considerable amounts on their borrowing facilities with the Bank to such an extent that by the end of September they had drawn almost all the funds available within their borrowing limits. Instead of raising these limits the Bank intervened in the money market for the first time, in September only in the day-to-day market but in December also in the market for weekly and monthly loans.

In 1977 monetary restrictions were eased with lending ceilings raised 3 per cent in February, the discount and rediscount rates lowered in March and a release by the National Bank of half the banks' special deposits in April. The lending ceiling was raised again by 2 per cent in June and by 3 per cent at the end of October and in late November the National Bank released 1.5 billion Krone of required reserves deposited on non-interest-bearing accounts between November 1975 and April 1976. In August the National Bank requested the banks to restrict consumer lending and, while keeping within the credit ceiling, to increase lending to trade and industry.

Commentary

While it could be argued that the absence of a developed money market and of a system of variable reserve requirements make it difficult for banking operations to be controlled by the central bank, nevertheless the use of credit ceilings both on their own and in conjunction with rediscounting and the special deposit system have reduced the banking system's manoeuvrability to at least the extent achieved by central banks operating elsewhere with access to a wider range of controls. Of course the strong argument for the use of credit ceilings in the Danish case is that the unpredictable flows of funds from overseas are of such magnitude that a method of restricting their effects on the domestic economy is necessary.

When the effectiveness of credit ceilings in restricting liquidity was reduced in the early seventies by the persistent exceeding of the ceilings on the part of some banks, the authorities moved towards making the voluntary agreements on these controls of legislative force, although further voluntary agreements were made which continued credit ceilings. In 1975, faced with substantial liquidity flows, the authorities set narrow borrowing limits for the banks and introduced a special deposits scheme which in 1976 became particularly restrictive.

By comparison with the position at the beginning of the seventies a single bank would have found its means of circumventing the credit ceiling restrictions largely eliminated and liquidity-minimising schemes like the special deposits scheme and the three-month deposit certificates operated consistently by the monetary authorities. The National Bank's intervention in the money market in late 1976, while making some funds available to those banks who were close to their borrowing limits, was apparently not symptomatic of a switch in policy technique because the 1977 policy moves were again accomplished through the use of ceilings and special deposits. It would be doubtful whether the money market yet exhibited sufficient depth to be used as a consistent base for monetary policy moves.

Further Reading

Krogstrup, Erik, 'Banking in Denmark' in H. W. Auburn (ed.), *Comparative Banking*, 3rd edn (Waterlow, England, 1966)
Morgan, E. Victor, Richard Harrington and George Zis, *Banking Systems and Monetary Policy in the EEC* (Financial Times Ltd, London, 1974) ch.2.

11 BANKING REGULATION IN NORWAY

'In Norway we have been rather reluctant to use customary money supply targets. We have put more emphasis upon the development of the liquidity of the banking system as an instrument for influencing the level of advances of commercial banks and savings banks.' (Interview with Knut Getz Wold, the Governor of the Bank of Norway, *The Banker*, July 1978, p.71.)

Institutional Framework

Within the Norwegian banking system commercial banks, savings banks and state banks, the Post Office Savings Bank, Post Giro and Norges Bank are the main institutions, but only the first two groups operate as deposit banks. Since 1950 there has been a substantial decline in the numbers of both savings banks (from 606 in 1950 to 384 in 1975) and commercial banks (from 89 to 27 over the same period) due to a number of mergers and takeovers within both groups. Of the commercial banks the big three — Den norske Creditbank, Christians Bank og Kreditkasse and Bergen Bank — dominate, having increased their proportion of commercial banking's total resources from 41.5 per cent in 1950 to 56.8 per cent in 1975. It has been the policy of the monetary authorities to limit the concentration of commercial banking while encouraging a stronger concentration within the savings bank group in particular to provide strong, independent regional banks. While the policy is not yet demonstrably successful with regard to the commercial banks, since 1970 there has been a growth in the strength of the regional savings banks to the extent that they are now a majority of the top ten savings banks. Nevertheless there remain a much larger number of savings banks than commercial banks, probably because of the consistent tradition that the savings banks serve their own local communities. Tradition has also given the savings banks a much higher proportion of long-term loans than the commercial banks who have favoured overdrafts and building loans and are also the main lenders to the distributive trades.

The savings banks are public-service institutions, but the commercial banks are joint-stock companies with not less than three shareholders if these are other banks, and not less than twenty shareholders otherwise. Each of the nine state banks ensures a reasonable supply of credit to such specific sectors of the economy as newspapers, housing, agriculture, education, fisheries and industries.

Norges Bank, the central bank, was established in 1816 as a joint-stock company, but in 1949 the government took all the shares. Implementation of monetary and credit policy is the task of the Ministry of Finance which sets the quantitative targets for credit supply, and of the Bank which investigates alternative means of reaching those targets and advises on the use of the various policy tools. In addition there is an Inspectorate of Banks, under Ministry of Finance supervision, which ensures that the practices of commercial and savings banks conform to the banking laws and are financially stable. Two separate co-operative bodies – the Section 15 Committee and the Open Market Committee – together with members appointed by the Norges Bank, advise on the issue of bearer bond loans (the former body) and on the Norges Bank's bond market transactions (the latter body).

While the impact of the above structure appears to enforce the Norges Bank's role as being under parliamentary direction and control, Erik Brofoss, governor of the Bank from 1954 to 1970, gave his opinion that the Bank had the right to be consulted, to make proposals, to raise questions on its own initiative and to criticise public policy if it felt that it should do so. The Bank, for example, not only advised against but subsequently sharply criticised the government's 1971 1 per cent devaluation of the currency. Axel Damman comments that it 'should not be easy for the government to act contrary to central bank advice; it should be politically inexpedient for it to do so'. In spite of the tradition of consultation between the authorities and the institutions, reform of the monetary control system has been accompanied by considerable disagreement. While this is most clearly instanced in the debate surrounding the 1965 Act, there is evidence of considerable debate and some discord since.

Policy Instruments and Their Use

The Act Authorising the Regulation of Monetary and Credit Conditions of 25 June 1965, known as the Monetary and Credit Policy Act, provided a number of monetary and credit instruments – liquidity reserve requirements, deposits against foreign liabilities, supplementary reserves, bond investment regulation, direct regulation of lending, the setting of maximum interest rates on loans and the regulation of bond issues.

Liquidity reserve requirements were of two kinds, 'primary' and 'secondary', both fixed as a proportion of bank liabilities. Section 5 of the 1965 Act which defined these two kinds of reserves was amended by Acts of 17 June 1966 and 30 June 1967. Primary liquid reserves were the bank cash holdings, their deposits on ordinary current account with Norges Bank, deposits on Post Office Giro account, and holdings of Norwegian Treasury bills, while secondary liquid reserves were the bank holdings of government and government-guaranteed bonds at book value. Under the same section the primary reserve ratio was to be not greater than 15 per cent and the aggregate of the two ratios not more than 25 per cent for the commercial banks, with the added proviso that the ratios could be varied according to the banks' resources and geographical location.

Separate deposits were to be maintained against increases in foreign liabilities, with the ratio able to be set differently for loans and deposits of over twelve months and those of shorter term. Section 8 of the 1965 Act required the banks to deposit a certain proportion of the growth of lending on a separate current account in Norges Bank, with this proportion able to be varied according to not only the banks' total resources and geographical location but also differently for various lending purposes.

Provision was made for the obligatory holding by banks of government bonds and other domestic bearer bonds and for these to be increased by a specified percentage of the growth of their total resources. Where the reserve requirements or the bond holding requirements were not fulfilled interest had to be paid on any reserve deficiency at a rate above the Norges Bank's discount rate.

Regulations stipulating the maximum rate of interest and commission were included as a policy tool and the banks were obliged to report their activities and interest rates to the Bank.

A measure already in existence prior to the Act, the Norges Bank's discount rate, was normally stable and relatively low and, as the Bank does not rediscount securities and borrowing from the Bank is only done by the commercial banks to iron out seasonal fluctuations, the discount rate is not of critical importance as a credit policy instrument.

From the formal coming into being of the Monetary and Credit Policy Act in January 1966, the government attempted to implement a combination of liquidity regulation and the maintenance of constant interest rates. In September 1966 the government introduced a supplementary reserve requirement of 50 per cent of the increase in loans and advances (other than for home building) calculated over the past twelve months' period. This move had a strong effect in reducing advances and, after the abolition of the supplementary reserve requirement in March 1967, bank lending was held in check by the annual government announcement of the target for the increase in bank loans and by the possibility of increased liquidity requirements.

In September 1969, to cope with not only the need to curb bank lending but also a strong expansion in government borrowing, Section 9 of the 1965 Act was used to make it obligatory for the banks to increase their holdings of domestic bearer bonds by 33 per cent of the growth in their total resources; the Norges Bank's discount rate was changed for only the second time since 1946 from 3.5 per cent to 4.5 per cent.

Section 15 of the Act provided for a key policy instrument – the regulation of the bond market – by giving the authorities power to decide the total volume of bond issues, their issue terms and their distribution among various borrowers.

Regulation of Banks in the 1970s

Monetary management and control were found to be more difficult during the early 1970s as unanticipated increases in liquidity pushed the actual credit supply well beyond its target figures. In 1970 the large increase in domestic liquidity was a predictable consequence of tax reform and was countered mainly by raising reserve requirements for the banks from 9 per cent to 16 per cent between June 1969 and October 1970 and, when the banks covered these increases by raising their investment in bonds, the government was readily able to finance its budget deficit. Supplementary reserve requirements were imposed on increases in lending beyond a stated percentage and minimum investments in bearer bonds were made obligatory for the banks.

Following the cessation in 1971 of Norges Bank's intervention in the foreign exchange market, the domestic money market became more significant. It is primarily an inter-bank market in which the banks use their excess liquidity for short-term lending to other banks.

Rules for the banks' automatic borrowing facilities from Norges Bank were put into operation at the beginning of 1971 for the purpose of evening out the short-term and seasonal fluctuations in bank liquidity that result from the bimonthly transfers of value-added tax and withholding tax to the Treasury, but with the additional purpose of discouraging the banks' use of these facilities to even out daily fluctuations in liquidity. Loan tranches of a specified percentage of total resources borrowed for seven days within a two-month period were established. Each loan was to be a minimum of a tenth of the loan tranche and be kept for seven days. Up to five such tranches could be used in each two-month period and a progressive interest rate was introduced as an inducement to the banks to show restraint in the use of these facilities.

In 1973, again faced with an unexpectedly high supply of liquidity to the banks, primarily due to the foreign exchange position, supplementary reserve requirements were enforced although the Norges Bank strongly put the view that primary reserve requirements were a more appropriate measure. The supplementary requirement was applied more leniently to those banks based in Northern Norway, but all the requirements were enforced again in December.

A subcommittee of the Credit Policy Liaison Committee reported at the beginning of November 1973 on possible changes in the structure of interest rates and the Ministry of Finance and Norges Bank worked out proposals for changes in interest rate policy during late 1973 and early 1974. In order to maintain a high level of investment in the postwar period, a relatively low and stable long-term interest rate had been considered important, but much of the justification for this no longer existed and the authorities were finding it necessary to restrict investment demand.

The Norges Bank discount rate was raised from 4.5 per cent to 5.5 per cent from 30 March 1974 and several interest rates on bills, bonds and loans were raised by approximately 1 per cent. It was emphasised in the government's White Paper of 29 March, *On Changes in Economic Policy for 1974*, that it was not intended to use variable interest rates as a monetary and credit instrument and that the current changes had only been made to counteract unintentional inequities.

New changes in the rules for banks' liquidity loans from Norges Bank were made in response to the shift to almost permanent use of the borrowing facilities by the banks from the latter half of 1973. Not only did the borrowing increase in its consistency but additional loan tranches had also to be granted and the consequent loan expansion quite seriously exceeded the budgeted amount. Proposals for amendments to the 1971 rules were discussed with the banks as well as with Norges Bank, and from 1 January 1975 a reduction was made in the volume of the automatic liquidity loans to the first three of the previous five loan tranches. Of these three loan tranches, the first became smaller but the interest rate stayed the same, the second became larger than previously but had a higher interest rate, and the third was unchanged but also had a higher interest rate. It was intended that these changes encourage the banks to maintain a higher level of liquidity than they had recently done.

Unexpectedly, demand pressure declined in early 1975 and banks' reserve positions were eroded by the growing current account deficit, and a number of measures were taken to ease the liquidity position of the banks. In January the supplementary reserve requirements were abolished and the primary reserve requirements were reduced and on

20 June these too were finally abolished. In May 1975 Norges Bank recommended that the obligatory bond holding requirement under Section 9 of the Monetary and Credit Policy Act be lowered from 30 per cent to 23 per cent and, to prevent the sale of the unblocked bonds from producing a fall in bond prices, Norges Bank agreed to increase its open-market operations to cope with these unblocked bonds. This proposal was implemented. Special terms were available from Norges Bank to banks wishing to lend to export industries for the purpose of stock building but by the latter half of the year the banks were able to finance these loans almost entirely from their own liquidity.

As a further part of the interest rate agreement between the credit institutions and the monetary authorities, made in 1974, deposit rates and the interest rate on overdrafts were increased by 0.5 per cent on 1 July 1975. Banks were allowed to raise the interest rates on first mortgage loans on dwellings and other housing loans by 0.5 per cent from 1 April 1976, providing that the repayment periods of the loans were lengthened to ensure that loan repayments did not rise. Other adjustments made were a lowering of the discount rate to 5 per cent from 6 October 1975 and a reduction of 0.5 per cent in the interest rate on Treasury bills. However, these latter changes were made as a step towards loosening the link between the discount rates and long-term interest rates in order to facilitate the use of the discount rate as a means for changing the short-term interest rates.

Norges Bank in its 1975 Annual Report (pp.18-22) noted a structural change in bank liquidity resulting from the changing exchange rate system. Liquidity reserve requirements being the main mechanism for influencing bank lending, the concept of free primary reserves was of critical importance. Free primary reserves are primary liquid assets less obligatory primary reserves, or the banks' minimum requirements less loans in Norges Bank. When no primary reserve requirements existed it was estimated that commercial banks held at least 3 per cent of their total resources in primary liquid assets. Under the fixed exchange rate system free reserves comprised free primary reserves plus net deposits with foreign banks which were regarded as a form of secondary liquid asset. Restrictions had occasionally been put on banks' foreign transactions because of this use as a liquid asset.

Since the advent of the currency 'snake' and more flexible exchange rates, banks trying to borrow abroad to increase liquidity or increasing their deposits abroad suffered serious foreign exchange losses, and even when central bank intervention in the foreign exchange markets was allowed in 1975 uncertainty about exchange rates had all but eliminated their use of foreign exchange liquidity. Nevertheless the banks do use the forward exchange market to minimise foreign exchange risk, and these forward rates are influenced by liquidity and inter-bank market interest rates so that there is still some link between the foreign exchange liquidity of the banks and domestic liquidity.

Although the primary reserve requirement was again the main instrument for the control of lending in 1976, more use was made of the technique of notifying the banks well in advance of the monetary authorities' targets for both lending and liquidity, with the result that the banks were provided with a more stable base for lending. In addition to the reintroduction of and subsequent increase in reserve requirements, the compulsory bond holding requirements for banks were tightened and the discount rate was raised by 1 per cent to 6 per cent. It was expected that the rise in the primary reserve requirement and the discount rate would signal the aim of a slow-down in lending, but in fact lending tightened so strongly that the automatic borrowing facilities were temporarily extended by widening the second loan tranche (interest rate 8 per cent) by an amount equal to the third loan tranche. As the banks' liquidity tightened they increased their resort to the special short-term credits for the finance of stock-building and in response Norges Bank shortened the maturity of these loans.

In December 1976 new rules for the automatic borrowing facilities were approved to be applied from 1 January 1977. The jump in interest rates from one tranche to the next had proved to be disruptive because the inter-bank rate tended to follow the changes in the interest rate on loans and the major change in the new rules was to increase the number of tranches to five, with a smoother escalation of interest rates. It was intended that the first two tranches be available for tax remittances to the Treasury and in three of the borrowing periods they were allowed to be larger for this purpose. Providing that the borrowing bank holds securities eligible as collateral, additional tranches granted on an individual basis may be used without collateral. Norges Bank commented that these new arrangements were made in order to facilitate the use of this borrowing arrangement as an active credit policy instrument.

Commentary

From at least the 1965 Monetary and Credit Policy Act, but more particularly during the 1970s, the area of manoeuvrability which the Norwegian banks appear to have had with respect to the management of their liquidity has been progressively eroded. In some cases this has been the unexpected consequence of changing circumstances when, for example, the move from fixed exchange rates to more flexible rates has all but eliminated the ability of the banks to increase or place their liquidity through foreign exchange markets. While Norges Bank remarked in its 1975 Annual Report that the banks have been able to use the forward exchange market to minimise foreign exchange risk, this use must be regarded as a means of insuring against unpredictable foreign exchange losses rather than as any source of potential liquidity.

In other cases the actions of the Norwegian monetary authorities have narrowed the scope for independent liquidity variation by the banks, for example in their changes in the rules for the banks' automatic borrowing facilities from Norges Bank and in the restriction of bank access to the special short-term funds for the finance of stock-building. Of course it may quite reasonably be argued that the actions of the Norwegian authorities over the past twelve years are consistent with a widening of the range and scope of the instruments of utility for monetary and credit control over the whole ambit of financial institutions, and not merely to increase control over the commercial banking sector. Nevertheless it is also true that the banks themselves have protested strongly on several occasions at various actions of the authorities which they felt threatened to narrow their sources of liquidity, and on other occasions at the lack of protection provided by the authorities. As an example of the latter, in 1972 the banks complained that their competitive position with the foreign banks in the provision of finance for activity on the Norwegian continental shelf was weakened because under the liquidity reserve requirements and the bond-investment obligation the domestic banks were forced to hold much of their resources in the form of low interest-bearing assets. There were protests from the banks during the negotiations for a Framework Agreement for 1960-4 and the banks withdrew from the Joint Consultation Council over the proposals for the 1965 Act on Monetary Control. The major bone of contention was the banks' preference for regulation through agreement in contrast to the government's preference for legal measures to facilitate the enforcement of a solution when agreement could not be reached.

In the subsequent uses of, and proposals to use, the supplementary reserve requirement under Section 8 of the 1965 Act, in particular in conjunction with primary reserve requirements, Norges Bank often argued to the Ministry of Finance that prolonged use of the Section 8 requirement would freeze the loan structure in the banking system. Certainly the strains of setting these requirements uniformly for all the banks were quite frequently seen to be too great and reduced requirements were specified according to total resources or geographical location.

The move in late 1976 to change the rules for automatic borrowing facilities, in order to minimise the disruptive effects which the interest rate jumps occurring under the old rules had caused, was made so as to facilitate the use of this instrument in credit policy and foreshadowed tighter central bank control of liquidity.

Further Reading

Damman, Axel, 'Monetary Policy in Norway' in Karel Holbik (ed.), *Monetary Policy in Twelve Industrial Countries* (Federal Reserve Bank of Boston, 1973)
Eide, Leif, *The Norwegian Monetary and Credit System* (Oslo, 1973)
Halsen, Martinus, 'Structural Changes in the Norwegian Credit System since 1950', Norges Bank *Economic Bulletin*, September 1977, pp.158-69
Norges Bank, *Economic Bulletin*, December 1976

12 BANKING REGULATION IN A UNITED EUROPE

> 'Europe is no nearer to EMU than in 1969. In fact if there has
> been any movement it has been backward.' (EEC Commission
> on Economic, Monetary and Financial Affairs, *Report of the
> Study Group 'Economic and Monetary Union 1980'*, March
> 1975.)

Although the Rome Treaty of 1957 which established the European
Economic Community made no specific provision for either a common
economic or a common monetary policy, a Monetary Committee was
established to monitor the monetary situation in member countries and
to formulate its views on these conditions. In March 1960, the Council
of Ministers of the EEC established a Countercyclical Policy Committee
and simultaneously asked member countries to inform the Commission
of the European Communities of those plans which might affect the
economic conditions in partner countries, with an exception made for
policies whose success required secrecy. In its October 1962 *Memorandum of the Commission on the Action Programme of the Community
for the Second Stage*, the Commission, in addition to recommending the
progressive introduction of common counter-cyclical policies, presented
proposals for increased co-ordination leading to the eventual establishment of a monetary and economic union, including a recommendation
that there be established a committee of governors of central banks of
member countries who would hold regular meetings and joint meetings
with finance ministers. It was to be the function of this committee to
exchange views not only on domestic monetary policies, but also on
proposed exchange rate changes and international monetary reforms.

It was not until the currency crises of the late 1960s that more formal
consideration was given to monetary union. A plan known as the Barre
plan was proposed by the Commission to the Council of Ministers which
accepted many of the proposals and issued a directive that members
ought to consult with each other with regard to short-term economic
policies and that a system of short-term monetary drawing rights be
established. Subsequently, on 26 January 1970, the Council agreed to
set up a short-term monetary support mechanism and to fix target
figures for four main economic aggregates as a step towards eventually
harmonising economic policies. The Werner Committee was appointed
to work out a plan to set up an economic and monetary union and

submitted its Final Report[1] to the EEC Council and Commission on 8 October in which it laid down a planned series of stages to achieve Economic and Monetary Union by 1980. In the Werner Committee's view the approach to monetary union involved three main elements: first, the progressive narrowing and eventual elimination of exchange rate margins so that a common currency was established; second, that foreign exchange reserves of the member countries be pooled; and third, that a common central banking system be organised following the pattern of the US Federal Reserve System with authority to conduct the Community's internal and external monetary policy and centralised management of the Community's foreign exchange reserves.

While the early discussions of the Commission and its various committees dating back to the Treaty of Rome are often criticised as giving scant attention to monetary union, the Werner Report was criticised for having given too much attention to monetary union and not enough to economic union. The Report proposed that the first stage of monetary union be accomplished over the three years 1971-3, with consultation procedures and the co-ordination of policy to be reinforced, a unified European capital market to be created after the liberalisation of capital movements, an immediate reduction of the margins of exchange rate fluctuations among member currencies, and the establishment of a European fund for monetary co-operation. Although the Commission generally agreed to the proposals for the first stage and the Council of Ministers adopted most of the proposals in February 1971, much of the rest of the Report did not meet with the agreement of all member countries and even the first stage was overtaken by the international monetary disarray surrounding the US suspension of dollar convertibility which frustrated the moves to narrow the exchange rate margins and to develop European capital markets.

The EEC countries did bring into effect the narrowing of currency margins in the 'snake-in-the-tunnel' scheme.

The progress of the snake has been tortuous with a number of members on various occasions finding themselves unable to keep within it and with a number of realignments of the parties within the snake. In the words of the Midland Bank[2] in its Winter 1977 *Review* (p.20):

The 'snake', having sloughed off its original skin, has in effect donned the raiment of a Deutschemark area. With the British and Irish pounds, the French franc, and the Italian lira all floated independently outside, while Norway, a non-member of EEC, still adheres, it has effectively lost its identity as an earnest of monetary union in the EEC.

In spite of the lack of success of this aspect of the union there have been other moves which give the promise if not the performance of greater monetary co-operation. The first directive on banking, adopted on 28 June 1973, on the Freedom of Establishment of Banks provided for the right of financial institutions to establish branches and offer their services throughout the EEC, with the member countries where the head offices of the institutions were situated retaining the primary responsibility for liquidity and solvency controls over the banks.

In early 1974, faced with the additional problems of the oil crisis and the international recession, the Commission established a study group under the chairmanship of Robert Marjolin to review the prospects of a European Monetary Union in the light of the change in economic circumstances since the Werner Report of 1970. It was the view of the Marjolin Report of 1975 that Europe had not progressed any further towards monetary union than it had been in 1969, that to attempt to establish monetary union by a series of small technical moves was not possible and that the transfer of the monetary policy-making powers of the EEC's national governments to Brussels would be politically unacceptable. The Marjolin Report proposed schemes to increase investment, to direct savings into financial rather than real assets, to encourage a convergence of regional disparities and to provide finance for, and eventually to remove, disequilibria in balances of payments.

In January 1976 a further report on the future of the EEC by the Belgian Prime Minister, Mr Tindemans,[3] was published in which it was suggested that those member countries able to proceed to monetary union ought to do so, while those not able to do so should be allowed to join the monetary union at a later date. A further recommendation was made that the 'snake' would have to be strengthened as a vital first step towards the convergence of monetary policies. The Tindemans Report was not generally accepted within the Community.

An unofficial document, 'The All Saints Day Manifesto to European Monetary Union', produced by a group of academic economists and published in *The Economist* on 1 November 1975, proposed an early introduction of a 'European money' as a parallel money alongside existing currencies, with certain safeguards concerning the purchasing power parity of the new currency.

With regard to the harmonisation of banking, an initial draft of the First Co-ordination Directive on the regulation of credit institutions was forwarded by the Commission to the Council of Ministers in December 1974, and following comments by other Community institutions on the draft it was forwarded to a Council working group for negotiation over certain points of difference. The directive was adopted during 1978 and will come fully into force in the Community two years after its adoption. The directive, which confirms that it is not feasible to attempt to establish a common European banking law at the present time, does attempt to identify those areas in which progress towards co-ordination and supervision could be achieved. A number of minimum qualifying conditions relating to the adequacy of capital and resources and the quality of management are suggested for credit institutions. Although the directive initially specified four statistical measures for liquidity and solvency for comparative purposes – the relation of capital and reserves to deposits, to risk-bearing assets and to fixed assets, and the relation of liabilities to liquid assets – and the Commission also wanted a statistical measure of foreign exchange exposure, negotiations within the Council's working group appear likely to result in no specific ratios being recommended.

Further proposals made in the directive include the principle that Community banks should be treated in the same way as those from non-member countries, and the creation of an advisory committee drawn from the Commission and the competent authorities in each member state which is to develop the implementation of co-ordination. However, while this draft directive has been moving along its protracted path, certain initiatives have occurred in other areas. In early 1977 a new scheme of information exchange on country risk lending was begun between the countries comprising the Group of Ten plus Luxembourg, Switzerland, Denmark and Ireland, under which banks provide information on three categories of loans (those maturing within one year, from one to two years, and beyond two years) extended to individual countries by all offices of the bank and by its subsidiaries. This Basle scheme of supervision is not the only one; there is also the Luxembourg or Dondelinger scheme organised by the banking supervisory authorities of the EEC which proposes an exchange of information on individual loans above 2.5 million US dollars.

The EEC Commission has also discussed a deposit insurance scheme with the banking authorities of its members, but it was agreed that the national schemes either proposed or already in existence would provide sufficient protection. Agreement was reached concerning freedom for foreign exchange transactions which was to see all private capital movements within the EEC freed from controls by the end of 1977. However, only Germany, Belgium and Luxembourg had put this into effect by December 1977.

While reaction to Roy Jenkins's Jean Monnet Lecture[4] in October

1977, which enumerated some strong economic advantages to be derived from monetary union, and to the November 1977 Conference on European Monetary Union in Leuven, Belgium, confirms the wide support within the Community for monetary union, there remain many wide-ranging variations between the EEC's banking systems. At least three different institutional frameworks came into existence in Europe and these have produced banking systems which are quite distinctive. In both the French and Italian systems the provision of finance for industry is primarily the prerogative of the national credit institutions and nationalised banks; in Germany the provision of bank credit and services by the commercial banks is so wide-ranging that the German commercial banks are often described as 'universal banks'; and in the Netherlands and in the United Kingdom the banks have traditionally been providers of short-term funds and only very recently have sought to widen their range of business.

Professor Revell[5] in a survey of housing finance in Europe describes the diversity of methods for its provision within Europe as probably greater than for any other type of finance. The UK, the Netherlands and Belgium provide most mortgage loan financing through short-term savings deposits, while in Denmark, Italy, Norway, Sweden and Finland the loans are financed by long-term funds. Even within these two general groups there is considerable diversity, although all institutional arrangements require borrowers to obtain at least two loans to raise the total amount needed.

With regard to the degree of independence of the central banks from government control there is also a very wide range within Europe, from almost maximum independence for the central banks of Germany and Switzerland to virtually complete control in France. Even in the area of minimum solvency requirements the range of the ratio of capital to assets is from 7.8 to 8.4 per cent in Denmark, through 2.6 to 3.2 per cent in Germany, to 0.7 to 0.8 per cent in France, although Fair[6] argues (p.82) that these differences are explicable on the grounds that those countries whose banks have low capital assets ratios have nationalised banks which are presumed to have the backing of the State in times of need.

Other important institutional differences between member countries include the existence of national Giro systems for payment and the relative strengths of money and capital markets, the latter being of particular importance in prescribing the extent to which indirect instruments of banking control may be implemented in the various banking systems.

Notes

1. 'Report to the Council and the Commission on the Realization by Stages of Economic and Monetary Union in the Community, Luxembourg, October 8th 1970', *Bulletin of the European Communities* (Supplement, 1970 (2)), cited as the 'Werner Report'.

2. Bela Belassa, 'Monetary Integration in the European Common Market' in 'European Monetary Union?', *Midland Bank Review* (Winter 1977).

3. Tindemans Report, *Bulletin of the European Communities*, Supplement 1/76 European Union, Report by Mr Leo Tindemans, Prime Minister of Belgium, to the European Council (January 1976).

4. Right Honourable Roy Jenkins, 'Europe's Present Challenge and Future Opportunity', Jean Monnet Lecture (Florence, October 1977), reprinted in *Lloyd's Bank Review* (January 1978).

5. Jack Revell, 'Housing Finance in Europe', *Three Banks' Review* (June 1977).

6. D. E. Fair, 'Clearing Banks and the Common Market', *Three Banks' Review* (December 1977).

Further Reading

Allen, Polly Reynolds, 'Planning a New Currency for Europe', *The Banker* (January 1978)

'Communication of the Commission to the Council on the Elaboration of a Plan for the Phased Establishment of an Economic and Monetary Union, Brussels, March 4th 1970', *Bulletin of the European Communities* (Supplement, 1970) (3), cited as 'Plan for an Economic and Monetary Union'

Dennis, G. E. J., 'European Monetary Union: In the Snake-pit', *The Banker* (October 1976)

'European Banking Systems – Balance Sheet Structures and Influences', *Midland Bank Review* (February 1973), pp.10-20

European Communities Monetary Committee, *Compendium of Community Monetary Texts* (Supplement, 1976)

Fair, D. E., 'Common Market Banking Developments', *Three Banks' Review* (December 1977)

McKinnon, Ronald I., 'On Securing a Common Monetary Policy in Europe', *Banca Nazionale del Lavoro Quarterly Review* (1977)

Morgan, E. Victor, Richard Harrington and George Zis, *Banking Systems and Monetary Policy in the EEC* (Financial Times Ltd, London, 1974), ch.15

OECD, *Capital Markets Study* (1967)

Pringle, Robin, 'Credit Information Exchange', *The Banker* (March 1977)

13 BANKING REGULATION IN THE UNITED STATES

> 'There is no help for us in the American system; its very essence and principle are faulty.' (Walter Bagehot, *Lombard Street* (John Murray, London, 1873), p.162.)

Institutional Structure

Banks in the United States comprise two groups of institutions, the commercial banks and the thrift institutions. This latter category includes savings banks, credit unions and savings and loan associations. Commercial banking in the USA operates under a dual system with federal and state regulations in force jointly. A federally chartered or national bank is chartered by the Comptroller of the Currency, while a state chartered bank is chartered by the state in which it is located. National banks are required to be members of the Federal Reserve System and to have their deposits insured by the Federal Deposit Insurance Corporation (FDIC). Although state banks are not required to join the Federal Reserve System, should they choose to do so they must meet the same capital requirements that national banks meet, have their deposits insured by the FDIC, and maintain the prescribed legal deposit reserve balances with the Federal Reserve Bank of their district.

Originally banks were chartered by the states and the 1864 National Bank Act provided that the national banks were subject to the locational restrictions of the state laws. The centralised US banking system was established by the Federal Reserve Act of 1913 and subsequently was refined by the Bank Acts of 1933 and 1935 respectively. Among the principal functions of the Federal Reserve System provided by the Federal Reserve Act were the regulation of the US money supply, the holding of the legal reserves of member banks and the examination and supervision of member banks chartered by the various states. The Federal Reserve System operates through the Board of Governors, the Federal Open Market Committee, the Federal Advisory Council, the Federal Reserve banks and their branches and the member banks, both state and national.

There are twelve Federal Reserve Banks established by the Act, those of Boston, New York, Philadelphia, Cleveland, Richmond, Atlanta, Chicago, St Louis, Minneapolis, Kansas City, Dallas and San Francisco.

These 'bankers' banks', whose main function is the control of the money supply, restrict their activities to transactions with other banks.

The Federal Reserve Board of Governors, whose seven members are appointed by the President and confirmed by the Senate, regulates, supervises and audits the twelve Federal Reserve Banks, regulates and supervises member banks, influences national monetary regulation, and reports to Congress on policy decisions and their application and on the difficulties of monetary policy. The Federal Banks elect five representatives to the Federal Open Market Committee to which the Federal Reserve Board of Governors also belong. It is the function of the Federal Open Market Committee to make decisions concerning open-market operations and advise other members of the Federal Reserve System on the co-ordinated use of monetary instruments. In addition the Federal Reserve Banks select the twelve members of the Federal Advisory Council which advises the Board of Governors on matters of interest to the Federal Reserve System.

The commercial banking system comprises almost 14,000 banks, only about 5,700 of which belong to the Federal Reserve System, although these member banks account for about 80 per cent of all commercial bank deposits. There are four possible regulation patterns to which commercial banks may be subject: national federally chartered banks which are automatically members of the Federal Reserve System and so are insured by the Federal Deposit Insurance Corporation (FDIC); state chartered banks with membership of the Federal Reserve System and accordingly insured by the FDIC; state banks that are insured by the FDIC but are not members of the Federal Reserve System; and state banks without either Federal Reserve membership or FDIC insurance. Although about three-fifths of the commercial banking system's total assets are held by banks under the first pattern of regulation, the largest number of banks (with a little over 20 per cent of the sector's total assets) operate under the third pattern. Only a small number of banks, holding only 1 per cent of total commercial banking assets, operate under the fourth pattern.

Banks joining the Federal Reserve System are required to subscribe 3 per cent of their capital and surplus to the capital of their Reserve Bank and to hold a further 3 per cent available subject to call. Among the obligations of the member banks are the maintenance of legally required reserves either on deposit without interest at the Reserve Bank or as cash held in their own vaults, and the remittance at par for checks drawn against them when presented for payment by a Reserve Bank. Included among member banks' main privileges are the ability to borrow from the Federal Reserve Banks when temporarily in need of funds (subject to criteria for this borrowing set by statute and regulation) and to obtain currency whenever required.

Over the past three decades the proportion of commercial banks belonging to the Federal Reserve System has been declining, the reason most frequently offered by departing banks being the cost of member reserve requirements compared to the reserve requirements of the different states for non-member banks. As Gilbert[1] has recently pointed out, while state reserve requirements for non-members (particularly for small banks) are not less than those for member banks, there is a significant difference in the types of assets which may be used to meet the legal reserve requirements. Most states allow reserve requirements to be met by vault cash, cash items in the process of collection and demand balances due from other commercial banks, but member banks are only able to use vault cash and collected reserve balances at the Reserve Banks to meet their reserve requirements.

From his study of 233 member banks served by the head office of the Federal Reserve Bank of St Louis, Gilbert finds that there are substantial costs (primarily transaction costs) associated with Federal Reserve membership, in particular for smaller banks. However, it appears that many smaller banks for whom the costs otherwise exceed the benefits might regard the retention of membership as justified by access to a lender of last resort facility through the Reserve Bank discount window. Large banks, for whom the existence of this facility may not be thought to be so critical, use more of the Reserve Bank services to the extent that these benefits would more than compensate for any opportunity costs on their reserve balances.

Because of the declining number of members the Federal Reserve System is restricted in its ability to impose heavily contractionary policies on its members by the need to keep member banks at levels of operation which do not disadvantage them by comparison with non-member banks. While to some extent the use of open-market operations as the major tool of policy enables the effects of policy moves to be felt throughout the financial markets in general, the constraint that banks may voluntarily leave the system at any time is at least as serious a limitation on the effectiveness of monetary instruments as obtains in any other country in this survey.

It is very often argued that small countries with comparatively small and underdeveloped money markets have a disadvantage in not being able to use open-market operations as a major tool; however, in the United States where open-market operations are possible, the voluntary nature of Federal Reserve membership imposes severe limits on the application of controls readily applicable in other countries.

Apart from commercial banks there are non-commercial banks or thrift institutions which include savings banks, credit unions and savings and loan associations. Savings banks, which aim to promote thrift and savings within a community, are mainly mutual savings banks with no capital structure, specialising in savings accounts, the funds from which are invested in long-term bonds, corporate preferred stocks and long-term mortgages. Normally savings banks accept deposits only from individuals with up to 40,000 dollars in each account insured by the FDIC. Credit unions, which mainly obtain funds from the sale of shares to members and from savings deposit accounts on which they pay interest, also promote thrift and saving and provide sources of credit for their members. Savings and loans associations are either state or federally chartered financial institutions which are organised either on a mutual basis with no capital stock structure or on a stock basis with a capital stock structure. These associations accept savings deposits on which they pay dividends or interest and the funds from these deposits are used to finance long-term mortgage loans. Up to 40,000 dollars in each savings and loan association account, for all federal and most state chartered associations, is insured by the Federal Savings and Loan Insurance Corporation (FSLIC).

Agreement corporations (which operate under an agreement between a commercial bank and the Federal Reserve) and Edge Act corporations exist to aid in the financing and stimulation of foreign commerce in the United States. They are governed by the Federal Reserve regulations and, except for limitations about the type of deposits they can accept and the type of investments they can make, they have the same powers and are subject to the same restrictions as domestic banks.

Recent proposals for reform of the financial structure include the elimination of a number of the existing distinctions between the banks and the thrift institutions, although it has been argued[2] that these distinctions are already narrowing.

Banking Regulation

Banking regulation in the United States has been described by Scott[3] as not only exceedingly detailed and comprehensive but also as defying simple and accurate generalisation, even on the federal level. Two distinct levels of regulation are applied to commercial banks; the first level, that of the bank chartering authority, defines the powers and regulates the activities of the banks established under it; while the second level of regulation, federal in origin, is directed towards controlling the money supply and influencing aggregate demand through control over the operations of banks. It is this second level of regulation that is the subject of interest here. The main tools of federal regulation in the USA have been open-market operations, discount policy and changes in reserve requirements, with the first two of these requiring co-ordination to be efficient.

Open-market operations are undertaken only on the initiative of the Federal Reserve through the Federal Open Market Committee. The Federal Reserve Bank of New York handles all open-market transactions for the Federal Reserve System, using approximately two dozen dealers in US government securities. Purchases and sales of government securities are made for the purpose of applying the degree of pressure or easement in the reserve position of banks that is consistent with the Open Market Committee's directives. Instructions given by the Open Market Committee are contained in either a continuing authority directive or a current policy directive. A continuing authority directive, which is reviewed at least annually, sets technical limits about the type of securities traded and the procedures and conditions for trading, while current policy directives are formulated at each meeting of the Open Market Committee. Since 1962 the Open Market Committee has also administered open-market operations in foreign currencies.

Open-market operations change the unborrowed reserves of member banks; that is, if the manager of the Federal Reserve open-market account buys securities or enters into repurchase agreements (which are purchases with an agreement to resell one to fifteen days later), the unborrowed reserves are increased, while if the manager sells securities or enters into matched sale-purchase agreements, the unborrowed reserves are decreased. If open-market operations withdraw reserves from the market, member banks may have to restore these reserves by borrowing. Marginal cost of these borrowed funds is given by the discount rate, the rate at which the commercial banks can borrow from the Federal Reserve Banks. For efficient management it is necessary that the discount mechanism be co-ordinated with open-market operations.

In the Federal Reserve System the member bank privilege of discounting with its Reserve Bank is subject to two constraints; first, that it must accept the interest or discount charge imposed, and second, that it must conform to the regulations relating to the eligibility of assets and the propriety of the bank's reason for borrowing. Regulation A of the Board of Governors provides *inter alia* that Federal Reserve credit is normally extended on a short-term basis to enable banks to cope with temporary shortfalls, that it is not to be used continuously as a source of credit, and that in each individual case the Federal Reserve Bank concerned will look at the purpose of the credit, at the pattern of loans and investments by the member bank, and at whether the bank is borrowing to gain a tax advantage, to profit from rate differentials or to extend undue credit to speculative areas.

Because of the large number of banks and the wide range of conditions under which they operate, the commercial banks have developed an organised market known as the federal funds market in which banks with excess free reserves offer to lend them on a day-to-day basis to banks short of reserves. Although this allows an additional source of funds for the banks when credit conditions are tight, the federal funds rate from this market may rise above the discount rate, thus encouraging member banks to use the discount facility. It has been usual to find that the discount rate typically follows other interest rates rather than leads them, although it is also usually held at a level below other interest rates. It is thought that a combination of the requirements of Regulation A and the tradition against borrowing from the Reserve Banks restricts borrowing to covering those needs which could not have reasonably been foreseen or against which preparation could not prudently have been made.

Congress first granted the Federal Reserve power to vary the minimum percentage reserve requirements against several classes of member bank domestic deposit liabilities in 1935. During the next two years the Reserve Banks doubled the percentage reserve requirements from their original level, but it has never been used to that extent since that period. Although the Federal Reserve has preferred increasingly to rely on openmarket operations, this may partly be in consequence of a constraint imposed by the Reserve System on its own use of these requirements – that it will make no changes in reserve requirements smaller than one-half of a percentage point. This limits its use to occasions when a large change is considered necessary and even then it is likely to be supplemented by open-market operations.

The OECD,[4] in its 1974 study of US monetary policy, commented that the device of varying reserve requirements is less useful to the Federal Reserve System than might appear at first because, quite apart from the increased flexibility of open-market operations, it is administratively asymmetrical, that is it affects all banks within a class regardless of their initial reserve positions, and it will result in banks adjusting their positions by substantial movements in money market assets.

Separate ratios are set for Reserve city banks and for country banks of under and over 5 million dollars in demand deposits, and for all classes of banks, savings deposits and other time deposits of under and over 5 million dollars have separate reserve requirement ratios. A further limitation on the use of variable reserve requirement ratios as a monetary policy tool is that, if the Federal Reserve's ratios were more stringent than those imposed by the states on non-member banks, there would be an exodus of banks from the Federal Reserve System.

Another policy tool which may usefully be used in combination with open-market operations is Regulation Q which gives the power to fix ceiling interest rates on bank deposits. From 1966 a distinction was made for the purpose of Regulation Q between large deposits of over 100,000 dollars and time and savings deposits below 100,000 dollars, and the ceiling for the latter category was maintained below that for the former category. Regulation Q interest rate controls may be used to shift funds between the banking sector and the money market, reducing the access of banks to deposit funds in times of monetary restraint and reducing the availability or raising the cost of bank loans in such times. These effects may be reduced if not eliminated to the extent that the banks may gain access to other sources of funds. In 1969 banks had recourse to the Eurodollar market, loan participation sales and the issuing of commercial paper through bank holding companies for additional funds. Reserve requirements were, however, imposed on these funds — maximum interest rates were suspended from June 1970 for large deposits with less than ninety-day maturities and from May 1973 for large deposits with ninety days or more to maturity.

As well as these general instruments the Federal Reserve has had legal authority since 1933 to restrain the undue use of bank credit to finance speculative purchases in securities, real estate or commodities and, since 1934, authority to limit the amounts that banks and others may lend on securities for these speculative purposes.

Banking Regulation in the 1970s

Early in 1970 the Federal Reserve shifted from its policy of restraint pursued in 1969, relying primarily on open-market operations to increase growth in the money supply. Maximum interest rates payable on time and savings deposits were raised as part of a co-ordinated move by the Federal Reserve and the other appropriate authorities to realign and increase the ceiling rates on deposits at banks and non-bank thrift institutions in relation to rates on competing market securities. Towards the middle of 1970, market uncertainties and illiquidities were alleviated by open-market operations, the availability of the discount window to assist banks to advance credit to businesses finding it hard to roll over maturing commercial paper, and the suspension of maximum rate ceilings on large CDs of short maturity.

Later in 1970 when more normal market conditions prevailed the Board of Governors acted to extend reserve requirements to funds obtained by banks through the issuing of commercial paper by their affiliates, and by Eurodollar borrowings.

When the short-term market rates fell below the discount rate in November, the Federal Reserve lowered the discount rate for the first time since April 1969, and then made two further reductions in early 1971 as market rates continued to drift downwards until the strong demand for credit reversed this movement. After August the Federal Reserve became less aggressive in the supplying of reserves and this helped tighten money market conditions which accentuated rising market interest rates to which the discount rate was adjusted.

The announcement of new economic policies by the President on 15 August reversed interest rate trends, but this decline was interrupted in November by congestion in the securities market which was relieved in part by large Federal Reserve purchases of Treasury coupon issues. In the last two months of 1971 the discount rate was reduced and as the Federal Reserve increased its supply of reserves short and long-term interest rates fell sharply.

The Open Market Committee in its day-to-day monetary operations during 1972 emphasised total member bank reserves less reserves required against US government and inter-bank deposits, that is, the reserves available to support private non-bank deposits. Early in 1972 open-market operations were used to expand these reserves (referred to as RPDs by the Federal Open Market Committee) but later in the year reserve provision by this means became more restrained and was replaced by increased borrowing by member banks from the Federal Reserve. Short-term interest rates rose by more than 2 per cent between February and the end of the year, although they did not reach the high levels of July 1971.

During 1972 technical changes were made to the regulations affecting the reserve positions of member banks, including a change to Regulation D which eliminated the distinction between Reserve city and country banks for reserve purposes and which introduced a new system of graduated reserve requirements for net demand deposits based entirely on the amount of deposits and applicable to all member banks.

Towards the end of 1972 the Federal Reserve began to resist excessive monetary expansion through open-market operations, and this resistance was intensified early in 1973 not only with open-market operations but also with a series of discount rate increases between the end of 1972 and late August 1973 and with several increases in reserve requirements. In 1973 the strong expansion in demand for credit was largely undeterred by the upward surge in interest rates. In response to the movement in market rates the discount rate was adjusted upwards in a series of steps to 7 per cent in July.

In July and August the Federal Reserve reduced the money supply and between July and September the growth in M_1 (notes and coin and demand deposits) fell almost to zero. Federal Reserve policy in the 1973 period of restraint differed from the policies implemented during the 1966 and 1969 periods of restraint, in that the Federal Reserve in 1973 preferred to avoid relying on reducing the availability of funds at banks and depended instead on the upward movement of interest rates to discourage demand for bank loans. In order to facilitate this latter process the Federal Reserve moved on 16 May to remove the ceiling rate on large denomination CDs.

Although money market interest rates peaked in September and eased from then until March 1974, the discount rate was maintained at 7.5 per cent and the growth in the money supply was held to minimal levels. The combination of recession and inflation posed difficulties for the Federal Reserve in 1974 and those policies which were implemented had to be modified on several occasions. The lessening of monetary restraint adopted in late 1973 was continued into early 1974, but by late February credit demand was again expanding rapidly and, when short-term market rates moved rapidly upwards, the discount rate was also raised.

Market uncertainty, generated by the difficulties and subsequent failure of the Franklin National Bank and the report of a major utility company that it was unable to borrow the funds needed to complete two new generating plants, led lenders to tighten their credit standards. As credit became not only tighter but also more costly there were fears of a liquidity crisis and the Federal Reserve responded with a shift to a more accommodative open-market policy which was readily reflected in a sharp, general decline in short-term market rates. Further assistance to banks was provided by the removal in September of the 3 per cent marginal reserve requirement from large time deposits and from large non-deposit liabilities of over four months to maturity.

When there was an unexpected deterioration in economic activity in the fourth quarter all of the main policy instruments were brought into operation: open-market operations were used to expand the banks' supply of non-borrowed reserves; reserve requirement ratios were reduced to allow for credit expansion; and the discount rate was reduced in order to lower the cost of reserves borrowed from the Reserve Banks.

During 1975 easier monetary policy was used in order to rebuild the economy's liquidity, not only by the usual method of open-market operations but also, as in the last quarter of 1974, by reductions in the discount rate and in member bank reserve requirements. As a consequence of these moves ample liquidity was available at reduced rates for the support of economic recovery at the beginning of 1976. Commercial banks had in addition to recovering liquidity made increased provision for potential loan losses and improved their capital ratios. Care was taken in the implementation of monetary policy that, while expansion in economic activity was to be facilitated, this was not to be done in such a way as to aggravate inflation.

Member bank reserve requirements on medium-term time deposits were reduced in early January and the discount rate was cut, but Federal Reserve policy became less accommodative in the second quarter when market interest rates rose and the money stock growth accelerated. These changes moderated towards mid-year and open-market operations resumed their accommodative trend and interest rates renewed their decline.

Proposals for Change: A Brief Review

The Report of the President's Commission on Financial Structure and Regulation in 1971, known as the Hunt Commission Report,[5] made a series of recommendations to remove what it called unnecessary regulatory restraints and suggested changes in the supervisory framework. The Commission recommended greater portfolio and liability for all of the depository institutions which for the commercial banks meant the abolition of the restrictions on real estate loans, the elimination of Regulation Q, and access to the management of agency accounts subject to SEC regulation. In the Commission's view these changes would improve the functioning of the private financial system.

From the recommendations of the Hunt Commission, the Treasury sponsored the Financial Institutions Act, which was first introduced in 1973 and was passed by the Senate in 1975. In the view of the Senate Banking Committee, the Financial Institutions Act would remove unnecessary and outdated regulations from depository institutions which would then allow them to provide new services and enable depositors to earn returns that reflected current market conditions. With regard to the commercial banks, the Financial Institutions Act provided that national banks (and all federal thrift institutions) would be allowed to pay interest on chequing accounts from 1 January 1978 subject to a possible delay (if conditions warranted in the view of the Federal Reserve) until 1 January 1980; that Regulation Q be eliminated five years from the effective date of the legislation; that banks could accept corporate savings accounts; that limits on the amounts and maturity of real estate loans made by national banks would be repealed; and that all banks be permitted to convert freely from federal to state charters and vice versa.

The House Committee on Banking, Currency and Housing, in a departure from the normal legislative procedure generated by its dissatisfaction with the narrow focus of the Financial Institutions Acts of 1973 and 1975, commissioned its own study, the Financial Institutions in the Nation's Economy Study (FINE) and drafted its own Financial Reform Act of 1976. The FINE study proposed that many of the activities of the Federal Reserve Board, the Federal Deposit Insurance Corporation and the Comptroller of Currency be combined into a super-agency – the Federal Depository Institutions Commission (FDIC) – which would have responsibility for the chartering, conversion, supervision and regulation of federally chartered depository institutions and their holding companies, state chartered banks and foreign banks. The FDIC was to be divided into two units, one to undertake the examination, supervisory and regulatory functions and the other to be charged with promoting competition. Responsibilities of the Federal Reserve Board would be reduced to the conduct of monetary policy and the regional reserve banks would be relieved of regulatory responsibility. The presidents of the regional reserve banks would assume the other responsibilities of the regional reserve banks and their boards would be replaced by advisory committees of representative depository institutions which would advise the Federal Reserve Board on how its monetary policy affected them.

Disclosure requirements for the commercial banks would be widened to include reports to the FDIC, by market area, of the amount of interest paid on loans, interest charged on loans, capital provisions, foreign activities and losses on loans, as well as the impact of holding company operations on their institution. Where it was not in conflict with state laws, inter-state branching would be allowed and where this was in conflict, branches would be allowed in all Standard Metropolitan Statistical Areas with populations of 2 million or more. Banks would be allowed to underwrite revenue bonds.

It was proposed that the activities of foreign banks within the USA would be limited to those allowed to domestic banks, which would mean that they could not underwrite corporate securities and that they would be subject to the 'closely related to banking' restrictions of the Bank Holding Company Act of 1970. With regard to US banks operating abroad, these would be subject to control and approval by the FDIC and foreign expansion would be approved only where the bank's capital was not endangered.

Meanwhile Senator Williams's Subcommittee on Securities of the Senate Banking Committee, having finished major legislation affecting the securities industry, has moved into a two-year study of the securities-related aspects of the Glass-Steagall Act which is also known as the Banking Act of 1933. Provisions of the securities-related sections of this Act include the following: banks may only engage in underwriting with respect to some government securities; organisations that under-write may not accept deposits; banks are prohibited from any affiliation with companies principally engaged in underwriting securities; and, apart from some government securities, bank authority to deal in secur-ities is restricted to the purchase and sale of securities and stock only on the orders, and for the accounts, of customers.

Although these and other proposals for reform reflect some conflict in their interpretations of the role of large banks − which are variously that their existing power and concentration is cause for concern, and that they ought to move into securities-related areas in order to broaden the process of capital-raising − one consistent view, widely reflected in all of these proposals, is that the existing highly segmented and over-lapping regulatory structure is inefficient.

Commentary

The voluntary nature of commercial bank membership in the Federal Reserve System is, as has been noted above, an inhibiting factor on strong Federal Reserve controls over the member banks in the system. Fischer Black[6] has commented that banks ought to be able to avoid the effects of most, if not all, of the regulations imposed on them but, as will be discussed below, this ability to evade may be derived from the type of controls which the Federal Reserve System is able to implement as well as from the nature of the System. Owing to the large money and capital markets in the United States, the use of open-market operations should be a much more reasonable proposition for that system than in most of the other countries we have surveyed.

The dual nature of the banking system complicates the assessment of its efficiency and there is no doubt that a simplification of this system could work towards making monetary policy more effective. It is arguable, as Fischer Black notes, that the individual bank is in fact very free to manage its own funds in the United States and in this sense it is freer than in any of the other systems surveyed.

Notes

1. R. Alton Gilbert, 'Utilization of Federal Reserve Bank Services by Member Banks: Implications for the Costs and Benefits of Membership', *Federal Reserve Bank of St Louis Review* (November 1975).
2. Cambridge Research Institute (Paul V. Teplitz, principal author), *Trends Affecting the U.S. Banking System* (Ballinger Publishing Co., Cambridge, Mass., 1976).
3. Kenneth E. Scott, 'The Dual Banking System: A Model of Competition in Regulation', *Stanford Law Review* (November 1977).
4. OECD, *Monetary Policy in the United States* (Paris, 1974).
5. Commission on Financial Structure and Regulation (The Hunt Commission), *Report* (US Government Printing Office, Washington, DC, December 1971).
6. Fischer Black, 'Banking and Interest Rates in a World without Money', *Journal of Bank Research* (Autumn 1970).

Further Reading

Black, Fischer, 'Bank Funds Management in an Efficient Market', *Journal of Financial Economics*, no.2 (1975)
Board of Governors of the Federal Reserve System, *The Federal Reserve System, Its Purposes and Functions* (Washington, DC, 1963)
Brown, Marilyn V., 'The Prospects for Banking Reform', *Financial Analysts Journal* (March-April 1976), pp.14-24
Chandler, Lester V. and Dwight M. Jaffee, 'Regulating the Regulators: A Review of the FINE Regulatory Reforms', *Journal of Money, Credit and Banking* (1977)
De Kock, M. H., *Central Banking*, 4th edn (Crosby Lockwood Staples, London, 1974)
De Pamphibs, D. M., 'The Short-Term Commercial Bank Adjustment Process and Federal Reserve Regulation', *New England Economic Review* (May-June 1974)
Gilbert, R. Alton, 'Bank Failures and Public Policy', *Federal Reserve Bank of St Louis Review* (November 1975)
— and Jean M. Lovati, 'Bank Reserve Requirements and Their Enforcement: A Comparison across States', *Federal Reserve Bank of St Louis Review* (March 1978)
Heggestad, Arnold A. and John J. Mingo, 'The Competitive Condition of U.S. Banking Markets and the Impact of Structural Reform', *Journal of Finance* (June 1977)
Holbik, K., *Monetary Policy in Twelve Industrial Countries* (Federal Reserve Bank of Boston, 1973)
Kunreuther, Judith B., 'Banking Structure in New York State: Progress and

Prospects', *Federal Reserve Bank of New York Monthly Review* (April 1976)

Melichar, Emanuel and Harriet Holderness, 'Seasonal Borrowing at the Federal Reserve Discount Window', *Agricultural Finance Review*, vol. 35 (October 1974)

Orsingher, Roger, *Banks of the World*, English translation (Macmillan, London, 1967)

Peat, Marwick, Mitchell and Co., *Establishing an Office of a Foreign Bank in the United States: A Guide for Foreign Banks*, 2nd edn (New York, 1977)

Pierce, James L., 'The FINE Study', *Journal of Money Credit and Banking* (1977)

Robinson, Roland I. and D. Wrightsman, *Financial Markets: The Accumulation and Allocation of Wealth* (McGraw-Hill, New York, 1974)

Rose, Peter, 'Exodus: Why Banks Are Leaving the Fed', *The Bankers Magazine* (Winter 1976), pp. 43-9

Schott, Francis, M., 'The Economist's Corner: A Qualified Yes to the Hunt Commission Report', *The Bankers Magazine*, (Summer 1972)

Shapiro, Edward, *Understanding Money* (Harcourt Brace Jovanovich, New York, 1975)

Sutch, Richard C. and Thom B. Thurston, 'Member Bank Borrowing from the Federal Reserve System and the Impact of Discount Policy', *Quarterly Review of Economics and Business*, vol. 16, no. 3 (Autumn 1976)

Young, Ralph A., *Instruments of Monetary Policy in the United States: the Role of the Federal Reserve System* (IMF, Washington, DC, 1973)

14 BANKING CONTROLS IN JAPAN

'[T] he role of the banking sector in Japan in providing credit is probably far greater than in most other industrial countries, making monetary controls a more significant part of government framework guidance of the economy.' (Francis A. Lees and Maximo Eng, *International Financial Markets*, Development of the Present System and Future Prospects, Praeger, New York, 1975, p.257.)

Institutional Framework

The main banks in Japan are the 'ordinary' banks, and commercial banks are either city banks or local banks. The thirteen city banks command 45 per cent of the economy's banking resources and, while based in large cities, they have networks of branch offices throughout the country. Local banks, each of which is based in a prefecture, conduct business mainly within their own and neighbouring prefectures. Although earlier the commercial banks dealt in long-term finance as well as in commercial banking proper, moves were made after the Second World War to shift their primary function to that of British banks' short-term finance. In 1952/3 long-term credit banks were established for the specific purpose of lending long-term funds which are raised by debentures. Nevertheless commercial banks still participate in long-term lending. They hold large quantities of debentures and much of their short-term lending is renewed into the medium and long term.

A characteristic of the city banks that has persisted since the 1950s is the condition of 'overloan' which has resulted from the tendency to indirect financing on the part of business corporations who have relied on excessive borrowings in relation to their comparatively inadequate own capital. The consequence of 'overloan' for the banks has been heavy dependence on borrowing from the Bank of Japan, call money and other external funds sources. (There are also seven trust banks which, though classified as ordinary banks under the Bank Law, perform long-term finance and financial management functions.)

The Bank of Japan is legally a special corporation whose current role as central bank may be said to date from the 1942 Bank of Japan Law which provided that the Bank's objects were 'the regulation of currency, the control and facilitation of credit and finance, and maintenance and fostering of a credit system, pursuant to the national policy'. The Policy

Board, comprising the Governor of the Bank, two non-voting government representatives and a member from each of the city banking, country banking, commerce and industry, and agriculture sectors, is responsible for all the main policy instruments except for changes in reserve ratios which need the approval of the Minister of Finance and changes in interest rate ceilings which require consultation with the Interest Adjustment Council.

While the Minister of Finance has the power to issue general directives and supervisory orders to the Bank including appointing the Bank's comptroller and in addition the government has general control over almost all the Bank's activities, the emphasis in the government-Bank relationship remains on mutual co-operation which does not require the use of the available government controls.

The business of commercial banks is limited under the Banking Law to the receipt of deposits, loans and advances, the discounting of bills, exchange transactions and ancillary activities such as the provision of safe custody. Later laws have permitted their entry into savings banks and trust business but few banks have moved into these areas.

Banking Regulation

Not unexpectedly, in view of the pronounced tendency to 'overloan', the primary instrument of monetary policy has been changes in the Bank rate, that is the discount rate of the Bank of Japan, which affects the rediscounting of commercial bills, the Bank's standard form of lending. By agreement with the banks, short-term lending rates have moved with the official discount rate since 1957. A lower discount rate than the rate on loans secured by others is set for commercial bills and interest rates on loans secured by government securities, specially designated securities and bills corresponding to commercial bills. As well as its cost effect, changes in the Bank rate usually signal a change in the direction of the Bank's monetary policy and accordingly have an 'announcement' effect.

Between the end of the Second World War and 1962 a limit on loans extended to each commercial bank by the Bank of Japan was set under the 'High Interest Rates Application System' which required higher interest rates to be applied when these limits were exceeded. Since 1962 the Bank of Japan has used the credit ceiling application system which, since it lacks legislative force, may only be used against those banks which are in debt to the Bank, that is, primarily the city banks and the long-term credit banks. For borrowings above the ceiling, which are only permitted when there is a reserve shortage, a penalty rate 4 per cent higher than Bank rate must be paid.

Owing to the underdeveloped state of the Japanese capital market, the Bank's purchases and sales of securities, at least until 1962, were only occasionally conducted with individual banks. In November 1962 the Bank decided to add a form of open-market operations to its monetary instruments by adopting a flexible policy of trading in bonds and debentures but still in direct negotiation with financial institutions. A more positive step towards the more usual type of open-market operations was taken in January and February 1966 with the issue of long-term government bonds, the reopening of the public bond and debenture markets, and the Bank's decision to buy and sell bonds and debentures at market prices without repurchase agreements.

Power to use reserve requirements was only granted to the Bank of Japan in 1957 and it was not used until 1959. Subject to the approval of the Minister of Finance the Bank may establish, alter or abolish the reserve ratio. The financial institutions covered by these requirements, which include commercial banks, long-term credit banks and trust banks, have to lodge a certain proportion of their deposits (different proportions for time deposits and for other deposits) in cash with the Bank. Although the legal maximum reserve ratio was set at 10 per cent the tendency to 'overloan' meant that the reserve ratios were very low indeed (only 1 or 2 per cent in 1969) compared to the levels set in other countries, and it appeared that this tool could only be a supplementary means of monetary control. In the period June to December 1971, however, the Committee on Financial System Research examined the operation of reserve requirements and from this came a revision of the law, in April 1972, which expanded the system. Application of the requirements was widened to bank debentures and principals of Trusts as well as deposits and the maximum limit of reserve ratios was raised from 10 per cent to 20 per cent.

From the time of this revision reserve requirements were used much more actively as a policy instrument, being raised an unprecedented five times between 1973 and 1975.

A type of moral suasion in the form of 'window guidance' was used as a credit rationing device. From 1954 to 1964 guidelines on loans granted by the Bank of Japan to commercial and long-term credit banks were determined on a monthly basis, based on estimates provided by the banks and the central bank. Apart from two gaps between June 1965 and September 1967 and during 1971-3 some form of window guidance has been used. From January 1973 until late in 1974 window guidance became increasingly more restrictive on banks and was widened to cover most financial institutions. Particular attention was paid to curbing loans for speculative uses.

Credit ceilings, reserve requirements and window guidance were the weapons used to restrict credit expansion and then to stabilise it at reduced levels from 1973 on, with some changes in the discount rate also being made. The emphasis on quantitative credit restrictions continues to be a notable feature of monetary policy in Japan.

Banking Regulation in the 1970s

The liquidity position of the city banks in particular progressively deteriorated during 1970 as a consequence of the tight monetary policy applied since September 1969. Requests to the city banks to reduce the year-to-year increase in loans were attached to a direct quantitative control, the increase to be reduced to 15 per cent by the end of June. The requests to other banks were merely moral suasion to reduce lending activity. City banks were forced to sell securities to fund loan demands.

During 1971 Bank rate was reduced four times and money market rates also declined, and although the Bank of Japan reduced its lending to commercial banks and sold special securities after August 1971 inflows of funds from the balance of payments surplus provided sufficient improvement in the liquidity of the city banks to allow expansion of their credit operations throughout 1971. As part of the government's seven-point programme announced on 23 May 1972 it was decided to further reduce interest rates by lowering the discount rate and the rates paid on time and savings deposits.

Continuously into 1972 the liquidity generated by the balance of payments surplus was allowed to flow unchecked into the money supply which grew by 25 per cent in that year. No changes were made in the reserve requirements for bank deposit liabilities but the discount rate and the interest rates on time and savings deposits were reduced in July 1972. Apart from 1965 it was usual for the authorities to meet recession with policies of monetary restraint and the easy monetary stance was rather unexpected. The results of the easy monetary policy were seen in the reduction in the business failure ratio, in the increased flow of funds into housing construction and in the expansion of bank credit and of new issues of securities. Among the groups advantaged by the expansion of bank credit, apart from housing, were small businesses, wholesale and retail trade, real estate and other services.

In January 1973 a change to a more restrictive monetary policy was signalled with the resumption of window guidance on the expansion of bank credit and an increase in reserve requirements on domestic yen deposits, but these quantitative controls were merely aimed at slowing the growth in credit expansion. Nevertheless, monetary policy was progressively tightened with the discount rate being raised in several steps from 4.25 per cent to 9 per cent, four further increases in reserve requirements and increasingly restrictive window guidance on allowed credit expansion.

Selective guidance on the pattern of bank credit was introduced in December 1973 and quickly became an important policy instrument used to restrict loans from non-essential uses. Owing to the effects of the easy monetary policy in the previous two years the non-bank private sector was quite liquid, with the result that the switch to monetary restraint took some time to be effective in slowing down the level of activity. It was only at the end of 1973 that the credit restrictions could be seen to have a clear impact on liquidity. During December 1973, in reaction to the oil crisis, guidelines were issued to major industries to stop new investments in equipment, initially for the period ending March 1974, but this was subsequently extended until September 1974.

Window guidance for allowed credit expansion continued to become more and more restrictive until late 1974, and selective guidance continued to be used to restrict loans for speculative and non-priority uses and to direct funds to residential construction and other hard-hit areas. In early 1975 the official discount rate was reduced in two steps and the window guidance ceilings on bank lending were eased up, although bank interest rates on lending remained high. Later in the year the discount rate was reduced still further, window guidance was allowed to become progressively more expansive and the minimum compulsory reserve requirements were reduced in November 1975. In reaction to the strong reduction in the discount rate bank lending rates declined.

During 1976 monetary policy became accommodating rather than easy and, while reserve requirements were reduced slightly in February, the official discount rate was not varied and only moderate increases in bank lending were facilitated by the increase in window guidance ceilings. When signs of hesitation in business investment and reduced business confidence became obvious in the early months of 1977, the authorities moved to ease monetary and financial conditions by lowering the interest rate structure and increasing bank borrowing facilities at the Bank of Japan. September 1977 saw a further easing of monetary policy when both the discount rate and bank reserve requirements were reduced. As a result of the lack of demand pressure on bank lending, the Bank of Japan suspended its window guidance system and introduced a new formula for bank lending control under which city banks, long-term credit banks and trust banks will submit their lending programmes to the Bank of Japan, which reserves the right to intervene in those cases where credit extensions may be considered excessive.

Required reserve ratios were reduced for time and other deposits from 1 October but credit demand had still not risen significantly by the year's end even though the interest rates on loans continued to decline.

Commentary

In the growing Japanese economy the city banks met the chronic shortage of funds by maintaining an almost continuous position of 'overloan', which favoured monetary policy founded on the discount rate. The Bank of Japan began in the early sixties to lay the foundations for the use of open-market operations. In common with other countries, however, Japan's banking system became more liquid in the early seventies so that attempts at monetary restraint took much more time to be effective. The Bank of Japan appears to have reacted very flexibly to the switch from 'overloan' to 'over-liquid' and last year introduced a new system to control bank lending. While it might, of course, be said the use of selective credit controls inhibits the banks' management of their funds, the banking system appears to have survived the strains of the oil crisis without undue difficulty and to be able to expand its growing international base.

Further Reading

De Kock, M. H., *Central Banking*, 4th edn (Crosby Lockwood Staples, London, 1974)

Euromoney, Special Survey on Japan, March 1975, March 1976, March 1977.

Federation of Bankers' Associations of Japan, *Banking Systems in Japan*, 5th edn (Tokyo, 1974)

Fukuda, Haruko, 'Japanese Banking at the Crossroads', *The Banker*, April 1973.

Mikitanii, Ryoichi, 'Monetary Policy in Japan' in K. Holbik, *Monetary Policy in Twelve Industrial Countries* (Federal Reserve Bank of Boston, 1973)

OECD, *Monetary Policy in Japan*, Monetary Studies Series

Ogawa, S., 'Banking in Japan' in H. W. Auburn (ed.), *Comparative Banking*, 3rd edn (Waterlow, England, 1966)

Presnall, L. S. (ed.), *Money and Banking in Japan* (Macmillan, London, 1974)

15 BANKING REGULATION AND REFORM IN CANADA

> '[A] more open and competitive banking system . . . carefully and equitably regulated . . . but not bound by restrictions which impede the response of the institutions to new situations, enforce a particular pattern of narrow specialization or shelter some enterprises from competitive pressures.' (The Porter Commission, *Report of the Royal Commission on Banking and Finance*, 1964, p.564.)

Institutional Framework

Ten privately owned banks with a network of more than 7,200 branches operate in Canada, of which the three largest – the Royal Bank of Canada, Canadian Imperial Bank of Commerce and the Bank of Montreal – represent some 62 per cent of the total assets of the banking sector while the largest five banks (the above and the Bank of Nova Scotia and the Toronto Dominion Bank) have consistently controlled over 90 per cent of the total assets of the industry. It is a distinctive characteristic of Canadian banking legislation that for the private or chartered banks the Bank Act is a corporate charter to be revised every ten years when all charters automatically expire. The chartered banks are able to act as both commercial banks and savings banks and traditionally have emphasised short-term lending in particular for the purpose of providing working capital for industry. Bank charters in earlier periods prohibited lending on the security of real property other than a subsequent security but successive revisions of the Bank Act have widened the ambit of bank lending.

The Bank of Canada was established as the central bank in 1934 following the Macmillan Commission of 1933, which had recommended its establishment while noting that the absence of a highly developed money market could limit its effectiveness in controlling currency and credit. Nevertheless the Commission suggested that the main operations of the Bank should include the purchase and sale of 90 or 120 days' prime Bank or commercial bills and Dominion and Provincial government securities of up to one year terms. Treasury bill tenders were in fact one of the first activities of the new Bank of Canada, although for some twenty years the chartered banks were the main private parties in the tender. In 1954, after improving the position of investment dealers with respect to participation in the money market, the Bank discontinued direct payment for securities that the banks sold to it and routed the payment through the clearing system. The Bank also changed the banks' legal cash reserve requirement from a daily 5 per cent to a monthly 8 per cent basis which allowed them more cash to invest in the money market. A further development in May 1956, in which, on the initiative of the Bank, the banks adopted a convention to work to a minimum monthly average ratio of cash, day loans and Treasury bills to deposits of 15 per cent, had the effect of increasing the banks' sensitivity in the money market. By these and other means the money market in Canada has been developed to the stage where it may be regarded as a focal point of Bank actions with regard to the economy's liquidity structure.

Before the 1967 amendment of the Bank of Canada Act the exact relationship between the central bank and the government was the subject of some controversy as the existing legislation appeared to give the Bank of Canada exclusive rights to direct monetary policy. Any possibility that such an interpretation could be made was removed by the provisions in the 1967 Act. These provided for regular consultation between the Governor of the Bank and the Minister of Finance and set out a formal procedure under which, should any disagreement between the bank and the government fail to be resolved, the government may after further consultation issue a written directive in specific terms and applicable for a specified period to the Bank as to the monetary policy it is required to follow. It is further provided that the directive be both published in the *Canada Gazette* and tabled in Parliament. Although this provision gives the government ultimate responsibility for monetary policy it is clear that the Bank remains responsible for its implications.

Management of the Bank is in the hands of a board of directors comprising a Governor and Deputy Governor and twelve directors. The Minister of Finance appoints the directors for three-year terms and they in turn appoint the Governor and Deputy Governor for terms of seven years each. There is an Executive Committee comprising the Governor, two directors and the Deputy Minister of Finance (who may not vote) with the same powers as the board, although its decisions must be submitted to the board at its next meeting.

A federal Crown corporation and a subsidiary of the Bank of Canada, the Industrial Development Bank (IDB) was set up by Act of Parliament in 1944 to give capital assistance in the development of new businesses and the expansion of small and medium-sized businesses unable to find finance elsewhere. In December 1974 the Federal Business Development Act established the Federal Business Development Bank (FBDB), which incorporates the IDB, to provide financial and advisory management services to small and medium-sized businesses.

Instruments of Regulation

The Bank of Canada Act which established the Bank of Canada also conferred on the Bank specific powers to enable it to regulate credit and currency. Revisions to the 1934 Act were made in 1936, 1938, 1954, and 1967. All banks operating in Canada are chartered by Parliament under the terms of the Bank Act, which is revised at approximately ten-year intervals, and is, at the end of 1977, again in the process of revision. The Bank Act regulates some internal aspects of bank operations as well as the banks' relationships with the public, the government and the Bank of Canada. The instruments of regulation described in this section are those in operation since the 1967 legislation and those changes made without the need for legislative revision.

Under the Bank of Canada Act the Bank may determine the total amount of cash reserves available to the chartered banks as a group and by that means control the rate of expansion of total assets and deposit liabilities of the banking system. The Bank Act requires that each chartered bank maintain a stipulated minimum average cash reserve which is calculated as a proportion of its domestic deposit liabilities in the form of Bank of Canada notes and deposits. From 1 February 1968 the minimum cash reserve requirement was set at 12 per cent of demand deposits and 4 per cent of other deposits. In addition the Bank of Canada may require the chartered banks to maintain a secondary reserve which the Bank may vary within certain limits. When first introduced, the secondary reserve, which comprises cash reserves in excess of the minimum requirements, Treasury bills and day-to-day loans to investment dealers, could not be more than 6 per cent of total deposits and could not be changed to exceed 12 per cent. In either introducing or increasing the secondary reserve requirement the Bank must provide at least one month's notice to the chartered banks and may not increase the requirement by more than 1 per cent a month.

A major method used by the Bank of Canada to change the level of cash reserves of the banks, and through them the amount of chartered bank deposits, is by the purchase and sale of government securities. This may occur either through open-market operations or by transfers of government deposits. This latter technique was described by the Bank of Canada in its submission to the Porter Commission in May 1962 as follows:

The Government of Canada maintains a deposit account with the Bank of Canada through which pass virtually all Government receipts and payments. If this were the only Government Bank balance it would fluctuate with the daily ebb and flow of Government receipts and payments ... In order to avoid this sort of disturbance the Government maintains deposit balances with the chartered banks as well as with the central bank and permits the Bank of Canada, with the concurrence of the Minister of Finance, to transfer balances between the Bank and the chartered banks.

Daily adjustment of the excess cash available to the banking system is made by the Bank of Canada in response to money market changes and moves in chartered bank cash, and the main instrument for making this adjustment is transfers of government deposits since the cash reserves of banks are affected the next day after these transfers are made. The strongest advantage which use of these transfers offers is that they do not have a direct money market impact and therefore are able to be used without any direct impact on the cost of credit.

Open-market operations are also used to alter cash reserves when it is reasonable to have a direct effect on prices and yields in the money market. Payment by the Bank for the securities it purchases in the market adds to the cash reserves of the chartered banks and allows them to expand both their assets and deposit liabilities. On the other hand, when the Bank sells securities this causes a reduction in the cash reserves of the banks which forces them to reduce their holdings of assets and liabilities.

The Bank of Canada may make loans or advances to chartered banks for terms of up to six months on the pledge by the latter of particular classes of securities and the bank is required to make public the minimum rate at which it is prepared to make loans or advances. Changes in the Bank rate are intended to signal desired changes in the direction of policy. Between 1935 and 1944 the rate was held constant at 2.5 per cent and from 1944 to 1955 it moved from 1.5 per cent to 2 per cent, too low a level to be of influence, but in 1955 and 1956 the Bank rate began to play a more significant role. Between that time and 1962 the Bank rate was held at a fixed 0.25 per cent margin above the average Treasury bill rate. In announcing this move the Bank stated that if the bill rate ceased to be the best indicator of conditions or that a change in monetary conditions could be better shown by another means the practice would be changed. In early 1962 a dual Bank rate system was set up under which money market dealers were able to borrow from the

Bank at the lower rate of 0.25 per cent above the most recent average Treasury bill yield or Bank rate, but the banks were only able to borrow at the Bank rate. As a result of this new system changes in the Bank rate became unable to affect short-term interest rates directly but nevertheless were able to function as a useful signal of the direction of monetary policy.

Use of moral suasion as a means of control dates from the year after the Bank of Canada commenced operations, but from then until the end of 1956 it was mainly used in the quantitative restriction of credit. As a qualitative control directing the control of credit to particular areas of the economy moral suasion has had most use since 1957. Because of the small number of chartered banks it is possible for the Bank to exert great influence merely through moral suasion.

Banking Regulation: the Past Ten Years

The Bank Act of 1967, which made substantial changes in the financial system, implemented in its various provisions the view expressed by the Porter Commission that allowing competition within the financial sector would allow the Bank to control that sector through the impact on chartered bank reserves. A number of changes were made to the controls over the assets and liabilities of the banks. In addition to accepting current and savings deposit accounts with chequing facilities and non-chequing fixed deposits, the Act empowered the banks to borrow by the sale of bank debentures with a minimum term of five years. Holders of these debentures could not use them as security for a loan and banks could only have a very limited amount of debentures outstanding in any one year.

From 1 January 1968 the Act removed the restrictions on maximum interest rates chargeable on loans and set the reserve requirement against current deposits at not less than an average of 12 per cent and against deposits 'payable after notice in Canadian currency' at not less than 4 per cent. In addition to these primary reserves the chartered banks were required to hold a secondary reserve comprising rates and deposits with the Bank of Canada, Treasury bills of less than a year's maturity, and day loans to certain investment dealers, against bank deposit liabilities to an amount varying between zero and 12 per cent, subject to a limit that in setting it above zero the first move could not be above 6 per cent. Reserve requirements were to be met over a two-week averaging period instead of the previous four-week period, with the Bank of Canada able to change the averaging period after 1 April 1968, if it wished.

Banks had been permitted to lend in the mortgage market under the provisions of the National Housing Act since 1954, and, under the 1967 Act, they were allowed to enter the general mortgage market. Some restrictions were imposed on interconnections between banks and other financial institutions. In particular bank ownership of any domestic corporation was limited to 10 per cent of the voting shares; no more than one-fifth of the directors of any company could become directors of a bank; after a two-year period a director of a trust or mortgage loan company accepting deposits from the public could neither be appointed nor elected director of a bank; and no individual or associated shareholders might vote more than 10 per cent of a bank's total shares outstanding.

Early in 1968 heavy selling pressure on the Canadian dollar was met by Bank moves to minimise the Canada-US interest rate differential by raising Bank rate in stages from 5 per cent to 7.5 per cent, but once the exchange crisis had eased, the Bank reverted to a more expansive monetary policy, but when no sign of inflation moderating was evident by autumn 1968 the Bank moved to monetary restraint. According to the Bank itself the 'more liquid asset' ratio, that is the ratio of cash reserves, day loans, Treasury bills, loans to brokers and investment dealers and Federal Government securities to total assets, 'is probably the best single indicator of monetary policy and conditions'.

Short-term market rates of interest rose and Bank rate was pushed up to 6.5 per cent in December and to 8 per cent by July 1969. Banks met the strong demand for credit by using up their substantial liquidity positions and the 'more liquid asset' ratio dropped from a peak 32.5 per cent in 1968 to 27.5 per cent in mid-1969. From June 1969 the minimum secondary reserve requirement was lifted and the Bank, by the use of moral suasion, made the banks agree not to compete strongly for large domestic term deposits and to give their lending preferences to small businesses and to housing.

In 1970 monetary policy progressively eased, although there was a complication during the second quarter when capital inflow rose coincidentally with rising bank liquidity and falling interest rates and the government issued 250 million dollars of Treasury bills. The Bank of Canada raised the minimum secondary ratio to 9 per cent of the chartered bank deposit liabilities and cut Bank rate to 7.5 per cent, in line with money market rates. Bank rate was further reduced to 7 per cent in May and to 6 per cent by November, although the Bank exercised some restraint from mid-November 1970 until January 1971 on the amount of cash reserves in excess of minimum requirements that were available to the banks. Monetary expansion continued to be fast and the Bank's policies made funds available at lower interest rates in

1971 than in 1970. From the middle of 1971 monetary policy was operated to contain bank liquidity without restricting the growth of bank credit, and the second half of the year saw a lower rate of increase in bank liquidity. Reductions were made in the required ratio of secondary reserves to domestic bank deposit liabilities in December 1971 and in January 1972 to 8 per cent because the Bank considered that the 9 per cent ratio was not necessary to maintain adequate control of bank liquidity. Weekly increases in outstanding Treasury bills were finished in November. Growth in the Bank's liquidity was modified in the autumn of 1971 by the success of the Canada Savings Bond campaign but monetary policy could be characterised as highly expansionary both in 1971 and in the first half of 1972. At the beginning of 1972 when Bank credit was growing rapidly the Bank held the banks' cash reserves at levels intended to reduce the banks' liquidity, and in order to continue to meet strong credit demands the banks bid aggressively for deposit funds, by this means contributing to the upward rise of short-term rates. Unfortunately some distortion appeared in the interest rate structure as short-term interest rates increased. Bank prime lending rates remained at 6 per cent making it profitable for investors to place funds on short-term bank deposit and for large borrowers to use bank credit instead of issuing short-term paper. Bank fixed deposits and bank loans rose particularly strongly in May and these moves and the distortion of the interest rate structure in general were the subject of discussion between the Bank and representatives of the chartered banks in May and June at their regular meetings. As a result the 'Winnipeg agreement' was made at the request of the banks and with the permission of the Minister of Finance, under Section 138 of the Bank Act, providing that rates of interest on deposits of 100,000 dollars or more for terms of up to 364 days would be limited to a maximum of 5.5 per cent. By August, as a result of this agreement, the distortions were virtually eliminated and the aggressive competition among the banks for deposits diminished.

During 1971 and 1973 the Bank's policy had been to encourage the chartered banks to lend freely in order to support growth in the economy. However, by late 1972 and early 1973 there were increasing signs that the limits of the economy's capacity were being reached and, accordingly, the Bank of Canada varied its policy to moderate the pace of credit expansion without threatening continued economic growth. In April the voluntary ceiling interest rate for large short-term deposits, set at 5.5 per cent in June 1972 under the Winnipeg agreement, was substantially increased to 8.5 per cent with the intention of improving the banks' competitive position for funds in the short-term money market. From April 1973 also the banks were urged to moderate their lending while still maintaining a reasonable flow of funds to housing, small business and less prosperous sectors of the economy. To accomplish this most banks adopted a dual lending rate structure under which the minimum lending rate to smaller borrowers (200,000 dollars or less) was lower than the prime rate for other borrowers.

Over half of the increase in domestic deposits in the banks during 1973 was in the form of personal fixed-term deposits and this was symptomatic of the banks' increased reliance on comparatively high-cost term deposits to finance growth. The required minimum secondary reserve ratio was held at 8 per cent throughout the year and this meant that the banks required increasing amounts of Treasury bills to meet this ratio. Bank rate was raised five times during the year to a peak of 7.25 per cent in September. The shift to a tighter monetary policy was not significantly reflected in credit expansion. However, it is difficult to identify the exact effects when the credit expansion reflected to a considerable extent a substitution of bank credit for short-term money market borrowing.

During 1974 until late summer the Bank of Canada pursued a policy of monetary restraint. In March and April, when interest rates on the money market were rising quickly, the Bank made considerable open market cash purchases of short and medium-term government bonds, increasing its portfolio of government securities by some 550 million dollars in only six weeks. Bank rate was raised in three moves from 7.25 per cent in April to 9.25 per cent in July. The 'Winnipeg agreement' ceiling was raised from 8.5 per cent to 10.5 per cent between the middle of April and the end of July. In early June the Bank sold government bonds when demand for new government bond issues exceeded the supply available.

Summer 1974 saw a strong down-turn in international interest rates which was reflected in declines in both short-term market rates and long-term bond yields after mid-August in Canada. These changing conditions led the Bank to move to a more accommodating policy stance. There was a reversal of the substitution process which had enabled the banks to attract funds into interest-bearing deposits when a new issue of savings bonds was offered in November 1974 at relatively attractive yields. The minimum secondary reserve ratio of the banks was reduced from 8 per cent to 7 per cent from 1 December and to 6 per cent from 30 December in a technical adjustment to the banks' tighter liquidity position after the November savings bond issue which had raised 5.975 billion dollars and the termination of weekly issues of Treasury bills in November. Any increases in the free liquidity of the banks resulting from these adjustments were offset by the Bank of Canada through its cash reserve management and open-market purchases of Treasury bills.

Money market interest rates continued to decline into 1975 and borrowing and lending rates continued to be revised downward. The structure of deposit rates under the Winnipeg agreement ceased to be a constraining influence and that agreement was terminated on 15 January 1975.

In the latter half of January short-term interest rates continued to fall and the Bank tightened its provision of cash reserves to the banks to moderate this decline, which came to an end in February. A further cut was made in the minimum secondary reserve ratio to 5.5 per cent at the end of February and the resulting rise in bank liquidity was offset at least in part by open-market purchases of Treasury bills by the Bank and cash management policy. There was a new issue of government bonds in March at a time when the market was deteriorating and the Bank supported the market by buying short and medium-term bonds. Further open-market purchases were made in April to moderate the upward pressure on interest rates at that time; when Bank rate was increased to 9 per cent in early September the move was interpreted as a signal that there would be further tightening in policy and interest rates moved up sharply. The Bank eased its cash reserve position to modify these rises and when rates moved down in September and October it moved into a series of bond switches encompassing a lengthening of term for the market.

Again in early 1976 strong downward pressure on interest rates appeared and the Bank tightened its cash management policy, sold short and medium-term bonds and reduced its holdings of Treasury bills. In February interest rates began to edge up again and Bank rate was raised to 9.5 per cent from early March. When this had the effect of pushing short-term market rates even higher the Bank purchased Treasury bills in the market and significantly increased the amount of excess cash reserves provided to the banks. After March the presence of foreign investors in the bond market put downward pressure on bond yields and in response the Bank became a net seller of short and medium-term bonds. Between June and October the Bank's operations concentrated on maintaining the prevailing level of interest rates. In October short-term rates began to decline and the Bank eased its restraint on bank cash reserve management, and in November reduced

Bank rate to 9 per cent. When the Bank rate move accelerated the decline in short-term rates the Bank purchased heavily in the market. From 22 December Bank rate was cut back to 8.5 per cent and the Bank sold a large amount of short and medium-term bonds and Treasury bills. Although Bank rate was reduced twice more to 7.5 per cent in May 1977 the Bank also used open-market sales of Treasury bills and management of bank excess reserves to stabilise interest rate movements as far as possible and, after May, to resist any tendency for short-term interest rates to move in either direction. No further policy moves were required to ensure that credit remained readily available and policy was accordingly restricted to dampening short-term interest rate moves.

Renewal of the Bank Act, which was due by the end of June 1977, was postponed until the end of the year. It appears, as Grant Reuber has noted, that four generally agreed objectives emerged as important from the wide-ranging discussions on the revision of the Act: first, that the public ought to be adequately protected against fraud and bad management; second, that the members of the banking system ought to be treated equally; third, that banking ought to be required to be as competitive as would be consistent with the provision of maximum service at minimum cost; and fourth, that the central bank be permitted to implement its monetary policies effectively and efficiently.

Two public policy documents relating to the revision of the Bank Act which are of interest are the Economic Council of Canada's study,[1] and the Department of Finance White Paper, *Canadian Banking Legislation*.[2] The primary aim of the Economic Council's recommendations is that financial institutions performing the same functions ought to be subject to common regulations in order to increase efficiency through competition. In the Council's view the lending and borrowing powers of all deposit institutions ought to be broadened to allow banks and others to undertake factoring, leasing and consumer, commercial and mortgage lending. Though the Council recommends that all deposit institutions have deposit insurance, it also proposes that they be required to satisfy liquidity ratios, a requirement which might be necessary if the deposit insurance premiums are allowed to vary with risk, as it suggests.

In the area of trust services, the Council departs from its proposal for common functions for all deposit institutions in arguing that the commercial lending banks offer a potential conflict with fiduciary responsibilities, and that the right to provide trust services ought not to extend to banks. New entrants into banking should be increased, in the Council's view, by allowing the establishment, subject to some size restrictions, of closely held domestic banks. To improve the effectiveness of monetary policy the Council proposes that all deposit institutions be subject to uniform statutory minimum cash ratios, although it notes that primary reserve requirements may not be essential for effective monetary control.

Certain of these latter proposals fit very uneasily indeed into the aim espoused by the Council and may increase rather than reduce both regulation and costs for deposit institutions. The second public policy document, the White Paper, is mainly concerned with the problems of the inequitable distribution of liquidity requirements and the limits to entry into the clearing system, as well as with the unregulated activities of foreign banks in Canada. In the White Paper it is proposed that the existing cash ratios imposed on the banks be extended to the deposit liabilities of all those institutions that accept domestic deposits or foreign currency deposits used domestically. Membership of the clearing system would be made compulsory for all institutions offering transferable deposits and, if this was accomplished, legal enforcement of cash requirements on non-bank deposit institutions would be facilitated.

Although it is proposed in the White Paper that banks be allowed wider interests for factoring, leasing and mortgage lending, no widening of the scope of the non-bank institutions is proposed and even the banks are to withdraw from mutual fund operations. The differences between the recommendations of the Economic Council and those of the Department of Finance are also reflected in the wide-ranging discussions among academicians, financial economists, and policy officials concerning proposed revision of the Bank Act.

The 1978 Bank Act and Associated Acts

In the 1978 Canadian Payments Association Act the White Paper proposal that all institutions accepting transferable deposits must join the new Canadian Payments Association was modified so that only the Bank of Canada, all chartered banks, and Quebec savings banks were required to join. Other deposit-accepting institutions were able to join the CPA if they wished and if they could meet the requirements of the Act. Apart from the Bank of Canada, every CPA member was to belong to the Canada Deposit Insurance Corporation, to have its deposits either insured or guaranteed under provincial legislation that also provides for inspection of financial institutions, or to belong to the Canadian Co-operative Credit Society. In contrast to the White Paper proposals CPA members were not required to maintain non-interest-bearing cash reserves or a specified level of clearing balances. However, from 1 July 1979 or a year after the Bank Act comes into operation the reserve requirement on Canadian dollar demand deposits was to be reduced gradually from 12 per cent to 10 per cent, and, while there was no change made to the 2 per cent requirement on the first 500 million dollars of Canadian dollar notice and term deposits of residents (except deposits of over a year if not encashable), on the remainder of Canadian dollar non-encashable notice deposits of residents the requirement was to be reduced gradually from 4 per cent to 3 per cent.

With regard to entry into banking, the Bank Act distinguishes between Schedule A banks, which are those now chartered under the Bank Act and those future banks with widely held capital stock, and Schedule B banks, which are those with closely held capital stock and all foreign bank subsidiaries. (The foreign bank proposals are outlined in Part 5 below.)

The operations of banks, once incorporated, are defined mainly along the lines proposed in the White Paper. More specifically, banks are permitted to buy and sell mortgages, bonds, debentures and other debt instruments for their own account and for customers, except that in the case of equities traded for customers this business must be executed by registered brokers through the exchanges. Banks may place their own equities with institutions with the Inspector of Banks' consent and may sell their own equities to the public.

As proposed in the White Paper, the Act permits banks to engage in leasing subject to regulations ensuring that leases are the functional equivalent of credit. The Act specifically authorises them to engage in factoring, while they are to be restricted in their provision of data processing services to those 'banking related'. No prohibition is placed on banks participating in loan syndicates but banks are specifically prohibited from engaging in trust activities in Canada and from managing mutual funds in the future.

Bank investment in Canadian corporations is limited on the general rule that operations are to be confined within the banks' own corporate structure, and by the requirement that banks may not acquire over 10 per cent of the voting shares of a Canadian corporation unless as authorised by the Bank Act. The Bank Act follows the proposals made in the White Paper by allowing banks to be sole owners of mortgage loan corporations engaged primarily in residential mortgage lending, and to be sole owners of Real Estate Investment Trust and MIC service corporations or to enter into partnership with other financial institutions to invest in these corporations. Banks may continue to be sole owners of those bank service corporations that only provide service to or hold real estate for the banks, and may also own venture capital corporations, although subject here to regulations limiting the extent of investments. A further White Paper proposal incorporated in the Act is the provision allowing banks to own up to 50 per cent of the voting shares in non-financial Canadian corporations, subject to the holding in excess of 10 per cent being disposed of within two years, unless extended by the Minister of Finance. Except for shares in trust or loan companies banks may temporarily exceed the 10 per cent limit for the new investments in Canadian financial corporations.

Under the associated Act, the Quebec Savings Bank Act, banks formerly limited to opening branches in the Province of Quebec are able to open branches anywhere in Canada and former limits on the size of their mortgage loans were released.

Commentary

The Bank of Canada has been able to use a wide range of instruments to control the banks, and, although in the past ten years their use has on occasion created distortions in the interest rate structure, in general policy intentions have been able to be implemented with reasonable speed. The use of government deposit transfers enables the Bank to change bank cash reserves without directly affecting the cost of credit, and this, together with the other available instruments, appears to provide a complete range of methods for influencing banking activity.

The tendency, observable at least from the 1967 Bank Act, for banks to operate in a widening range of areas appears to be further reflected in the new Bank Act. If the Economic Council's proposals are adopted the Canadian banks will be moving increasingly towards the 'universal bank' of the German type, able to service the corporate sector's every financial need.

Under regulatory controls in the past decade the individual bank often was forced to bid quite aggressively for deposit funds in times of strong credit demand and it had to direct some lending to certain areas favoured by the Bank of Canada. Further, because of the interest rate distortions and their subsequent reversal, a bank needed to adapt its funds management policies very quickly in order to obtain an advantage from these conditions. Owing to the range of instruments available to the Bank of Canada it appears to have been very difficult for an individual bank to be able to predict the combination of instruments used and, as a consequence of these different pressures, a prejudice for some excess liquidity holdings by a bank appears unavoidable. Nevertheless, on those occasions when bank liquidity rose the Bank of Canada consistently moved to offset this rise by cash reserve management and by open-market operations.

Dean and Schwindt point to a major political problem concerning regulatory policy, that the non-bank financial institutions generally operate under provincial and not federal charter as the banks do, with the result that federal legislation can only liberalise chartering regulations and procedures in order to encourage non-banks to seek charters. Dean and Schwindt also note that the 1967 Act's removal of some restrictions from banks proved to be beneficial to consumers as well as to banks and there does appear to be a case for widening the allowed scope of bank activities. As in so many other countries, the inequities resulting from the failure of non-banks to be subject to the same regulatory controls as banks provide an argument for allowing banks to widen their range of activities, as well as the obvious case for extending bank controls to non-banks.

Notes

1. Economic Council of Canada, *Efficiency and Regulation: A Study of Deposit Institutions* (1976).
2. *Finance Canada, White Paper on the Revision of Canadian Banking Legislation* (Ottawa, August 1976).

Further Reading

Baum, D. J., *The Banks of Canada in the Commonwealth Caribbean* (Praeger Publishers, New York)

Binhammer, H. H. and Jane Williams, *Deposit-Taking Institutions: Innovation and the Process of Change* (Economic Council of Canada, 1976)

Bond, D. E. and R. A. Shearer, *The Economics of the Canadian Financial System: Theory, Policy and Institutions* (Prentice-Hall, Toronto, 1972)

Botha, D. J. J., 'The Canadian Money Market I: Institutional Developments', and 'II: Instruments of Monetary Policy', *South African Journal of Economics* (1972)

Cairns, J. P., H. H. Binhammer and R. W. Boadway, *Canadian Banking and Monetary Policy* (McGraw-Hill Ryerson, Toronto, 1972)

Canada, *Report of the Royal Commission on Banking and Finance* (Ottawa, 1964)

Chant, John, James Dean, J. A. Galbraith, Douglas D. Peters, John W. Popkin, G. L. Reuber, Henri-Paul Rousseau and J. E. Toten, 'Comments on the 1977 Bank Act', *Canadian Public Policy*, Summer 1976

Crick, W. F. (ed.), *Commonwealth Banking Systems* (Clarendon, Oxford, 1965)

De Kock, M. H., *Central Banking*, 4th edn (Crosby Lockwood Staples, London, 1974)

Dean, James W. and R. Schwindt, 'Bank Act Revision in Canada: Past and Potential Effects on Market Structure and Competition', *Banca Nazionale del*

Lavoro Quarterly Review, no.116, 1976

Galbraith, J. A., *Canadian Banking* (Ryerson, Toronto, 1970)

— and A. L. Guthrie, 'Canadian Banking Legislation Ottawa Style: Principles or Pragmatism', *Canadian Public Policy*, Winter 1977

Gestin, B. R., 'Understanding Banking in Canada', *The Bankers Magazine*, Winter 1976

Green, D. W., *The Canadian Financial System since 1965* (University of Wales Press, Bangor, 1974)

Neufeld, E. P., *The Financial System of Canada* (Macmillan, Toronto, 1972)

O'Brien, J. W. and G. Lerner, *Canadian Money and Banking*, 2nd edn (McGraw-Hill, Toronto)

Orsingher, Roger, *Banks of the World*, English translation (Macmillan, London, 1967)

Pattison, John C., 'Bank Deposit Competition: The Canadian Experience', *The Bankers Magazine*, January 1970

Pesando, James E. and Lawrence B. Smith, 'Monetary Policy in Canada' in K. Holbik (ed.), *Monetary Policy in Twelve Industrial Countries* (Federal Reserve Bank of Boston, 1973)

Powell, D. J., 'Banking in Canada' in H. W. Auburn (ed.), *Comparative Banking*, 3rd edn (Waterlow, England, 1966)

Reuber, G. L., 'Comment', *Canadian Public Policy*, Summer 1976.

16 BANKING REGULATION IN SOUTH AFRICA

'The excessive reliance on monetary measures in the past, of course, restricted the main activities of the banks and affected their profitability. It provided moreover, an important stimulant to the bank to diversify . . . [and] Diversification has transformed commercial banks in South Africa . . . into organizations offering a full range of financial and related services.' (F. J. C. Cronje, 'South African Banks and the Franzsen Report', *The Banker*, 1972, pp.1057-8.)

Institutional Framework

In South Africa credit facilities are provided by commercial banks, merchant banks, savings banks, general banks, hire-purchase banks and discount houses, mining institutions, the Industrial Development Corporation of South Africa and the Post Office Savings Bank. The commercial banking sector, dominant among financial institutions until 1945, declined in relative importance during the fifties and sixties, partly due to the enforcing of monetary controls on the commercial banks through the Banking Act of 1942 while most other financial institutions were untouched by such controls. Barclays National Bank, the Standard Bank of South Africa, Nedbank, Volkskas Beperk, and the Trust Bank of Africa are the five largest banks. Although the commercial banks originally concentrated on the provision of short-term financing they have consistently obtained a large proportion of their funds in the form of savings and time deposits and on this basis have been able to enter the field of medium-term credit to commerce and industry. Diversification of commercial banking into hire-purchase lending, insurance, leasing, factoring and other financial activities and by the acquisition of equity in enterprises in non-financial areas occurred in the 1960s and early 1970s, although the banks are required not to invest beyond the field of banking to an extent exceeding their paid-up capital and reserves.

The tendency to a high degree of concentration in commercial banking has changed its pattern in recent years as the strong growth of the smaller three of the five largest banks and the aggressive competition of banks outside the five for savings and time deposits tend to reduce the domination of the two largest banks.

Other financial institutions which must comply with the same requirements as the commercial banks are hire-purchase banks, savings banks and general banks. Hire-purchase banks concentrate primarily on the financing of hire-purchase transactions, while the savings banks make small loans to individuals for domestic purposes. General banks were established to provide services not provided by the commercial banks, in particular long-term loans for industrial development purposes, underwriting of share issues, and the discounting of hire-purchase paper. Although some general banks have quite extensive branch systems they do not usually provide current account facilities. There are two hire-purchase banks, eight savings banks and eighteen general banks registered with the Registrar of Banks, as well as three discount houses which specialise in the mobilisation of call money, and ten merchant banks which were only taken under the general system of banking regulation by the Bank Act of 1965.

The South African Reserve Bank was the only central bank in the British Commonwealth outside London when it began operations in 1921. Control of the Bank, which is a limited liability company with a share capital of 2 million rands contributed by between 800 and 900 shareholders, is in the hands of a board of twelve directors, six (including the Governor and three Deputy Governors) appointed by the government and six elected by shareholders to represent commerce, industry, non-commercial bank finance and agriculture. Operating in close co-operation with the Minister of Finance and the Treasury, the Reserve Bank nevertheless has considerable independence with respect to the control of credit.

Act 33 of 1949 set up the National Finance Corporation for the purpose of developing a broad and active money market. In performing that function it accepts call deposits from financial institutions, the government, the South African Railways, the Post Office and local government in minimum amounts of 100,000 rands and it absorbs surplus funds in the money market in times of excess liquidity, if necessary with the assistance of the Reserve Bank. With its board comprising senior representatives of all types of financial institutions, the Reserve Bank and the Treasury, it is a unique forum for the discussion of activities in the finance sector.

Control of Banking

Prior to the Bank Act of 1972 which is discussed in the next section, the Reserve Bank had statutory instruments in the form of cash reserve requirements and liquid asset requirements, and non-statutory instruments in the form of discount policy, credit ceilings, deposit rate controls and, of course, the use of moral suasion. The 1965 Bank Act required that banks hold a fixed percentage of their short term liabilities (8 per cent) as a cash reserve deposit with the Reserve Bank and a variable liquid asset requirement, set initially at 30 per cent of bank short-term liabilities to the public, 20 per cent of their medium-term liabilities and 5 per cent of their long-term liabilities, to be held in the form of liquid assets.

Owing to serious difficulties experienced by one of the commercial banks in 1921 in meeting its cash reserve requirement and the gold cover that it was required to hold against its own bank notes, the Reserve Bank very early in its existence fulfilled the role of lender of last resort. It advances funds to the banking system or discounts money market paper at the discount rate.

The direct control of credit by the imposition of maximum limits or ceilings on bank lending was first introduced in October 1965, although this power had existed since the passing of the Currency and Exchange Act in 1933. As well as empowering the setting of credit ceilings the Currency and Exchange Act also allows the Reserve Bank to determine the maximum rates which deposit-receiving institutions may pay on deposits. Under the Limitation and Disclosure of Finance Charges Act of 1968, the maximum interest rates which financial institutions may charge for loans to the public are prescribed.

Taking into consideration both general market conditions and its own policy objectives, the monetary authority directly determines the interest rates on government maturities of three years and longer, but at the short end of the market the Treasury bill rate is controlled indirectly. It is a tender rate determined each Friday by a tender on a previously announced issue of Treasury bills, in which both the Reserve Bank and the National Finance Corporation may participate.

Use of these instruments may be instanced by monetary policy operations in 1965. A penalty discount rate over Bank rate was imposed on bank borrowing from the Reserve Bank by those banks extending excessive or non-essential credit in March 1965, and later in the same month deposit rate control was enforced on all banks. In the latter half of 1965 tap Treasury bills were introduced to mop up excess liquidity, credit ceilings were imposed to limit lending and guidelines were given to direct the restricted amount of lending to farmers and exporters.

Critics of the range of instruments available and their use, who have included the *Economist* (1962), the Franzsen Committee (1970), and the Technical Committee on Banking and Building Society Legislation (1972), have been mainly concerned with the wide range of assets able to be regarded as liquid assets and with the lack of open-market operations by the Bank. Liquid assets, as either provided specifically by legislation or approved by the Registrar of Banks comprise Reserve Bank notes; subsidiary coin, gold coin and bullion; demand deposits with the National Finance Corporation and demand deposits with other banks; loans to discount houses repayable on demand; Treasury bills; government securities of less than three years maturity; bills issued by and advances to the Land Bank which, at the lender's option, may be converted into bills; Land Bank debentures of less than three years maturity; debentures or notes issued by the Industrial Development Corporation for financing capital goods exports, which have a three-year currency and are guaranteed by the government; acceptances of a bank discountable by the Reserve Bank; self-liquidating bills or promissory notes arising out of the movement of goods with a maturity not greater than 120 days or, in the case of agricultural bills, not greater than six months, and which are discountable by the Reserve Bank; and Reserve Bank securities with a maturity of not more than three years.

While the Franzsen Report recommended the institution of open-market operations,[1] the use of which required the abolition of the rigid interest rate structure, elsewhere in the same Report the continued control of both interest and deposit rates was recommended. Professor Strydom observes that this contradiction 'is deeply imbedded in the thinking of the architects of monetary policy in South Africa'.[2]

An opposite view was presented by the South Africa Reserve Bank in its report for 1970/1 in a commentary on a longer-term view of monetary policy since 1964 in which it is stated (on p.27) that 'the facts show clearly that monetary policy supplemented by fiscal measures has in fact contributed importantly to economic stability over this period'.[3]

Regulation of Banks in the 1970s

During 1969 and early 1970 there was a strong decline in the liquidity of the commercial banks, as monetary policy measures such as reserve requirements were tightened to reduce banking liquidity so that the credit ceiling could be removed and control directed through changes in liquid assets and statutory reserves. Pressure on interest rates resulting from the Reserve Bank's request to commercial banks to hold the rate on deposits of twelve months or longer at no more than 7 per cent made it very difficult for smaller banks to attract sufficient funds to meet their liquidity needs, and some of them raised their rates. The Governor of the Reserve Bank met with the heads of financial institutions on 30 April 1970 and it was agreed that 7 per cent should remain the maximum rate paid except for those institutions with total assets of under 10 million rands who were allowed to pay a maximum of 7.25 per cent per annum.

Concessions to the banks, in the form of raising the ceiling on banks' discounts and advances and some reduction in the holding of liquid assets against medium-term liabilities, failed to make the banks hold their advances within prescribed limits and in February 1971 the Reserve Bank announced that it would require additional cash reserves, interest-free, from banks exceeding their ceilings.

While the credit ceilings remained at their March 1971 level until March 1972, quite substantial increases in the ceilings were then announced on 29 March, and all banks were given a concession to exceed the ceilings on their discounts and advances by 5 per cent and the ceilings on their investments by 10 per cent in order to facilitate the extending of new credit for production and exports. Bank credit failed to rise in response to this stimulus owing to a lack of demand caused by a low level of economic activity and high interest rates.

Short-term money market rates jumped from August 1971 but subsequently dropped even more sharply in the first half of 1972. In contrast deposit interest rates were relatively stable. However, these were subject to Reserve Bank control from 30 March 1972 in an endeavour to avoid an interest rate war amongst financial institutions after ceiling controls had been removed. An unfortunate result of the imposition of interest rate control was that funds were diverted to the grey market.

In the 1972/3 financial year monetary policy could be categorised as cautiously expansive. Ceilings on bank deposits were abolished from 1 November 1972 when the amended Banks Act of 1972 was implemented. Supplementary cash and liquid asset requirements were laid down in the new Act. It was now necessary for the banks to hold a minimum cash reserve balance at the Reserve Bank of 8 per cent of the banks' short-term liabilities to the public; a supplementary cash balance with the National Finance Corporation of 10 per cent of the banks' short-term liabilities to the public; and liquid assets including cash reserves amounting to 45 per cent of the banks' short-term liabilities to the public, 28 per cent of their medium-term liabilities to the public, and 10 per cent of their acceptance liabilities. Further, the Act imposed a 20 per cent limit on the extent to which liquid bankers' acceptances and trade and agricultural bills may be included with liquid asset requirements.

Short-term interest rates declined from early 1972 until well into

1973. The Treasury bill rate fell from 6 per cent at the end of 1971 to 2.57 per cent in July 1973. The supplementary cash requirement with the National Finance Corporation was reduced from March 1973 to 7 per cent. From excess liquidity and little demand for credit at the beginning of 1973, increasing demand for credit and substantial outflows of capital from South Africa created an acute shortage of liquidity from August 1973 onwards, and most banks were forced to borrow from the Reserve Bank by the end of the year.

In order at least partly to alleviate the shortage of funds the Reserve Bank extended open-market operations, although commercial bank deposit rates were increased by the banks to the maximum allowed under deposit rate control in line with the conservative monetary policy aim of raising interest rates to levels prevailing overseas.

In the first half of 1974 the banks raised their ratio of long-term deposits to total liabilities and reduced the relative share of short-term deposits to total liabilities, which generated a flow of funds sufficient to increase lending. Interest rates rose very quickly from their low in August 1973 and by August 1974 Treasury bills were at 5.84 per cent and ninety-one-day negotiable certificates of deposit rates rose from 3.25 per cent in July 1973 to 12 per cent at the beginning of August 1974. The maximum deposit interest rates were revised in January and June, and in August the Bank rate was increased to 8 per cent and banks moved their prime overdraft rate to 10.5 per cent. In the August Budget speech it was announced that the maximum finance charge had been raised from 12 per cent to 14 per cent under the provisions of the Limitation and Disclosure of Finance Charges Act.

It should be noted that most of the swings in liquidity were generated by changes external to the economy as speculative capital flows put pressure on the rand, and it was mainly on occasions when the financing of international trade switched from foreign to domestic sources that shifts in monetary policy occurred. In latter 1974 the monetary authorities allowed the downward drift in interest rates to occur, but continued balance of payments problems and the necessity to contain inflation forced the taking of an increasingly restrictive monetary stance as mid-1975 was reached. A new agreement was made between the Reserve Bank and the commercial banks in July 1975 concerning the relationship between the Bank rate and the banks' prime overdraft rate, that the latter would be the lowest overdraft charged and that it would maintain a firm relationship with the Bank rate. No clearing bank would have an effective prime rate of more than 3.5 per cent or less than 2.5 per cent above Bank rate, while for its part the Reserve Bank indicated that the

Bank rate would in future bear a closer relationship to market short-term interest rates.

On 11 August 1975 a number of measures affecting the banks were announced as part of a package to limit leads and lags in trade payments and to encourage foreign capital inflows. The Bank rate was increased from 8 to 8.5 per cent and liquidity requirements against short-term liabilities were raised from 45 to 49 per cent from 21 August. On 30 September it was announced that from 21 October the liquidity ratio against short-term liabilities was to increase to 55 per cent and the ratio against medium-term liabilities to 30 per cent. Further, supplementary liquid assets equal to at least 20 per cent of the increase in short-term liabilities and 10 per cent of the increase in medium-term liabilities since the end of September had to be held from 21 November. In order to limit the excessive increase in bank credit to the private sector which was linked to abnormally large purchases of foreign exchange from the Reserve Bank, in February 1976 the Reserve Bank imposed direct quantitative restrictions on bank credit to the private sector. Using 31 December as a base, these restrictions were to limit the increase in discounts, loans and advances to the private sector, and the increase in investment in certain private sector securities for each bank to a maximum of 1.5 per cent to the end of March 1976 and to 0.5 per cent per month after that. Following representations by the associations of bankers, an easing of these restrictions was announced on 3 March which raised the maximum to the end of March to 3.5 per cent, and after this date the ceiling was to be raised by 0.5 per cent of the December base figure each month.

The Bank rate was raised again from 8.5 per cent to 9 per cent in July which allowed banks to raise their prime overdraft rate to a maximum of 12.5 per cent. In June it had been announced that the maximum rates payable on deposits would now apply to all individual deposits of 1 million rands or less instead of to those of 250,000 rands or less. The combined effect of heavily restrictive liquid asset requirements and high interest rates forced one bank, Rondalia, into curatorship in November. Under the Banks Act the Minister of Finance is empowered to appoint a curator, with the powers of a judicial manager appointed to a trading company under the Companies Act, to any bank in financial difficulties if he thinks it in the public interest. Rondalia's curator explained that the bank had moved heavily into instalment finance in an attempt to overcome declining profitability, but that the fixed return on its large portfolio of instalment credit in combination with the higher deposit rates in the money market further restricted profit.

Rand Bank was caught by the collapse of a property venture, Glen Avil, to which it had directly lent 4.3 million rands and advanced 5.7 million rands under promissory notes, and was also placed under curatorship. As the Chairman of the Reserve Bank commented in his 1977 address to shareholders, 'a lack of confidence in smaller banking institutions developed and substantial amounts of deposits were switched to the larger banks'.

In February lifeboat facilities were arranged with the five largest banks, establishing a fund of 55 million rands with the National Finance Corporation of South Africa for special loans to smaller banking institutions experiencing liquidity problems, but this arrangement was terminated in August.

The smallest of the Big Five, Trust Bank of Africa, was the subject of a successful bid for control at a price one-third less than the historical low price of its shares, and Bankorp, the new holder, announced that shareholders could expect no dividends for years to come.

A revision to the deposit interest rate control regulations reduced the exemption limit back to amounts of 250,000 rands or more and the ceilings on bank lending to the private sector were tightened again in March 1977 when the 0.5 per cent increase allowed per month was suspended, although the monthly increase was reintroduced again in September, when banks whose combined ceiling figure did not exceed 10 million rands were exempted from the ceiling requirement. In order to hold domestic short-term interest rates comparable with those overseas the Reserve Bank made open-market sales of government securities to banks and others.

Commentary

During 1976 and 1977 the South African banking system suffered a serious crisis, partly due to the effects of overinvestment in property but made the more serious by the impact of regulatory constraints on small banks. Under the Banks Act the banks are required to hold both cash and liquid assets in large amounts which are increased as the maturities of bank deposits become shorter. If deposits are reduced, as occurred for a number of banks when the public became anxious about the property exposure of banks in general, banks may move their liquid assets to the South African Reserve Bank as well as reducing their other assets. As deposits fall so they reduce their assets, charging any losses incurred in the process against earnings or, if necessary, against capital and reserves which themselves must be held at a specified minimum level. In circumstances where the economy is in a down-turn, assets may not be able to be reduced along with deposits and loans will need to be called in. It is here that the need to be liquid may threaten solvency. Of course, the larger and more diversified the interests of a bank, the less likely it is to be vulnerable here. Again, it is the larger banks that may more readily move into other areas of finance to compensate for declining profitability produced by the rise in liquid asset requirements and the various credit ceilings.

An individual large bank could gain from these conditions to the disadvantage of smaller banks whose survival this system of regulatory controls appears to threaten seriously. It could be argued that several strong banks would make the banking system more able to cope with the heavy cyclical fluctuations which the South African economy has faced in the 1970s than the current, more polyglot, collection of banks, but the interests of shareholders as well as of depositors suggest that this is probably not the best way to achieve that end.

Notes

1. Barclays D.C.O. Economics Department, 'The Franzsen Commission Report', *The Banker* (1972).
2. P. D. F. Strydom, 'Some Observations on Monetary Policy', *South African Journal of Economics*, vol.41 (1973), pp.234-56.
3. South African Reserve Bank, *Annual Report, 1970/1*.

Further Reading

Cronje, F. J. C., 'South African Banks and the Franzsen Report', *The Banker*, 1972
Goodhuys, D. W., 'Has Monetary Policy Failed?', *South African Journal of Economics*, vol.40 (1972), pp.77-83
Greenblo, Alan, 'South Africa's Banks Lick Their Wounds', *The Banker*, October 1977
Kantor, B., 'The Evolution of Monetary Policy in South Africa', *South African Journal of Economics*, vol.39 (March 1971), pp.42-73
— 'South African Financial Structure', Supplement to *The Standard Bank Review*, September 1972
Laight, J. C., 'Hire purchase, Savings and General Banks', Supplement to *The Standard Bank Review*, December 1974
Meier, G., 'Commercial Banking in South Africa', Supplement to *The Standard Bank Review*, March 1973
Official Yearbook of the Republic of South Africa, 1962, 1973, 1976
Oxford, G. M. F., 'An Interpretation of Banking Developments in the Past Year', Supplement to *The Standard Bank Review*, June 1974
South African Reserve Bank, Economic Department, 'The South African Reserve

Bank: Its History, Functions and Growth', Supplement to *The Standard Bank Review*, December 1972

Strydom, P. D. F., 'Monetary Legislation in South Africa: An Analysis', *South African Journal of Economics*, vol.42 (1974), pp.1-11

17 THE BANKING SYSTEM IN AUSTRALIA

'The Australian banking system, like that of Great Britain and
most countries other than the United States, is dominated by a
few large banks each with a wide network of branches.' (F. J.
Garlick and M. R. Hills, 'The Australian Banking System — A
Competitive Oligopoly?', *The Bankers Magazine of Australasia*,
June 1975, p.375.)

The Institutional Framework

The major financial institutions in Australia are the Reserve Bank, the
trading banks, the savings banks, life insurance offices, finance companies, public and private pension funds, short-term money market
dealers, building societies and pastoral finance companies. There are
seven major trading banks: the Commonwealth Trading Bank (which is
a government bank), the Australia and New Zealand Bank Ltd, the
Bank of Adelaide, the Bank of New South Wales, the Commercial Bank
of Australia Ltd, the Commercial Banking Company of Sydney Ltd, and
the National Bank of Australasia Ltd. There are other cheque-paying
banks but these are either not subject to the requirements of the Banking Act or have less requirements to meet than the major trading banks.

The major trading banks have wide branch networks and each
operates a savings bank subsidiary. Significant changes within the
Australian financial sector in the 1960s were the relative decline in the
importance of the trading banks as sources of finance; the substantial
expansion in the then comparatively unregulated non-bank financial
intermediaries and the growth of savings banks. In response to the
growth in significance of the non-bank financial intermediaries the
1974 Financial Corporations Act provided a framework within which
the government can introduce controls over the asset ratios, interest
rates and lending policies of these institutions.

Australia's central bank is the Reserve Bank of Australia which came
into operation on 14 January 1960 by virtue of the Reserve Bank Act
and the Banking Act. Division 2 of the Banking Act obliges the Reserve
Bank to exercise its powers and functions for the protection of the
depositors of the banks that are subject to the Act. The Bank is the sole
issuing authority for Australian notes and acts as agent for the Treasury
in the distribution of coin to banks.

Bank advances, although also made by the loan system, are primarily made in Australia by the overdraft system under which a customer who is granted an advance is given a maximum limit to which he is allowed to overdraw his current account at the bank. This may result, as in 1971, in overdraft limits being expanded but the funds not being drawn upon for some time. In general the trading banks are short-term lenders to individuals and to business.

Monetary Controls Affecting the Trading Banks

Direct regulation of trading bank activities is achieved by reserve requirements, interest rate policy and advance policy. More indirectly, open-market operations may be used.

In regulating trading bank liquidity the Reserve Bank has the use of the Statutory Reserve Deposit system (SRDs) and the liquid assets and government securities (LGS) convention. The LGS assets consist of notes and coin, cash held at the Reserve Bank, Commonwealth Treasury bills and notes and other Australian government securities. This ratio of LGS assets to deposits is termed a convention because it has no legislative base, but is merely a formal expression of firm undertakings between the Reserve Bank and the trading banks first made in 1956. By these undertakings each bank agreed to ensure that its LGS ratio would not fall below an agreed minimum level, which was uniform for all banks, and that if it did fall below this level the bank would borrow short-term from the Reserve Bank. In consideration of this agreement, the Reserve Bank agreed to operate the Statutory Reserve requirements in such a way that the banks which followed Reserve Bank policy would be able to maintain their LGS ratios above the agreed minimum.

The second arm of liquidity regulation is the Statutory Reserve Deposit system, established in 1960, which requires each trading bank to maintain an SRD account with the Reserve Bank for which the Reserve Bank determines the minimum level of deposit, which is equal to a stated percentage of the bank's current level of Australian deposits. The SRD ratio is uniform for all the trading banks and may be increased to not more than 25 per cent of deposits with one day's notice, or to a ratio greater than 25 per cent of deposits with forty-five days' notice and subject to certain conditions.

Initially at a minimum level of 14 per cent, the LGS ratio has been at 18 per cent since 1962. Its main purpose is to place some restrictions on the banks' disposition of assets which will affect their responses to changes in the SRD ratio. To the extent that the banks hold LGS assets above the minimum level, they are able to meet a call to SRD accounts merely by running down their holdings of these assets and not otherwise adjusting their assets. But as LGS holdings approach the minimum level the banks find themselves forced to reduce their other assets, especially loans. The Reserve Bank, in outlining its functions and operations, says that, with the existence of the LGS convention, an increase in the SRD ratio will tend to have a stronger and more immediate effect on bank lending to the private sector.

Apart from influence on interest rates through the use of open-market operations, the Reserve Bank is given authority under the Banking Act (with the approval of the Treasurer) to make regulations controlling rates of interest paid and received by banks. While bank interest rates have not been formally determined under the Banking Act, various maximum rates for both trading banks and savings banks have been established from time to time. Trading banks observe a uniform maximum overdraft rate applied since 1972 only to loans drawn against limits of less than 50,000 dollars. A schedule of rates applies to fixed deposits.

Banking legislation also empowers the Reserve Bank to determine the advance or lending policy of banks with reference to both the volume of bank credit provided and its distribution, but in practice the Bank relies on the co-operation of banks in changing their lending as directed by policy. Nevertheless one of the studies of the early 1960s credit squeeze in Australia[1] argues that the apparent ineffectiveness of restrictive monetary policy then may be at least partly explained by the failure of the trading banks to contract their lending in response to explicit Reserve Bank directives. Although quantitative advance policy has been used there appears to be more frequent recourse to qualitative advance policy, that is to directing the flow of bank credit either towards or away from specific classes of borrowers.

Through SRD accounts, and calls from other bank assets, the Term Loan Fund and the Farm Development Loan Fund are funded. The former's resources are used to make loans for capital expenditure on production for fixed terms of from three to eight years, while the latter fund was established to provide the rural sector, especially small producers, with improved access to medium and long-term finance.

The Reserve Bank may also influence the banks and the financial markets by the use of open-market operations, undertaken by the Bank with stockbrokers, authorised money market dealers and on the stock exchanges themselves.

In the 1971 Mills Memorial Lecture,[2] the then Governor of the Reserve Bank of Australia, (now Sir) John Phillips presented the view that monetary policy should not focus on banks but should have a general impact throughout the financial system and for this reason open-market operations must be regarded as an essential ingredient of any monetary .policy package. Only a few years before, Harcourt, Karmel and Wallace[3] in an Australian macroeconomics textbook had noted that the LM/IS framework could not be considered appropriate in the case of Australia because there was not really a money market in existence. By 1971, however, Phillips was able to say that the Reserve Bank 'had cultivated assiduously the market for government securities and promoted institutional developments conducive to open market operations'.

Between 1958 and 1970 the Reserve Bank and the government had created the short-term money market and the commercial bills market, extended the range of maturities of conventional bonds, introduced new types of securities and, by permitting certain tax advantages, had encouraged the insurance companies to participate in the bond market.

The existence of these features of the Australian market was sufficient justification for Governor John Phillips to claim in his 1971 lecture that, 'As a rough rule, and depending on the circumstances, we would nowadays tend to look first at the more pervasive instruments of open market operations and interest rates, and then at direct influence on lending and direct liquidity controls.'

In 1969 the range of trading bank deposit facilities was enlarged and renegotiable certificates of deposits (CDs) were introduced in March for sums of 50,000 dollars and over for terms from three months to two years. Further, in August the term-deposit structure was changed to allow separate rate structures for large, that is over 100,000 dollars (reduced to 50,000 dollars in March 1970), and small deposits.

From December 1970 trading banks were allowed to accept interest-bearing deposits for periods beyond two years and up to four years. Term deposits which were only 22.5 per cent of total trading bank deposits in 1959/60 had risen to 57 per cent by 1976. It is important to note that this has increased banking costs and may be seen as one of the factors speeding up the move to computerise banking operations as a means of improving efficiency.

Regulations in the 1970s

The Reserve Bank's 1970 monetary policy package directives were in restraint of new lending and included calls to SRDs, increases in interest rates on deposits and loans and an increase in the long-term bond rate, but in contrast to the greatly lagged effects of similar restraints in 1960 this package was successful to the extent that in late 1971 these restraints were lifted. In December 1971 official constraints on bank lending were removed and banks were encouraged to increase their lending when the SRD ratio was reduced to 7.1 per cent, the lowest ratio since the SRD system was introduced in January 1960. By comparison with the 18 per cent minimum LGS convention the trading banks held 29.1 per cent in those assets so that their immediate response to the removal of constraints was to increase new approvals of overdraft limits quite sharply, although business took some time to draw on these funds. Interest rates turned downwards in late 1971, and in February 1972 similar reductions in trading banks' lending and deposit rates were authorised. In addition the Reserve Bank removed the upper interest rate limit on transactions exceeding 50,000 dollars. These moves were described in the Bank's 1972 annual report as a conscious policy shift intended to make the banks more competitive with other financial institutions beyond the Bank's direct control.

In spite of this change in policy stance the domestic economy proved, in the words of the Treasurer in the 1972 Budget speech, 'hard to budge from its too subdued growth path', but a combination of interest rate differentials between Europe and Australia and speculation in advance of the revaluation of Australia's dollar produced a substantial capital inflow which kept pushing up the rate of growth of the money supply, so that in January 1973 the Bank's LGS ratio had risen to 34.1 per cent.

While under the Liberal-Country Party coalition there had been a move towards market-oriented monetary controls, the Labour Party, which governed from December 1972 to November 1975, preferred to utilise more direct controls, in particular the SRD ratio. In 1973 two calls of 0.5 per cent each to SRD in April 1973 were an early indication that the authorities were worried about the overexpansion of the economy and from the middle of the year much stronger action was taken. Early in July the Bank announced that two further calls of 1 per cent each would be made to SRD accounts in August. Bond rates were increased in the July Commonwealth Government Loan and in September the government announced that the Bank would pursue open-market sales of government securities, an announcement which had the effect of pushing market yields up to 8.5 per cent, which became the new long-term (twenty years) rate for the October Commonwealth Loan. On 14 September the Bank announced that the maximum rate which trading banks could offer on term deposits would be increased from 6.5 per cent to 8 per cent and that the interest rate ceiling previously applied to certificates of deposits would be removed and their maximum term extended from two to four years. At the same time the maximum overdraft rate on loans of less than 50,000 dollars was increased from

7.75 per cent to 9.5 per cent. Owing to the government's stated desire that home-buyers of moderate means should be shielded from the full impact of interest rate increases, bank lending rates generally only rose by 1 per cent.

These restrictive monetary policies in combination with restrictions on capital inflow which switched demand to domestic sources produced a strong credit squeeze in the first half of 1974. When, in response to the continuing demand for funds, the banks moved into competing with the non-bank intermediaries for deposits in order to try to hold their LGS ratios above the minimum level, this only served to exacerbate market pressures which pushed interest rates up.

The second half of 1974 witnessed a switch to an expansionary monetary policy in an attempt to counter the recession in the economy, with reductions in SRD and a lowering of short-term Treasury note yield which improved the level of bank deposits and advances as banks were able to reduce interest rates on CDs. Liquidity continued to rise throughout 1975, and although the trading banks had been observing lending objectives intended to restrict the flow of finance since the beginning of the year, four calls of 1 per cent each were made to SRD accounts in July, August, September and November 1975.

When the government changed in late 1975 there was an almost immediate switch from a comparatively easy monetary policy to a much firmer policy of restraint. In January 1976 Australian savings bonds were introduced to finance part of the government deficit by drawing on the exceptionally high level of household saving. Interest rates on the bonds were pitched very competitively and large amounts of the issue were taken up by the public. The minimum LGS ratio of the trading banks was increased, until the end of March 1977, from 18 per cent to 23 per cent of deposits and the maximum interest rate on loans of less than 50,000 dollars was reduced. Resulting pressure on trading bank liquidity was increased in the June quarter when there was a seasonal run-down in liquidity, made stronger by the deferred February instalment of company tax. The Bank reduced the SRD ratio to ease the pressure and in addition offered to purchase commercial bills or lend on non-penal terms to the trading banks. Little use was made of these two alternatives although their availability assisted in bank fund management during this time.

Throughout 1976 an important aim of monetary policy was to restrain the growth of lending and as part of the measures taken in November 1976 the SRD ratio was raised by 1 per cent, and the banks were asked to contain new lending below the level of new overdraft approvals, which had been about 100 million dollars a week, and to continue to reduce unused limits. The interest rate payable on SRD accounts with the Reserve Bank was increased from 0.75 per cent per annum to 2.5 per cent per annum. Between 30 December and 2 February 1977 the SRD ratio was raised from 6 per cent to 10 per cent.

Until the beginning of April 1977 the higher required LGS ratio of 23 per cent acted as a restriction on free liquidity, but when this ratio resumed its normal minimum of 18 per cent it was quickly eroded by seasonal flows of funds to the government and the actual LGS ratio of the trading banks fell from about 30.3 per cent in March to 21.5 per cent in June. Where individual banks found liquidity exceptionally tight, they were able to acquire some funds at least from the inter-bank lending market which was developing. The decline in bank liquidity was not, as had been customary, arrested in the September quarter and the banks' LGS ratio fell for the first time in a September quarter since 1974.

Commentary

In the past decade the Australian trading banks have undertaken substantial diversification outside the traditional banking area, beginning with the move to bank-affiliated finance companies, and at the same time regulation initially confined to banking has spread to the general financial sector. The move towards market-oriented monetary controls, begun with the development of the short-term money market in the late fifties, was halted in the years of the Labour government (December 1972 to November 1975), who favoured more direct controls. The problem of lags in the effect of monetary policy has bothered successive governments since the 1960s' credit squeeze and it appears to be necessary for SRD and LGS ratios to be used even in conjunction with open-market operations, although by themselves these ratios are difficult to use with any degree of finesse because of the wide range of actual liquidity ratios held by the banks.

It appears that individual banks, although finding pure banking sufficiently limiting to want to diversify, do in fact have plenty of time in which to accommodate themselves to changes in monetary policy.

Notes

1. M. S. Henderson, 'A Sectional Investigation of the 1960 Credit Squeeze', *Australian Economic Papers*, vol. 4 (June-December 1965).

2. J. G. Phillips, 'Developments in Monetary Theory and Policy', R. C. Mills Memorial Lecture (1971).

3. G. C. Harcourt, P. H. Karmel and R. H. Wallace, *Economic Activity* (Cambridge University Press, Cambridge, 1967).

Further Reading

Arndt, H. W. and C. P. Harris, *The Australian Trading Banks*, 5th edn (Cheshire, Melbourne, 1977)

'Banking and Monetary Policy – from Freedom to Restraint', *Bank of N.S.W. Review*, no.11 (July 1974)

'Banking and National Policy – Australia', *ANZ Bank Quarterly Survey*, various issues, 1968-77

Phillips, J. G., *The Banker*, December 1969.

Sanders, D. N., 'Australian Monetary Policy: Recent Developments and Current Thinking' in J. W. Nevile and D. W. Stammer (eds.), *Inflation and Unemployment* (Penguin, Harmondsworth, 1972)

Sharpe, Ian G., 'An Evaluation of the Controls Governing Australian Banks', *Economic Monograph* no.337, Economic Society of Australia and New Zealand, N.S.W. Branch, April 1973

18 THE DEVELOPMENT OF BANKING IN PAPUA NEW GUINEA

'One of our first priorities will be to show that a central bank can be a positive influence in identifying, monitoring and dealing with some, at least, of the economic and financial problems that face a developing country. We recognise that there will be difficulties in this task of delineating for ourselves a role, particularly because, in Papua New Guinea, there has been no prior experience of an independent central bank managing an independent banking system.' (Extract from an Address by Governor Henry on 1 January 1973 commemorating the establishment of the Bank of Papua New Guinea.)

Institutional Framework

The PNG banking sector was until 1973 merely an extension of the Australian banking system. Four Australian trading banks and their savings bank subsidiaries provided banking services within Papua New Guinea: the Bank of NSW was the first bank, with its first branch established in Port Moresby in 1910; and it was followed by the Commonwealth Bank of Australia in 1916, the Australia and New Zealand Bank Ltd in 1953 and the National Bank of Australasia Ltd in 1957. These banks primarily serviced the needs of Australian companies operating in Papua New Guinea, and those of planters and the local government. It was only in the 1970s, with government plans to localise the foreign-dominated economy by providing for the promotion of indigenous enterprise, that this direction changed.

In December 1972, a special Committee on Banking in Papua New Guinea, established jointly by the PNG and Australian governments, submitted its final report and in the following April the two governments announced the principles on which the PNG banking system was to be established.

These were that responsibility for the control of the PNG financial sector should be vested in the domestic authorities as soon as possible; that a central bank (later announced that this would be called the Bank of Papua New Guinea) should be established on the basis of the Reserve Bank of Australia's Port Moresby office; that a national banking institution (later named the Papua New Guinea Banking Corporation) should be established within the economy to assume the domestic business of the Commonwealth Banking Corporation, except where financial and contractual considerations prevented this move; that the Papua New Guinea Banking Corporation should provide a full range of banking services and operate as far as possible under the guidance of commercial considerations; that savings banking and trading banking in the economy should not be legally or institutionally separated; and that those private commercial banks in operation within the economy should be allowed to continue operations subject to appropriate changes in structure.

In September 1973 a Central Banking Ordinance and a Banks and Financial Institutions Ordinance were passed by the House of Assembly and the Bank of Papua New Guinea was formally established to take control of the banking system on 1 November 1973. The Papua New Guinea Banking Corporation took over the PNG assets and operations of the Commonwealth Banking Corporation, except for the Port Moresby branch which retained the business of a single customer, Bougainville Copper Ltd. In early 1974 the three other commercial banks began to incorporate locally with the National Bank, becoming the Bank of South Pacific Ltd.

The Bank of Papua New Guinea was given a charter to control both banks and other financial intermediaries, together with wide powers of inspection if it has any doubt about financial stability. With regard to the regulation of banking, the Bank has broad powers to give direction about the size, purpose and conditions of bank lending; to establish liquidity and other financial ratios; to impose special statutory deposit requirements; to control interest rates and to deal in government securities.

Under the terms of the Banks and Financial Institutions Act a system of licensing was applied to banks, requiring specified minimum capital funds to guarantee the strength of their financial bases. As part of the central bank's encouragement to the banks to make their operations appropriate to the needs of Papua New Guinea, the Bank approved the establishment of branches at twenty-three new locations and asked the banks to direct their lending policies towards an emphasis on assessing the viability of individual projects, and away from the borrower's ability to provide tangible collateral.

From 1 March 1974 the Bank required the banks to retain at least 15 per cent of their deposit liabilities in the form of specified liquid assets which were to include a minimum of 2 per cent in Papua New Guinea liquid assets. It was intended that this 2 per cent minimum be progressively increased to help retain within the country funds mobilised by the banking system. The paucity of demand within Papua New

Guinea for substantial short-term loan funds was reflected in a tendency for the banks to invest substantial funds in demand deposits in Australia.

In order to reduce this movement of funds the Bank and the Papua New Guinea Department of Finance introduced a series of short-dated (91-day and 182-day) Treasury bills. The size of these issues was limited by the government's own restricted use of short-term finance.

Until 19 April 1975 the Bank's ability to control the money supply and interest rates was limited by the use of Australian currency, but from that date the introduction of a Papua New Guinean currency, the kina, was introduced. This step alone did not localise the economy's monetary base, and the Bank supported the development of a local money market, the centralisation in its hands of foreign currency holdings and the establishment of a framework for foreign currency dealings in order to accomplish this objective.

Following the introduction of short-dated Treasury bills in October 1974, the local component of the liquidity ratio was raised to 5 per cent, but the Treasury bills were not sufficient to meet the banks' local investment needs. Accordingly, in May 1975, two more kina-denominated investment facilities were introduced for the commercial banks: a call facility allowing the banks to place funds with the Bank overnight or for periods of up to thirty days at an interest rate initially geared to Australian short-term money market rates; and an interest-bearing deposit facility allowing the banks to deposit funds with the Bank for periods from thirty days to twelve months at interest rates set by the Bank. The approval previously available to include deposits with overseas banks as 15 per cent of liquid funds was withdrawn on 1 October 1975, effectively localising all liquid assets needed to meet the minimum requirement.

There were a number of measures used to direct lending more to Papua New Guineans, including the introduction of a rule for the Papua New Guinea Development Bank under which it would normally lend to foreign borrowers no more than 25 per cent of paid-up capital; the sponsoring of the Village Economic Development Fund under which the government makes capital grants to supplement loan funds for approved projects; and the introduction of a Credit Guarantee Scheme administered by the Papua New Guinea Banking Corporation.

In 1976 it was again realised that the range of domestic liquid investments available to the banks was limited and in May more flexibility was introduced by reducing the rediscount rate on the rediscount facilities offered by the Bank for Treasury bills, allowing banks to deal in these bills between themselves, easing the penalties on banks for breaking term deposits with the Bank of Papua New Guinea, stabilising the rates offered to the banks on call and on term deposits, and initiating moves to amend the Central Banking Act to enable the banks to lend between themselves to even out liquidity pressures. These latter amendments to the Central Banking Act were made in September 1976.

The effects of the seasonal demand for funds (by the coffee industry in particular) on commercial bank liquidity in both 1975 and 1976 led these banks to alleviate the pressure by increasing their off-shore borrowings. In order to reduce this potential for seasonal dependence on external funds, the Bank agreed in May 1977 to make short-term loans available to the banks during the period of high seasonal demand for finance in order to enable the banks to hold their liquidity ratios at least at the minimum agreed level.

Between January and May 1977 the statutory minimum liquidity ratio for the commercial banks was raised from 15 per cent to 25 per cent of deposits, not as support for a policy of restraint, but as a means of ensuring more flexibility for monetary control in the future.

Use of Banking Controls since Independence

The continued use of the Australian dollar as the Papua New Guinea currency until April 1975 virtually kept the Papua New Guinea banking system as an off-shore extension of the Australian banking network, primarily oriented to satisfying the requirements of expatriates, and denied the Papua New Guinea central bank effective control of the money supply and interest rates within the economy. Further, the Papua New Guinea economy was not fully monetised, which was another limitation on the effectiveness of credit policy within the economy.

Even in the December quarter of 1975 major impact was being made on the banking system by the large increase in advances thought to be associated with the transmission of funds to Australia prior to the end of the dual currency period. Therefore it is only really in 1976 that it is possible to consider the supervision of the local banking sector as a distinct entity.

In March 1976 the Bank of Papua New Guinea issued guidelines to the banks on their lending priorities, suggesting that preference in lending be given to enterprises involved in import-substitution and to those with large Papua New Guinean equity, and low priority to the financing of consumer goods imports. Foreign companies intending to invest in Papua New Guinea were expected to bring as much of their own funds with them as possible.

By the end of 1976 the commercial banking sector had a high level of liquidity and the Bank of Papua New Guines took this opportunity to raise the required minimum ratio of liquid assets to deposits that commercial banks had to observe to the maximum level of 25 per cent. In the December quarter of 1976 the Bank reduced the interest rates it offered on call and term deposits to the commercial banks, and the banks were asked to reduce their average rate of interest on loans by the same amount.

Further Reading

Baldwin, George B., *Papua New Guinea, Its Economic Situation and Prospects for Development* (World Bank, Washington, 1977)
Bank of Papua New Guinea, *Annual Report*, various years
Reserve Bank of Australia, *Annual Report*, various years

19 CHANGING BANKING REGULATIONS IN NEW ZEALAND

Institutional Framework

There are five commercial or trading banks, twelve trustees savings banks, the Post Office Savings Bank, and savings banks operated by the commercial banks in the New Zealand banking system. Of the five commercial or trading banks, the Bank of New Zealand (wholly state-owned) and the National Bank of New Zealand are incorporated by special New Zealand legislation (though the latter bank is domiciled in England), while the Australia and New Zealand Banking Group, the Bank of New South Wales and the Commercial Bank of Australia Ltd are primarily Australian institutions. Approximately 40 per cent of the liquid assets of the New Zealand financial system are held by the trading banks. (Although term lending has been a growth area recently, trading banks primarily provide short-term finance.)

Regulation of Banking

Under the ceilings system for bank advances which operated from 1942 to June 1973 (although qualitative directives are still used), the Reserve Bank set ceilings for individual categories of borrowers at monthly intervals for six to twelve months ahead. Unless some special exception was made, the banks were penalised if these official ceilings were exceeded. It was usual until 1969 for this system to involve raising the banks' reserve ratios to a level which forced them to borrow from the Reserve Bank to meet increased requirements at a penalty rate.

In October 1969 this system was replaced by a scheme under which each bank was penalised according to the level of its non-priority sector advances in relation to the official ceilings for those advances. From late 1969 until March 1971 non-priority sector advances almost continuously exceeded their ceilings and the banks were penalised. In June 1973 a Reserve Assets Ratio Scheme was introduced for the trading banks in place of the ceiling and minimum cash ratio systems. This scheme requires each bank to ensure that holdings of reserve assets do not fall below a minimum variable percentage of their deposits. Reserve assets are defined as demand and time deposits held at the Reserve Bank plus holdings of notes and all forms of government securities. These ratios are determined monthly according to policy, seasonal and other transient influences. This scheme was modified by the introduction in late 1974 of a special deposits system under which the Reserve Bank lends to trading banks an amount up to a specified limit which is determined by the Bank on a monthly basis. The effect of this was to maintain the reserve asset ratio at a constant level with the level of special deposits approved by the Bank becoming the variable element. An additional 50 million NZ dollars of special deposits was made available in December 1974 to assist growth.

Instruments of Control over Trading Banks

The rates charged by trading banks on overdrafts were set at a minimum of 4 per cent and a maximum of 5 per cent between August 1941 and February 1956, but banks were then allowed to determine rates on individual transactions subject to an overall average on all transactions not greater than 5 per cent. This average was raised to 6 per cent in 1967. No interest was payable on deposits of less than thirty days. While rates on term deposits have been regulated, the rate offered on large deposits of 25,000 dollars and above was freed from control in June 1969 and rates on deposits of over two years were freed in October 1970.

In March 1972 general controls on interest rates were reintroduced by the Interest on Deposits Regulations which set maximum rates ranging from 4.5 per cent on demand deposits to 7.25 per cent on deposits of six years or more. The May 1974 New Interest on Deposits Schedule raised all but the short-term interest rates, but the March 1976 series of monetary measures included the revocation of the Interest on Deposits Regulations as well as the abolition of control over trading bank overdraft lending rates.

From 1943 until June 1965 the trading banks were not permitted to increase their holdings of government securities, and between June 1965 and June 1969 these holdings could be increased in step with the increase in time deposits up to a limit of 6 per cent of total deposits. In June 1969 the banks were allowed to invest freely in government securities and, following the introduction of Treasury bills in October 1969, they were permitted to invest in these as well, provided that they maintained their statutory minimum cash balances with the Reserve Bank.

A major control over trading bank activities was the restriction until 1963 of their lending to the provision of short-term overdraft and bill-discounting facilities. Term loans were allowed on a limited scale after 1963 and from October 1970 both the amount and the purpose of the loans became almost completely unrestricted.

Under the ceilings system for bank advances which operated from 1942 until June 1973 the Reserve Bank set ceilings for individual categories of borrowers at monthly intervals for six to twelve months ahead. Unless some special exception was made, the banks were penalised if these official ceilings were exceeded. In 1965 this selective advance policy was made more flexible when bank advances were divided into two categories; 'top-tier', that is specified export producers such as farmers, stock and station agents, freezing companies and wool-buyers, and 'bottom-tier', made up of all other categories. In general bank advances to top-tier borrowers were subject to wider but much less restrictive control than were advances to bottom-tier borrowers. This system of quantitative control was abolished in June 1973 with the introduction of the Reserve Assets Ratio Scheme (which is discussed in the next section) although the Reserve Bank still issues qualitative directives.

Since 1934 cash balances have had to be held by banks with the Reserve Bank equivalent to at least 7 per cent of demand deposits and 3 per cent of time deposits, although flexible rates were used between 1952 and October 1969, and from the latter date normal minimum reserve ratios of 8 per cent of demand and 3 per cent of time deposits were required. The system of cash ratios was abolished in 1973.

Changes in Banking Policy

Following requests from the trading banks and recommendations by the Monetary and Economic Council, the government proposed a review of monetary policy in 1967 and the changes resulting from this official review were announced in the 1969 Budget. These changes confirmed the progressive reduction of direct restraints on trading bank activities which had begun in 1965. Restrictions on banks' ability to invest in government securities were removed, the variable cash ratios became a statutory minimum cash requirement, and individual banks were allowed to determine their rates for deposits for terms greater than two years. The maximum permitted interest rate on two-year deposits below 25,000 dollars was raised to 4.8 per cent a year.

In 1970 the ceilings set for bottom-tier or non-priority lending, which were very tight, were reinforced in June by an increase in the Reserve Bank's interest rate on penal borrowing from 7 per cent to 8.5 per cent, and again later in the year by the introduction of a new system which related the interest rate charged to the amount of each bank's penal borrowing. The tight monetary policy continued into 1971 and by October there were fears that the shortage of liquidity would inhibit needed investment in the economy. In response the government raised the growth rate suggested for trading bank credit from 9 per cent to 11 per cent for the year ending June 1972, but by January the rate of growth of bank lending had not reached half that rate and so the Bank rate was reduced from 7 per cent to 6 per cent to indicate an easing of monetary policy.

The Interest on Deposits Regulations introduced on 28 March 1972 set interest rates ranging from 4.5 per cent on demand deposits to a maximum of 7.25 per cent for six years or longer. A new type of deposit instrument, the transferable certificate of deposit with minimum amounts of 7,000 dollars and a minimum term of twenty-five months, was introduced in December.

After June 1972 banks were asked to lend more freely and were given a guideline of 8 per cent for the growth of lending between June and December 1972, but this was not reached. Advances rose sharply in 1973 and in June of that year a new method of controlling trading bank activities was introduced, which has been said to be the final break with the old system directed to rigid controls over trading bank operations.

This new method, the Reserve Assets Ratio Scheme, required each bank to arrange its assets and liabilities so as to ensure that its average holdings of specified reserve assets over any month do not fall below specified proportions of demand and time deposits in the previous month. A trading bank's reserve assets were defined, for the purpose of the scheme, as deposits at the Reserve Bank and holdings of all forms of government securities and notes. Acting on the advice of the Reserve Bank, the Minister of Finance establishes the level of the reserve assets ratios which is then promulgated monthly. It is intended that the ratios selected should reflect whether official policy is neutral, restraining or expansive. There is a lower asset requirement against time deposits in order that a bank may reduce its required holding of liquid assets and support a higher level of lending by converting holdings of demand deposits to time deposits or by encouraging time deposits from other sources. On the introduction of the scheme the ratio against demand deposits was set at two and a half times the ratio against time deposits.

It was intended that the Reserve Bank would give at least three months' notice of a change in ratio policy. Any shortfall in a bank's reserve requirement must be borrowed from the Reserve Bank at a rate of interest sufficiently high to make the banks exhaust all other alternatives before falling back on the Reserve Bank as lender of last resort.

In August 1973 prior notice was given of a 2 per cent point increase in the ratios to be made on 1 December, in response to which the trading banks competed more strenuously for deposits and reduced the growth in their lending in the last five months of the year. Because the trading banks are able to borrow from each other if they have a cash shortage, the total working balances of all the trading banks combined only need to cover net cash outflows in the system due to government cash surpluses or drains in the balance of overseas payments.

From the viewpoint of the trading banks themselves the Reserve Asset Scheme has allowed them much more scope than hitherto in the management of their own funds, although it is still open to the Reserve Bank to direct them to follow official lending priorities, and in fact in December 1973 the banks were instructed to give priority in lending to exporters and importers.

Legislative amendments to the Reserve Bank Act in September 1973 extended the scope of official powers to the rest of the financial system.

As liquidity tightened in 1974 the resulting pressure on money markets pushed the uncontrolled interest rates up, and those subject to the Interest on Deposits Regulations to the maximum allowed by the regulations. When the margin between the controlled and uncontrolled interest rates widened to unacceptable levels in May 1974, the Regulations were amended to increase the attractiveness of medium and long-term financial assets. More specifically, the maximum rate was reached at four years instead of six years, secured borrowings for five years or longer were freed from the regulations and a margin of 0.5 per cent was introduced between the Regulation rates and the rates trading banks were permitted to pay on deposits.

Apart from the continued directions concerning priority lending to the banks, there was also some modification made to the Reserve Assets Ratio Scheme in October 1974 in order to make available to the trading banks funds to support lending to priority areas. Reserve asset ratios were held at 22 per cent of demand deposits and 9 per cent of time deposits respectively, with the Reserve Bank making special deposits available to finance increased lending to priority areas where necessary. Justification for this modification at a time when the banks still had reserve assets was that the banks' ratio of advances to deposits was in excess of 80 per cent, which was considered to be the maximum prudent level. It was intended that the special deposits scheme should merely avoid an undesirable tightening in bank lending and not indicate any relaxation in the policy of monetary restraint, although in December 1974 it appeared that some easing of policy constraints was taking place when the government authorised further deposits to the trading banks to prevent the seasonal tightening in March, and allowed another

50 million dollars of special deposits to be made available to the banks to facilitate growth. Special deposits were used extensively by the banks in March 1975 but following that the ratio of advances to deposits steadily declined and little further use was made of them.

Trading banks' reserve asset ratios were raised from 1 July 1975 to 27 per cent of demand deposits and 11 per cent of time deposits, and on 30 July further monetary policy measures were announced. With respect to the trading banks, the measures required that they keep lending tight while still giving priority to exporters, but exempted trading bank deposits of three years or more from the Interest Regulations.

In the 'March 2 package' of early 1976, major reform of the New Zealand financial system was implemented with the stated aim of providing the traditional financial institutions with the means to attract funds back from the higher cost, uncontrolled markets. Controls on trading bank overdraft rates were abolished as were ceilings on interest rates for all deposits other than those with either savings or trading banks for amounts up to 12,000 dollars for terms of less than three years. Rates charged on overdrafts moved up in response to the announcement of the package, and trading banks, savings banks and finance companies found that fixed-term deposits grew rapidly. In the year ending January 1977 term deposits in the trading banks rose by 32 per cent compared to the 9 per cent growth in demand deposits.

Between March and December 1976 the government continued its mildly restrictive monetary policy, but the continued expansion in lending led to a Reserve Bank directive to the banks to reduce heavily their lending to non-priority areas.

In its Annual Report for the year ending 31 March 1977, the Reserve Bank commented that difficulties and inefficiencies were involved in the application of variable reserve requirements to the financial sector simultaneously with the maintenance of below-market rates of interest on the securities the sector must hold, particularly the reduction of competitiveness of the institutions subject to these controls. The Reserve Bank Report further noted the need for interest rates on government securities to be adjusted more often and more flexibly in line with market rates, a change which would reduce the reliance on periodical reserve asset requirement adjustments. In the light of this need the Bank planned to begin limited open-market operations.

In early December 1976 formal instructions were given to the trading banks to reduce substantially their lending to non-priority areas and, in reinforcement of these instructions, the Reserve Bank raised its rates for lending to the trading banks and warned that after 30 April 1977 the rate would be related to the current short-term money market rate plus a margin. The special deposits scheme was formally abolished, having been in abeyance for some time.

In October 1977 the Minister of Finance announced a number of measures to ease monetary conditions which were intended to complement the reforms of March 1976. Trading banks were directed to give a high priority to credit for those companies having difficulty in financing existing stock levels, and the reserve asset policy was eased to allow the banks an additional margin of 'free reserves' with which to achieve this provision of credit. Interest rates on one and two-year government securities were reduced and small upward adjustments were made, at the same time, to Treasury bill rates in order to rationalise the rate structure for government securities and to facilitate wider use of the Treasury bill as a market instrument. The Reserve Bank agreed to reduce its lending rate for borrowing by the trading banks for the purposes of their reserve asset ratios.

The Minister of Finance announced, in the same package, the introduction of a compensatory deposit scheme in March 1978 under which the Reserve Bank was to ex-deposit with the trading banks the large new flows of funds to the government in that month, which were to be repaid by the banks between then and the end of May. It was the intention of this scheme to reduce the substantial fluctuations which usually occurred in March and to ease the pressure on short-term interest rates. Trading banks were also to be permitted to invest in local authority stock, although these assets were not to comprise part of their reserve assets.

Commentary

In mid-1973 there was a major shift in the pattern of New Zealand's banking regulation with the removal of credit ceilings after over twenty years of use. The introduction of the Reserve Assets Ratio Scheme and its provision that the Reserve Bank should give at least a quarter's notice of a change in ratio policy allowed the banks substantial scope in their own liquidity management and time to minimise disruption to their business when policy changed. Most of the interest rate ceilings were abolished in 1976 and this enabled the banks to attract funds back from the non-bank sector.

The Reserve Assets Ratio Scheme allows the banks to borrow from each other, to convert demand deposits to time deposits or to encourage new time deposits in order to meet their requirements, although the banks' ability to follow the last two options was limited by the persistence of interest rate controls until 1976. Management of bank funds was still subject to some limits with the Reserve Bank's qualitative directions concerning lending being continued consistently after 1973.

This shift to more elastic restraints was necessary in order to reverse the decline of the trading banks in favour of the unregulated non-bank intermediaries, and the 1976 'March 2 package' and its elimination of most interest rate limits was a further means of allowing the banks to attract funds back from the non-bank sector. Official regulatory powers were widened to include the non-bank sector in 1973.

Certainly by comparison with the experience of banks in most European countries during the seventies, banks in New Zealand experienced a significant easing of central bank intervention in their activities and a welcome increased scope for liquidity management during the same period, although qualitative restrictions were still applied.

Further Reading

Crick, W. F. (ed.), *Commonwealth Banking Systems* (Clarendon, Oxford, 1965)

Deane, R. S., 'Papers on Monetary Policy, Credit Creation, Economic Objectives and the Reserve Bank', *Research Paper No. 9* (Reserve Bank of New Zealand, December 1972)

—, D. Grindell and A. C. Fenwick, 'Financial Asset Behaviour and Government Financing Transactions in New Zealand', *Research Paper No. 11* (Reserve Bank of New Zealand, April 1973)

— and M. A. Lumsden, 'A Model of the New Zealand Monetary Sector', *Research Paper No. 2* (Reserve Bank of New Zealand, December 1971)

De Kock, M. H., *Central Banking*, 4th edn (Crosby Lockwood Staples, London, 1974)

Hawke, G. R., *Between Governments and Banks: A History of the Reserve Bank of New Zealand* (Shearer, Wellington, 1973)

Simkin, C. G. F., 'Banking in New Zealand' in R. S. Sayers (ed.), *Banking in the British Commonwealth* (Oxford, 1954)

20 THE NEW BANKING SYSTEM IN INDONESIA

'Although Indonesia does lack various types of financing, such as long-term credits, it does not lack a fairly wide variety of financial institutions. The problem is largely one of properly utilizing existing institutions.' ('Indonesia' in Robert F. Emery, *The Financial Institutions of Southeast Asia*, Praeger, New York, 1970, p.220.)

Institutional Structure

In 1967 and 1968 legislation setting up a new banking system was promulgated in Indonesia. A 1968 Act provided that Bank Indonesia as the central bank should abandon its commercial activities. Article 30 of the same Act provided that the central bank was to provide guidance to banks by means of, *inter alia*, 'stipulating general provisions on the solvability [sic] and liquidity of banks' and 'directives for sound banking management'. The Central Banking Act also provided for the establishment of a Monetary Council comprising the Ministers of Finance and Economics and the Governor of Bank Indonesia to govern and co-ordinate the implementation of the monetary policy determined by the government.

Five categories of banks exist in Indonesia: state banks, national private banks, private foreign banks, banks jointly owned by local governments and the private sector, and banks owned jointly by Indonesian nationals and foreigners. More generally these may be described as either commercial banks; development banks which are state owned, private, or owned by local governments or jointly owned by local governments and private individuals; savings banks either state or private; and other secondary banks including village banks, paddy banks, market banks, employees banks and co-operative banks.

The 1968 legislation provided that the state banks which had been merged into the Bank Negara Indonesia were to become independent commercial banks. Article 3 of the Principal Regulations on Banking defined commercial banks as 'banks collecting funds primarily in the form of demand and time deposits and the main operation of which is the lending of money by means of short-term credits'. In December 1968 there were 122 head offices and 177 branch offices of national private commercial banks in Indonesia.

In October 1968 the central bank implemented an interest rate policy of raising interest rates on twelve-month deposits to 6 per cent a month in order to divert the public's cash into the banking system. The Bank Indonesia subsidised a third of the interest paid on six and twelve months' deposits for the state banks.

A selective credit policy designed to divert bank lending to the production sectors, especially foodstuffs, textiles and exportables, had been in operation since 1966 and Regulation No. 5/1960 provided quantitative credit restrictions which set the ratio between a bank's liquid assets and its liabilities payable on demand at not less than 30 per cent, with not less than 10 per cent of the liabilities payable on demand to be in a current account with the central bank. The commercial banks were also required to provide information and written reports to the central bank on the organisational structure of their credit operations and the type and character of both deposits and loans.

Demand deposits are the major source of funds for the private commercial banks, who usually pay interest on the minimum balance of these deposits. Under government regulations government enterprises are not permitted to deposit funds in a private bank and so these banks rely entirely on the private sector for their deposits. Most loans are comparatively short-term, with loans for two months very common and not many for longer than a year. At the time of the new banking system legislation private banks were substantially increasing their lending, although the state banks were granting 70 per cent and private banks 30 per cent in 1968.

Developments in the Regulation of Banking after 1968

In 1969 Government Regulation No. 8 provided that national commercial banks in operation satisfactorily for not less than five years could be authorised by Bank Indonesia to operate as foreign exchange banks.

A number of national private commercial banks contravened the cash ratio requirement and the provision requiring deposits with the central bank and difficulties in the repayment of loans, a decline in the amount of capital of the banks, and poor administration resulting in bank failures affected the public's confidence in the banking system. In reaction to these problems the Bank Indonesia established a new policy in November 1969 which was designed to both improve the infrastructure of banking and to assist the national private commercial banks. The 30 per cent cash ratio and the 10 per cent required deposit with Bank Indonesia, previously computed on daily positions, were now computed on the average daily positions over a week and the monthly interest imposed for contraventions of these ratios was reduced from 10 per cent to 2.5 per cent. Further, the banks were given the opportunity to invest their excess liquid assets in secondary reserves on special deposit account with the Bank at 1 per cent a month interest or in Bank Indonesia certificates, and the overdraft fine was reduced from 1 per cent a day to 6 per cent a month.

In order to assist the national private commercial banks the Bank Indonesia granted liquidity credits to these banks for the expansion of their activities in all sectors except importing, in exchange for the implementation of improved capital structure and management plans by these banks. Another new regulation required the banks to comply with conditions which would enable them to participate in clearing operations. The result here was to provide the central bank through these operations with more recent and detailed information on the operations and financial positions of the banks.

In 1970 the Bank Indonesia took further measures to assist the national private banks in their liquidity difficulties. In particular it granted liquidity credits to the banks to enable them to settle clearing deficits and meet the reserve requirements with the Bank. In order to be eligible for these credits the banks had to submit periodic reports without window-dressing to the Bank and to refrain from providing cross-clearing facilities to their customers.

A revision was made to the reserve requirements in March 1971 which removed Bank Indonesia certificates from the liquid assets definition and allowed 10 per cent of savings deposits and of time deposits to be counted as current liabilities.

Mergers of banks were encouraged in order to allow the growth of sizable banks, and in 1971 Bank Indonesia undertook to grant loans under the terms of remortgage and to provide special loans to cover emergencies and clearing liquidity facilities. From 5 January 1972 Bank Indonesia raised the cash ratios on deposits and savings from 3 per cent to 5 per cent in the case of private commercial banks and to 10 per cent for state commercial banks with a penal rate of 3 per cent a month to be charged on contraventions.

Domestic banks were permitted from 1972 to carry out cash operations outside their regular bank offices but foreign banks could not do so. As well as encouraging mergers Bank Indonesia urged inter-bank co-operation in the form of joint financing and encouraged co-operation between national private banks and state banks and between the former and foreign banks.

In spite of the continued support of the Bank Indonesia, by March 1974 the five state commercial banks were still the major banks with

78.6 per cent of the resources and the role of the private national banks was still very small scale. In April 1974 a number of monetary measures were undertaken as part of a programme to restore financial stability. A ceiling was imposed on increases in net domestic assets for each bank, 33 per cent for state banks and 34 per cent for national private banks. Inter-bank accounts were excluded from the definition of legal reserve assets and the minimum reserve requirement, that is the ratio of legal reserve assets in a given currency to current liabilities in that currency, was set at 30 per cent for both rupiah and foreign exchange accounts. New regulations also required that banks failing to report at the set times pay a fixed penalty, that banks failing to maintain the required minimum pay an interest penalty of 3 per cent a month on the shortfall, and that an additional 2 per cent a month interest would be charged on shortfalls hidden by false reports.

In order to encourage the banks to meet the minimum liquidity requirements the Bank decided to pay interest on rupiah clearing accounts and on bank deposits in foreign exchange for all amounts in excess of the minimum requirements. When this was introduced in July 1974 the interest rate on the minimum daily balance of excess reserves held over the course of a month was set at 10 per cent per annum calculated monthly and paid once a year.

The ceiling imposed on the net assets of banks was successful in reducing the expansion of credit to only 26 per cent during the 1974/75 year and a ceiling of 34 per cent was set for the increase in bank credit for 1975/76, although the realised increase in this latter year was only 25 per cent. In addition, qualitative measures were implemented to direct lending to the priority sectors of small businesses and exporters in particular. New regulations were set for the granting of liquidity credits by the Bank in the form of a refinancing facility, the total of which was linked to the sound condition or reliability of the banks and their activities in providing guidance to certain major clients. National private banks classified as 'healthy' could obtain liquidity credits as a refinancing facility of up to 100 per cent of their own capital, and up to 200 per cent if they had guided certain major clients.

In March 1971 there were 145 commercial banks but as a result of mergers, encouraged by favourable government tax provisions, and the withdrawal of permits for some of the 11 foreign banks, that number had declined to 107 banks with 949 offices by 1976.

Commentary

In the 1968 legislation establishing the new banking system, the role of commercial banks was defined along the lines of the British tradition, with their main business of short-term lending. However, in strong contrast to the position in most of the economies surveyed in this Part, the Indonesian authorities have supported the merging of banks as well as other forms of co-operation between banks.

Liquidity difficulties have been a persistent problem for the national private banks and Bank Negara Indonesia has had to adopt a policy of providing liquidity loans to many of these banks, as well as encouraging the development of sizable banks by merging. It was the Bank's intention to encourage domestic banks in preference to foreign banks and to direct lending to the priority sectors of export and small business.

In common with many other central banks Bank Negara wished to use reserve requirements as a control mechanism but the implementation of these has been complicated not only by the liquidity difficulties of the banks but by their attempts at window-dressing and cross-clearing to obscure their real positions. As the private banks become stronger, the regulatory mechanism should be able to be used without the Bank Negara providing liquidity credits. In view of the incentives, including tax relief, offered to these banks if they merge into larger, more viable units, it would appear to be only a matter of time before the system comprises sufficient viable units to enable this application of regulatory controls.

Further Reading

Emery, Robert F., *The Financial Institution of Southeast Asia: A Country-by-Country Analysis*, Praeger Special Studies in International Economics and Development (Praeger Publishers, New York, 1970)

21 THE DEVELOPMENT OF BANKING REGULATION IN MALAYSIA

'The authorities have proceeded cautiously in establishing new institutions, and they have enacted without undue delay new regulatory legislation when they found such action necessary to protect the general public.' ('Malaysia' in Robert F. Emery, *The Financial Institutions of Southeast Asia*, Praeger, New York, 1970, p.348.)

Institutional Framework

A mission from the World Bank which visited the then Federation of Malaysia in 1954 recommended the establishment of a central bank which would replace the Currency Board as the monetary authority of the country. First instituted in 1906, the Currency Board's function was restricted to the issue and redemption of currency in exchange for sterling at a fixed rate. In the view of the World Bank mission the existence of the Currency Board as monetary authority excluded the exercise of discretionary control over the money and credit system of the economy. On the advice of the World Bank mission, Mr G. M. Watson of the Bank of England and Sir Sidney Caine of the University of Malaya were invited to enquire into the problems of central banking in Malaya and to advise on legislation to establish a central bank. Their report, the Watson-Caine Report, was released in September 1956 and its legislative recommendations were the basis for the Central Bank of Malaysia Ordinance 1958, under which the Central Bank of Malaysia, Bank Negara Malaysia, was established on 26 January 1959. Bank Negara Malaysia is a corporate body with capital of 20 million Malaysian dollars fully subscribed by the government. Its jurisdiction was extended to all parts of Malaysia on 21 January 1965, following the formation of Malaysia.

Direction of the Bank is in the hands of a seven-member board of directors (maximum of ten members), including the Governor, the Deputy Governor and the Permanent Secretary to the Treasury. All members are appointed by the state for a term of from three to five years. The powers and functions of the Bank are governed not only by the aforementioned Ordinance but also by the 1958 Banking Ordinance which deals with commercial banking operations. In 1972, in an outline of the proposed 1973 Banking Act, the Bank commented that the general policy reflected in the 1958 Banking Ordinance, 'regarding the supervision and regulation of the banking system in the country had been to provide only a very broad legislative framework, within which the supervision and regulation of commercial banks could be undertaken and to rely largely on moral suasion for the purpose of establishing a sound, modern and progressive banking system.'

At the end of 1957 there were twenty commercial banks in operation, twelve of them foreign, with seventy-seven of the eighty-eight offices attached to the foreign banks. By the end of 1977 domestic banks were twenty of the thirty-seven commercial banks in operation with almost two-thirds of the 429 banking offices in Malaysia and with almost half of the total assets of the banking system, compared to 20 per cent in 1957. Commercial banks are the largest Malaysian financial institutions, providing some 70 per cent of the total credit extended by the financial sector. By 1970 deposits in the commercial banks were 50 per cent fixed deposits, 32 per cent current and 18 per cent savings.

Primary instruments of control given to the Bank Negara Malaysia by the Ordinances were variable minimum reserve requirements, a liquidity ratio, control of bank interest rates and qualitative control of credit. In addition to the exercise of these powers, the Bank has established clearing house facilities, promoted the development of money and discount markets and encouraged the commercial banks to move out of sterling balances and overseas securities and into local loans and investments including the establishment of branches throughout the country.

Quite uncommonly among the central banks in lesser-developed economies, the Bank Negara Malaysia is not dominated by the Ministry of Finance even though the Minister of Finance is authorised under the 1958 Ordinance to issue directives to the board of directors on any policy matter.

In an address at the Tenth Anniversary Commemoration of the establishment of the Bank on 26 January 1969, the Governor, Tan Sri Ismail bin Mohamed Ali, noted that the only references in the 1958 Ordinances to relations between the Bank and the government provide merely that the Bank be banker and financial agent of the government, that it may grant the government temporary advances and that the Bank board should keep the Minister of Finance informed of the monetary and banking policy pursued or to be pursued by the Bank. Governor Ismail has recently characterised his working relationship with the government as 'being independent within Government but not of Government' (p.8).[1]

Apart from Bank Negara Malaysia and the commercial banks, the Malaysian banking system also includes the finance companies that are licensed as borrowing companies, merchant banks (the first of which was only established in 1970), discount houses and the National Savings Bank.

There is an annual conference of commercial banks with the central bank and seminars with the central bank and the top management of a group of two or three banks at a time.

In 1974 the government reconstructed the Post Office Savings Bank into a National Savings Bank intended to promote and mobilise savings and to utilise these funds for investments which would support the economic development of the country.

Instruments of Control

The two 1958 Ordinances gave the Bank Negara Malaysia power to set variable minimum reserve requirements, a liquidity ratio, control of bank interest rates and qualitative control of credit. Commercial banks are required to hold statutory reserves in the form of balances with the Bank.

Initially these minimum reserve requirements were set as 4 per cent of their total deposit liabilities. As a supplement to this requirement there is the obligation that the banks must hold a certain proportion of their total deposit liabilities in the form of liquid assets which are defined as cash in hand and with the Bank, net balances with banks and money at call in Malaysia, Treasury bills, government securities, bills discounted and bills receivable and cheques purchased payable in Malaysia. In addition commercial banks are required to hold at least 50 per cent of their savings deposits in longer-term government securities and in housing loans to individuals and approved financial intermediaries.

Interest rates on both advances and deposits are the subject of central bank control. Apart from the general motive of encouraging longer-term savings and helping to stabilise deposits, the Bank has made changes in these rates on a number of occasions in order to stem any possible outflow of funds overseas. Qualitative control of credit or moral suasion has been the major tool used by the Bank, mainly because it is by this means that it may encourage lending to those areas which it wishes to see developed.

Bank Negara Malaysia does not formally declare a Bank rate but in its place the rediscount rate for Treasury bills of ninety-one days by the Bank has emerged as the effective Bank rate since both commercial banks and other institutions may rediscount Treasury bills with Bank Negara at any time, although the rediscount rates contain an element of penalty.

Because of its belief that an efficient banking system is a vital infrastructure for economic development the Bank has given active encouragement to the commercial banks to expand their branch networks to serve every area of the country. The Bank is also promoting the development of the Malaysian money market by making available suitable financial instruments, promoting the establishment of dealers and providing lender of last resort facilities.

Banking Regulation in the 1970s

In 1970 domestic credit expansion by the commercial banks was 250 per cent more than that extended in 1969. However, total deposits of the banks did not rise even as rapidly as in 1969 so that during 1970 the liquidity ratio of the banks suffered a substantial decline. In the view of the authorities this credit expansion was timely as there was a reduction in funds from the external sector during the year. It was felt that commercial banks ought to undertake more long-term financing in the form of term loans rather than overdrafts, and accordingly the Bank encouraged the extension of these loans and allowed the banks to accept medium-term fixed deposits for up to three year terms in order to generate the necessary funds.

Two separate liquidity ratios continued to be required from the commercial banks: a minimum ratio of 50 per cent of savings deposits to be held in the form of government securities and housing loans and a minimum ratio of 20 per cent in liquid assets against total non-savings deposits. Half of this latter requirement had to be in actual liquid assets, that is, cash, cash at Bank, net balances with banks, money at call and Treasury bills. Other liquid assets are government securities and bills discounted or purchased and bills receivable.

When the Second Malaysia Plan, 1971-75, was launched a review of the role of commercial banks was made in the light of their expected support of the development process. Bank Negara Malaysia emphasised the important role of the commercial banks in the Plan at the twelfth annual conference between the Bank and the commercial banks and subsequently the Bank initiated a series of seminars with the top management of a group of two or three banks at a time, beginning with Bank Bumiputra Malaysia Berhad and Malayan Banking Berhad in January 1972. Particular attention was paid at these meetings to the finance of agriculture and of small-scale enterprises, whether urban or rural. The Bank drew attention to the emphasis on collateral for loans, with emphasis on the viability of the particular project and knowledge of the character and background of borrowers.

During 1971 the liquidity position of the banks increased significantly and the Bank lowered interest rates without changing either the reserve or liquidity requirements in order to encourage bank credit to expand at a faster rate. Nevertheless the slow-down continued into 1972 and monetary policy continued its generally easy stance. Interest rates on loans and deposits were reduced and short-term interest rates were revised downwards in line with the declining trend in these rates internationally. Some excess liquidity in the hands of the banks was drained off from 16 October 1972 when the statutory reserve ratio was raised from 5 per cent to 8.5 per cent and the banks were told that more funds would be frozen if they failed to increase loans and advances. In its 1972 Annual Report the Bank noted that the 'stigma associated with frequent recourse to the Central Bank for accommodation either through the rediscount window or by taking advantage of the Central Bank's refinancing facilities requires to be dispelled' (p.30).

Surprisingly, in the light of this comment, the substantial amendments to Malaysia's banking legislation passed by Parliament in February 1973 contained no reference to this aspect.

Most of the changes made in the 1973 amendments to the 1958 banking legislation were concerned with widening the Bank's flexibility in the use of policy instruments. Under the 1958 legislation the statutory reserve requirement and directives concerning lending policies had to be applied uniformly to all banks, but this was changed in the 1973 amendments to allow the Bank to differentiate its policies according to different categories of banks, whether this is defined by size or location or both.

Following a January 1972 seminar on banking development and later discussions a credit guarantee corporation, the Credit Guarantee Corporation Berhad, was incorporated on 5 July to provide guarantee cover of 69 per cent to the commercial banks in their lending to small-scale enterprises, with a paid-up capital of 2 million dollars, four-fifths subscribed by the commercial banks and one-fifth by the Bank. In general the loans eligible for guarantee are those for the purposes of working capital or the purchase of capital assets with a ceiling of between 5,000 dollars and 25,000 dollars dependent on the size of the enterprise as well as the purpose of the loan.

A surge in bank loans and advances in late 1972 and early 1973 was primarily for the finance of consumption and of stock market transactions and the Bank attempted to change market sentiment and expectations in April and May by raising the lending and borrowing rates of the banks moderately and by giving directives on the quality and preferred direction of lending. Substantial capital inflow increased the banking system's ability to lend and from June 1973 lending to manufacturing, construction and commerce in particular expanded in response to strong demand from these areas. Interest rates on the longer-term deposits were raised again in August and the liquidity ratio was raised from 20 per cent to 25 per cent of total (non-savings) deposits to reduce the level of free reserves held by the banks.

By the end of the year there were sufficient strains on the capacity of various sectors of the economy for a change in the direction of monetary policy towards restraint to be necessary and on 17 December a series of measures were implemented. A policy directive to the banks to direct new loans and advances to increasing the capacity of production in the economy was given more bite by raising the interest rates on deposits and loans, increasing the statutory reserve requirement from 8.5 per cent to 10 per cent of total deposits from 16 January 1974, and changing the composition of assets the banks had to maintain against 50 per cent of their savings deposits to require that an amount equal to 3 per cent of total savings deposits must be in the form of small loans under the credit guarantee scheme operated by the Credit Guarantee Corporation.

In early 1974 the government became concerned with a tendency to hoard in the economy which was exacerbating supply shortages in food and essential materials, and on 1 March the Bank directed the commercial banks to review their pattern of credit to ensure that these facilities were not being used to finance hoarding. On 24 April a package of monetary measures was introduced as part of the government's anti-inflationary programme, once again lifting the interest rates on deposits and on lending rates; raising, this time to 5 per cent, the proportion of total savings deposits that had to be in the form of small loans under the credit guarantee scheme of the Credit Guarantee Corporation by 30 June; and limiting the rate of growth of bank loans and advances in 1974 to 20 per cent above the 31 December 1973 level (an increase of about 1,000 million dollars).

These measures did succeed in moderating the growth of bank credit and moving the direction of lending to that intended by the Bank. However, the latter body remained concerned that small borrowers, intending home owners and the bumiputra community might not have ready access to credit. For this reason the Bank announced on 11 July that loans to the bumiputra community, to small borrowers under the credit guarantee scheme of the Credit Guarantee Corporation, and loans to the government and a Bank-approved list of government corporations and agencies, were excluded from the calculation of the increase in loans for 1974. Subsequently, when, as a result of the falling price of rubber, the producers agreed to a voluntary scheme to increase their inventory of rubber, bank loans to finance this stockpile were also exempted from the calculation.

Towards the end of 1974 there was evidence that the monetary situation could become more relaxed with the emergence of recessionary trends in the economy. However, domestic inflation had not been reduced sufficiently to justify too relaxed a monetary policy and for this reason only selective relaxation was announced together with the November Budget. For the commercial banks the annual growth ceilings for loans and advances to manufacturing and housing loans to individuals were raised to 40 per cent above the level at 31 December 1973, the requirement to maintain 5 per cent of total savings deposits in small loans under the Credit Guarantee Corporation scheme was lifted to 10 per cent, and the banks were directed to promote longer-term fixed deposits and savings deposits.

As the worldwide recession was mirrored increasingly in the Malaysian economy in late 1974 and early 1975 the demand for bank credit dropped appreciably and in response monetary policy moved to greater ease in February with a decrease in the maximum rate for fixed deposits and in lending rate, a cut of 1.5 percentage points in the statutory reserve requirement, and abolition of the system of credit growth ceilings, although a minimum of 10 per cent of total savings deposits was required to be in small loans under the credit guarantee scheme of the Credit Guarantee Corporation by the end of June.

In order to ensure that lending was directed to suitable avenues, a minimum of 50 per cent of the net loans and advances extended during the year were to be to the bumiputra community, the manufacturing industry and for home ownership by individuals. Positive reaction to these measures in the form of increasing bank loans and advances was confined to February and credit demand weakened throughout March and April.

In an endeavour to restore a stronger demand for bank credit, new monetary measures were announced on 30 April including a reduction in the maximum interest rates on fixed deposits and on lending, a further 1.5 percentage point reduction in the statutory reserve requirement and a directive to increase their lending to manufacturing. The February and April measures together produced a growing expansion in bank credit from May, and in August the Bank moved for the third time in 1975 to easing policy further with further interest rate reductions, not only for fixed deposits and lending, but also for savings deposits. From

16 February 1976 the statutory reserve requirement was further reduced to 6 per cent of their total deposits.

During 1975 loans to the sectors designated priority lending by Bank Negara Malaysia represented 56.8 per cent of the total increase in loans for that year by comparison with the minimum requirement of 50 per cent. Nevertheless the Bank commented in its 1975 Annual Report on its concern with four trends in the recent growth of the banking system: the dilution of the capital base of the banking system; a moderate deterioration in the quality of bank assets in some areas of the system; a lack of professionalism in the management of the banking industry; and the slow response in the banking system to the adoption of modern techniques and the provision of modern banking services. The first of these trends was a consequence of the rapid expansion of the commercial banking system, whose time and savings deposits had increased by twenty-seven times its 1957 figure by the end of 1975, but whose expansion of credit grew faster than the growth of deposits in the period 1970-75. This resulted in the ratio of loans to deposits rising from 66 per cent in January 1970 to almost 80 per cent at the end of 1975 and in the ratio of shareholders' funds less fixed assets to total deposits declining from 10.1 per cent in 1971 to 7.5 per cent in 1975.

With regard to the quality of assets, this became an area of concern in relation to some commercial banks when, during 1973, the very rapid expansion of bank loans spilled over in some cases into loans for property development and some other areas whose viability was dependent on the overexpansive period of 1973 continuing, and the value of whose borrowings suffered deterioration in the more recessionary period of 1975. In 1976 the Bank compelled the reorganisation of a few banks overcommitted in these directions. Lack of professionalism was evident in several directions, not only in the proliferation of too many small banks but in the ineffectiveness of boards of management in larger banks, in the practice of excessive lending to board members, and the extremely limited powers with which branch managers were endowed.

It was hoped by the Bank that mergers and takeovers among the banks would facilitate their adoption of modern techniques and their expansion of banking services, but the danger inherent in the other trends led the Bank and the government to revise and tighten banking legislation to deal with these problems.

The policy of monetary ease followed in 1975 was continued in 1976, but private investment tended to a reduced growth level. In an endeavour to expand productive capacity the Bank reduced the statutory reserve requirement from 7 per cent to 6 per cent from early February and offered the commercial banks a facility for rediscounting bills drawn on the export of goods manufactured in Malaysia.

When, despite an overall expansion in the volume of bank credit, loans to agriculture, mining and manufacture continued at a comparatively low level, the Bank announced a series of monetary measures to correct this imbalance to operate from 1 October. Commercial banks were required to extend a minimum of 20 per cent of the growth in loans, advances and trade bills to the bumiputra community, 10 per cent for agricultural food production, 25 per cent to the manufacturing sector and 10 per cent for housing loans to individuals. For new loans to the bumiputra community not guaranteed by the Credit Guarantee Corporation and of less than 500,000 dollars each, for unguaranteed loans of 150,000 dollars or less to small-scale enterprises, and for new loans for individual homes where house and land did not exceed 200,000 dollars in value, a maximum rate of interest of 10 per cent per annum was set.

Under the rediscounting facility, the Bank undertook to refinance for a maximum three months credit extended by the banks to exporters of goods manufactured in Malaysia. With the prevailing prime lending rate at 8 per cent, the maximum rate chargeable by the banks under this facility was 5.5 per cent and refinancing was available from the Bank at 4 per cent per annum. This attempt to increase the banks' recourse to rediscount was only modestly successful in the year of its introduction.

Bank Negara Malaysia forced a number of banks to restructure their equity capital and revise the composition of their boards of directors where there was either malpractice or evidence of unsatisfactory operations. In some cases loans were recalled or suspended as the Bank undertook more intensive investigation of the operations and practices of the commercial banks.

Monetary expansion slowed during the first quarter of 1977, but the commercial banks continued to be highly liquid. By May the authorities were becoming concerned with the slow growth of private investment and in order to strengthen its recovery the Minister of Finance, after consultation with the Bank Negara Malaysia and the commercial banks, announced a further relaxation of monetary policy in the form of a reduction of percentage points on loans and advances and of 0.5 percentage points on all but twelve-month deposits which were also reduced 1 percentage point.

Commentary

The substantial influence of Tan Sri Ismail bin Mohamed Ali, the long-serving Governor of the Bank Negara Malaysia, not only on the Bank but also on the Malaysian banking and financial system has been the most significant feature of banking in Malaysia since 1962. In contrast to the policies pursued in most of the other countries surveyed here, the Bank has consciously sought to encourage mergers and takeovers in an endeavour to expedite the adoption of modern techniques and to widen the range of banking services offered. Further, the Bank has provided the incentives for banks to move into long-term lending, to widen their branch networks and to encourage lending to the bumiputra sector of the economy. While the Bank has increased the flexibility of its controls, it has still to achieve an efficient banking system.

Note

1. 'Talking to Bank Negara's Governor Ismail' in 'Malaysia — A Survey', *Euromoney*, March 1978.

Further Reading

Emery, Robert F., *The Financial Institutions of Southeast Asia: A Country-by-Country Study* (Praeger Publishers, New York, 1970)
Malaysia, *Official Year Book*
Sheng-Yi, Lee, *The Monetary and Banking Development of Malaysia and Singapore* (Singapore University Press, 1974)
'The Malaysian Banking System: Good and Liquid' in 'Malaysia — A Survey', *Euromoney*, March 1978
Van Boetzelaer, Jan-Otto, 'The Malaysian Central Bank Lays Down the Law', *Euromoney*, South-East Asia Supplement, May 1976

22 BANKING IN THE ARAB REPUBLIC OF EGYPT

'The changing position of the commercial banks after 1956 had three aspects: sequestration, Egyptianization, and finally full nationalization. These three aspects were intertwined.' (Donald C. Mead, *Growth and Structural Change in the Egyptian Economy* (Publication of the Economic Growth Center, Yale University, Irwin, Illinois, 1967), p.195.)

Development of the Modern Egyptian Banking System

When Egypt left the sterling exchange standard in July 1947 the dependence of foreign banks operating in Egypt on foreign funds was gradually reduced and they were forced to have recourse increasingly to the National Bank of Egypt to meet seasonal financial requirements. Further, under a gentlemen's agreement, banks began to hold cash balances with the National Bank and supplied it with information on their monthly positions, providing here a basis from which future credit control might be developed.

The National Bank of Egypt, which originated as a commercial bank and a bank of issue in 1898, had started to move towards central bank status from the 1940s when the government agreed that the Bank's control over commercial banks should be extended and that its administration should be Egyptianised. However, it was not until 1951 (law No. 57) that the National Bank became a *de jure* central bank and ceased its minor commercial bank activities.

Under Law No. 57 the Bank was given responsibility for the stabilisation of the value of the Egyptian currency and for credit and it was authorised to act as a lender of last resort. Commercial banks were required to maintain a minimum cash reserve ratio with the National Bank, the level of which was first set at 15 per cent with changes in it to be determined by the Supreme Committee for Currency, Credit and Exchange.

Following the political events of 1956 and the subsequent sequestration of those British and French banks operating in Egypt, the Law No. 22 of 1957 was promulgated, which provided that banking operations could only be carried out by Egyptian joint-stock companies with paid-up capital of not less than 500,000 Egyptian pounds each. Shares in these companies were to be nominative and always held by Egyptians, to whom membership of boards of directors and managerial posts were also to be confined. A year's delay was allowed to foreign banks, but sequestrated banks had to comply within a month. Prior to the promulgation of this law, foreign banks had held 51.4 per cent of deposits.

In order to provide banking legislation of a more comprehensive nature and able to cover a broader area of the financial sector, the 1957 Banking and Credit Law, Law No. 163 authorised the National Bank of Egypt to regulate the availability and cost of credit to meet the needs of the economy, to take measures to alleviate general or local economic and financial disturbances, and to ensure, by means of control, the soundness of banks' financial positions. Under this law the National Bank became government banker, was charged with the management of public debt and became adviser to the government on the flotation of local or foreign loans.

A bank was required to keep assets in Egypt at least equal to its liabilities to Egyptian creditors, in addition to an amount equal to its paid-up capital. Further, under the 1957 law the activities of commercial banks were defined as the acceptance of demand deposits or time deposits payable within a year, but they were not authorised to deal in movables, real estate or their own shares (except in the settlement of debts due to them) nor were they permitted to own shares representing more than 25 per cent of the capital of any joint-stock company.

The National Bank was also authorised to establish general regulations for non-commercial banks, that is, for those whose basic activities did not include the acceptance of sight deposits. The Supreme Committee's credit control powers were now conferred on the National Bank.

In 1960 and 1961 Law No. 250 of 1960 revamped the central bank and banks were brought into public ownership. Under Law No. 250, the National Bank of Egypt, until then a central bank undertaking commercial operations, was divided into two separate banking entities: one to carry out central banking functions proper as the Central Bank of Egypt; and the second to conduct ordinary commercial banking operations and to retain the name of National Bank of Egypt. The Central Bank of Egypt was provided with the traditional array of instruments for credit control available under the 1957 law and the new law authorised further rediscounting and open-market operations and other measures of selective credit control. The legal status of the Central Bank was changed from that of a joint-stock company to that of a public institution with an autonomous legal entity.

Three major banks were nationalised in 1960, the National Bank of Egypt and the Misr Bank in February, and Banque Belge et Internationale (which became the Bank of Port Said) in December. In July 1961 all other banks and financial institutions were nationalised and in 1963 a series of mergers was introduced which resulted by October 1963 in the reduction of banks to five commercial banks, three mortgage banks, an industrial bank and the Agricultural Co-operative Credit Organisation. The five big commercial banks were the National Bank of Egypt, Misr Bank, the Bank of Cairo, the Bank of Alexandria and the Bank of Port Said.

In 1964 the business of public sector companies and organisations was distributed among those five banks with the effect that competition for this business was abolished. Only the marketing of agricultural crops was left to all banks because of their large financing requirements. Following the success of this sectoral distribution, it was decided to improve upon the specialisation and at the same time reduce the number of operating commercial banks to four.

A presidential decree of September 1971, which came into force in July, allocated foreign trade business, all import and export banking and the banking business of certain export-marketed agricultural products to the National Bank of Egypt, which by the end of 1973 had almost 50 per cent of the aggregate funds of commercial banks. The Misr Bank, which had been created in 1920 as the first purely national bank, was merged with the Port Said Bank and domestic trade business, including the financing of the cotton and rice crops, was allocated to it. The Bank of Alexandria, originally established in 1957 to take over the local branches of Barclays Bank (D.C.O.), with which the Industrial Bank was merged, was allocated the business of the productive units engaged in industry, agriculture and the crafts. The Bank of Cairo, which had been established in 1952, was allotted the business of the services sector. Individuals and private sector establishments were able to deal with all four banks.

While commercial bank lending is normally short-term, some commercial bank loans have become revolving and therefore of a long-term nature. Loans and advances are granted either against collateral (crops or other merchandise), on personal guarantees or are otherwise secured, but with the substantial growth of the public sector since the nationalisation measures of the early sixties, unsecured loans and advances to the public sector have become a major part of bank lending.

The remainder of the banking sector comprises two real estate banks — Crédit Foncier Egyptien and Arab Land Bank — seventeen agricultural co-operative credit banks and three other banks, the Arab African Bank, the Arab International Bank and the Nasser Bank Authority. These

latter three banks are not subject to central bank control. The Arab
African Bank, jointly owned with Kuwait, makes investments in Arab
and African countries and undertakes banking business in foreign
currencies subject to the limit that such corporations in Egypt must be
effected through local banks. The Arab International Bank, a joint
venture between Egypt, the United Arab Emirates, Libya and Oman,
provides full banking operations in convertible currencies, although it
must also channel local operations through local banks. The Nasser
Bank Authority's operations are not of a commercial nature.

The 1974 Arab and Foreign Investment Law provided for the setting
up of new banks, provided that they were either investment and commercial banks transacting in free currencies, or joint venture banks, with
at least 51 per cent Egyptian shareholdings, making local currency transactions. Among the new banks entering under this law were the Bank of
America, which opened a Cairo branch to deal in foreign currency
transactions, and an Egyptian Rumanian bank owned 51 per cent by
Misr Bank and 49 per cent by three Rumanian banks. By 1978 approximately twenty foreign banks were resident in Egypt. However, they have
not been instrumental in providing needed private corporate finance or
medium-term investment funds and they have provided competition for
both the customers and the qualified staff of the local banks. It remains
to be seen whether further entry will be encouraged.

Law No. 120 of 1957 gave the boards of directors of all public sector
banks, including the Central Bank of Egypt, full authority in their
management in accordance with national economic planning. The fixing
of interest rates on deposits and loans, it was provided, was no longer
to be restricted to a 7 per cent ceiling. The Central Bank of Egypt is
described in the 1957 Law as an autonomous public legal entity and it
is further provided that the governor may not be relieved of his duties
during his period of appointment.

Instruments of Banking Control

The Central Bank of Egypt has a wide range of instruments under its
control. It is able to grant exceptional loans to banks on the collateral
of their assets, in the event of a financial emergency, and, under normal
conditions, the Central Bank accepts Treasury bills and commercial bills
for rediscount within limits fixed in the light of each bank's financial
position. The refinancing of bank loans through the Central Bank occurred increasingly after 1966 when the specialisation of banks in
financing sectors often created a disparity between sectoral needs and
bank resources. The discount rate was originally 3 per cent for prime

commercial bills but this was raised to 5 per cent in May 1962. The possibility of open-market operations being used to manipulate the cash resources of the banking system became remote after the 1961 national-isation measures which created a large public sector with financial needs.

The more important regulatory tools have been the reserve and liquidity ratios. Section 41 of the Banking and Credit Law No. 163 of 1957 provided that all commercial banks should hold a proportion of their deposits in an interest-free account with the Central Bank. In the early sixties the reserve ratio was set at 12.5 per cent, reducing to 10 per cent during the period of active seasonal financing of cotton. As a result of the Stabilisation Agreement between Egypt and the IMF in 1962, the Central Bank raised the ratio to 17.5 per cent from July 1962 and in 1966 this ratio was raised to 20 per cent, with a reduction to 17.5 per cent in the cotton financing season.

The commercial banks are also required to maintain a liquidity ratio of not less than 30 per cent. This ratio represents the ratio of cash, government securities and other liquid assets to all types of deposits plus letters of guarantee and amounts due to banks and correspondents. It has been usual for both reserve and liquidity ratios to be kept at much more than the required levels. For example, in 1973 the reserve ratio was 20.8 per cent and the liquidity ratio was 50.1 per cent, and in 1974 the ratios were 20.5 per cent and 58.5 per cent respectively.

During periods of expansion it is usual for the Central Bank to raise the level of credit by reducing interest rates and raising credit ceilings and it may also vary the reserve and liquidity ratios. The interest rate schedule of the commercial banks was revised in 1962 with the conclu-sion of the Stabilisation Agreement with the IMF, and a maximum debtor interest rate of 6 per cent (5.5 per cent for cotton financing) was set. Maximum rates were removed by the 1975 law.

While insufficient information is available to enable a detailed exam-ination of the operation of monetary policy in Egypt in recent years to be made, the National Bank of Egypt has provided in a series of special studies in its *Economic Bulletin* some discussion of the factors which have affected the National Bank's loans, bills discounted and deposit activity over the period 1962 to 1973 which enables some identification of the influence of policies to be made. This discussion is briefly sum-marised below.

With respect to loans, the National Bank refers to the regulations imposed subsequent to the Stabilisation Agreement, that is, the setting of ceilings on the loan facilities that could be provided by commercial banks, the lifting of bank rate from 3 per cent to 5 per cent and the lifting of the reserve ratio to 17.5 per cent. In the National Bank's view the effect of these moves was to be seen in the general decline in the rate of growth of loans granted over this period, even though deposits were growing at a much faster rate. In 1973, the National Bank's specialisation became foreign trade operations and its loan balances in other sectors were moved to other banks.

Turning now to deposits, total commercial bank deposits grew by 145 per cent between 1962 and 1973 and for the National Bank they grew by 141 per cent over the same period. The liquidity ratio recorded a low of 35.8 per cent in 1967 and a high of 91.3 per cent in 1961. After 1965 the Central Bank required Treasury bills to cover the note issue and this had the effect of lowering the liquidity ratio held from that time on. The rate of deposit utilisation was 63 per cent over this period with a peak of 96 per cent reached in 1963. This rate declined after 1968 as loans were held back while deposits continued to grow.

Commentary

In several respects the reorganisation of the Egyptian banking system to provide for sectoral specialisation in the provision of finance could be regarded as a useful strategy for developing economies to follow in the development of their financial sectors, although politically the strategy may not be usable. Once the influence of foreign banks was removed by sequestration and Egyptianisation, there arose the problem of competition for business. One of the consequences of this process in the case of other countries has been that the sectors that require most funding for development are not those offering the most profitable and least-risk investments. In the Egyptian case, the division of business between the four commercial banks meant that each bank had to specialise in its allotted area. Although disparities between a sector's financial requirements and a bank's resources could arise, further funding could be provided by the Central Bank. Certainly this specialisation has the advantage of providing an incentive for each bank to maximise its information flow concerning conditions in its own sector in order to sustain a profitable flow of lending.

It is interesting that foreign banks appear to have been allowed limited entry under the 1974 Arab and Foreign Investment Law in order to supply much-needed funds for private companies and for medium-term investment. However, these might be seen as areas of clear shortfall in funding if the banks met all the requirements of the sectors to which they were allocated.

Further Reading

Central Bank of Egypt, *Credit and Banking Developments*, Cairo
—, *Economic Review, 1961-1975*
Hansen, Bent and K. Nashashibi, *Egypt* (New York, 1975)
Mabro, Robert, *The Egyptian Economy 1952-72*
Mead, Donald C., *Growth and Structural Change in the Egyptian Economy*
    (Irwin, Illinois, 1967)
National Bank of Egypt, *Economic Bulletin*, various issues
Sanchiz, J. C., 'Money and banking in the U.A.R.', *IMF Staff Papers*, vol.12
    (1965)
Thorn, Philip and Farida Mazhar, *Banking Structures and Sources of Finance in
    the Middle East* (Banker Research Unit, 1975)

23 CONCLUSION

From the survey undertaken in this Part, it is apparent that no consistent pattern is revealed along which domestic banking regulation may be seen to be moving. Any tendency that may have occurred within the past decade in Europe to move towards indirect controls has been washed away in the wake of the substantial capital movements across borders from which all of Europe appears to have suffered to some extent. While the retreat from indirect controls has been towards more direct controls, the individual regulatory frameworks of the various countries have provided a diversity of even these controls.

The contrast in forms of regulation preferred becomes even stronger when we include the countries outside Europe and discover that, while Germany has moved to eliminate almost all the ability of its banks to manage their own liquidity, New Zealand has at almost the same time lifted its quite restrictive system of regulation, in part because it prevented banks from managing their own liquidity, and has given the banks much wider scope in liquidity management.

It might be argued that the move by several countries, including Australia, towards the use of open-market operations suggests that with sufficient governmental support the whole menu of regulatory constraints may be open to most countries. However, the experience of stronger swings in economic activity in the 1970s has not provided ideal conditions for the use of open-market operations within comparatively small open economies, a perhaps unfortunate timing which may minimise the chances of further experiments in this direction.

One factor which may be seen as enforcing a certain diversity in the use of regulatory constraints is the difference in regulatory bases from which central banks may operate. For example detailed regulations are imposed by legislation in France, but the Bank of England and the Banque Nationale de Belgique have tended to use consultation in place of coercion and their powers have developed from custom rather than from legislative endowment.

Part 3

INTRODUCING REGULATION INTO THE MODEL OF UNCONTROLLED BANKING

'All these controls and restrictions prove surprisingly easy to defeat or to get around, often by the most respectable means. The only effective way to operate is by restricting the credit base.' ('The Debate over Money Supply', *The Economist*, 26 October 1968, p.17.)

1 INTRODUCTION

In Part 2 the regulation of banking in nineteen countries and within a united Europe was examined, with particular emphasis on those regulatory constraints that are imposed and varied as part of the implementation of monetary policy and their impact on the operation of an individual commercial bank within each economy. It is the purpose of this Part to introduce into the model of the unregulated bank, which was developed in Part 1, the main forms of regulatory control found in the last Part. We are interested in identifying the minimum and the maximum possible effects of the various regulations, since the competitive structure of banking, the institutional environment and the pattern of overall regulation will determine for each individual economy where, between these possible effects, the actual effect will lie. Further, as we are only looking at the effects on an individual commercial bank, we assume for simplicity that the other banks within the industry will react as our bank does, in order that their positions within the industry may be maintained. Of course, this assumption may need to be varied in the case of some competitive structures, but we assume that the industry is composed of several at least medium-sized banks, that is, it is an oligopoly whose members will be anxious to maintain their relative positions within the industry.

Before moving to introduce the various regulatory controls both singly and in some combinations into our model, we will first briefly outline the prudential regulations commonly imposed on banks. This is necessary not only because certain originally prudential regulations are used as part of the implementation of monetary policy in many countries, but also because at best the distinction between prudential and other controls is often difficult to draw. Revell[1] comments that there is no such thing as the ideal system of prudential regulation because the financial structure of the economy, the operational methods of institutions and tradition will all have their effects in a regulatory system.

The first element of a minimal prudential regulation system is the passing of legislation providing the supervisory authorities with the power to regulate banks which will be licensed or authorised under that legislation. For the second element it is usual for solvency and liquidity ratios to be specified to ensure (to the satisfaction of the authorities) that each bank meets those minimum standards of solvency and liquidity which ought to be sufficient to enable it to cope with the normal risks of business. In order to cope with losses which might not reasonably be foreseen in such a way as to provide protection for depositors, the supervisory authorities may agree to act as lender of last resort or institute a scheme of deposit insurance. Hirsch[2] argues that the presence of central bank support raises the possibility of excessive risk-taking by banks, or moral hazard. To check this the monetary authorities may provide moral suasion or gentlemen's agreements, or they may use market controls. In Hirsch's view the latter strategy is very difficult to apply evenly.

G. R. Hall[3] points out a weakness in the design of much prudential regulation when he says that the intent of such regulation is to minimise the rate of failure of financial institutions, but that it may be necessary to allow the rate of failure to increase in order to obtain a more competitive industry. Revell[4] (p.137) suggests that a system of regulation designed to minimise failures ought to place most emphasis on supervisory techniques designed to provide an early warning of potential difficulties to the authorities. In his view this would mean an informal, discretionary form of supervision rather than a rigid system of formal regulations.

From the viewpoint of the present study, it is apparent that the lack of a standard system of prudential regulation makes it difficult to isolate correctly those elements of any regulatory system which are merely prudential from those either occasionally or consistently used for monetary policy purposes. This problem is returned to later in this Part when we examine the overall effectiveness of the regulation of banks.

Prior to that, however, we introduce separately four types of regulatory constraint commonly used within the economies surveyed in Part 2; reserve requirements, interest rate constraints, credit ceilings, and market controls. In each case, following a brief consideration of the limitations and use of the constraint, it is introduced into the model and its minimum and maximum effects on the individual bank are explored and compared with the unregulated bank model. Next, certain combinations of constraints are illustrated in order to present situations closer to the real world where the operation of several constraints in combination is much more often used than a single constraint.

One further change implied by the introduction of regulatory constraints is in the role of capital, which assumes much more significance for a regulated bank, at least in part because banks are subject to capital supervision. We reassess the role of capital in a regulated bank before moving on to discuss Fischer Black's argument[5] that those policies of bank funds' management that are optimal in an unregulated environment must also be considered optimal in regulated environments like the USA where it is not difficult for banks to avoid regulatory controls. It is shown that although this argument only partly depends on the particular regulatory environment in the USA, there is sufficient evidence to support the contrary view that banking operations are modified by the presence of regulation.

One of the results of the forms of regulation commonly imposed has been that banks have often been limited to non-price forms of competition, and we examine the effects that these forms may have on the efficiency of the industry.

Finally we discuss the moves towards diversification which have characterised the operations of banks in many countries over the past twenty years, looking first at within-economy diversification and, second, at diversification to escape from the main effects of domestic cycles and of the cyclical pattern of regulatory controls, which has involved the spread of operations overseas.

Notes

1. Jack Revell, *Solvency and Regulation of Banks*, Bangor Occasional Papers in Economics No. 5 (University of Wales Press, 1975).
2. F. Hirsch, 'The Bagehot Problem', *Manchester School* (1978).
3. G. R. Hall in Federal Reserve Bank of Boston, *Policies for a More Competitive Financial System*, Conference Series No. 8 (1972).
4. Revell, *Solvency and Regulation of Banks*.
5. Fischer Black, 'Bank Funds Management in an Efficient Market', *Journal of Financial Economics*, vol. 2 (1975), pp. 323-39.

Further Reading

Black, Fischer, 'Banking and Interest Rates in a World without Money', *Journal of Bank Research* (1970), pp. 9-20

2 THE IMPACT OF RESERVE REQUIREMENTS

> '[T] his class of control liquidity ratios and the "Special
> Deposits" system has been so far purely ritualistic; owing to
> the flexibility of the banks' investment ratios the effective
> control is the regulation of advances and not any liquidity
> ratio.' (Richard S. Sayers, 'The British Monetary Scene since
> Radcliffe' in *Monetary and Credit Policy and the Banking
> Community* (Almquist and Wiksell, Stockholm, 1966),
> pp.108-9.)

It will be apparent from the survey of banking regulations in nineteen
countries undertaken in the last Part that reserve requirements are a
common means for the control of banks in many countries. Although it
has been suggested in our earlier discussion of the operations of an unregulated bank (see Part 1 above), that a bank would hold a prudent
amount of reserves to protect its business, it is highly probable that the
reserve requirements imposed by a central bank would exceed those
which an unregulated bank would hold. Further, the narratives of
changes in banking regulation during the 1970s suggest very strongly
that the main use of reserve requirements has been to attempt to reduce
the liquidity of the banks in situations where this would almost automatically have followed into increased lending, but that when reserve
requirements are eased it is often at times when the demand for loans
by the private sector is very weak and more enticement than the mere
availability of funds is necessary to generate their interest.

Other disadvantages of the use of reserve requirements primarily
relate to their effect on the development of government securities
markets which is an essential prerequisite for the use of open-market
operations as an instrument of monetary policy. It was argued that
liquidity ratios successfully removed a large part of the government
securities acquired by the banking system from postwar inflation from
money markets and central banks. However, the persistence of these
ratios has not only held substantial amounts of government securities
outside the markets but also has influenced monetary authorities to
hold down interest rates.

The *Economist*, commenting in 1965 on the use of liquidity ratios
for monetary policy,[1] said that when this use was proposed in the 1950s
it was assumed that the Treasury could control the volume of its bills

outstanding, but the possibility of other components of liquid assets expanding was ignored with the result that, when the increase in commercial bills was reflected in deposits, both sides of the ratio increased, rendering it ineffectual in controlling credit expansion.

A refinement of reserve requirements, the cash reserve ratio, although originally merely a solvency requirement and not a monetary policy variable, was turned to by monetary authorities in the 1960s when the more general reserve requirements appeared to be of inadequate force. Owing to its previous use as a solvency requirement, however, there were restrictions imposed on its ready use by central banks – for example, in Belgium the Ministry of Finance must approve of its application.

With the cash reserve refinement available, a central bank, as well as changing the absolute level of reserves held by banks as a proportion of their deposits, may vary the form in which those reserves may be held. Consequently a bank must be concerned not only with the possibility of reserve requirements being increased, but also with the possibility that its earning power on those reserves may be diminished and even removed altogether by central bank action.

An obvious consequence of the use of reserve requirements as a technique of monetary control is that, as far as possible, banks will wish to modify the potential for immediate impact on their lending through reserve requirement changes by holding an amount of free reserves over and above the imposed reserve levels to be used, if thought necessary by the bank, to absorb reserve requirement changes. One implication of the holding or the availability of a level of free reserves is that the intention of a switch in central bank policy could be either defeated entirely or have its effects seriously reduced. The changes in Nederlandsche Bank's credit control system to enable it to reduce, and eliminate if necessary, the free margin of liquidity held by banks, are only one example of central bank response to a banking system found to be too well able to manipulate its free reserves to achieve, on occasions, total immunity from policy changes. We will look at the effect of such changes in regulations shortly in the context of the model.

Quadrant IV of our unregulated bank diagram must now be re-labelled 'earnings on reserves' instead of 'earnings on free reserves' to permit the incorporation of reserve requirements into the model (Figure 5). By comparison with the position of the unregulated bank and on the plausible assumption that the reserve requirements would exceed those which an unregulated bank would hold, the EF function will shift down to $E'F'$ and will modify its shape by taking until D_T' to move into income-earning assets and by moving its peak to the left of D_3 at D_C.

Figure 5

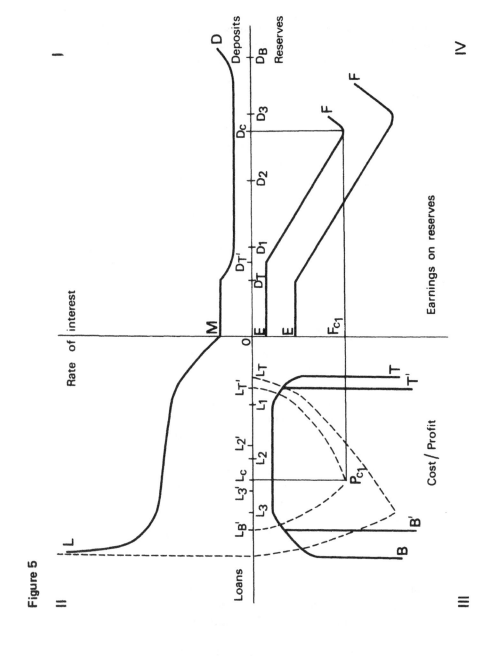

The shift down in the EF function is justified by the usual feature of reserve requirements that the minimum level of pure liquidity required would be above that held by an unregulated bank, and earnings on total reserves would fall accordingly. In addition the bank will not now earn other than minimal income on its reserves until a higher level of reserves is held than in its unregulated state, and this will be responsible for the shift in the position at which peak earnings on reserves are achieved.

The main other changes which the introduction of reserve requirements will make to the bank's operations relate to the minimum viable level of operations and to the level of profits. With regard to the minimum viable level of operations, the introduction of reserve requirements will influence the bank to regard its critical minimum level of operations − that which will prevent a real risk of takeover − as higher than when it was unregulated, probably at L_T', because only from that stage may reserves be safely invested so as to contribute meaningfully to profit. At the same time the proportion of deposits able to be loaned out by the bank will be reduced by the increased level of reserves. In combination these last two effects will reduce the area of the loan function on which the bank would prefer to operate, to that area to the left of L_T' and to the right of L_B'.

Finally the structure of the BT and the profit functions will be altered in response to the imposition of reserve requirements, in that the bank will not begin to earn profits until beyond L_T' instead of L_T and will not wish to expand its business beyond the level of loans L_B'. Further, it will be unable to earn as much on its reserve holdings as it previously did. In combination the result may be that the profit function is reduced in its potential peak and in the level of business for which it is now appropriate. If it is thought that the reduction in the peak profit potential from the unregulated to the regulated state is too severe, a moment's reflection that, for example, in Australia in early 1976 the rate of interest on government securities exceeded 10 per cent while the rate paid on statutory deposits was only 0.75 per cent per annum, will strengthen the point made.

After the introduction of reserve requirements, it can be seen from the figure that any move towards the elimination of free reserves will further reduce the profit potential of the bank. Where this is thought to be a possible course of policy it may have the additional consequence of making the bank less willing to pursue all of its lending opportunities. The alternative approaches to management under a reserve requirement system may be seen in the current position of certain of Australia's trading banks. The Commercial Banking Company of Sydney in its report for the 1977 year commented on the almost non-existent margin of free liquidity which it held simply as evidence that it felt that better profit could be gained by using what otherwise would be a free margin elsewhere in its business. In contrast the other Australian trading banks in the same year held a wide free liquidity margin. Without imputing such a motive in the present case, it should be mentioned that the absence of a margin of free liquidity in the case of another of the Australian trading banks had earlier in the 1970s slowed the imposition of a heavier SRD ratio on all the banks.

If we compare the operation of the bank subject to reserve requirements with the operation of the unregulated bank, two possible results may occur in consequence of the introduction of this regulatory restraint. First, it appears that if reserve requirements are likely to be a consistent instrument of policy the bank will wish to diversify into other areas in order to retain the profit potential it had in its unregulated state; and second, since the bank will not be able to maintain the same proportion of loans to deposits as hitherto, there may now be a clear role for other financial intermediaries to play in the provision of loans.

Notice that if the bank seeks to minimise the effect of changes in reserve requirements it will be necessary for it to hold a much larger level of free reserves in order to be able to achieve this aim. It is quite likely that this will involve a shift in the bank's balance sheet which reduces its loan content and raises its reserve holdings. Therefore, even minimising the effect of reserve requirements changes will affect the bank's operations.

Note

1. *Economist*, 'Whatever Happened to Credit Control?', 19 June 1965, p.viii.

Further Reading

Sayers, Richard S., 'The British Monetary Scene since Radcliffe' in *Monetary and Credit Policy and the Banking Community* (Almquist and Wiksell, Stockholm, 1966)

3 THE EFFECT OF INTEREST RATE CONSTRAINTS

'Banks are free to pay lower rates than the ceiling rates, but competition and tight credit conditions usually ensure that actual rates are at ceiling levels.' (Dwayne Wrightsman, *An Introduction to Monetary Theory and Policy*, 2nd edn (The Free Press, 1976), p.50.)

Because open-market operations are considered separately, the analysis in this chapter is confined to the impact of limits exercised by monetary authorities on the interest rates charged by banks on lending and those payable by banks on (primarily) time deposits. Interest rate constraints may be fine-tuned to affect particular classes of lenders and borrowers, but we are more concerned here with the impact of maximum interest rates set on lending *in toto* and of maximum interest rates imposed on time deposits (as for example is done in the USA by Regulation Q). To the extent that there are lags in the implementation of almost all monetary controls, it is not unexpected to find that the official adjustment of maximum rates lagged behind the swift-moving events of the early 1970s. This often created disparities between banking rates and market rates which produced substantial flows of funds between the banking sector and the money market which, on occasion, inverted the usual interest rate structure.

Where maximum rates are imposed on both deposits and loans, the scope for a bank to relate riskiness to interest rates on the loan side is very limited and it is likely in these circumstances that a bank will favour lending to those areas of business which provide minimal risk. This limitation of lending will provide an impetus for non-bank financial intermediaries to service these sectors. As exemplified by the case of South Africa in 1976, the combination of restrictive reserve requirements and high rates of interest payable on lending and borrowing can prove of particular difficulty to smaller banks. And in inflationary situations small savers will be disadvantaged by the lag between market rates of interest and the more slowly adjusted rates offered by the banks. Of course, while the small saver in such a situation will often leave his money in a bank because of his lack of expertise in the money market, large depositors will very quickly switch their funds between banks and the market to get the best return, even to the extent that (as occurred in the UK in 1973 and 1974) they may borrow from the banks at agreed overdraft rates and deposit the funds thus acquired elsewhere in the financial markets at a higher rate. The management of a bank is of course made much harder if, as in the conditions just described, deposit flows may be substantially reduced while the demand for loans rises.

In contrast to the effects of adding reserve requirements to the original model, the consequences of alternatively placing interest rate constraints on the bank are primarily confined to the loan area of operations. As will be apparent from Figure 6 it is unlikely that the setting of maximum interest rates will have much influence on the bank's preferred rates of interest on deposits, but if there was a large discrepancy between the maximum allowed and the actual rates paid on deposits, while the maximum and actual rates charged on loans were identical, there would be room for other financial intermediaries to come into existence.

The impact of the imposition of a ceiling rate of interest on loans, shown in Figure 6 quadrant II, will be to raise the possible rate at low levels of activity but to restrict the rate on all other levels of loans. This has the effect of reducing the scope for the possible expansion of bank lending to a position well to the right of the original L_3, how far to the right being dependent on the extent to which the bank wishes to maximise profits. Owing to the maximum rate of interest payable on loans there will be little incentive for the bank to expand its lending to areas of risk and, again, there will be scope for other non-bank financial intermediaries to emerge to serve this need.

A further implication of the enforcing of a maximum interest rate on loans may be that the bank may well be tempted to reduce its loans and increase its investment of reserves as a source of revenue. Provided that the bank limits its loan business to the minimal risk areas it is unlikely that the level of liquidity of its reserves need be maintained at its original level, and some scope for increasing the income-earning portion of reserves is likely to be found. Interest-rate constraints may in fact operate for the benefit of the bank by deterring it from approaching the riskier area of loans.

Leaving aside any variation in the investment of free reserves, Figure 6 depicts the probable reaction to the implementation of maximum interest rates. The impact of a maximum interest rate of M' will not be felt unless it generates a growth of competitors to the banks; however, if M'' is the maximum interest rate allowed on loans then clearly there is a reduction in revenue from loans for the bank's preferred level of operation, between L_1 and L_3. This reduction in revenue will be reflected

Figure 6

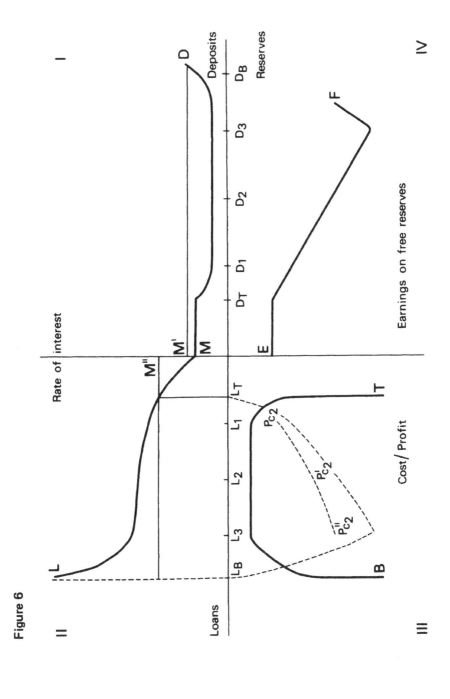

in the bank's profit function which not only shifts down but will also be appropriate over a smaller area of operations, because, at levels of lending in excess of L_3, the difference between the maximum rate of interest allowed and the rate required to compensate for the increased risk of this business is too great for the bank to feel able to operate. The new maximum level of profit is smaller than the pre-constraint level, but the slope of the profit curve is now less steep and the bank may prefer the less than profit-maximising level of operation in order to minimise the difference between the maximum interest rate and the rates the bank would wish to charge as a free agent.

4 THE OPERATION OF CREDIT CEILINGS AS A CONSTRAINT

> 'Quantitative restrictions must not be allowed to be antici-
> pated; they must "sneak up" on the market quickly and
> unexpectedly to be effective.' (James Duesenberry, 'Com-
> ments', *Brookings Papers on Economic Activity*, no.2, 1971.)

The continued use of credit ceilings as a regulatory constraint in many of the countries surveyed in Part 2 suggests that by no means all countries have found that their central banks are able to restrain aggregate demand significantly by using the more market-oriented measures. Nevertheless the impact of quantitative restrictions on bank lending for an economy as a whole is analogous to the imposition of rationing in a commodity market with all its attendant inefficiencies. It has the effect of promoting evasion, it tends to become ineffective when implemented for long periods, it encourages the banks to lend only to those areas characterised by least risk while other areas usually require urgent access to credit and, accordingly, it increases the loss of bank business to other financial institutions which are not subject to this control.

A major argument used to justify quantitative restrictions or credit ceilings has been that these restrictions speedily result in banks rationing credit and then increasing their interest rates on lending with a consequently early effect on aggregate demand. By comparison open-market operations, for example, take much more time, as banks may be able by selling off securities to postpone the adoption of tighter lending policies, and in consequence the flow-through of restraint to aggregate demand may be reduced or spread over a longer period of time than desired by the monetary authorities.

A secondary, but related, argument is that open-market operations (for example) used for constraint will push the entire interest rate structure upward at least in the short term, while credit ceilings in contrast will ration some credit demand at least out of the bank market, with smaller interest rate increases quite possibly confined to the banking sector.

Except in the case where banks react to the imposition of credit ceilings by reducing lending to companies which are indifferent to whether they borrow from the banks or from non-bank financial intermediaries, which may mean that no significant effect occurs on aggregate demand, the other possible reactions of banks to the imposition of credit ceilings will result in a depressing effect on aggregate demand. Even in the exception noted, it is rather unlikely that companies which previously borrowed from banks could shift to non-bank sources of funds at exactly the same interest rates, and the extent to which they were unable to obtain the same supply at the same cost would make them reluctant to shift and this unattractiveness or unavailability of substitutes would have a depressing effect on demand.

In common with one possible result of the imposition of maximum interest rates on lending, it is possible that the imposition of credit ceilings will merely remove a bank's interest in the riskier area of loans altogether and leave the maximum profit potential untouched. Reference to the use that has been made of credit ceilings, particularly in some European countries, does suggest however that they usually do limit bank business quite significantly. The effect of credit ceilings in use has been quite asymmetrical, that is, their imposition is a successful means of limiting growth whereas the releasing of credit ceilings is of itself generally unable to encourage a stronger demand for bank credit.

It is interesting to enquire whether this asymmetry is due to a wider impact of the control than is often considered to occur. That is, if the imposition of credit ceilings is directed primarily at the siphoning off of the speculative excesses of demand it might be expected that a subsequent release of the ceilings would find a response in increased demand. Looking at the cases in which ceilings have been imposed, however, it appears that in reality the imposition of ceilings has a strong impact in denying access to credit to the private sector and that their failure to obtain credit is reflected in a significant reduction in their planned expenditure which will reduce not only present demand but expected future demand. With these reduced horizons, it is unlikely that a subsequent release of ceilings will generate an immediate response. In fact in the impact of its release, the use of credit ceilings exhibits all of the lags considered to be attendant on the more general forms of control in effecting constraint.

While central bankers can point to the advantages of simplicity, directness and certainty in the effects of credit ceilings and to the fact that often the mere knowledge of the existence of ceilings makes clients refrain from applying for credit, these short-run advantages appear to be more than offset by the technique's adverse effects on inter-bank competition and by the likelihood that it would encourage the growth of uncontrolled intermediaries for the provision of credit.

In the past decade there has been a move, particularly among the

European central banks, to increase their use of credit ceilings as a response to the large increases in bank liquidity provided by balance of payments surpluses. The presence of overdraft limits creates, in Benston's[1] words (p.16), 'the specter of loans made without warning by customers', which will complicate the enforcement of restrictive ceilings. Further, as Wold[2] has noted (p.65), in the case of Norway the operation of credit ceilings on banks encouraged an increase in new financial institutions whose variety of form made it a complex task to have them included in the voluntary agreement on credit ceilings.

From the point of view of the individual bank, then, the impact of credit ceilings on the demand for credit may be of longer duration than the ceilings themselves. A second form of credit restriction which is used more often than restrictions over total lending is control over the composition of lending which is usually termed qualitative restriction or selective control. This form of control alters the incidence of restrictive monetary policies rather than their efficacy. It may be argued that in some cases qualitative credit restrictions are imposed to direct bank lending towards areas to which, in a free market situation, the banks would have lent little or nothing, and away from areas to which they have normally been the main source of funds. For example, one could imagine that banks in the United Kingdom in 1974 might have felt, in the face of selective requests to limit lending in the areas of property development, speculation and personal expenditure, and realising that manufacturers might be about to make particularly heavy demands on them owing to a need to offset their deteriorating financial positions, that the riskiness of their loan structure might be increased more than they would wish. In fact, the manufacturing sector's demand for funds did not eventuate to the extent feared, and lending to services increased to the extent that borrowing by manufacturing declined.

In introducing credit ceilings as a constraint on an otherwise unregulated bank, the main change will be to modify the effective area of the loan function which the bank may service. This may be shown in Figure 7 by moving the line which rises vertically from L_B in quadrant II to the right. We may look at the effects of three alternative credit ceilings at L_3, L_2 and L_1 respectively. At a ceiling of L_3 only the riskier areas of lending are eliminated for the bank, and its maximum profit position is still attainable. Moving to a credit ceiling of L_2, however, profit is seriously affected and there will be a number of loans which the bank would like to service but which will have to be foregone. While the bank may not be reluctant to lose that group of loans represented by the distance between L_B and L_3, for it would have raised its interest

Figure 7

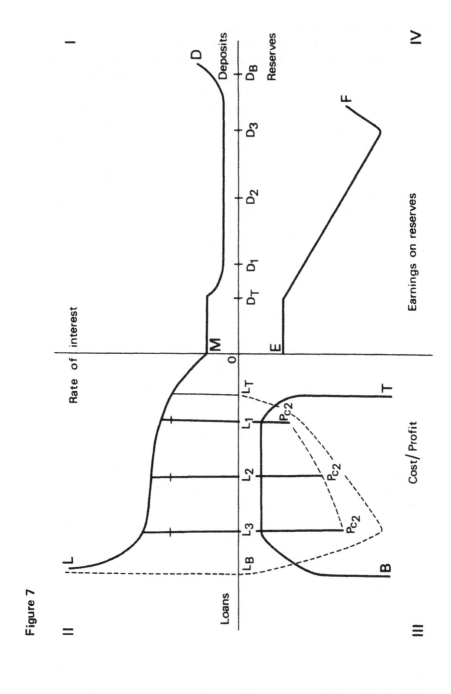

on those loans before providing them, once the credit ceiling is imposed at L_2 the bank will lose business which may be provided by another non-bank intermediary. If the non-bank intermediary concerned continues to be unregulated, a number of the bank's customers (some adversely affected by the imposition of the credit ceiling and others only fearing a future adverse effect) will be attracted to this non-bank intermediary, whether it charges the same interest as a bank or more than that rate.

It may be argued that restricting the credit ceiling to L_1 would be the equivalent of subsidising the competitors of banks in the provision of loans. Of course, such a limit may be proposed and then reduced as a result of the bargaining between the central bank and the commercial banks which often attends the proposed implementation of credit ceilings.

Notes

1. George J. Benston, 'Overdraft Banking: Its Implications for Monetary Policy, the Commercial Banking Industry and Individual Banks', *Journal of Bank Research*, vol.3, no.1 (1972), pp.7-25.
2. Knut Getz Wold, 'Selective Measures of Monetary and Credit Policy', *Monetary and Credit Policy and the Banking Community* (Almquist and Wiksell, Stockholm, 1966).

Further Reading

Dorrance, Graeme S. and William H. White, 'Alternative Forms of Monetary Ceilings for Stabilization Purposes', *IMF Staff Papers*, vol.9 (November 1962)

5 THE IMPACT OF INDIRECT OR MARKET CONTROLS

> 'If we take into consideration the total liquidity of the banking system open-market transactions as practised in the Netherlands and . . . Germany are of qualitative rather than quantitative significance. This is tantamount to the saying that in general these transactions in no way influence the total volume of liquidity at the disposal of the banking system (cash and potential liquidity) but merely its composition.' (EEC, *The Instruments of Monetary Policy* (1962), pp.38-9.)

The classification of open-market operations and discount-rate policy as indirect controls reflects the fact that, although the first instrument in particular directly affects bank reserves, the banks must pass on this response to their customers for its impact to be generally felt in the economy. In an economy with a sufficiently developed government securities market to allow open-market operations to be implemented without either flooding the market or entirely depriving it of funds, this tool may be regarded as more flexible in both timing and adjustment than alternative tools, although its more indirect nature may reduce its effectiveness.

Open-market sales of government securities by the monetary authorities have the effect, when the sales are to the commercial banks, of substitution on the asset side of their balance sheets by reducing their deposits with the central bank and increasing their holdings of government securities, and, when the sales are to the public, there is a reduction on both sides of commercial bank balance sheets as deposits with the central bank (an asset) are reduced and the public's current or demand deposits (a liability) fall by the amount of the sales. On the other hand, if the monetary authorities decide to make open-market purchases, this will have the result, if the purchases are from banks, of reducing their holdings of government securities and increasing their holding of reserves, and, if the purchases are from the public, the payment received by them will be deposited with the commercial banks who in turn will forward the cheques to the monetary authorities and have the amount credited to their deposit balances with the central bank. Where the banks themselves are the sellers, their deposit liabilities are unchanged by the process and their excess reserves rise by the amount of the sale, but where the public are the sellers the banks acquire an additional amount of reserves through their acceptance of the public's deposit of the funds from selling, and the proportion of additional reserve holdings required by the additional deposits will be added to their required reserves so that their excess reserves will be less than the amount deposited by the proportion of required reserves.

Of prime interest here is the purchase or sale directly from the commercial banks and their possible means of offsetting its effects. Open-market purchases will increase commercial bank reserves by the amount of the purchase; however the banks may elect to increase their excess reserves in order to provide a source of funds to continue their flow of loans on the next occasion that the monetary authorities sell securities to the commercial banks. It could be argued that if the banks fail to put their excess reserves to work they are reducing their overall return on their funds until the time of their potential use, and when the reserves are used it will be in a time of monetary tightening which might be expected to affect adversely the riskiness of loans. The contrary argument is that banks ought to be allowed to manage their loan portfolios as they wish, and that the holding of excess reserves should merely be an insurance of that freedom obtained by the premium of interest foregone on the excess reserves.

In the opposite situation where open-market sales are made, it is the intention of the monetary authorities that these be reflected in the reduction of commercial bank loans and securities. However, the commercial banks may adjust instead by simply reducing their excess reserves or by replacing the reserves lost by borrowing additional reserves, in the US situation at the Federal Reserve's discount window. Of course it is up to the Federal Reserve to set the discount rate, and it may be able to make it an expensive proposition for banks to increase their reserves by raising the discount rate (although the banks may find other sources for borrowing) when they wish to reduce the money supply, and to reduce the discount rate below alternative rates for securing funds when they wish the banks to borrow to increase their reserves.

It appears that if the banks elect to build up excess reserves sufficient to allow them to maintain a constant lending pattern regardless of cyclical variation in monetary policy, the economy, or both, they will be able to ignore discount rate changes except so far as these on occasion may allow the banks to obtain funds more cheaply than from alternative sources. The monetary authorities may use their other tools, in particular reserve requirements, in order to lower bank holdings of excess reserves down to the level at which open-market operations will

be of influence. Should these be insufficient, there could be implementation of the type of control scheme used in West Germany where all
excess reserve holdings were reduced to an insignificant level and the
banks had to rely on the money market, from which the Bundesbank
withdrew its operations, with the result that not only bank lending but
also non-bank demand for credit were reduced.

It is common among many of the countries surveyed in the last Part
that government securities markets have been too inactive and discon-
tinuous to allow regular two-way bank transactions to occur in sufficient
volume to support open-market operations. In those economies where
the banks normally pay interest on demand and other short-term deposits, it is quite difficult for non-bank markets for Treasury bills to be
developed.

A further difficulty common to central banks in small open economies arises where the gold and foreign exchange reserves held by the
central bank normally exceed the bank-note circulation, with the result
that 'its grip on the market must be well-nigh nonexistent'[1] (p.38) and
its influence cannot depend only on manipulation of the bond market.
In the view of the 1962 EEC paper,[2] open-market operations as used in
West Germany and the Netherlands influenced only the composition of
total liquidity and not its volume because those operations proved unable to drain the banking system of cash.

Nevertheless, owing to the potential for less palatable controls to be
implemented where open-market operations were seen to be of little
effect, it appears reasonable to expect that open-market operations
would be seen to have some effect on the activities of an individual
bank. On this assumption it is possible to introduce the effects of open-
market operations on the activities of our otherwise unregulated bank.
Assuming that the monetary authorities sell securities to the bank, this
will result in a switch between their holdings of government securities
and their deposits with the central bank or other cash holdings which
will reduce the liquidity of their asset structure. In order to regain the
liquidity foregone by this adjustment, the bank may reduce its loans
rather than run down its reserves.

In the case of small, open economies it is apparent that open-market
operations will not be a sufficient means for central banks to supply the
reserve base if the process of discounting is used.

Discounting may be defined as the extension of central bank credit at
the initiative of the commercial banks. Its effects are limited in periods
of excess demand and abundant bank liquidity, although it is often a
useful adjunct to other policies. The main criticism of discount rates and

quotas as a policy tool is that they are traditionally a path to central bank resources to which the banks gain access as a right rather than as a privilege, and their setting is often a matter of bargaining between the central banks and the commercial banks. Further, to the extent that discount quotas become part of the banking sector's liquid assets, it will be difficult for the central bank to reduce them without considerable disruption when the individual banks operate close to their ceilings.

For a majority of the countries discussed in the last Part, none of the central banks are able to use open-market operations to supply the reserve base of the banks and, instead, this base is supplied by central bank credit provided at the initiative of the banks rather than of the central banks. Logue[3] describes the 'paradox' of discount ceilings and quotas as follows: '. . . if the banks are pressing against the ceilings, the situation is as if the global ceiling were zero, and if the banks are below their ceilings, the supply of central bank credit is perfectly elastic within the available margin.' (pp.60-1).

In the light of the obvious limitations of discount policy it would appear that the only change required to our original model to incorporate the presence of discount facilities would be to reduce the level of reserve holdings by an individual bank as more reserves could be acquired from the central bank if necessary.

Notes

1. M. W. Holtrop, 'Monetary Policy in an Open Economy: Its Objectives, Instruments, Limitations and Dilemmas', *Princeton Essays in International Finance*, no.43 (September 1963).

2. EEC, *The Instruments of Monetary Policy* (1962).

3. R. Logue, 'Imported Inflation and the International Adjustment Process', PhD thesis, George Washington University, 1969, University Microfilms International, Michigan.

6 THE ROLE OF CAPITAL UNDER REGULATION

'The fundamental role of bank capital, the role of all capital, is to provide the investment funds for productive assets . . . and to protect creditors by absorbing losses which management has been unable to anticipate.' (J. Carey, 'The Role of Bank Capital', *Journal of Bank Research*, Autumn 1975, p.167.)

The role of capital assumes more significance for a regulated bank than for an unregulated bank, partly because banks are subject to capital supervision. It was argued in relation to the unregulated bank that, providing it maintained the average ratio of capital to deposits, it did not need to consider its capital as a significant variable. To be more reasonable, the type and range of a bank's activities will assist in the determination of an adequate ratio of capital to deposits. For example, where a bank specialises in lending to a particular industry or region in the economy it might consider itself more vulnerable to loss than banks servicing a wider clientele and might maintain a very conservative capital ratio for this reason. Again, a bank that is heavily reliant on an inter-bank market for funds ought to maintain a relatively high capital base to allow itself to avoid liquidity shortages in that market.

The extent to which a bank has government backing may be an even more important factor than those already mentioned, because a bank which is completely nationalised, as are the national banks of France, may rely on government support rather than on its own capital. This factor explains why the national banks of India and Egypt are able to maintain capital to deposits ratios of below 2 per cent. Higher capital ratios are maintained by those banks, such as the UK clearing banks, which have tacit rather than complete government support.

In discussing the supervision of the UK banking system in 1975, George Blunden of the Bank of England[1] said that in assessing the capital adequacy of a bank it is necessary to ensure as a first priority that shareholders' funds should provide full coverage for investments in fixed assets, in subsidiaries and in related trading companies, and that in general capital and reserves ought to provide the general infrastructure of the bank's business as well as protection for depositors against losses.

Taggart[2] compares the bank capital decision under two hypothetical situations in which direct supervision of bank capital is assumed away, in order to demonstrate the influence of certain features of bank regulation on the capital decisions of banks. In the first hypothetical case, the bank operates under reserve requirements and without the US Regulation Q prohibition on interest rates on deposits. Here deposits and capital are alternative sources of funds for the purchase of assets, but acquiring deposits would obligate the bank to make interest payments and to meet the reserve requirement as well as producing profits from charges for cheque clearing and book-keeping. Two opposing effects would occur here as profits would encourage deposits relative to capital at the same time as the reserve requirement would tend to discourage deposits. If new capital was raised as an alternative source of funds, this would reduce the probability of bank failure to the advantage of depositors who may be prepared to accept a lower interest rate as a trade-off for this increased safety. Existing shareholders, on the other hand, would require that their expected stream of income and/or capital gains not be jeopardised by the raising of new capital. The bank would vary its mix of deposits and capital in order to balance all of these costs and benefits.

The second of Taggart's cases assumes that there are reserve requirements, a prohibition of interest on deposits and the full insurance of all deposits by the government in return for a fee paid by the banks proportional to their deposits. In these circumstances depositors would not consider a bank's capital position as relevant to the safety of their deposits, though the deposit insurance agency would benefit by a reduction of its own potential losses if a bank raised more capital. For the bank the interest prohibition would enable it to raise funds by increasing deposits at less than the market rate for funds and it would prefer this to raising new capital which offered no similar incentive and would not affect the safety of depositors.

Taggart argues that the presence of the deposit insurance system in the USA leads banks to prefer deposits to capital but that this preference is affected by two additional features of the US system; the limit of FDIC protection to 40,000 dollars per account and the supervision by regulatory authorities of bank capital positions. Watson, First Deputy Controller of the Currency,[3] lists eight factors taken into consideration by the US Comptroller of Currency in measuring capital adequacy. These factors are quality of management; the liquidity of assets, the history of both earnings and their retention; the character of management; the burden of occupancy expense; the volatility of the deposit structure; the quality of operating procedures; and the capacity of a bank to meet the present and future requirements of its trade area. The capital adequacy ratio was defined by the Comptroller to be the ratio of equity capital to total liabilities.

In looking at the Franklin and US National Bank of San Diego failures and the near failure of the Security National Bank of Hempstead, New York, Watson comments that 'three classic conditions' were present in each of these cases — the mismanagement of asset and liability maturities, loan losses higher than average and an abnormally low return on assets. Watson[4] concludes that 'this seems to support the premise that there is no amount of capital that will salvage a bank which is grossly mismanaged' (p.171).

Friedman and Formuzis[5] in an examination of the deposit-protection incentive for maintaining or increasing bank capital, argue that this incentive is probably only of significance in the case of small banks, and that for larger banks only depositors with balances well above the deposit-insurance level of 40,000 dollars will have any incentive to react to changes in the ratio of capital to liabilities and they are, Friedman and Formuzis suggest, only likely to find the ratio rewarding in the event of failure.

Perhaps it is more reasonable to make deposit insurance of one form or another take over the deposit-protection aspect of banking operations, and to allow capital to be considered adequate when it gives full coverage for investment in fixed assets, in subsidiaries and in related trading companies, as the UK authorities feel is the first priority requirement. Once the deposit-protection aspect is otherwise coped with, there is no reason for the regulation of capital to be considered as a monetary policy instrument and it regains its correct place as part of the fixed regulations on solvency and liquidity.

Notes

1. George Blunden, 'The Capital and Liquidity Adequacy of Banks', *Bank of England Quarterly Bulletin* (September 1975).

2. Robert A. J. Taggart, 'Regulatory Influences on Bank Capital', *New England Economic Review* (September/October 1977).

3. Justin T. Watson, 'A Regulatory View of Capital Adequacy', *Journal of Bank Research* (Autumn 1975).

4. Ibid.

5. Benjamin M. Friedman and Peter Formuzis, 'Bank Capital: The Deposit-Protection Incentive', *Journal of Bank Research* (Autumn 1975).

Further Reading

Carey, Gerard V., 'Reassessing the Role of Bank Capital', *Journal of Bank Research*, Autumn 1975
Gallant, Richard A., 'Approaches to Capital Planning', *Journal of Bank Research*, Autumn 1975
Taggart, Robert A. J. and S. I. Greenbaum, 'Bank Capital and Public Regulation', *Journal of Money, Credit and Banking*, May 1978

7 THE COMBINATION OF CONSTRAINTS

It is not the intention here to provide a taxonomy of the possible combinations of constraints, but simply to illustrate the way in which our model is able to cope with the combination of several constraints. The reader will doubtless wish to introduce the combination of constraints appropriate to his own banking system.

In Figure 8 we show an interpretation of the impact of the combination of reserve requirements and maximum interest rate constraints on the operations of a previously unregulated bank. First, the major impact of the introduction of reserve requirements will be the shift of the EF function to $E'F'$ and the corresponding shifts of the takeover and bankruptcy constraints to L_T' and L_B' respectively and the associated downward shift of the profit function. Second, the introduction of the maximum interest rate constraint of M'' will prevent the bank from operating on the loan functions LM'' and LQ_2M'' and effectively limit loan expansion beyond L_c.

In combination the two constraints will have the effect of establishing a new loan function LQ_1M'', although it can be seen that the only feasible operating region along this function will be confined to the area to the right of L_c. The bank's level of operations will be somewhere between L_1 and L_c where these levels of loans are now a smaller proportion of total deposits than when the bank faced no constraints. In addition, the bank will be prevented by the combined operation of these constraints from simply making up any shortfall on profit resulting from the limitation of loan business by increasing the earning capacity of reserves, since these are also reduced. The profit function no longer offers the potential for its unregulated maximum levels.

Note that only a minimal variation of this combination of reserve requirements and maximum interest rates is necessary to replicate the 1976 difficulties presented to small banks in South Africa by their Reserve Bank's combination of these forms of constraints.

If we compare the operations of a bank in the unregulated world as depicted in Part 1 with the operations of a bank under the above combination of constraints, we may see some of the effects of regulation. For the unregulated bank, the main difficulties with which it will be faced are uncertainty about the flow of funds, the assessment of risk on loans and the maintenance of a prudent level of liquidity in reserves.

Figure 8

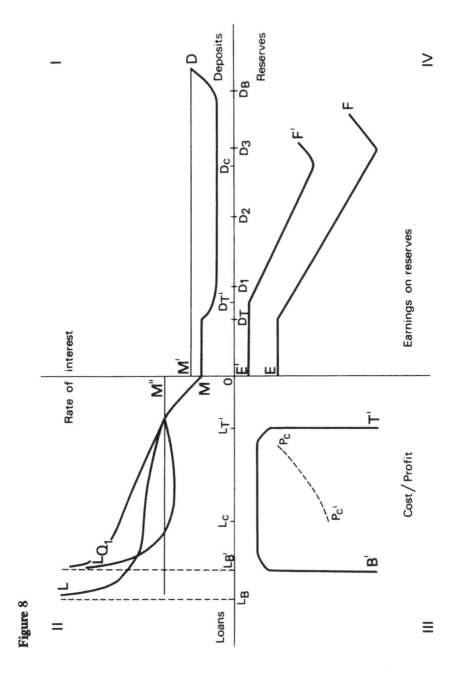

One impact of the above combination of regulatory constraints is to modify part of these difficulties, in that one consequence of the application of maximum interest rate ceilings is to allow the bank to restrict its loans to that level for which the ceiling rate is equal to the rate which it would have charged under unregulated conditions. Nevertheless, while the risk of bankruptcy is reduced by the elimination of these riskier loans from the bank's business, the same constraint does seem to reduce the bank's potential for maximising profit. This last result may be influenced mainly by the interest rate ceilings but it is reinforced by the combination of reserve ratios which alter the structure of the BT function so as to reduce the range of attainable profits for the bank.

Within the context of our model, we may also illustrate an even more restrictive combination of constraints, a ceiling on credit and qualitative directions on the composition of lending. In Figure 9 we show the credit ceiling of L_2 (as in Figure 7) which will seriously affect both the volume of loans and the profit and in addition will cause a shift in the bank's loan function in order to reflect qualitative directions as to the disposition of credit from the central bank.

Two possible shifts in the loan function are shown; firstly LQ_1 which reflects either increasing risk or increasing costs in servicing the change in the composition of loans (increasing costs if a switch to smaller loans to consumers from larger loans to business is implied); and secondly LQ_2 which suggests that less risk or cost will be involved in the new composition of loans. The combination of the L_2 limit to credit and the LQ_2 loan function will limit the bank's business and reduce its profit, while the L_2 limit and LQ_1 loan function may enable the bank to maintain its original profit function but only at the expense of the increased risk inherent in that function.

With the combination of constraints illustrated first in this chapter, one of the effects of regulation was to reduce the riskiness of loans, but with the present combination that riskiness seems to be increased. One reaction to this second combination of constraints is that the bank may attempt to make up the shortfall in profit caused by the limitation of its loan business, by increasing the earning capacity on its reserves.

Apart from providing the incentive to diversify its business, it appears that regulatory constraints on banks reduce the possibility of price competition between banks while at the same time strengthening the case for non-price competition and product augmentation. A common attribute of these new forms of competition is their emphasis on providing a service while simultaneously overcoming some of the impositions

Figure 9

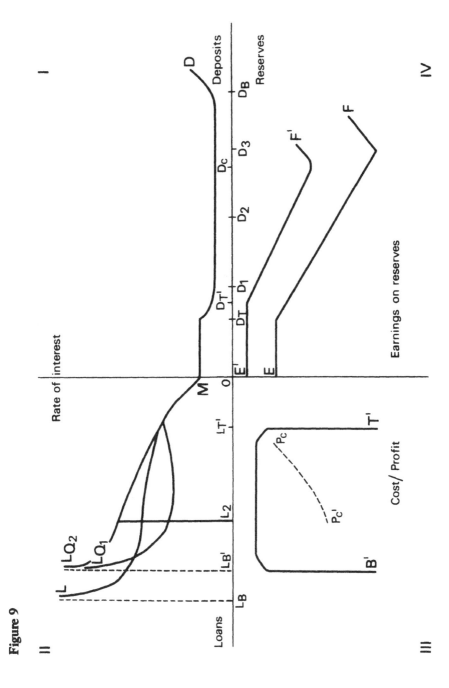

which regulation makes on a bank's preferred position in an unregulated environment.

It is apparent from both of the combinations of constraints illustrated here that the introduction of non-bank financial intermediaries into the economy is necessary to satisfy the demands of the riskier classes of borrower which the banks are unable to service. New intermediaries will create further competition for the banks to the extent that they are able to provide depositor facilities. This will create a need for banks to expand their range of convenience-type services in order to continue to attract deposits, now a more necessary strategy because of the relatively higher level of both deposits and loans which must be attained under regulatory conditions to overcome the takeover constraint.

Non-price competition is likely to raise the costs of banking services to consumers because of the 'lock-in' effect of this type of competition. This effect occurs by the following process; let us assume that one bank decides to introduce a travel department in order to entice to itself a bigger share of the market. The bank will incur costs in setting up the travel department but it will be expected that these costs will be re-couped by the additional business generated. However, other banks anxious to reduce the possible competitive advantage gained by the bank originating the travel department idea will also move to add a travel department to their organisations. That is, each bank in the in-dustry will incur the costs of setting up a travel department in order to reduce the competitive advantage it feels will otherwise accrue to the bank which first introduces it. Of course, it is possible that the banks will be able to gain business from outside their usual customers from their travel departments; however, the gain to each bank will be small, and possibly not sufficient to provide a return on the establishment cost for all the banks. Nevertheless all banks will continue their pro-vision of this service because if they eliminate it, other banks may gain a competitive advantage. This 'lock-in' effect of non-price competition will over time be reflected in increased costs to the users of bank services.

This reaction simply confirms that regulation reinforces the tendency of banking towards oligopoly, although this point depends on regulation being effective and not readily evaded. This problem is examined in the next chapter.

8 IS REGULATION EFFECTIVE?

'... it is relatively easy to get around most of the regulations that are applied to banks.' (F. Black, 'Bank Funds Management in an Efficient Market', *Journal of Financial Economics*, vol.2 (1975), pp.338-9.)

Fischer Black argues that those bank funds management policies which would be optimal in an unregulated environment are also optimal in such regulated environments as the United States on the grounds that banks may avoid the intended impact of regulations applied to them. While there are special circumstances which may make this a reasonable conclusion in the US case, it is important to consider the potential applicability of this argument to other economies because of its implications for the general issue of control.

In Fischer Black's two main papers on this subject,[1] he takes all forms of regulatory constraints as if they were imposed for control purposes rather than as a form or forms of prudential regulation. This confusion is unfortunate because no rational banker would wish to avoid prudential regulation since his bank's acceptance of it places it on par with other banks in the industry in the eyes of the public. Further, there is no distinction made between reserve requirements which are prudentially required and those varied as part of the monetary policy process.

In this chapter the special circumstances of the USA will be examined first, before attention is turned to the general applicability of Black's argument to banks in other countries and finally to the extent to which individual measures of control may be avoided.

One critical characteristic of the US banking system which renders it unusual among the world's systems is that the regulation of banks at the federal level is only implemented on those banks that voluntarily elect to become members of the Federal Reserve System. It is open to banks in the system to withdraw from membership. In exchange for submitting to regulatory controls, member banks gain access to the Federal Reserve discount window and the federal deposit insurance scheme. As noted in our discussion of US banking regulation in Part 2, the proportion of commercial banks belonging to the Federal Reserve System has been declining over the past three decades. The main reason for leaving the system offered by departing banks has been the cost of member reserve requirements by comparison with those requirements imposed by the various states. The exodus of banks from the system is of sufficient continuity and magnitude to restrict the Federal Reserve in its ability to impose regulatory constraints to an extent that disadvantages member banks in relation to non-member banks.

Although the Federal Reserve's use of open-market operations as the primary policy tool does facilitate the spread of the influence of policies throughout the financial sector of the economy, the particular impact on banks is nowhere near as severe as if regulatory constraints more directly limiting credit were used.

Looked at in the context of the US banking environment, Black's argument[2] appears to have some content; that is, that it is possible for banks 'to get around most of the regulations' (p.339). Black follows the case put by Harry Johnson[3] that reserve requirements place an implicit tax on banks, but he allows (and Johnson seems not to) that there may be a logical rationale for this tax to the extent that it may be sufficient to equalise the untaxed value of services provided by banks to holders of demand deposits so that the taxation of deposits and debt securities would be equivalent.

It may be seen from the simplified model of regulatory constraints developed in this Part that the most critical of the constraints seem to be those that affect the quantity of credit that the banks are able to extend. Such constraints should obviously be reflected in reductions in the total amount of credit extended by banks and in consequence if banks are able to continue lending to their old, pre-constraint level, it will become clear to the central bank that the level of constraint applied to credit is insufficient and further constraints will be applied. While this possibility is of greatest strength where direct controls over total credit are a commonly applied constraint and the gain from obvious evasion would then be a very short-term one, even under a less limiting system of control the inadequacy of these controls reflected in the maintenance of credit levels will eventually lead the authorities to investigate other alternatives. For example, it is noteworthy that one of the reasons for the move by the West German monetary authorities to eliminate bank reserve holdings as far as possible was to ensure that banks would have to restrict credit when the authorities moved to a restrictive policy stance.

In general terms, then, the wholesale evasion of regulatory constraints where possible by banks appears to offer only short-run advantages, and as we shall see in the next chapter, these gains are more easily achieved and persist longer if they are achieved by diversification rather than by evasion.

This leaves one remaining problem; the identification of the constraint or constraints whose effects are not easy for the banks to avoid or minimise. Ruth Logue,[4] in an interesting study of the instruments of monetary policy and their use in the adjustment process to imported inflation in European economies, notes Tobin's comment that '. . . it must be assumed that each member . . . commands monetary and fiscal instruments adequate to manage total demand and fulfill its adjustment obligations. If, for political, constitutional, or traditional reasons, this assumption is not met by various members of the group, the system cannot work'[5] (p.205).

We have already discussed in Part 2 the reaction of monetary authorities in various European economies to large capital inflows, and from this survey it is apparent that open-market operations proved to be ineffective and that most central banks were forced to vary their usual regulatory preferences to provide for direct restrictions on the earning assets of commercial banks as a means of coping with inflationary pressure. Those central banks which used discount policy found that this did not give them control over the quantity of credit available, as access at the initiative of commercial banks became a right rather than a withdrawable privilege and central banks were left with only the price of that credit, the discount rate, as a variable factor. Liquidity ratios also proved insufficient in themselves to restrain credit and had to be supplemented by other measures. Logue[6] comments (p.67) that liquidity ratios had an additional result in that they inhibited the development of government securities markets because they immobilised quantities of this debt and because they encouraged low interest rates on national debt. This result has been varied in those countries like Belgium and France which have separated bank holdings of government securities into different tranches in attempts to develop the basis for open-market operations.

Lack of legislative force behind central bank desires to raise the cash reserve requirements of banks in order to restrict bank liquidity was a problem for most central banks, particularly because increasing reserve requirements were very unpopular with the commercial banks themselves which were unlikely to agree voluntarily to their imposition. The restriction of the credit base is the most effective weapon in the armoury of monetary policy instruments.

Throughout this discussion we have assumed implicitly that a regulatory constraint is 'effective' if its effects are not able to be avoided by a bank. However, this is a stronger assumption than it is really necessary to make. It is the stated purpose of much regulation in this area to influence rather than to formally control bank operations. There is within the US system a widely-regarded 'announcement effect' for changes in the direction of monetary policy and in this, and in many other countries, the public's knowledge of the existence or recent variation of constraints is instrumental in modifying public demand for credit.

There is one further important point which has been glossed over in the above discussion and that is that monetary policy changes either reflect or exacerbate (if not, as Friedman believes, actually cause) the cyclical fluctuations of an economy and, therefore, even if individual constraints may be evaded or their effects minimised, the business of the bank will be reduced by a domestic contraction. This point is of particular relevance to our discussion of diversification by banks, to which we move in the next chapter.

Notes

1. Fischer Black, 'Bank Funds Management in an Efficient Market', *Journal of Financial Economics*, vol.2, no.4 (1975); Fischer Black, 'Banking and Interest Rates in a World without Money', *Journal of Bank Research*, vol.1 (Autumn 1970).

2. Black, 'Bank Funds Management'.

3. Harry G. Johnson, 'Reserve Requirements and Monetary Control', *Economic Council of Canada Discussion Paper No. 66* (October 1976).

4. Ruth Logue, 'Imported Inflation and the International Adjustment Process', PhD thesis, George Washington University, 1969, University Microfilms International, Michigan.

5. J. Tobin, 'Adjustment Responsibilities of Surplus and Deficit Countries' in W. Felher, F. Mochlup, R. Triffin *et al.*, *Maintaining and Restoring Balance of International Payments* (Princeton University Press, Princeton, NJ, 1966).

6. Logue, 'Imported Inflation'.

9 DIVERSIFICATION: DOMESTIC AND INTERNATIONAL

A bank, like other businesses, may find a number of reasons for and a number of methods of diversification. Many commercial banks, originally only concerned with short-term lending, were able to move into the provision of medium and long-term funds as their first form of diversification. A strong reason for diversifying its interests away from pure banking activities does appear to derive from the impact of regulation, because this option allows the bank to reduce the effects of regulatory constraints on its total business without having to reap a subsequent harvest of heavy restrictions. One limitation of importance here is that a bank's operations may be constrained by the terms of its charter or licence; for example, in the United States multistate branching by bank holding companies is restricted by the Bank Holding Company Act of 1970 and activities allowed by bank holding companies in the same Act are those 'closely related to banking or managing or controlling banks'. These limitations may be more apparent than real, for as Nadler[1] describes, bank holding companies have been allowed to make mortgage, finance or factoring loans; act as investment advisers for mortgage and real estate trusts; lease personal property directly or as an agent or broker; provide the services of an insurance agent or broker (so long as they are provided at the holding company's offices); perform trust company functions; provide courier services; provide credit life insurance and credit accident and health insurance which is related directly to the bank holding company's credit extensions; act as management consultants to certain non-affiliated banks; and invest in the equity or debt of corporations or projects primarily devoted to the provision of community welfare.

The American Banker in a series of studies in 1975 of the nationwide operations of large US banks described the extensive operations achieved by these banks in spite of the restrictive branching requirements to which their banking operations were subject. For instance, Citibank had 284 offices in 164 cities in 34 states and the District of Columbia, most of which it gained through consumer finance, mortgage banking and leasing subsidiaries.

Such diversification is justified for reasons other than merely circumventing branching restrictions. By providing services of a financial or related type to its customers a bank is able to secure the continuous patronage of its customers. Several advantages accrue to the bank from the provision of a wide range of services to customers. First, the information costs are reduced in the case of loans made to customers for whom the bank provides other services, because through these other services it will acquire information about its customers. Second, by the provision of wider services to its customers, the more of these services a customer uses, then the less likely it is that the customer will be attracted away by the cheaper provision elsewhere of a single service. This factor is critical where there is significant competition from non-bank financial intermediaries. Third, there may be positive advantages for the bank in providing travel facilities, for example because it acquires the customer's traveller's cheques and foreign currency business at the same time. Fourth, diversification in the form of the provision of other financial services may enable a bank to use its financial expertise to allow flows of funds from these areas to provide a counter-balance to the less stable flows from the regulated area of pure banking.

There are certain possible disadvantages that may occur in consequence of diversification. First, diversification may result in the dilution of management and therefore of control; second, it may result in the dilution of capital; and third, it may impinge on liquidity. These disadvantages occur, however, in the diversification process only if it is poorly handled and it may be argued that the tradition of financial experience in commercial banks will lead them to handle the process of diversification prudently. There is a possibility, however, that additional services provided by a bank in a process of diversification will produce the same result as other forms of non-price competition often produce within oligopolistic industries — that the bank will find itself unable to remove a service, once adopted, for fear of losing a competitive advantage. Care must be taken here to distinguish the provision of services as a principal by comparison with that as an agent. Should a bank feel that too much capital or management is involved in the provision of certain services it is open to it in very many of these areas to continue to offer the service or services as an agent for another enterprise which is mainly in that area of business. This move will minimise cost and management while maintaining the service to manufacturing companies that have themselves diversified overseas.

In the past, unless domestic banks were able to provide a fuller service than merely through correspondent banks abroad, they ran the risk that the correspondent banks would begin to service those needs as a full bank rather than as a correspondent, and the domestic banks might even have lost the business entirely. Of course, this spread into multi-national operations offered other advantages as well; there was little regulation of 'foreign' banks and scarcely any restriction on their range of activities (which explains the tendency for banks operating outside their original domestic base to provide a wider range of services outside), and it was possible to stabilise the flow of funds for the bank as a whole as recourse could be had to several countries for funds, since the cyclical experiences of countries do not necessarily closely coincide even under the managed floating exchange rate system.

Consistently with the earlier discussion (in Part 1) of banking as the provision of a retailed service, it can be seen that both domestic and multinational diversification is the equivalent of providing additional services in response to demand. While some commercial banks were able to become general financial merchants or retailers within their own domestic environment, as were the German 'universal' banks, many more were restricted domestically not only from providing wider services but even in some cases from extending their provision of loans into the long-term area. For the domestic monetary authorities it often seemed unreasonable that banks with a lender of last resort facility available to them in relation to their banking business should attempt to widen the scope of their business beyond pure banking, and, even by implication, carry the privilege of having a lender of last resort facility with them. Their reluctance is reflected in the many legislative prohibitions on the ambit of the operations of banks.

In these circumstances the shaking off of the shackles of both tradition and central bank reluctance very often appeared to be well beyond the patience or the resources of commercial banks, who commonly faced the intrusion of the less shackled or totally unshackled non-bank financial intermediaries into banks' traditional areas and the consequent threat to the volume and profitability of banking. Having diversified domestically as far as was allowed within their domestic environment, the attractions of branching out into other economies and away from at least domestic controls (and usually from discretionary controls entirely) were primarily those of operating as virtually unregulated banks.

As we have noted in the last chapter, the attempt to avoid domestic regulatory controls entirely appears to provide only a very short-run advantage, and we shall investigate in the remaining two Parts the extent to which multinational banks have been able in the past and will be able in the future to avoid regulatory controls.

Note

1. Paul S. Nadler, 'The Territorial Hunger of Our Major Banks', *Harvard Business Review*, vol.52 (March 1974).

Further Reading

Barnes, Burton, 'The Fine Edge of Prohibition: Interstate and Foreign Banking in the United States', *Banking Law Journal*, vol.93, no.8 (September 1976)
Hughes, Evan, 'How Much Diversification?', *Journal of Institute of Bankers* (December 1974)
McLeod, George M. and James E. McGookey, *Travel – A Logical Banking Service*, a Research Study issued jointly by Stonier Graduate School of Banking of the American Bankers Association and the Financial Publishing Co. of Boston (Boston, 1972)

10 CONCLUSION

In this Part we have introduced into our model of the previously un-regulated bank the main forms of regulatory control which were encountered in the survey made in Part 2. Although, as already noted, the problem of discriminating between purely prudential regulations and those used either occasionally or consistently for monetary policy purposes complicates both the identification of the latter and therefore also their effects, it is possible to proceed along the lines followed here and to identify the minimum and maximum effects of the various constraints. Of more importance, however, is a consideration of the effects of combinations of constraints as this is more usually the position in the real world.

It is apparent from the analysis presented that the critical regulatory constraints from the viewpoint of an individual bank are those affecting the quantity of business. Quite apart from the consequences of such constraints on profits, the failure to satisfy the demand (for loans in particular) allows for the growth of other financial intermediaries to satisfy that demand. Owing to our focus here only on commercial banks we have only mentioned in passing the growth of non-bank financial intermediaries, but a moment's reflection will suggest that their presence only heightens the general effects of regulation. That is, the presence of unregulated financial intermediaries will reinforce the tendencies away from price competition and towards non-price competition and will justify banks diversifying into unregulated forms of financial intermediation.

Note that in an unregulated state, banks would supply all of the financial requirements of the community and would not require diversification in order to maintain adequate profit levels. The unregulated state is a least-cost position in comparison with the regulated state, even if we discard the possibility that economies of scale may prevail at the higher volume of business possible in the unregulated state, because non-price competition and product augmentation both have the effect of raising the cost of banking services to customers. If the move to a regulated state has been supported on the grounds that it will reduce the possibility of a monopoly arising in industry, it must be admitted that the costs of the competition permitted under the regulated state may be more expensive than allowing a monopoly.

Of course the bankruptcy constraint, which appears important in the unregulated state, is virtually removed under most systems of regulation by the central bank's provision of a lender of last resort facility, although the prudential regulation which forms the basis for this provision might be matched by a voluntary deposit insurance scheme in an unregulated banking industry.

While we have shown dubious regard for the argument that regulation may be avoided entirely and successfully within a domestic economy, there is no doubt that a major impetus towards multinational banking has been given by the absence of regulation for 'foreign' banks in many economies.

It is quite inadequate to regard multinational banks as simply the original domestic bank operating similarly in more countries. In terms of our earlier discussion of banking as the retailing of services, it may be said that banks add additional services in order to serve new markets. In serving these new markets, different types of risk become important, and it is to a discussion of these in particular that we turn in the next Part.

Part 4

THE MOVE TO MULTINATIONAL BANKING

'In the aftermath of the shocks of 1974, the collapse of Herstatt, the consolidation of the OPEC cartel and the phenomenon of recession and inflation at the same time, 1975 was a year of major adjustments in our business.' (Robert N. Bee, 'Looking Ahead in International Banking', *Journal of Commercial Bank Lending*, March 1976, p.31.)

1 INTRODUCTION

To this point this book has been concerned with the operations of domestic banks within their own frontiers. In this Part the move to multinational banking is examined in some detail. For most domestic banks their first experience in transactions external to their country of operation came through their dealings in foreign exchange, and in the financing of trade for their domestic customers. That is, the base from which most multinational banking operations developed was their own customers' foreign exchange and trade requirements in other countries.

Although the base has been usually the same, different circumstances have led the domestic banks of different countries to move to multi-nationalism at different paces and by different methods. This move is explored for four economies, Norway, the Netherlands, Japan and the United Kingdom, in the second chapter in this Part. From this exploration it is evident that, while the type of overseas operation preferred has been primarily determined by the individual bank's experience in international transactions, the timing and extent of the move have been primarily influenced by domestic restrictions.

In considering the nature of multinational banking we are not forced to move away from the retailing paradigm. In fact, the very diversity of the forms of multinational banking supports the idea that banks, as retailers of services in differing localities, choose to provide that mix of services which is most appropriate for each particular location. At the end of the earlier chapter on banking as the retailing of services, the point was made that production theory and portfolio theory could yield useful insights into particular types of banking operations.

A case in point within the multinational banking arena is the type of consortium bank which is concerned with the management of loan port-folios and investments on a multi-country basis, using the European financial markets as its main area of operation. To the extent that these markets are efficient capital markets, portfolio theory is the appropriate paradigm. In the present study, however, the main concern is with the wide area covered by multinational banking, so that we do not pursue the development of this paradigm.

Following the discussion of the creation and main forms and operations of multinational banking, attention is directed in the remainder of this Part to particular aspects of the operation of multinational banks which differ from those of most purely domestic banks. A major part of multinational banking comprises banking within host-country markets. However, these operations bear quite a close resemblance to the domestic-base operations. The main distinction drawn is often that in host-countries they tend to provide wholesale banking functions, but this does less than justice to the differentiations in services provided in various markets. These differentiations are matched by those provided by a number of purely domestic banks within their own markets.

The particular aspects of host-country banking that differ from those of purely domestic banks are most clearly instanced by the operations of banks within the Euromarkets. As these activities are the subject of present moves towards prudential regulation, to which purely domestic banks are already subject, it is thought that examining the main aspects of these operations, and the risks involved, would be of interest and use.

We begin by examining roll-over risk and mismatching, which earlier studies allege comprise the main risk area for the Eurobanks. We are able to show that this risk is more apparent than real for the core of the market, although it may be more critical for the peripheral participants.

Of more importance to all multinational banks, not only to those operating within the Euromarkets, are the several aspects of foreign exchange risk, specifically banking risk, currency risk, country risk and sovereign risk. Normally the first two might be classified as short-term and the latter two as longer-term risks. Information flows and the management problems of these banks are also discussed.

A very elementary diagrammatic illustration of some aspects of multinational bank operations is provided to draw attention to those areas of risk considered to be particular to these banks. That is, it is intended to provide a contrast with the model of the purely domestic bank and to emphasise a critical point for the potential regulators of multinational banks, that they are likely to be as vulnerable to price regulations as domestic banks have conventionally been to quantitative regulations. This distinction may lead to quite disastrous results if regulations are imposed without taking it into account.

2 FROM INTERNATIONAL TO MULTINATIONAL BANKING

'The foreign expansion of a nation's banks is bound up with
the extension of its foreign trade, and consequently the commercial banks have been the principal ones to expand abroad.'
(C. W. Phelps, *The Foreign Expansion of American Banks*,
1927 (Arno Press Reprint, New York, 1976), p.vii.)

International banking activities are carried on by domestic banks in
most countries of the world through their dealings in foreign exchange
and the financing of foreign trade. As a general rule banks meet the
requirements of their domestic customers' foreign exchange and trade
dealings through the use of the services of their networks of overseas
correspondents. The correspondent bank, usually a bank native to the
foreign market but sometimes the branch of a larger bank in that foreign
market, agrees to act as agent and divides the commission on transactions with the originating bank. It is usual for the correspondent
relationship to exist where the amount of business involved is neither
very substantial nor continuous and in such cases the originating bank
is able, without undertaking the expense of setting up its own branches
in every country with which its customers have business, to take advantage of its correspondents' local knowledge and expertise.

Quite often, although a domestic bank will operate through a wide
network of correspondent banks, it may have more continuous business
with a few foreign cities and decide to locate representatives there. It
has been accurately said that representative offices are service stations
rather than branches which do not accept deposits nor compete with
native banks for banking business, but rather provide a liaison service
with correspondents, keep the originating bank supplied with information about foreign exchange and local conditions, and provide both
assistance and information to customers of the originating bank passing
through the city.

Where the business transacted by a domestic bank with a particular
foreign country becomes substantial but the originating bank is reluctant
to establish a subsidiary or branch there, a stronger connection than is
possible with either correspondents or representatives may be achieved
by securing a commandite or an affiliate interest in that country. Foreign
expansion is achieved by the commandite method when an originating

bank buys an interest, usually a controlling interest, in a bank domestic to the foreign market in which it wishes to accommodate expanding business. In acquiring a commandite, the originating bank obtains simple and cheap access to foreign markets and is able to restrict the risk of its foreign operations to the capital invested to obtain its interest in the foreign bank. There may be further advantages to the commandite method if the country in which an interest is to be obtained has restricted the establishment of branch banks or placed branches at a substantial tax disadvantage with local banks.

The most serious problem encountered in attempting to expand abroad by the commandite method is that many countries prohibit the acquisition of domestic commercial banks by foreign interests, although many allow this type of acquisition to occur in the case of merchant banks and non-bank financial intermediaries. Foreign countries are less inhibited about entry where the interest obtained in a foreign commercial bank is small and not able to be used as a means of eventually gaining control. This latter process establishes an affiliate for the originating bank in the foreign country concerned without providing control over the affiliate's affairs.

Whether a commandite or an affiliate relationship is established the originating bank gains an interest in the foreign country, but due to its distance from the management of its interest it may find that this lack of an administrative connection is not in its own interests. This is not necessarily a problem if the main purpose of acquiring the interest is merely to allow access to funds from the foreign country at the lower rates applicable to a well-established domestic bank, but should the originating bank wish to direct its foreign operations the establishment of subsidiaries or branches would be more appropriate.

A form of affiliate operation favoured by a number of foreign banks wishing to enter the USA has been the establishment of broker-dealer security operations in New York. From these affiliates foreign banks are not only able to acquire first-hand information about the US capital markets, but also may be able to participate in the underwriting and' trading of securities (a practice which domestic US banks are stopped from combining with banking under the Glass-Steagall Act) and in the provision of merger and investment services to both US and foreign clients. Where foreign banks service clients with substantial investments in US securities and very little interest in commodities this is probably the ideal form of representation for a foreign bank to have overseas.

Any banking contact short of a subsidiary or branch may be sufficient when a bank's customers have only intermittent foreign transactions, but when customers expand their own businesses overseas and banks wish to follow in order to meet their customers' requirements there is a strong case for establishing subsidiaries or branches. The distinction between a subsidiary and a branch is that the former, like a correspondent bank, a commandite, or an affiliate, is legally distinct from the parent bank, while the latter is not a separate institution and is regarded as an integral part of the parent bank. In other words, to deal with a subsidiary is to deal with an institution distinct from its parent bank, but to deal with a branch is to deal with the parent bank itself.

A subsidiary, as a separately incorporated entity even if wholly owned by its parent bank, is usually chartered in its country of operation. The risk for the parent bank is normally limited by the amounts invested in the subsidiary itself. Subsidiaries normally perform all the business usually performed by the banks native to the place of their establishment and, therefore, do compete with the domestic banks. Certain state regulations within the USA, which either prevent foreign banks from establishing branches or place them at a disadvantage *vis-à-vis* domestic banks, have encouraged the establishment of state-chartered subsidiaries by foreign banks. One form of subsidiary which is owned by a number of banks is the consortium bank which is the subject of a later chapter.

For a foreign bank wishing to operate within the USA there is an important taxation distinction made between foreign branches and foreign subsidiaries. A branch is able to remit profits to its head office without incurring any additional US tax liability, but a US subsidiary of a foreign corporation must withhold tax at the rate of 30 per cent on dividends paid to its foreign parent where the foreign parent is not itself engaged in business in the United States. Within the United States a subsidiary of a foreign bank does, to some degree, involve its parent bank as well as itself in meeting some provisions of the Bank Holding Company Act and some regulations of the Board of Governors of the Federal Reserve System.

In the case of consortium banks and other forms of subsidiaries operating within the United Kingdom, parent banks have been required to provide certain guarantees concerning their support for their subsidiaries. In these circumstances the parent bank's risk in the operations of its foreign subsidiaries cannot be restricted simply to its investment and, commensurately, the advantages of a subsidiary over a branch are reduced.

Of course, a major case for preferring the subsidiary type of relationship may be reluctance on the part of the parent bank to accept complete responsibility for the operations of an enterprise over which direct control is very difficult to enforce, not merely due to distance but to the often quite different commercial environment of a foreign country. In these circumstances the different nature of the expertise required in the operations of the subsidiary, by comparison with that available in the parent bank, may lead to the latter making inappropriate risk estimates of the subsidiary enterprise. Here a limit on the parent company's risk to the extent of its investment, such as offered *prima facie* by the subsidiary form of organisation, appears a reasonable alternative for a parent bank. If this advantage is eliminated by the monetary authorities of host countries, perhaps the consortium bank type of subsidiary would have heightened appeal, with the risks divided among a number of parent banks.

Within the USA, those foreign banks which want to provide retail banking services including the acceptance of deposits from the public usually establish a state-chartered banking subsidiary which is on equal terms with regard to both powers and restrictions with domestic banks.

Branches are the more usual form of organisation for foreign banks wishing to provide wholesale banking facilities within the USA. Branch banks constitute the maximum intrusion possible for a foreign bank into the banking sector of a host country since branches are integral parts of the parent bank. It is usual for branches to be able to provide the full range of banking services, although within the United States branches of foreign banks have tended to restrict themselves to the provision of wholesale services. In contrast Eurobanks tend to have both investment and commercial banking objectives.

Stuart Robinson in his study *Multinational Banking*[1] notes four main reasons for the establishment of foreign branches rather than some alternative form of representation by US banks. First, he suggests that the guarantee provided to branch depositors by the asset structure of the parent bank may be important for wholesale banking operations; second, that large corporate customers may be attracted to a branch on the grounds that it should be able to marshall more funds for lending; third, that a parent bank is able to exercise 'maximum effective control' over a branch; and finally that this is the traditional pattern of overseas expansion by banks. Robinson is unable to find much support for this last argument, although one possible line of support may be derived from the requirement that where a foreign bank establishes a branch within the US there must be reciprocity for US banks in that country. This requirement would seem to imply that no impediments would inhibit the establishment of branch banks in these reciprocal countries, although there may be restrictions on other forms of representation by banks.

This tradition suggests that less prior investigation may be necessary for the establishment of a branch than other forms of representation.

There is an implication from the above discussion that multinational banks are merely the extension of the operations of an originally purely domestic bank to a number of countries, but, as we shall see later in this Part, this implication does less than justice to the multiplicity of multinational banking operations. Before looking further at the nature of multinational banking, in the next chapter we examine in more detail the move to multinationalism by the banks of four economies, in order to demonstrate that the timing of the move tends to vary in response to domestic developments.

Note

1. S. Robinson Jun., *Multinational Banking* (A. W. Sijthoff, Leiden, 1972).

Further Reading

Phelps, C. W., *The Foreign Expansion of American Banks*, 1927 (Arno Press Reprint, New York, 1976)

3 MOVING INTO MULTINATIONAL BANKING

'The rapid pace of expansion in international banking has transformed the world's principal commercial banks into truly multinational enterprises.' (George W. Mitchell, 'How the Fed sees Multinational Bank Regulation', *The Banker*, 1973, p.757.)

While the motives for moving to a multinational form of operations have been discussed in very general terms earlier in this Part, in this chapter we examine a little more closely this move by the banks of four economies – Norway which is a small rather open economy, the Netherlands, a medium-sized economy, and Japan and the UK, both larger, open economies. It is hoped that this examination will shed further light on the particular circumstances which have encouraged domestic banks to move into a multinational sphere of operations. Although undoubtedly the move has been made by banks based in very many countries, the timing in particular cases often varies owing to domestic developments.

Owing to the significance of international trade for the Norwegian economy, a system of correspondent banks dates from early times for the Norwegian banks. The oldest of the overseas banking establishments, in which Norwegian banks still participate, was established in Zurich in 1958. It was Finanzierungsgesellschaft Viking in which Bergens Privatbank was the original Norwegian shareholder, later joined by Felleshanken and Andresens Bank. Six years later in 1964 Bergens Privatbank participated in the establishment of the Banque Scandinave en Swisse in Geneva and Den norske Creditbank in the establishment of Nordfinanz-Bank Zurich in Zurich. In 1967 Den norske Creditbank bought equity in the Paris-based Banque Nordique de Commerce, Paris, which later became the Manufacturers Hanover Banque Nordique. It was not until 1970, however, that Norwegian banks participated in completely Nordic-owned banks and not until May 1973 that a completely Norwegian-owned bank was established abroad, when Christians Bank og Kreditkasse International SA was established in Luxembourg as a subsidiary of Christians Bank og Kreditkasse.

Although the shipping sector has traditionally been the sector of the Norwegian economy most involved internationally, it appears that the services of correspondent banks were sufficient to provide the necessary banking facilities without encouraging the Norwegian banks to move into

292

other forms of international representation. The catalyst for increased participation in banking abroad appears to have been the significant expansion of manufacturing activity abroad, while the catalyst for the establishment of fully owned subsidiaries abroad seems to have been the oil activity in the North Sea.

The argument that both of these areas could have been effectively serviced by the existing domestic banks may be countered by two other arguments, one of general relevance, the second relating to the particular conditions under which Norway's domestic banks operate. The more general argument is that manufacturing industry in an overseas expansion normally requires from its bank both services and information in those foreign countries which, if not provided by a branch, affiliate or subsidiary of the domestic bank, are likely to be obtained from a bank local to each foreign country, with consequent loss of business for the domestic bank. A correspondent bank could readily become the bank used in its own right by a manufacturing company.

The second argument is that because of certain provisions of the Norwegian Monetary and Credit Policy Act, it is difficult for Norwegian banks to provide international banking services at rates competitive to those of external banks. Specifically, the Monetary and Credit Policy Act 1965 provides that banks must hold a stipulated proportion of their total assets in very liquid form and that they are obliged to maintain a significant holding of low-yielding Norwegian government bonds and other Norwegian bearer bonds in proportion to their total assets.

The Norwegian banks themselves argued in 1972 that the consequence of these two requirements was that they had to hold a larger part of their total resources in low interest-bearing assets than did banks based in other countries and that this weakened their competitive position in relation to these foreign banks, not only by making loans from Norwegian banks relatively more expensive but also by reducing their ability to attract the placement of funds by the business sector.

The first of the Norwegian banks' moves abroad was for the particular purpose of financing Norwegian shipping (Finanzierungsgesellschaft Viking) and a later venture involving Den norske Creditbank, Ship Mortgage International established in Amsterdam in 1968, had the same rationale. Other moves appear to have the servicing of other areas of the Norwegian economy, in particular manufacturing, in mind.

Joint ventures with other banks were the logical form for initial moves abroad to take in the light of the lack of experience of the Norwegian banks in operating outside their own economy. Once some experience was gained from participation in joint venture operations, the lack of direct control over joint venture operations became a relevant factor, for the larger banks in particular, in the move to establish wholly owned subsidiaries, sometimes owned by one Norwegian bank, sometimes by several Norwegian banks with one of them as majority shareholder.

A further feature of Norwegian banking legislation inhibited any moves there might have been to establish branches in other countries, that feature being that a branch, as an integral part of the parent bank, would be subject to the same requirements of liquidity reserves and bond investment as the parent bank. Subsidiaries would not be subject to these requirements.

The causes of the shift from basing overseas ventures of joint or single form in Switzerland to basing them in Luxembourg in particular from 1973 onwards, rather than basing them in London as many other banks have done, relate to market access and to regulatory requirements. Switzerland was a centre for long-term capital in Europe in the late 1950s but during the 1960s the growth of the Eurodollar market made London a much more important centre. Luxembourg, as well as allowing access to the Eurodollar market as London would, has the other advantage of minimal banking legislation and, therefore, minimal requirements of the banks establishing subsidiaries there.

Direct investment in other countries by Norwegian companies and individuals has always required the permission of the foreign exchange authorities. Norges Bank has been given the authority to make these decisions by the Ministry of Commerce. Minority interests in foreign banks or other financial institutions only required this permission for direct investment, but the establishment of wholly owned subsidiaries brought Section 9 of the Commercial Bank Act into operation. This requires a bank to obtain permission from the King to establish a branch outside its home municipality. Each case is decided individually by the Ministry of Finance, having consulted with Norges Bank and the State Inspectorate of Banks. Since Christians Bank og Kreditkasse obtained permission in 1973 no bank has been refused permission.

In contrast to Norway's quite recent foray into multinational banking, Dutch banks have a much longer history of multinational activities. Algemene Bank Nederland's ancestor, the Netherlands Trading Society established by King William I in the nineteenth century, opened its first office in Batavia (now Jakarta) and from there developed a network of representation in Asia. Before their nationalisation by the Indonesian government, the Bank had more than twenty branches within Indonesia.

Several of Algemene Bank Nederland's mergers have assisted its development of a wide overseas network. For example, Hollandsche Bank-Unie, which it acquired in 1968, had sixteen branches in South America, while the Mees and Hope Group, acquired in 1975, had African interests concentrated in the Commercial Bank of Zambia and was a partner in a Singapore merchant bank and in an Indonesian merchant bank with Morgan Guaranty. In its own right Algemene Bank Nederland (ABN) has usually made its overseas expansion in its own name and with complete control of the enterprises in question. It has, however, joined a group called Associated Banks of Europe Corporation (ABECOR) in Brussels, the other members of which are Dresdner Bank, Bayerische Hypotheken-und Wechsel-Bank and Banque de Bruxelles. ABECOR has established an investment bank in the USA.

The second of the large Dutch banks, Amsterdam-Rotterdam Bank (AMRO), originated from the merger of two almost entirely domestic banks which had normally used foreign banks as correspondents. Amsterdamsche Bank, prior to its 1964 merger with Rotterdamsche Bankvereeniging to form AMRO, had been working with other European banks in the European Advisory Committee and AMRO became a member of EBIC (European Banks International Company), the first of the European consortium banks which resulted from the Advisory Committee. EBIC established the Australian Euro-Pacific Finance Corporation and the European-Asian Bank, among other enterprises.

Even the large bank, Rabobank, a combination of agricultural co-operative banks, with no history of international activities, began to develop international connections in the seventies, establishing Rabomerica International Bank in partnership with the Bank of America with a capital of 40 million US dollars, and combining with other European co-operative banks in the establishment of London and Continental Bankers, a London-based merchant bank.

As with the Netherlands' banks, multinational movements by the British clearing banks have not taken by any means the same form. The multinational operations of Barclays Bank date from the 1920s when it founded a new bank, Barclays Bank Dominion, Colonial and Overseas which amalgamated the operations of the Colonial Bank, the Anglo-Egyptian Bank and the National Bank of South Africa. The new bank operated extensive branch networks in Africa, in particular in South Africa and Nigeria. Barclays also operated a subsidiary, Barclays Bank SA in France, had a majority holding in a Swiss bank and was represented by a number of branches in the Caribbean from the 1920s onward. Further moves by Barclays into Europe occurred in the early 1960s but it was not until 1972 that it was able to provide full banking services in

Belgium, the Netherlands and Italy.

In 1965 a new subsidiary, Barclays Bank California, was established in California which extended its operations to forty offices in California and one in the Cayman Islands. A planned takeover of the twenty-nine branch Long Island Trust Company in 1973 was frustrated by the US authorities. Barclays was, however, allowed to take over a smaller bank in New York State which was re-named Barclays Bank of New York and now has twenty-five offices in that state.

Most of Barclays Bank's overseas ventures are wholly or almost wholly owned by the parent bank including ventures in Africa, Jamaica, Australia, Belgium (hire purchase and personal loans) and Canada. Other interests in which Barclays has a majority holding include Israel, Trinidad and Tobago, Swaziland, Netherlands Antilles and Egypt. In addition Barclays has some interests in consortium banks with specialised interests, for example the International Energy Bank and the Iran Overseas Investment Bank.

In contrast, the Midland Bank has been the pioneer of the modern consortium banking movement, beginning with the Midland and International Banks Ltd (MAIBL) in 1964 and going on to participate in the European American Banking Corporation in 1968, in the European Banks International Company in 1970 and in similar area-based ventures, the Banque Européene pour l'Amérique Latine and the Euro-Pacific Finance Corporation. It was not until 1973 that the Midland Bank began to establish its own representation in Belgium and later Japan and in 1975 it purchased a shareholding in the Standard Chartered Bank of South Africa.

Lloyds Bank's main international thrust began with its 1955 purchase of the National Provincial Bank's holding in their joint venture, Lloyds and National Provincial Foreign Bank which had a minor European branch network. In 1966 Lloyds purchased the National Bank of New Zealand and in 1971 Lloyds Bank (Europe) merged with the British Bank of London and South America to form Lloyds and BOLSA International, more than half-owned by Lloyds. Following the renaming of Lloyds and BOLSA as Lloyds Bank International the bank extended its interests into the USA and South East Asia. Through its international arm, Lloyds has branches in Egypt, West Germany, Japan, Singapore, Belgium, France and Monaco as well as in Central America, Latin America and the Caribbean.

When National Provincial sold its share of the international joint venture to Lloyds in 1955 it was left without overseas interests other than one of its parent bank's, the Westminster Bank's limited European representation. Since then it has participated in the Orion consortium, in the Roy West Banking Corporation based in the Bahamas, and, through the International Westminster Bank, it has branches in the Bahamas, Belgium, France, West Germany, Greece, Japan, Singapore and the USA as well as representative offices in Australia, Bahrain, Canada, Hong Kong, Spain and the USSR.

It can be seen from the timing patterns of multinational spread for the Netherlands and British banks that the sixties and the seventies have seen the most extensive movement abroad in both cases. Now all of the large banks have multinational representations. The banks which have moved more recently abroad have tended to use the consortium and other participatory forms to a greater extent than those with a longer history of international representation.

In 1960 Japan's banks had only twenty overseas branches with the main overseas ventures of large Japanese banks then being the Bank of Tokyo's 70 per cent interest in the New York based Bank of Tokyo Trust Co., and 50.3 per cent of the San Francisco based Bank of Tokyo in California; Fuji Bank's small interests in South America; Sumitomi Bank of California (57.3 per cent holding) based in San Francisco and its 15 per cent interest in the City Bank of Honolulu.

The common pattern of international spread, the establishment of offices overseas to cater for the needs of domestic corporations expanding overseas, was reflected in Japanese banking interests overseas until the mid-1960s. Overseas operations were primarily concerned with foreign exchange business and short-term finance for trade transactions. Certainly the major concentration of Japanese banks was on coping with a serious shortage of funds in a situation of continuing growth of the economy until the mid-1960s. The Ministry of Finance reinforced this general lack of participation in the growth of world banking with tight control over the foreign exchange transactions of banks and the Ministry's preference for the Bank of Tokyo to be involved in most overseas offices because it was the only bank specialising in foreign exchange and servicing the government's overseas financial affairs. A further restraint was the Ministry of Finance preference that the Japanese banks only acquire minor participations in international investment banks.

Increased internationalisation of Japanese banking was, however, encouraged after 1965 by the strong rise in foreign exchange reserves, and in the early seventies Japanese banks began to pursue three new approaches to this area: the establishment of local companies as in California and Hong Kong; the establishment of joint ventures with local participation; and participation in wider multinational banks.

Japanese international investment banks have been another significant development since the Banque Européenne de Tokyo SA was established by the Bank of Tokyo in Paris in November 1968 and six other Japanese banks became shareholders in 1969. Three banks, the Sanwa, the Mitzui and the Dai-Ichi Kengyo Banks combined with Nomura Securities to form the Associated Japanese Bank (International) Ltd in 1970.

Main areas of interest for the joint ventures by Japanese banks in partnership with local companies were Australia, where merchant banks have been established (foreign banks may not operate as trading banks in Australia); South-East Asia, particularly Bangkok, Hong Kong, and Singapore; and Sao Banks in Brazil. Participation by Japanese banks in consortium banks have included Mitsubishi's interest in the Orion group and Sumitomi in the Société Financielle Européenne (SFE) based in Luxembourg.

The Japanese interest in ship-building has been supported by an investment bank sponsored by Dai-Ichi Kengyo Bank to finance ships built for export and the formation of an international ship-leasing company in Kogin.

It is apparent from this survey of the move to multinational banking in four economies that the type of overseas operations domestic banks have opted for has depended on their own experience in international transactions. The timing of the move and the extent of the overseas spread have been primarily influenced by domestic restrictions.

For banks with little previous international experience the consortium approach appears to offer several advantages and it is to this particular form of multinational banking that we turn in the next chapter.

Further Reading

Channon, Derek F., *British Banking Strategy and the Challenge* (Macmillan, London, 1977)

Gordon, Cadogan A., 'British Banking in New York', *The Banker* (July 1969)

'How British Strategies Differ', *The Banker* (August 1974)

Iwasa, Yoshizane, 'Japan Ventures into Southeast Asia', *Columbia Journal of World Business* (November-December 1967)

Juel, Steiner, 'Norwegian Banks Abroad', *Norges Bank Economic Bulletin*, vol.47, no.3 (September 1976)

Komatsubara, T., 'Overseas Activities of Japanese Banks', *The Banker* (May 1970)

'Multinationalization of Japanese firms – (4) Banking and Securities', *The Oriental Economist* (March 1973)

Nishiyama, S., 'Internationalization of Banking Business', *Euromoney* (October 1973)

Steuber, Ursel, *International Banking*, English translation, (A. W. Sijthoff-Leyden,

Netherlands, 1976)

Takeuchi, Ichiro, 'Japanese Banks Overseas', *The Bankers Magazine*, vol. 204 (October 1967)

—, 'Japanese Banking Overseas', *Euromoney*, Supplement (March 1972)

4 THE NATURE OF MULTINATIONAL BANKING

'The need to provide comprehensive banking services for the multinational corporation is producing structural changes in the banking world along yet another dimension: a tendency to move away from traditional specialization towards a 'supermarket' approach to banking.' (Thibaut de Saint-Phalle and John Heptonstall, 'International Banking Services in Europe — a User's View', *Euromoney*, February 1973, pp.4-5.)

In Part 1 the view was advanced that domestic banking could be most appropriately considered as the retailing of services. This view is further supported when applied to multinational banking, although multinational banking has even very recently been described as taking three quite separate forms. It is implicit in the description of the movement from international to multinational banking that the early activities of multinational banks derived from the needs of the multinational manufacturers that the banks crossed frontiers to continue to serve. Having moved into multinational operations it quickly became obvious to the banks concerned that they were able to by-pass some of the limitations on their operations imposed by regulation within their original domestic environment. For example, US-based banks were able to escape from their domestic restrictions and move into the investment banking field abroad. Among the reasons why banks operating multinationally have found it not only possible but also advantageous to offer a wider range of services than they did within their original domestic operation are: purely regulatory differences between domestic banks and foreign banks operating within the same country (usually involving the exclusion of foreign banks from some forms of regulation including deposit insurance); the ability of multinational banks to base their operations in countries where there are tax savings; and genuine economies derived from increasing the average size of transactions and thereby lowering transaction costs.

While moving into multinational operations enabled some banks at least to escape from the limitations of their domestic environment, there was an off-setting disadvantage to be overcome, that of additional competition. At first, as happened when the US banks began to increase their business within Britain in the 1960s, the multinationals added a competitive edge to the market into which they moved. Subsequently

300

the reaction of local banks increased the competitiveness of the markets.

It is reasonable to describe the multinational banks as the new generation of banks, in the sense that they are able to provide a wider range of services than the purely domestic banks of most countries. Although attempts have been made to divide multinational banks into wholesale, retail and service types,[1] this distinction seems to do less than justice to the wide range of functions performed by many multinational banks. The basic definition of multinational banking, that it is the operating of a bank within a number of different countries, perhaps only needs variation to the extent of incorporating the point made by Stuart Robinson[2] (pp.10-11) that, certainly in the case of the USA, the commercial banks have been the most active participants in the field of multinational banking. This point was also made apparent in the last chapter's discussion about the move from international to multinational banking and its obvious commercial bank base domestically.

Nevertheless the nature of the services offered by a bank operating multinationally tend to be of wider scope than those of their originating domestic banks, both in the time-span of lending and in the services provided. A bank moving into multinational operations may take the opportunity to diversify into investment banking activities such as dealing in securities; it may develop specialist financial expertise in such areas as shipping; it may become a participant within international interbank markets and deal in spot and forward exchange markets for a number of currencies on its own account and on behalf of clients; it may move into the management and underwriting of bonds and long-term loans; and it may develop innovative methods of financing for the benefit of multinational companies.

Within the Eurocurrency markets the banks could place surplus funds in the inter-bank markets; participate in Eurocurrency syndicated loans as leaders or as syndicate members: extend their lending on a rollover or fixed rate basis to governments or their instrumentalities as well as to individuals and to corporations; extend their operations into Eurobonds, by underwriting and selling or by fulfilling the function of a secondary market; arrange the multi-currency placements of fixed-rate debt; and provide lease and export finance as well as portfolio management for international markets.

There is perhaps more scope still for the development away from those tasks detailed above, which tend to fall into the two categories of credit extension and money movement, and into the area of financially oriented company services. Examples of such services include the legal, fiscal and financial structuring of international operations, the development of international cash management systems, the provision of project manager services, and the identification, evaluation and negotiation of acquisitions, mergers and joint ventures.

This provision of comprehensive services of wider scope than the original domestic banks' is partly generated by the wide-ranging demands of multinational corporations, but also, at least partly, by the banks' increasing need to diversify their services sufficiently to prevent potential customers from merely shopping around for the lowest price of finance. Further, operating multinationally, besides providing greater opportunities for diversification and the spreading of risk, enables banks to transact in such a way as to minimise the effects that a down-turn in any single country of operation might have on their overall operations. It may be argued that this latter strategy may be less effective in the future: the changed international monetary system may result in a more synchronised tendency for business cycles in at least the developed economies.

In terms of the view taken of domestic bank operations, that they are in essence the retailing of services, the move to multinational operations may be interpreted as a move away from the traditional specialisation of those services, often reinforced by legislation in the country of origin, towards the provision of supermarket or universal banking services.

Notes

1. H. Grubel, 'A Theory of Multinational Banking', *Banca Nazionale del Lavoro Quarterly Review* (March 1978).

2. Stuart Robinson, *Multinational Banking* (A. W. Sijthoff, Leiden, 1972).

5 CONSORTIUM BANKING

'Many consortium banks were founded with a particular objective in view only to develop in an adjacent but somewhat
different direction.' (S. M. Yassukovich, 'Consortium Banks
on Course', *The Banker*, February 1976, p.167.)

It is necessary, first of all, to distinguish between a consortium of banks
and a consortium bank. A consortium of banks, that is, a group of banks
each operating in its own name, may combine to finance a particular
loan transaction. In contrast, a consortium bank is a pooling of some
resources of several banks, usually based on doing business in a number
of countries, to form a separate entity, in which no bank will hold over
45 per cent share-holding, to operate within a defined area or to provide a particular service or services. Although a number of consortium
banks have created some innovative borrowing devices, consortium
banks as a group do not offer unique services. The consortium banks
are a rather heterogeneous collection in terms of their styles of operation and the range of services they offer, but many modern consortium
banks were established to provide medium-term Eurodollar loans.

As already mentioned, the switch in the US role from largest debtor
to major creditor in the world economy, which coincided with the
authority given by the Federal Reserve Bank of 1913 to national banks
to form overseas branches and to accept foreign drafts, resulted in
expansion of the overseas activities of US banks. In a study of this
expansionary movement, Clyde Phelps[1] noted that American foreign
banking corporations formed by a large number of US interests included
Continental Banking and Trust Company of Panama, Mercantile Bank
of America, American Foreign Banking Corporation and the Bank of
Central and South America. Of these, the American Foreign Banking
Corporation was a clear precursor of the modern consortium bank.

The American Foreign Banking Corporation, incorporated in New
York State in 1917, had thirty-four US and one Canadian bank as shareholders. It established seventeen foreign branches, mostly in Europe
and Latin America, and acquired two further Latin American branches
from the Commercial National Bank of Washington, D.C. During 1922
it disposed of all of its branches except for three which were subsequently acquired in 1925 by the Chase National Bank of New York,
one of AFBC's original shareholders.

Although the eighty-one foreign branches were established and two were acquired by the American foreign banking corporations listed above, by 1927 those subsidiaries not already liquidated (mostly voluntarily) had been absorbed by the US banks themselves. While Phelps attributes this lack of success to the unduly rapid expansion and to the lack of trained management personnel, H. P. Willis writing in 1925[2] (p.164) commented:

> It soon appeared that the bank shareholders in such institutions were inclined to suspect one another, or to fear that through some lack of loyalty one or other of them would be disadvantaged through the knowledge of transactions or operations gained by the foreign trade bank in which it took stock and to which it agreed to shift presumably much of its foreign business. This factor, therefore, operated quite as strongly as any other in retarding the success of the proposed system of foreign trade banks.

Regular co-operation between banks on an international level did of course occur between the 1920s and 1963, but the first of the modern consortium banks could be said to have been established by the 1963 agreement between the Midland Bank, Amsterdamsche-Bank (subsequently Amsterdam-Rotterdam Bank), Banque de la Société Générale, Banca Commerciale Italiana, Société Générale de Banque and Creditanstalt Bankverein which set up the European Banks International Company in Brussels for the purpose of providing medium-term Eurodollar loans to European industry.

The organisation usually regarded as the pioneer of modern consortium banking, certainly for the medium-term Eurocurrency market, is the Midland and International Bank, known as MAIBL, established in London in 1964 with four partners, Midland Bank (45 per cent), Toronto Dominion (26 per cent), the Commercial Bank of Australia (10 per cent) and the Standard Bank of South Africa (19 per cent). In 1967 the Société Financière Européenne was set up in Paris to provide medium and long-term loans to European-based multinational companies. Its participants were Algemene Bank Nederland NU (16.65 per cent), Banca Nazionale del Lavoro (16.65 per cent), Bank of America (16.65 per cent), Banque Nationale de Paris (16.65 per cent), Barclays Bank (16.65 per cent) and Dresdner Bank AG (16.65 per cent). Even more widely based in its shareholding was the International Commercial Bank (announced in June 1967) which was based in London. Commerzbank AG (12 per cent), The First National Bank of Chicago (22 per cent), the Hong Kong and Shanghai Banking Corporation (22 per cent), Irving Trust Company (22 per cent) and National Westminster Bank Ltd (22 per cent) were its shareholders and its main function was the provision of medium-term sterling, dollar and Eurocurrency lending.

Bank of America together with Banque Lambert, Banque Nationale de Paris and Commerzbank AG formed United Overseas Bank SA in Geneva in December 1960, and World Banking Corporation in Nassau in 1963 with its above three partners and F. Van Lanschot, Skandinaviska Banken and Toronto Dominion Bank.

Banks based in New York, Lausanne, Paris, Luxembourg, Brussels, Oslo, Dusseldorf, Milan, Liverpool, Geneva and Stockholm formed the Lausanne-based Compagnie Internationale de Crédit à Moyen Terme in July 1967 to underwrite medium-term promissory notes, initially in US dollars, of companies introduced by participating banks and to operate in the secondary market for these notes.

The consortium banks in the medium-term Eurocurrency market arrange Euromoney loans of from two to eight years by placing the borrower's paper with other banks. While this paper is sold without recourse to the bank which made the issue, the issuing bank will try and pitch the rate in order to take the borrower's status into account. Loans are usually on a six-month roll-over basis, with the minimum rate 0.5 per cent over the LIBO rate usually charged to oil companies and a normal prime rate of 0.75 per cent. Several of the consortium banks prefer to make their own loans and Western American Bank tended to take loans itself and then sell off participations in them.

A number of strong advantages may accrue to banks which set up consortium banks but there are also a number of disadvantages. For many banks, even those which are large within their own domestic economy, lack of size and of an extensive and preferably world-wide branch network limit their ability to become multinational on their own account. Those banks whose entire experience has been within a domestic market, and those banks which are state-controlled, have found that participation in a consortium bank overcomes any lack of experience, and in the latter case political problems of embarking on multinational banking in their own right.

One strong justification for consortium banks lies in their specialisation and expertise, since when they concentrate on lending to a particular area they are able to be better informed of both political risks and economic conditions in that area. That lending within Eurocurrency markets particularly is too often made on the basis of reputation and too seldom on the basis of financial analysis and knowledge of the borrower is a common criticism of banking operations in these areas, and makes the case for consortium banks and their increased knowledge in specialised areas much stronger.

It might be argued that the costs of entry to some markets have stimulated the formation of consortium banks, but a better case may be made in terms of the absolute size of loans required in many cases. Ship finance is an obvious example. Although within the Eurocredit market loans of between 50 million dollars and 200 million dollars are quite usual, and while participation and syndication are often used, many banks regard the provision of a loan by a consortium bank as safer because of the latter's relatively large capital base and the substantial resources of its shareholders.

Certain disadvantages which consortium banks may have appear to derive primarily from their parentage. If the parent or shareholder banks interfere too much in the operation, or, on the other hand, if they use the consortium bank as a place into which to unload their less useful executive talent, the bank will find it difficult to run as an efficient organisation. Equally, unless the consortium bank's functions are clearly defined, it may find that it lacks the expertise for the transactions in which it takes part. A bank becoming a partner in a consortium bank should be able to provide expertise either for specialised functions or in particular regions, and these functions ought to be well defined.

Richard Dyson,[3] the deputy chairman of Barclays Bank International, was quoted in the December 1974 issue of *Euromoney*, concerning the problems of consortium banking, which in his view were the loss of individual control over a sector of the participating banks' operations and dissension among partners over major policy decisions. Dyson further commented that cohesion and effective direction were difficult to accomplish when there were a number of banks in a consortium, but that divesting itself of the entanglements of a consortium may be very hard for a bank, particularly if it wishes to maintain cordial relationships with its partners in the enterprise.

Evan Hughes, commenting on the difficulties of Western American Bank (Europe),[4] described the probable fate of a number of consortium banks as a partial dismemberment. In the case of Western American, the bank was finding it either too difficult or too expensive to acquire deposits to fund some of its loans and the parent banks had purchased these loans from the consortium bank. Hughes argues that in such situations the parent banks discover that their obligations reach beyond those of shareholders, when, as they possess a more stable deposit base and can borrow more cheaply, they are able to fund the consortium bank's loans more cheaply than it can and in doing so they acquire the risks and the necessity for credit assessment and other specialised services which they became partners in a consortium to avoid.

An example of the problems that may arise within a consortium, as well as an example of their resolution, is the Orion banking group's experience. The Orion group had been established in 1970 by National Westminster Bank, Chase Manhattan, Mitsubishi Bank, Credito Italiano, the Royal Bank of Canada and the Westdeutsche Landesbank. The Euromarket operating arm of the group, Orion Termbank, London, was set up in 1971 with 21.5 per cent shareholding by each of Chase Manhattan, National Westminster Bank, Royal Bank of Canada and Westdeutsche Landesbank Girozentrale and 7 per cent by each of Credito Italiano and Mitsubishi Bank. Three other operating entities were also established: Orion Bank for investment banking; Orion Pacific which had no shareholding relationship with Orion Bank, and Orion Leasing. This fragmentation of the group into four separate operations, apart from requiring more time and money to organise than a single operation, separated the profitable commercial banking division from the less successful bond market operations.

In 1974 Orion withdrew from making a market in Eurobonds, but it appears to have been the appointment of David Montagu of the UK Samuel Montagu Bank as chairman which most changed the operation of Orion. Montagu's first move was to combine the four areas of operations by merging Orion Bank and Orion Termbank, acquiring the whole shareholding in Orion Leasing and a majority holding in Orion Pacific. This new combined operation eschewed retail banking, bullion dealing and investment management and concentrated on large transactions in developing an investment banking operation on top of its strong and profitable commercial banking base. In combining the investment and commercial banking functions, Orion Bank was able to concentrate the considerable expertise of its staff on large transactions and to make use of its shareholder relations in, for example, lead managing most 1975-6 Canadian dollar issues made from London, in part with the assistance of its shareholder, the Royal Bank of Canada. Montagu is quoted as saying of Orion's operations that

If we want to package and project finance operations from the cradle to the grave we should be able, theoretically, to put together, in house, very substantial syndicated, roll-over bank loans to start with and bond them out in one of six or eight different markets, wherever it's appropriate over the next five years.

The key to success in consortium banking, as in the Euromarkets in general, seems to be dependent on the employment of experts who have substantial personal contacts within the markets, and who will assist the bank to acquire a 'name' in the market on the basis of which lending and syndication is done.

In consequence of the turmoil associated with the failure of the National Bank of San Diego in 1973 and those of Franklin National Bank and Bankhaus I.D. Herstatt in 1974, greater regard was given within the Euromarkets to credit-worthiness. Funding through the inter-bank market had been made at the standard LIBO (London Inter-Bank Offered) rate but the market rearranged its funding into three tiers of operation, differentiated by interest costs. Industry leaders such as Chase Manhattan were able to acquire funds at less than the LIBO rate, while in the second tier most of the large European and US banks were able to acquire funds at the LIBO rate, and in the third tier the new banks, including some Japanese and Italian banks and consortium banks, were asked to pay a premium on the LIBO rate for funds, with the precise premium depending on the reputation of the particular bank.

Because the acceptance of a rate in excess of LIBO was regarded by banks as an admission of relatively lower credit-worthiness, many banks who were rated in the third tier declined to borrow these funds and, as a result, had to cut their growth or acquire funds from their parent banks in the case of some consortium banks such as Western American. Orion Bank alleges that it was spared this problem because the negotiation of its funds was handled by A. J. ('Spike') Wright, an acquisition from its shareholder, National Westminster Bank, who had substantial connections with the London money market.

It is apparent that it must be the essence of successful consortium banking to combine their shareholders' best-qualified personnel in the proposed area of specialisation or to employ personnel who are expert in this area and, in either case, to allow them sufficient resources to compete for business with existing banks.

Hall[5] points to a contrast in the styles of two large consortium banks, Orion and the European Banking Company, although both share a dislike of the appellation 'consortium' sufficiently to have refused to join the London Consortium Banks' Association. The contrast lies in the latter enterprise's concentration on project finance, foreign exchange and floating rate notes, all areas that overlap those of its parent banks, while Orion has established its own identity, within the Eurobond and Eurocredit markets, which is complementary rather than competitive to those of its parent banks. Hall's article begins with the example of

London Multinational Bank, which has just (early 1978) been revamped by its shareholders into a wholly owned merchant banking subsidiary of one of the shareholders, apparently because since the consortium's formation its parent banks had become more knowledgeable and active in the same areas in which the consortium bank operated.

In order to ensure short-term viability and long-term survival it appears that a consortium bank should specialise in a particular area or aspect of operations that may gain clientele for its parents or provide its own clientele with services the consortium's parent banks cannot supply. That is, if its contribution is in general terms complementary to those of its parents and it either provides a satisfactory return on their investment or provides certain services for its parents in the markets, there is considerable long-term potential for the consortium bank.

One final problem, of particular importance in the case of consortium banks, which became apparent in the 1973-4 difficulties, was that of the provision of a lender of last resort in cases where no single central bank appears to be the appropriate authority for a multinational bank. Since this question is of some importance in the more general context of the regulation of multinational banking, its discussion is postponed until the next Part.

In the remainder of this Part attention is turned to particular aspects of the operation of multinational banks which differ from those of most purely domestic banks and which are instanced most clearly by bank operations within the Euromarkets.

Consortium Banks Lists as Contributors to the UK Banking Statistics, October 1977

Anglo-Romanian Bank Ltd
Associated Japanese Bank (International) Ltd
Atlantic International Bank Ltd
Banco Urquijo Hispano Americana Ltd
Banque Française de Crédit Internationale Ltd
Euro-Latinamerican Bank Ltd
European Arab Bank Ltd
European Banking Company Ltd
European Brazilian Bank Ltd
International Commercial Bank Ltd
International Energy Bank Ltd
International Mexican Bank Ltd
Iran Overseas Investment Bank Ltd
Italian International Bank Ltd

Italian International Bank (Channel Island) Ltd
Japan International Bank Ltd
Libra Bank Ltd
London Interstate Bank Ltd
London Multinational Bank Ltd
Midland and International Banks Ltd
Nordic Bank Ltd
Orion Bank Ltd
Orion Bank (Guernsey) Ltd
Saudi International Bank (Al-Bank Al-Saudi Al-Alami Ltd)
Scandinavian Bank Ltd
UBAF Bank Ltd
The United Bank of Kuwait Ltd
United International Bank Ltd
Western American Bank (Europe) Ltd

Notes

1. Clyde Phelps, *The Foreign Expansion of American Banks*, 1st edn 1927 (Arno Press Reprint, New York, 1976).
2. S. Robinson Jun., *Multinational Banking* (A.W. Sijthoff, Leiden, 1972).
3. R. Dyson, Interview in *Euromoney* (December 1974).
4. Evan Hughes, 'A Fresh Look at Consortium Banking', *Journal of the Institute of Bankers* (June 1975).
5. William Hall, 'Consortium Banks Struggle for Survival', *Institutional Investor* (March 1978).

Further Reading

Blanden, Michael, 'Consortium banks – the Honeymoon Is Over', *The Banker* (November 1974)
Burr, Rosemary, 'Consortium Banks at the Crossroads', *The Banker* (November 1977)
Channon, Derek F., *British Banking Strategy and the International Challenge* (Macmillan, London, 1977), ch.9
'Consortium Banks Grow Up', *The Banker* (November 1973)
Faith, Nicholas, 'Consortium Banking at the Crossroads', *Euromoney* (December 1974)
—, 'Profile: David Montagu, Chairman, Orion Bank', *The Bankers Magazine* (February 1975)
Fallon, Padriac, 'How David Montagu Gave a Lead to Orion Bank', *Euromoney* (May 1976)
McDonough, William J., 'Bank Consortium Lending to Developing Countries', *Euromoney* (January 1973)

Overend, Gurney, 'Multinational Consortia Banks', *Euromoney* (September 1970)
Parker, Carol, 'Consortium Banks Find the Going Tough', *Eurofile*, Supplement
　to *The Banker* (April 1978)
Von Clemm, M., 'The Rise of Consortium Banking', *Harvard Business Review*
　(May-June 1971)
Weissmuller, A. A., 'London Consortium Banks', *Journal of the Institute of
Bankers* (August 1974)
'Where Do Consortium Banks Go from Here?', *The Banker* (August 1975)
Yassukovich, S. M., 'Consortium Banks on Course', *The Banker* (February 1976)

6 ROLL-OVER RISK AND MISMATCHING

'The main risk that Eurobanks are likely to face is that of
interest-rate fluctuations if they choose to be unmatched in
the maturity structure of their loans and deposits.' (J. Hewson,
*Liquidity Creation and Distribution in the Eurocurrency
Markets* (Lexington, 1975).)

In order to discuss this aspect of multinational bank operations it is first
of all necessary to outline the system of roll-over credits and the range
of terms on which they may be offered. Roll-over credits are those
medium (occasionally long) term credits with variable interest rates
which are adjusted at agreed intervals to changes in the current market
rates for short-term credits. Primarily if not entirely Eurocurrency loans,
the interest rate cost of these roll-over credits is reviewed usually every
six months and adjusted to moves in the London Inter-Bank Offered
Rate or LIBOR. It is possible for the borrower to choose between several
currencies, to fix the credit in terms of a currency cocktail or composite
currency unit, or he may have an option to change the currency in
which the loan is denominated in order to benefit from more favourable
interest rates. Some roll-over loans also offer the borrower a right to
terminate without incurring a penalty payment and (within the same
agreement) allow the borrower to refinance the loan later if market
conditions become more favourable. Included in the interest rate stated
in the contract is the spread between the basic interest rate and the
interest rate payable by the borrower, which represents the lending
bank's profit margin.

Lenders in the medium-term market are normally banks who have as
their sources of funds short-term Eurocurrency deposits; three to six
month inter-bank loans from other Eurobanks and funds from the issue
of short and medium Eurodollar certificates of deposit (CDs) in London;
short and medium-term Eurodollar notes and medium-term Eurobonds;
and, in the case of consortium banks, lines of credit from their shareholder banks. Although Eurocredit loans may be for amounts of 500,000
US dollars and above, the most common size is from 20 million dollars
to 50 million dollars and, on occasion, upwards of 200 million dollars.
Because the size of the average Eurocredit loan makes it imprudent for
a single bank to take up the whole amount, it is the practice for these
loans to be spread among a number of banks by either the bank which

originates the loan offering participations in it to other banks or selecting members of a syndicate to syndicate the loan while the originating bank acts as manager.

Within their portfolios of loans multinational banks may hold some loan syndications, some loans generated by their own management, and, in the case of consortium banks, loans made available through contacts from shareholder banks. The banks will, of course, want a diversity of maturity structure within their loan portfolios.

Roll-over risks derive from those operations by which a bank borrows short-term funds and re-lends them on a long-term basis, that is, these risks arise from the existence of an unmatched position in the maturity structure of a bank's loans and deposits. There are two ways in which roll-over risk may arise: first, where short-term interest rates rise before a group of loans reach maturity and the bank's margin is either squeezed or eliminated altogether; and second, in a situation where a short-fall in a bank's portfolio becomes apparent to potential lenders who will then require a higher interest rate than hitherto to provide funds. Related to the roll-over risk is the additional problem that the desired funds may be unavailable on roll-over dates and the bank may be committed to the loan.

John Hewson argues in his book[1] that the multinational banks tend to have nearly matched amounts of assets and liabilities in every maturity class, that banks do not normally have to be concerned about the availability of funds at the roll-over dates and that roll-over risk is reduced by the use of the LIBO rate as a base for floating interest rates. These conclusions must, however, be modified in the light of the events of 1973-4 and subsequent changes in the market. No doubt the continued dynamism of the market whose operations we are discussing may consign the conclusions of the following analysis to the same fate in future years. Equally the essence of the quotation which begins this chapter has been replaced more recently by the larger risk which exchange rate variations have now assumed.

In the remainder of this chapter we will examine in turn the pre and post-1974 situations, mismatching and possible solutions to this difficulty, and the problem of inadequate or too expensive funding.

For those multinational banks, in particular the consortium banks, that are dependent on the flow of inter-bank deposits as sources of funds, this dependence is described by Davis[2] as an aggravation of the maturity mismatch which was a natural consequence of the extension of loan maturities to ten years and beyond.

Table 1. Maturity Analysis of the Net Position in millions of US Dollars of Foreign Assets and Liabilities of UK Banks as a Percentage of Total Liabilities

				MATURITY PERIOD			
	Less than 8 days	8 days to less than 1 month	1 month to less than 3 months	3 months to less than 6 months	6 months to less than 1 year	1 year to less than 3 years	3 years and over
Date							
September 1973							
British banks	(2.05)	0.119	(2.05)	(0.898)	(1.10)	3.78	2.86
Consortium banks	(4.41)	(2.23)	(8.69)	(7.89)	(1.12)	9.84	16.11
Total UK banks	(4.17)	(0.620)	(1.32)	(0.022)	(0.61)	2.33	4.63
March 1974							
British banks	(2.56)	(0.013)	(4.08)	(2.73)	(0.72)	4.64	5.58
Consortium banks	(3.10)	(5.65)	(9.47)	(7.45)	(0.26)	8.27	19.25
Total UK banks	(3.25)	(1.29)	(3.83)	(0.969)	0.125	2.85	6.54
May 1974							
British banks	(1.03)	(3.03)	(4.27)	(2.96)	(0.759)	4.69	7.38
Consortium banks	(5.02)	(8.45)	(8.91)	(8.12)	1.29	9.55	20.38
Total UK banks	(3.63)	(3.06)	(2.02)	(1.88)	0.433	2.95	7.12
August 1974							
British banks	0.28	(4.57)	(6.77)	(4.22)	0.170	5.69	10.10
Consortium banks	(2.00)	(10.61)	(13.38)	(10.48)	1.42	11.41	24.30
Total UK banks	(4.38)	(2.72)	(3.52)	(1.82)	0.623	3.43	8.41
November 1974							
British banks	(1.85)	(3.94)	(6.63)	(4.79)	0.495	5.37	11.81
Consortium banks	(6.86)	(11.68)	(15.18)	(7.93)	1.75	11.87	29.11
Total UK banks	(4.75)	(3.56)	(4.07)	(1.83)	0.434	3.34	10.53
February 1975							
British banks	(3.16)	(4.78)	(7.94)	(5.82)	0.013	6.75	16.92
Consortium banks	(3.21)	(11.23)	(16.37)	(8.54)	2.30	11.38	27.76
Total UK banks	(5.48)	(2.89)	(5.13)	(2.63)	0.239	3.87	12.66
May 1975							
British banks	(4.22)	(3.65)	(9.49)	(5.28)	(2.61)	6.40	19.84
Consortium banks	(4.57)	(8.56)	(14.61)	(10.36)	0.904	11.05	29.58
Total UK banks	(6.69)	(2.24)	(4.31)	(2.69)	(0.659)	3.68	13.20
August 1975							
British banks	(4.81)	(3.63)	(8.64)	(6.91)	(1.49)	5.98	20.10
Consortium banks	(4.41)	(8.82)	(14.07)	(10.91)	(1.03)	12.31	29.92
Total UK banks	(4.69)	(2.34)	(4.65)	(3.57)	(0.887)	3.78	12.43

Date	Less than 8 days	8 days to less than 1 month	1 month to less than 3 months	3 months to less than 6 months	6 months to less than 1 year	1 year to less than 3 years	3 years and over
November 1975							
British banks	(4.58)	(5.12)	(7.15)	(7.18)	(2.32)	6.67	20.10
Consortium banks	(5.57)	(6.58)	(14.11)	(12.75)	(1.02)	13.11	30.10
Total UK banks	(3.73)	(2.82)	(5.22)	(4.30)	(0.658)	3.93	12.87
February 1976							
British banks	(4.6)	(5.12)	(8.42)	(7.84)	(1.65)	7.81	20.71
Consortium banks	(5.08)	(7.94)	(16.19)	(11.27)	0.31	13.72	29.58
Total UK banks	(4.08)	(4.26)	(4.81)	(3.50)	(0.269)	4.20	12.87
May 1976							
British banks	(3.61)	(5.32)	(9.30)	(6.96)	(1.93)	8.17	20.04
Consortium banks	(5.11)	(8.38)	(13.43)	(10.52)	(1.24)	15.48	26.31
Total UK banks	(4.41)	(3.78)	(4.41)	(3.55)	(0.798)	4.28	12.89
August 1976							
British banks	(5.76)	(4.41)	(8.92)	(7.25)	(1.25)	7.67	21.13
Consortium banks	(5.39)	(8.13)	(13.54)	(11.72)	0.38	14.80	26.71
Total UK banks	(4.15)	(3.96)	(5.38)	(3.11)	(0.35)	4.35	12.78
November 1976							
British banks	(5.23)	(5.97)	(7.27)	(5.99)	(2.51)	8.91	19.00
Consortium banks	(6.00)	(9.02)	(14.27)	(9.34)	0.61	15.44	25.25
Total UK banks	(4.88)	(3.91)	(5.27)	(2.72)	(0.35)	4.71	12.62
February 1977							
British banks	(5.34)	(4.13)	(6.96)	(7.90)	(2.94)	8.25	19.70
Consortium banks	(5.30)	(8.12)	(12.80)	(11.86)	0.4	16.59	24.27
Total UK banks	(5.56)	(3.78)	(4.85)	(2.88)	(0.034)	4.95	12.31
May 1977							
British banks	(5.46)	(5.27)	(8.29)	(5.88)	(2.39)	8.36	20.32
Consortium banks	(4.79)	(10.48)	(11.20)	(9.88)	(0.89)	16.34	23.16
Total UK banks	(4.02)	(4.32)	(5.09)	(2.85)	(0.90)	5.03	12.35
August 1977							
British banks	(4.11)	(4.26)	(7.42)	(8.47)	(2.21)	8.83	19.41
Consortium banks	(4.68)	(7.76)	(12.55)	(13.02)	0.27	17.64	22.97
Total UK banks	(5.01)	(3.97)	(4.76)	(2.34)	(0.59)	5.10	11.79
November 1977							
British banks	(5.86)	(4.33)	(8.82)	(6.19)	(1.79)	8.52	19.41
Consortium banks	(5.80)	(8.47)	(13.43)	(11.55)	1.68	17.17	22.01
Total UK banks	(6.02)	(3.36)	(5.54)	(2.38)	0.03	5.04	11.92

Source: calculated from Bank of England *Quarterly Bulletin*, various issues, tables on maturity analysis of liabilities and claims of UK banks and certain other institutions in foreign currencies.

Notes to Table 1

British banks are all banks with majority UK ownership (excluding consortium
banks where there is foreign participation) including the London clearing banks,
the Scottish clearing banks, the Northern Ireland banks, the accepting houses and
their subsidiaries and offices in the Channel Islands, the Isle of Man, and Northern
Ireland. Consortium banks are defined as banks which are owned by other banks
at least one of which is an overseas bank and in which no one bank has a direct
shareholding of more than 50 per cent.

The total UK banking sector for the purposes of this table includes as well as
the banks certain other institutions in the UK with permission to accept deposits
and make loans in foreign currencies. Other than these the UK banking sector
comprises British banks and the UK branches and subsidiaries of American banks
including those in the Channel Islands, the UK branches of Japanese banks, all
other branches and subsidiaries of foreign banks, including Channel Island subsidiaries, the consortium banks and the members of the London Discount Market
Association.

Although mismatching on roll-over maturities is not documented, it
is possible to estimate the extent of mismatching with respect to final
maturities from tables published by the Bank of England in their
quarterly bulletin from which we can derive a sectoral analysis of the
net position by final maturity of assets and liabilities as a percentage of
total liabilities. The final maturities range from less than eight days up
to three years and over, and lending is classified according to the period
remaining to the ultimate maturity date of the loan rather than to the
next roll-over date. The Bank specifically notes that the maturity
analysis figures merely yield 'periodic snapshots of the position on a
particular day'. Figures were available for the period September 1973
to February 1978 and calculations are shown in Table 1.

Steven Davis,[3] discussing a similar analysis over the shorter period
August 1974 to May 1975, which compared only the overall UK banking sector and the consortium banks, concluded that the net lending
mismatch for the consortium banks was greater than for the overall UK
banking sector and noted that the May 1975 figures showed that 27 per
cent of the consortium banks' liabilities comprised the excess of claims
of over three years to maturity, while excess claims of the same maturity
comprised only 13 per cent of the liabilities of the overall UK banking
sector. Davis attributed the comparatively heavy mismatch for the consortium banks to a combination of a longer average life of loans and a
relative lack of access to short-term deposits of three to six months
duration.

There are a number of noteworthy features apparent from an analysis
of Table 1. First, it is apparent that the three groups of banks have all
become net borrowers for a longer range of maturities than prior to

May 1975. The banks are now net borrowers for the maturities ranging from less than eight days to under one year, compared to maturities from less than eight days to up to six months prior to May 1975. Second, at the other end of the range the consortium banks and the British banks both increased their lending mismatch over the period for the three years and over maturity. Third, while the consortium banks increased their lending mismatch in the one year to less than three year maturity by some 80 per cent over the period, the British banks have even more substantially increased their lending mismatch at the longest maturity, from 2.86 per cent in September 1973 to over 20 per cent from August 1975. Fourth, the other interesting feature of the consortium bank figures in Table 1 has been the tendency for the borrowing mismatch to increase in the one month to less than three months, and the three months to less than six months maturities. In the light of Davis's comment on the earlier period, that there may have been some lack of access to short-term deposits on the part of the consortium banks, it appears that over the latter period covered by Table 1 the more typical inter-bank deposit of three, six or twelve months has been in consistent supply. Fifth, the combined lending mismatch for the two longest maturities for the consortium banks rose from 24 per cent in September 1973 to 42 per cent in August 1975 and has averaged 39 per cent or over after that date.

The figures reported in Table 1 raise the question of why a bank might elect to run a mismatched maturity book. A bank may judge, on the basis of its experience in the money market, that interest rates are going to move in a particular direction and mismatch in order to take advantage of this special knowledge. For example, a judgement that interest rates are going to fall would result in a bank deciding to lend money at rates fixed for a year and to provide cover for these loans by borrowing on a monthly basis. A bank may also be tempted to borrow short to fund longer loans if it sees that short-term deposit rates are lower than deposits with six or twelve-month maturities. Or a bank may merely decide to refrain from matching a number of small transactions until a sufficient position has accumulated to be matched up at better wholesale rates.

Banks mismatching do in fact face two quite separable risks: first, the risk of an adverse movement in interest rates, and second, the risk that deposit funds may not be available on the market. In assessing the nature of both of these it is necessary to distinguish between the periods before and after mid-1974. It is probable that the pre-1974 situation is as described by Hewson[4] with one exception, which will be discussed below. In the pre-1974 situation, although an individual bank could find difficulty on occasions in gaining funds at roll-over dates, the more serious risk was that of interest-rate fluctuations if the bank was unmatched in the maturity structure of its loans and deposits.

More specifically, if potential lenders become concerned about the viability of a bank's portfolio they may require a premium over and above the normal rate to supply funds to the bank to enable it to complete its roll-over commitments. Prior to mid-1974 it could be argued that a bank might face a trimming of its profit rate but would not be denied liquidity.

Nevertheless if we refer to calculations provided by David Ashby[5] and Steven Davis[6] it is apparent that attempts to derive profits from mismatching based on mechanical rules, including riding the yield curve, or attempts to profit from the premium of the three months deposit rate over the one month deposit rate, ceased to produce any neutral or positive result from 1969 onwards. Although, of course, other mechanistic approaches could have produced more positive results, the potential for mismatching to achieve profits appears to have required, on the basis of the results reported in the two papers noted above, increasing expertise as banks moved into the 1970s.

From mid-1974, a period which Hewson would classify as abnormal rather than normal, the cumulation of the San Diego, Franklin and Herstatt difficulties and the UK secondary banking crisis of 1973/4 led to some serious reassessments by the participants in the funds side of the market. Perhaps coincidentally, flows of money, in search of a stable exchange rate after the dismemberment of the fixed exchange rate system in 1973 (more on this point in the next chapter), moved from country to country often exacerbating interest rate differentials.

The threat to roll-over operations came from both sides in this environment and first to the pure interest rate risk. Rising interest rates threatened many mismatchings with either substantially reduced profits or actual losses, and the market reaction to increased uncertainty was to reorganise itself into a series of tiers differentiated by the money costs for banks to raise funds. In the case of a number of banks, including a number of consortium banks, it became very important for them not to classify their status as 'third tier' by accepting the necessity of paying a high premium to acquire deposit funds. Many banks were able to accomplish the necessary funding either by recourse to their parent banks (in the case of consortia) or widening their search for deposits outside the market, or simply (where possible) by using up reserves or manoeuvring within their asset structure to find funds. Certainly some economising on recourse to deposits from the market appeared necessary because of the reduced flow of funds on the inter-bank market due to uncertainty. Thus the second aspect of roll-over operations, liquidity, was also under threat for a sizable part of the market.

During the European summer and autumn of 1974 the debtors' market became a creditors' market with a reduction in roll-over credits, a restriction of the market to only the largest banks and a reduction in loan maturities from twelve years to five years or less. The reduction in maturity did not necessarily improve the viability of a number of loans since loans for a shorter time period tended not to be attached to a source of repayment income, while the ten to twelve year loans had tended to be self-liquidating. Banks restricted their unmatched foreign currency positions and raised the spreads on their loans. Within the loans advanced the pattern was shifting from mainly corporate to public sector institutions which, while it reduced commercial risk, required banks to assess country and sovereign risks.

By mid-1975 the multi-tiered interest rate structure had levelled out, although it had not yet disappeared, and the reversion of short-term rates to their more normal position below long-term rates encouraged growth in the long-term Eurobond market, where borrowers were able to fix the cost of borrowing for the life of a loan. The average maturity of Eurocredit loans remained shorter into 1976 but the multi-tiered rates disappeared, and in the view of the Bank for International Settlements it had become a buyers' market for the banks as they became over-liquid and tried to substitute international lending for the still stagnating domestic demand. Again, as in 1975, the public sector was the major borrower and concern about the flow-on effects of the Herstatt crisis had been overtaken by concern about the indebtedness of deficit countries to banks through the Euromarkets.

In 1976, a main feature of the markets was the decline in spreads, especially on medium-term credits, and increased caution concerning borrowing by the less developed countries particularly where this was done for balance of payments financing. In the Eurobond market the cost of borrowing declined and average maturities were finally extended to over nine years with longest maturities up to fifteen years. Most customers were governments or semi-government institutions.

The margin over LIBOR declined from 1.25 per cent immediately after Herstatt and 1.375 per cent in 1975 to under 1 per cent in early 1977. Since mid-1974 there had been an increased concentration within both the lending and borrowing sides of the Eurocredit market. Within the borrowing side ten countries took over half the publicised Eurocredits –

in descending order of importance they were Britain, Brazil, Mexico, Italy, France, Spain, Iran, Algeria, Venezuela and Indonesia. Within the lending side, Mendelsohn[7] suggests that only twenty banks arranged two-thirds of the publicised Eurocredits in 1976 and 1977 (and provided about a third of the money). Tables provided in the *Institutional Investor*, in *Euromoney* and in the OECD *Financial Market Trends* confirm the tendency for names such as Citicorp, Chase, Deutsche, Crédit Suisse, Libra, Dresdner to dominate the market. This domination is reinforced by the ability of larger banks to secure funds below the LIBO rate from outside depositors and within their own enterprises to acquire interest-free deposits from their branches. Lesser banks pay closer to the LIBO rate, so that the spreads they quote on loans represent usually their profit margin, but for the larger banks there is a profit margin even at LIBO rate. This difference in the cost of access to funds appears to make the position of lesser banks much less profitable at times when spreads narrow, but perhaps only turns the larger banks to their own branches for funds in order to maintain and even improve their profit margins at those times.

Looking at the downward trend of margins in at least the first half of 1978 in the light of the above information it would appear that the present trend will enforce still further concentration within the lending side of the market. Only the lesser banks will find the reduction of margins unpalatable. The essential core of the market will merely switch their sources of deposits and continue their profitable business. Neither roll-over risk nor mismatching appear to be of critical concern to the core of the market, only to its peripheral participants. On the other hand, foreign exchange risks, to which we now turn, may be important to both core and peripheral participants.

Notes

1. John Hewson, *Liquidity Creation and Distribution in the Eurocurrency Markets* (Lexington, 1975).

2. Steven I. Davis, *The Euro-Bank* (Macmillan, London, 1976).

3. Ibid.

4. Hewson, *Liquidity Creation and Distribution*.

5. David F. Ashby, 'Analysing the Maturity Structure of the Eurodollar Market', *The Banker* (July 1973).

6. Davis, *The Euro-Bank*.

7. M. S. Mendelsohn, 'Eurocurrency Loans – Still Money to Be Made', *Eurofile*, Supplement to *The Banker* (June 1978).

Further Reading

Campbell, Mary, 'Maturity Structures of the Eurocurrency Markets', *The Banker* (April 1975)

Davis, Steven I., 'A Buyer's Market in Eurodollars', *Harvard Business Review* (May-June 1973)

—, 'Eurobank Profits – Four Prosperous Years – for Some', *Euromoney* (November 1977)

Einzig, Paul, *Roll-Over Credits – The System of Adaptable Interest Rates* (Macmillan, London, 1973)

'Euromarkets Survey', *The Banker* (January 1977)

Gilbert, Nick, 'Capital Adequacy and the Eurocurrency Markets', *Euromoney* (November 1975)

Hewson, John and E. Sakakibara, *The Eurocurrency Markets and Their Implications* (Lexington, D.C. Heath, 1975)

'How Precarious Are the Euromarkets?', *Euromoney* (July 1974)

O'Brien, Lord, 'The Prospects for the Euromarkets', *Euromoney* (September 1975)

OECD, *Financial Market Trends* (1977 and 1978)

Pakenham, Kevin, 'The Medium-Term Rollover Credit and Economic Fluctuations', *Euromoney* (November 1975)

Park, Dr Yoon S., 'A New Philosophy for Euromarket Banks', *Euromoney* (June 1975)

Sakakibara, Eisuke, 'A Broader Perspective on the Euromarkets', *Euromoney* (November 1975)

Van den Adel, Dr M., 'As the Sources of Euromarket Funds Change, So Do the Borrowers', *Euromoney* (June 1975)

—, 'Euromarkets – Activity Moves from the Long to the Short End', *Euromoney* (November 1977)

—, 'The Jumbos and the Mammoths Confront More Choosy Bankers', *Euromoney* (March 1977)

7 FOREIGN EXCHANGE TRANSACTIONS: BANKING RISK AND CURRENCY RISK

'The coalescence of private expectations regarding correctly aligned exchange rates is interrupted because official intervention is so unpredictable.' (Ronald McKinnon, 'Floating Foreign Exchange Rates 1973-74: The Emperor's New Clothes' in K. Brunner and A. H. Meltzer (eds.), *Institutional Arrangements and the Inflation Problem* (North-Holland, Amsterdam, 1976).)

Due to the substantial changes that occurred in the international monetary system in the early seventies, foreign exchange risk must now be regarded as the most important risk facing banks, as well as companies, which operate across countries. In order to analyse the effect of these changed conditions it is first necessary to outline the nature of the changes which have occurred.

Under the fixed exchange rate system in the form in which it limped into the seventies, the US dollar, which was regarded as the reserve currency, provided a stable base for international transactions. For most economies a change in their exchange rate was a last resort policy to be adopted only when every other policy had failed to restore external equilibrium, with the result that by the time an exchange rate was changed at least the direction of the change, if not the exact amount of it, would be common knowledge. There was a tendency for countries to attach their currency to a leader currency, such as the US dollar, the pound sterling or the French franc, with which their currency moved. In order for the fixed rate system to operate efficiently with only one reserve currency it was necessary that this currency fulfil two increasingly divergent aims, it must be stable and it must be in constant supply. The second aim could only really be accomplished if the US continually ran a balance of payments deficit — but this threatened the stability of its value.

The advantage of a reserve currency under the fixed exchange rate system was that while the US agreed to the dollar's convertibility into gold it offered a relatively riskless asset on which to base transactions. For example, the US dollar acted as an intermediary currency in much forward exchange trading and was the numeraire in which other exchange rates were normally stated. Towards the end of the sixties a combination of internal inflation, capital outflows and continuous deficits in the balance of payments created foreign exchange difficulties for the USA and when none of these difficulties eased the US was forced to suspend convertibility of the dollar, in August 1971. Foreign exchange markets closed while attempts to create a stable system were discussed but no agreement was reached and exchange rates were allowed to seek their own levels within some controls. In December 1971 the Smithsonian agreement attempted to specify conditions for a new system: the US dollar was devalued and other currencies were revalued upwards in relation to it and exchange values were to be maintained within 4.5 per cent around parity level. In June 1972 the United Kingdom suspended its participation in the Smithsonian agreement and allowed the pound to float, and in February 1973 the USA devalued the dollar and shortly afterwards the EEC countries agreed to jointly float their currencies: these events between them meant complete abandonment of the Smithsonian agreement.

Between 1971 and 1973 the increased uncertainty concerning international monetary arrangements was reflected in the move by some countries to allow their currencies to float freely. Other countries also moved to allow their currencies to float but they held reserves in order to be able to enter the exchange rate market if, in their opinion, their exchange rate floated to an 'inappropriate' level. After 1973 more and more economies were forced into some form of managed floating or dirty floating because of the sharp fluctuations which were occurring in the exchange rates of the major currencies with which their rates had hitherto been linked.

In these circumstances the case for simply allowing all exchange rates to float freely to find their appropriate equilibrium levels might seem strong to an impartial observer. However, the uncertainty which had prevailed in foreign exchange markets since the late sixties, and the unexpected and sharp fluctuations which had occurred in major currencies in the early seventies, suggested to most governments that allowing their currencies to float freely might be opening up a veritable Pandora's box which they would be ill-equipped to handle. Because of these problems the safest alternative for most governments was to elect to use a form of managed floating, that is to allow the exchange rate to float but to continue to hold foreign exchange reserves as a basis for intervention in the foreign exchange markets, if it was thought to be necessary.

A number of characteristics of this new era of managed floating have been very different from those of even the crisis-ridden fixed exchange rate regime of 1970-1: historically high movements in spot exchange rates have been experienced with even 1 per cent moves on a day-to-day basis not unusual; bid-ask spreads in spot exchange markets have widened significantly but bid-ask spreads in forward exchange markets have increased to such an extent that the longest regularly quoted forward exchange rate is now only twelve months, with three months the standard maturity; government intervention has been at a level at least as high as under the fixed exchange system; and relationships between exchange rates can no longer be regarded as stable.

Under managed floating, by comparison with either the fixed or purely floating alternatives, any pressure from any quarter on the exchange rate of a country may be met by any one of three alternatives: no action at all, thus allowing the exchange rate to move; supporting the rate by either the use of foreign exchange reserves or borrowing to increase the level of those reserves. Under a fixed rate system pressure on the exchange rate would be met by a series of policy moves designed to maintain the exchange rate, among which would be the use of reserves, and only if all of this failed would the exchange rate be changed. Under a purely floating rate immediate adjustment of the rate in response to pressure would mean that the exchange rate would be subject to minuscule adjustments over time too small to incite speculative activity.

The switch from fixed exchange rates to managed floating rates has changed the nature of both components of the exchange rate risk for multinational banks, that is of both banking risk and currency risk. Banking risk arises when a bank, as a result of a foreign currency transaction, holds a foreign currency unhedged against exchange rate changes. Currency risk is the risk of unexpected fluctuations in exchange rates.

In its normal operations a multinational bank will be involved in currency conversions, and to facilitate these a bank will hold a portfolio of accounts overseas in foreign currencies. Because most inter-bank transactions and in fact most international trade take place in a few recognised currencies a bank will concentrate its accounts on those currencies. Prior to the advent of managed floating a bank would use an intermediary currency such as the US dollar as a riskless asset base, in particular for forward exchange transactions. For example, a bank acting as agent in a transaction in which an Italian importer wanted to buy Australian dollars forward (there is no forward market in Australian dollars) would have to find a third currency in which to transact so that he could sell lira forward for that third currency and then sell the third currency forward for Australian dollars or hold the third currency until the date of the lira forward contract and then convert to Australian dollars. If the third currency had been US dollars and the operation carried out under the fixed exchange rate system, there would have been no risk in using the dollar as an intermediary.

The same transaction under managed floating is much more complex because the absence of a riskless intermediary currency requires either a search for a currency stable in relation to the Italian lira and the Australian dollar, or an expensive negotiation to directly link the two currencies which have no formal market links. The use of sterling could commend itself here as an intermediary with the bank, but this adds a third currency whose future moves are uncertain. Under the fixed rate a bank could convert its part of the transaction to a holding of riskless US dollars, but now it must either cover its position on the forward market (and have to renegotiate this on more than one occasion if the contract extends beyond a year) or hold its uncovered position in a currency of whose future moves it is quite uncertain. The breadth of information on foreign currencies which a bank requires to operate under managed floating is significantly increased over that necessary under the fixed system.

The above discussion has been in terms of transactions risk but there is the additional problem of translation risk for multinational enterprises operating in several currencies. Again, under the fixed system the US dollar was a safe currency in which balance sheets and income statements could be stated. At present, even should a bank cover its transaction risk in foreign currencies, there is still a substantial risk that a loss will occur in translating the result into a balance sheet in US dollars. Of course, this represents a strong argument for hedging against economic exposure, rather than taking transaction and translation risks separately.

The limitation to this approach from a single bank's point of view is that it may be seen to be unhedged in numerous transactions because it has an equal and opposite exposure elsewhere which will not be apparent to outsiders. In an environment where the risk of foreign exchange loss is seen to be greater than before, it is possible that it may give the impression of being more rather than less exposed to risk and to be more willing rather than less willing to take net positions in foreign currencies.

The plethora of official restrictions on the net foreign exchange positions of banks in a number of countries have been attempts to reduce the risk of insolvency as a result of foreign exchange losses. These losses have tended to influence some banks away from undertaking any net foreign exchange exposure at all. This has had the effect of narrowing the range of market participants and may be a contributory factor to wider bid-ask spreads in both spot and forward markets.

Turning now to pure currency risk, that is the risk of unexpected fluctuations in exchange rates, the nature of this has also changed with the move to managed floating rates. Under fixed rates it was quite common for exchange rate changes to be preceded, to use McKinnon's term,[1] by a 'coalescence of private expectations regarding correctly aligned exchange rates' which were then validated by the exchange rate moves. Under managed floating rates official intervention in the form of the use of reserves and exchange rate changes in unpredictable proportions defies orderly prediction of exchange rate changes.

From the point of view of the multinational banks the managed floating exchange rates system either creates or exacerbates three problems relevant to currency risk: first, the policy of restricting their range of foreign currency holdings to a few internationally traded currencies is less successful now there is no tendency towards a stable relationship between any two currencies or within any group of currencies; second, there is the danger inherent in lending that the borrower may be in an unmatched position, and for this reason, possibly, the prudent limits of bank lending may be exceeded or at least a contingent liability may arise without the bank's knowledge; and, third, the reduction in the time periods for which forward cover is available and the widening of bid-ask spreads have meant that forward cover is not as cheaply or readily obtainable as under the fixed system.

McKinnon (pp.87-8) notes one further difficulty that may arise from the last problem: payments uncertainty and fear of insolvency due to the new exchange rate system may lead companies to prefer the more certain cash foreign exchange transactions over forward contracting. The strength of this reaction generally will determine whether companies will need to provide the full funding for foreign transactions in cash as opposed to the margin requirement for forward trading, and also whether banks will be faced with a switch in demand away from the comparatively long-run forward contracts to a demand for much shorter term credit and for current deposits in foreign currencies.

Both of these effects raise the capital requirements for banks and companies which could be expected to limit the operations of both forms of enterprise.

It can be seen that banking risk, that is the risk of insolvency on the part of banks, and currency risk, that is the risk of unexpected fluctuations in exchange rate, either changed in nature or increased as a consequence of the change from a fixed exchange rate system to one of managed floating. These considerations form only part of the exchange risk problem. We ought also now to consider country risk and sovereign risk.

Note

1. Ronald McKinnon, 'Floating Foreign Exchange Rates 1973-74: The Emperor's New Clothes' in K. Brunner and A.H. Meltzer (eds.), *Institutional Arrangements and the Inflation Problem* (North-Holland, Amsterdam, 1976).

Further Reading

Clendenning, E. Wayne, *The Euro-Currency Markets and the International Activities of Canadian Banks* (Economic Council of Canada, 1976)
Davis, Steven I., *The Euro-bank* (Macmillan, London, 1976)
Hewson, J., *Liquidity Creation and Distribution in the Eurocurrency Markets* (Lexington, 1975)
Hirsch, F. and D. Higham, 'Floating Rates – Expectations and Experience', *Three Banks Review* (June 1974)
Nadelmann, Kurt H., 'Rehabilitating International Bankruptcy Law: Lessons Taught by Herstatt and Company', *New York University Law Review*, vol.52, no.1 (April 1977)

8 FOREIGN EXCHANGE TRANSACTIONS: COUNTRY RISK

'Countries do not disappear. Even Indonesia or Chile or Ghana
didn't go down the drain. We rescheduled their debts and we
fully expect to do the same in 1975 for Brazil or Gabon or
Greece. Everyone will get repaid in the end and there will be no
apocalypse.' (Neil McInnes, 'Financial Time Bomb', *Barron's*,
25 November 1974, p.9.)

The development of the oil crisis from late 1973 and its impact on
certain less developed economies brought into sharp relief the problems
of both country risk and sovereign risk for lenders. In order to be able
to evaluate the nature of these risks and the reasons for their growth in
importance it is necessary firstly to look at the nature of the oil crisis.
From the four-fold increase in the price level made by OPEC between
late 1973 and early 1974 the OPEC group derived a substantial balance
of payments surplus which it was beyond their own economies to
absorb. This surplus was of course mirrored in the deficits incurred by
the oil-consuming countries.

As much of the surplus was held in such currencies as the US dollar,
the value of which might have declined if the entire surplus was kept
out of the world monetary system, it was in the interests of OPEC that
at least most of the surplus be 'recycled' to the rest of the world. Investment of the OPEC surplus in the rest of the world was restricted by the
nationalistic tendencies of many countries which refused to allow those
funds to be invested, other than minimally, in real estate or in public
companies within their boundaries. The alternative long-term investment, that of bonds, did not at the time of the first investment of the
surplus offer a reasonable alternative for either lenders or borrowers. In
the inflationary environment of the time, with interest rates at historically high levels and with short-term deposit rates then exceeding the
returns on bonds, lenders were reluctant to accept long-term returns
lower than those available on short-term investments, and borrowers
were unwilling to offer rates sufficient to attract funds. Owing to the
lack of an effective secondary market for bonds, lenders also faced the
possibility, unrealistic for many OPEC governments, of being locked
into a bond investment for its full term.

For all of these reasons the major investment of funds was made in short-term maturities through a number of international banks, in part in the Eurocurrency markets, where the short-term funds were re-lent in the form of roll-over credits to governments of oil-consuming countries. One impact of this large increase in deposit funds and their transmission into loans of immediate concern to banks was that an increased capital base for these operations was needed at a time when these funds were not only difficult to raise, but also very expensive. Further, this inter-mediation exposed the banks more than previously to both country and sovereign risk. Country risk is the credit risk associated with dealing with the commercial arm of a foreign government or directly with a foreign government. This risk has three aspects: prudent limits, loan quality and information requirements. There are two elements inherent in the estimation of the prudent level for loans to an individual country: first, the risk of excessive debt in absolute amounts, where a country may have an aggregate level of debt of sufficient size to make the re-financing of it in the commercial market difficult and eventually impossible; and second, the risk that although total borrowing is only of modest size, the debt maturing in a particular month or year may be too large to be readily re-financed in the commercial bank market.

A country's ability to repay may be analysed in a manner com-parable to the analysis of corporate ability to repay, that is cash flow, liquidity and leverage are relevant but they are described by different terms with reference to an economy. To be more specific, the balance of payments is the equivalent of a cash flow statement, reserves are a country's liquidity and its leverage is a function of its debt burden.

There are three potential sources from which a country may acquire the funds to repay its loans; first, it may be able to generate sufficient foreign exchange from its exports of goods and services to allow a sur-plus to pay back its maturing loans after it has paid for its imports; second, it may be able to attract foreign aid, loan funds or direct invest-ment which are large enough to offset any shortfall on its balance of payments; and, third, it may have some foreign exchange reserves with which it may meet temporary shortfalls. If the first source is consistently unable to generate surplus funds over and above that needed for imports, the country's ability to hold reserves, and to attract foreign aid, loans or direct investment will be seriously threatened. Accordingly, analysis of the country's trade pattern is critical to any decision concerning its ability to repay loans, and a conventional means of analysis is to con-centrate on the country's export/import ratio.

Four factors contribute to low or unstable export/import ratios for many less-developed economies: price instability, supply instability, dependence on a few exports and dependence on a consistently high level of imports. Within the export structure of many developing economies, agricultural products and minerals often dominate and these share the characteristic of widely fluctuating prices in world markets. Since these price fluctuations in world markets do not have a significant relationship with the costs of production, their presence makes it very difficult to predict export revenues. In those cases where agricultural production is the major export base, supply instability may occur through good and bad harvests and this problem may be exacerbated when one or very few agricultural products comprise a substantial part of total exports.

On the import side, it is often very difficult for developing economies to hold their imports below very high levels because the imports are either food or essential inputs. It is here that the rise in oil prices has been very significant as many developing countries, as well as many developed ones, are reliant on imported oil as a source of energy. In combination with the higher prices for imported food during the world inflation of the early seventies, the oil price rise seriously reduced the export/import ratio for a number of countries.

Quite apart from the trade account, attention must be given to the services aspect of the balance of payments, in particular to dividend and interest, freight and insurance among the outflows, and flows from tourism among the inflows. And an analysis of the capital account will also be important in establishing the country's means of financing current account deficits. Account ought to be taken of the country's IMF borrowing rights in this analysis.

Loan quality, the second aspect of country risk, might be described as varying with currency movements. For example, loan quality will be lower if a country devalues its currency and is committed to pay for its loans in another currency. Should an economy which has substantial debts denominated in US dollars devalue by 20 per cent relative to the US dollar, then not only is its debt larger in terms of its own currency, but interest payments on that debt will also be relatively larger. In these circumstances it may be said that the quality of existing loans declines.

Information requirements are of particular significance in the analysis of a country's debt servicing although they are clearly also relevant elsewhere. Publicly available data sufficient to enable accurate analysis of debt-servicing have at least a two-year time lag where they become available. Further, even the data that then become available are deficient concerning debt burden and servicing in that they exclude external and private debt, exclusions which are likely to lead to understatement of the debt burden, and what is more they include only debt service paid rather than payable so that delinquent payments have the effect of reducing the ratio. All of this information is derived from the public data issued by the country concerned. Errors and omissions in this information are more likely to occur for countries with a short experience of providing detailed economic and financial data. Calculations based on the data may be additionally complicated if a potential lender feels that the current exchange rate is inappropriate. Quite apart from the possibility that these calculations may be based on inaccurate or incomplete information *ab initio*, these calculations may become outdated very quickly.

If a country is unable to repay its loans it may be able to reschedule its debts, arrange repayment guarantees or find a third party prepared to act as guarantor for its loans. Between 1956 and 1976 ten countries – Argentina, Brazil, Chile, Ghana, Indonesia, India, Peru, Pakistan, Turkey and Zaire – made a total of thirty-three multilateral reschedulings of debt. Excluded from this list are bilateral reschedulings and a very small multilateral rescheduling by Cambodia. In 1975, 1976 and 1977 only two reorganisations of debt a year occurred.

It is of interest to look at the cases of two countries, Zambia and Zaire, both of which have been cause for concern in international banking circles in recent years, with Zaire likely to continue to be a problem for some time yet.

Of the group of less-developed economies, Zaire is potentially one of the richest, already ranking among the leading producers of copper, cobalt, zinc, industrial diamonds and tin. Nevertheless it shares with other less fortunate developing economies the problem of a minimal infrastructure, little managerial expertise, a shortage of capital, and dependence on the revenue from a single export – copper – for a viable balance of payments position. Some 500 million US dollars in commercial bank debt was raised by Zaire between 1969 and 1974, with the 169 per cent rise in copper prices between late 1972 and mid-1974 encouraging the country to arrange a significant number of loans to be repaid in 1975. When the copper price fell back further than it had risen and the price of imported oil rose four-fold with the oil crisis, Zaire was forced into arrears on payments to both official lenders and private banks by 1975. The list of creditors included the IMF and the World Bank, as well as many commercial banks. It appears that the main problem lay in the bunching of repayments in 1975, the year in which Zaire was least able to meet them. Matters were further complicated for the creditor banks when it became very difficult for bankers and journalists to obtain visas to visit Zaire, and this, together with a complete silence from the official sources within Zaire, threatened to push the extended delay in meeting interest payments towards a *de facto* default.

In April 1976 a Paris Club met and rescheduled the official debt over ten years with a three-year period of grace, and at the end of the same month representatives of the private commercial banks met in London but were unable to agree to a united approach by the ninety-eight banks to which Zaire was indebted. The other creditor banks were dismayed to learn in July that the United States Exim Bank had apparently been able to reach a preferential agreement which was in technical breach of the negative pledge clauses in commercial banks' loan agreements. At the same time Zaire's official sources made it known that, in the absence of any move by creditor banks for a different agreement, Zaire wished to reschedule its private debt in the same manner that it had rescheduled its official debt.

By July the thirteen agent banks representing the ninety-eight creditor banks had invited representatives of the Zaire government to meet with them and in September a delegation led by Governor Sambura of the Banque du Zaire met with the agent banks in London. The delegation provided a substantial amount of detailed information which the agent banks set up two sub-committees to analyse. From the reports of these two committees it was clear to the agent banks that any proposal made to Zaire should avoid either re-financing or rescheduling and this had the added advantage of avoiding the setting of a precedent for other countries in like difficulties.

The Zaire delegation and the agent banks met in New York in October and agreed on the general outline of an agreement and on 5 November a memorandum of understanding was signed in London between Zaire and the agent banks. In this memorandum it was provided that, in order to re-establish its credit-worthiness, Zaire would pay the then outstanding interest of some 40 million dollars on its medium-term syndicated bank debt before the end of November; it would commence negotiations with the IMF and become eligible to draw under the higher IMF credit tranches by 1 April 1977; and it would begin to make provision for the payment of arrears of principal on its medium-term syndicated bank debt in order to provide the 50 million dollars due for payment to the banks by the end of February 1977.

This arrangement to restore Zaire's credit standing and enable it to borrow to sponsor continued development included an undertaking that, in return for the placing of 110 million dollars to 115 million dollars in a special account with the Bank for International Settlements to provide for the principal rescheduled arrears, Citibank would organise as far as possible a management group to raise 250 million dollars needed in order to service Zaire's debt.

Dr Irving Friedman, who was a participant in the negotiations, points out[1] that the IMF standby was important in the re-establishment of Zaire's credit-worthiness because it would indicate that there was international scrutiny and monitoring of Zaire's economic situation, and further that Zaire's agreement to repay arrears to the private banks would encourage the view that Zaire gave the highest priority to honouring its private bank debts and keep this area of lending available in the future. As well as the financial arrangements detailed above, Zaire made a series of major changes in its economy ranging from the reorganisation of the management of its internal transportation to the returning of plantations to their original owners. These changes, together with the eventual recovery in copper prices and the financial arrangements, may be sufficient to allow Zaire not only to re-establish its credit-worthiness but to enable it to attract the necessary financial resources on which to base its economic revival.

Zambia shares with Zaire the chief exports of copper (which ranks first for both economies), lead, zinc and cobalt. In the words of Zambia's Permanent Secretary to the Minister of Finance, Zambia is 'a landlocked single product economy with acute transport difficulties, whose principal product has fallen on hard times in a world market initially depressed'. This had not been the position between 1964 and 1970 when, in this period following independence, Zambia's balance of payments was consistently in surplus and an average rate of real annual growth of 9 per cent was achieved with minimal resort to external finance. The early seventies saw a considerable change of fortune for Zambia, with the problems of deteriorating terms of trade being exacerbated by the sudden 25 per cent decline in copper production capacity caused by the Mufulisa mine disaster, although there were sufficient international reserves to cushion these effects in the short term. Between 1971 and 1973 total external long-term debt remained virtually unchanged and a new 86.9 million dollars in short-term debt was provided by the IMF at low interest, however, the composition of the debt changed. In 1970/1 only 10 per cent of total long-term indebtedness comprised borrowing from commercial banks, but in 1973 this rose to 41.2 per cent and thereafter remained above 30 per cent.

Zambia prematurely redeemed its nationalisation bonds, a redemption which necessitated borrowing 150 million dollars on the Eurocurrency market in 1973. The most serious change in Zambia's external debt situation, however, occurred in 1975 when there was a current account deficit of 611 million dollars, an amount equal to 72.6 per cent of export earnings. As the country's international reserves were by then at a low level, this shortfall was financed by long-term debt, included in which was 346 million dollars of Eurocurrency loans from commercial banks, and by short-term borrowing which rose to 236 million dollars — and payments of 159 million dollars had still to be deferred. Although the debt service ratio was only a low 12.2 per cent in 1975, the country in effect could not meet current payments.

The major cause of this acceleration in foreign debt was the fall in copper and other export prices to which 87.5 per cent of the change in the current account was attributable. In the first half of 1976 there were some signs of improvement with the price of copper thought to.be easing upwards. However, when the foreign exchange reserves halved in the six months to June 1976, the Zambian authorities devalued the kwacha by 20 per cent (and pegged it to the SDR instead of the US dollar) in July and in August raised several more loans overseas to pay for essential imports, and moved to reduce deferred payments to their trading partners and promote export diversification. The loans raised included a standby arrangement with the IMF and a loan from the World Bank.

Although there was a significant improvement in the current account deficit, which fell from 99 million dollars in 1975 to 52 million dollars in 1976, the mining sector was providing no revenue and inflation, of the mainly imported variety, was rising strongly. In 1977 inflation reached 24 per cent; the two major copper producers both unsuccessfully sought medium-term credits; copper prices failed to improve; and the government was forced to take further measures to attempt to rescue the situation.

Zambia had increased state participation in industry in 1966 when, owing to the difficult situation in Rhodesia, it was found that a large number of foreign companies with Rhodesian subsidiaries were setting up in Zambia. By the early 1970s, Zimco, the state industrial holding company, controlled 80 per cent of the country's industry and private foreign investment was discouraged. In 1975 the government began to re-examine the need for foreign investment and in early 1977 President Kaunda officially stated that Zambia welcomed foreign investment and that it could either take the form of joining a project with a parastatal organisation, or going into partnership with a Zambian company, or establishing an operation entirely by itself without any local participation. The Industrial Development Act of August 1977 provided incentives which included tax relief for investors in manufacturing industry and immunity from nationalisation other than 'in the highest national interest'.

Zimco had pursued the government's fixed prices until its substantial loss in 1976, and its move to more rational pricing in late 1976 under the management of Dominic Mulaisho allowed foreign-owned business in at competitive prices.

In the view of the government a useful strategy to reduce the import bill was to promote import substitution in agriculture, but it remains to be seen whether the primarily subsistence farmers can be encouraged to produce a surplus. In order to reduce the borrowing requirements of the mining companies, a government committee recommended certain cost-saving measures and decided, in early 1978, to devalue the kwacha by 10 per cent, minimising the inflationary impact by having the Bank of Zambia absorb the cost to importers.

At the same time a programme of financing was negotiated with the IMF which provided a two-year stand-by arrangement of 250 million dollars, of which 61 million dollars was to be made available on board approval, 60 million dollars to be drawn immediately under the IMF's compensatory financing facility, a further 19 million dollars in June 1978, and 47 million dollars in repurchases due in 1978 were re-scheduled. As part of the agreement with the IMF Zambia agreed to targets on domestic credit expansion and external borrowing.

From an examination of both of the above cases it is possible to elicit the main dangers that may arise for lending banks in such situations. First, there is from the evidence a danger that substantial short-term funding by an economy may result in the bunching of maturities at inappropriate times, with the risk that at the least interest payments may fall into arrears and at worst (so far) some form of rescheduling may be necessary.

Second, in both cases interest payments at various points fell into arrears without any notice to the creditor banks. The time pattern of cash flows for the banks are thus unexpectedly varied. In these circumstances a lender may be forced to decide quickly and without adequate information on the country's credit-worthiness and on its (the lender's) attitude to refinancing. Third, as Duff and Peacock[2] note (p.71), in cases such as Zaire's, even if lenders are able to write refinancing agreements which specify certain domestic policy measures within the borrowing country, these are unlikely to affect the borrower's ability to repay, which will be a function of export revenues which it is not within the country's ability to repay. Fourth, while lending banks may be able to identify a reasonable maturity schedule of debt in relation to a particular country's foreign earnings, earnings of most less-developed economies are often subject to unpredictable fluctuations and a country's maturity schedule may change quite quickly if it elects to raise significant amounts of short-term debt. Fifth, it is apparent that lenders may be locked in to continuous support of a country in order to ensure that they are eventually repaid. Finally, there is the problem mentioned in the discussion of Zaire that an individual creditor bank may insist upon an attempt to be repaid in full with the threat that it may call a formal default unless paid. In order to prevent the borrowing country from being forced into default, the other lenders may have to buy out the other bank's debt.

Notes

1. Dr Irving S. Friedman, 'Country Risk: The Lessons of Zaire', *The Banker* (February 1978).
2. Deelan Duff and Ian Peacock, 'Refinancing of Sovereign Debt', *The Banker* (January 1978).

Further Reading

Brackenridge, A. Bruce, 'Country Exposure, Country Limits and Lending to LDC's', *Journal of Commercial Bank Lending* (July 1977)

Calhoun, jun., Alexander D., 'Eurodollar Loan Agreements: An Introduction and Discussion of Some Special Problems', *Journal of Commercial Bank Lending* (September 1977)

Cleveland, H. B. and W. H. B. Brittain, 'Are the LDC's in over Their Heads?', *Foreign Affairs* (July 1977)

Corse, C. T., 'International Term Loan Agreements and Loan Syndications', *Journal of Commercial Bank Lending* (March 1978)

Costanzo, G. A., 'Lending to Developing Countries – Why the Gloom Is Overdone', *The Banker* (June 1976)

Duff, Deelan and Ian Peacock, 'A Cash-Flow Approach to Sovereign Risk Analysis', *The Banker* (January 1977)

Jecker, Rolf, 'Assessment of the Risks from a Developing Country's Point of View: Zambia', *Aussenwirtschaft* (Fasc-1, 1978)

Latour, Pierre, 'The Three Countries on the Edge of Default', *Euromoney* (February 1976)

Meynell, Charles, 'No, We're Not Zaire', *Euromoney* (May 1977)

Moore, B. W., '20% Devaluation Brings Stability', *Euromoney* (November 1976)

Mueller, P. Henry, 'Sighting in on International Lending', *Journal of Commercial Bank Lending* (November 1972)

Pakenham, Kevin, 'The Debts of Less Developed Countries – The Challenge for Commercial Banks', *Journal of Commercial Bank Lending* (May 1976)

Walusiku, Francis, 'Zambia Tries to Sidestep Disaster', *Euromoney* (May 1978)

9 EXCHANGE RATE RISK: SOVEREIGN RISK

'The lender can and should negotiate for disclaimers and waivers of sovereign privilege. But even a belt, suspenders and bullet proof vest leave vulnerable areas exposed, and governments can be dirty fighters.' (Henry Harfield, 'Legal Aspects of International Lending', in F. John Mathis (ed.), *Offshore Lending by U.S. Commercial Banks* (Robert Morris Associates, New York, 1977).)

Sovereign risk, often called the legal counterpart of country risk, may be defined as the risk of loss through the expropriation of assets by a foreign government, the institution of exchange controls which prohibit the cross-country transfer of funds, or through a government's renunciation of a debt obligation. The extent to which sovereign risk exists is clearly always difficult to evaluate since it involves a government's continued willingness to repay a loan in contrast to the more readily calculated country risk which measures its ability to repay.

Sovereign governments have three privileges which are important here: first, they are not able to be sued without their own consent in either their own courts or the courts of another country; second, normally the courts of one country will not sit in judgement concerning the acts or omissions of the government of another country that occur within the latter country's territory; and third, the property of a government or its instrumentality is immune so that even if a judgement is obtained against a foreign government, that judgement may not be enforceable.

It is argued that commercial banks are justified in ignoring this risk, firstly, because no major default of this type has occurred in the past decade, and, secondly, because repudiation of debt may result in the country concerned being barred from access to the international capital markets, a fate it is thought few countries could afford.

Firm belief in these two principles is hard to justify in the face of a series of cases, for example the recent court decisions in the UK, the Federal Republic of Germany and the United States which were required when, following a change of government in Nigeria, sellers of cement originally ordered by the former Nigerian government remained unpaid.

In the remainder of this chapter, recent changes in the doctrine of sovereign immunity in the UK and in the USA will be discussed. It will be seen that these recent developments are likely to lead to more predictable decisions in the area of foreign sovereign immunity which may reduce the nature of this risk.

The Foreign Sovereign Immunities Act of 1976, which became law in the USA on 22 October of that year, represents the final stage of a shift from the doctrine of absolute sovereign immunity to the doctrine of restrictive sovereign immunity in that country.

The doctrine of absolute sovereign immunity derives from the concept of absolute sovereignty, which holds that '[T]he courts of a country will not implead a foreign sovereign, that is, they will not by their process make him against his will a party to legal proceedings whether the proceedings involve process against his person or seek to recover from him specific property or damages' (per Lord Atkin, *Compania Naviera Vascongado* v. *S.S. 'Cristina'* [1938] A.C. 485, 490).

In the USA this doctrine began to be eroded because of the increased involvement of states in commerce and trading activities. The trend away from the doctrine became clearer with the Supreme Court decisions *Ex parte Republic of Peru*, 318 U.S. 578 (1936) and *Mexico* v. *Hoffman*, 324 U.S. 30 (1945), in both of which the Court indicated that sovereign immunity should not be determined judicially but should rather be the decision of the State Department that it ought to be an executive decision, 'it is therefore not for the courts to deny an immunity which our government has seen fit to allow, or to allow an immunity on new grounds which the government has not seen fit to recognize' (*Ex parte Peru*, 318 U.S. 578-88).

The next significant development was the issue by the State Department of the 'Tate Letter' on 19 May 1952, in which it was declared that it was to be State Department policy to decline immunity to friendly foreign sovereigns in suits which arose from private or commercial activity. In the legislative history provided with the 1976 Act it was noted that the effect of the Tate letter was to leave the initiative to the foreign state to elect whether to go to court or to the State Department.

Although, subsequent to the Tate letter, US courts tended to deny sovereign immunity in cases arising from purely commercial transactions, the USA continued to adhere to the absolute theory of foreign sovereign immunity with regard to the execution of judgements. In a letter to the court in *Weilmann* v. *Chase Manhattan Bank*, 21 Misc. 2d. 1086, 192 N.Y.S. 2d. 469 (Sup. Ct. 1959) the State Department said, *inter alia*,

. . . even when the attachment of the property of a foreign sovereign is not prohibited for the purpose of jurisdiction, nevertheless the property so attached and levied upon cannot be retained to satisfy a judgement ensuing from the suit because in the Department's view under international law the property of a foreign sovereign is immune from execution even in a case where the foreign sovereign is not immune from suit.

To some extent the extreme limitation on recovery that this would suggest was reduced when most states complied with judgements made against them.

Most prevalent in the litigation in the area of sovereign immunity following the Tate letter were those involving the commercial activitie of foreign sovereigns, of which *Victory Transport Inc.* v. *Comisaria General Le Abastecimientos y Transportes*, 336 F. 2d. 354 (2d. Cir. 1964) cert. denied, 381 U.S. 934 (1965) was the leading judgement. In that case the Comisaria General, a branch of the Spanish Ministry of Commerce, had entered into a charter agreement with Victory Transport which contained the New York Produce Arbitration Clause providing for arbitration. The charter concerning the carrying of a surplus wheat cargo to Spanish ports was found by the Second Circuit to be a commercial and private act rather than a strictly public act which would have allowed sovereign immunity to the Comisaria General. In affirming this decision the Court of Appeals provided five categories for which it would allow a claim of sovereign immunity. These were internal administrative acts such as the expulsion of an alien, legislative acts like nationalisation, acts concerning the armed forces, acts concerning diplomatic activity and public loans. This approach has been followed in a number of subsequent decisions.

The Foreign Sovereign Immunities Act of 1976, though stated as deriving from the development of the restrictive doctrine of sovereign immunity, nevertheless produced some significant changes in the existing law; for example, in contrast to the classification of the activities of foreign sovereigns on the basis of the nature and purpose of the activities proposed in the *Victory Transport* case, the Act preferred that the test be the nature and not the purpose of the activities. This change has the effect of rendering what had developed as the leading interpretation of that problem of no significant value once the Act came into force.

The Act was intended to accomplish four objectives: first, to codify the restrictive principle of sovereign immunity which limits the immunity of a foreign state to its public acts (*jure imperii*) alone; second, to ensure that this principle is applied in litigation before US courts by transferring the determination of sovereign immunity from the executive branch to the judicial branch; third, to provide a statutory procedure to make service upon, and obtain *in personam* judgement upon, a foreign state which would render unnecessary the practice of seizing and attaching property to obtain jurisdiction; and fourth, partly to remedy the problems of obtaining execution of a judgement.

In the House Hearings on the Bill, the Legal Adviser provides an explanation for shifting the interpretation of commercial activity to the courts, as follows:

> We realize that we probably could not draft legislation which would satisfactorily delineate that line of demarcation between commercial and governmental. We therefore thought it was the better part of valor to recognize our inability to do that definitively and to leave it to the courts with very modest guidance. (H.R. Rep. No. 1487, 94th Cong., 2d. Sessions, 1976, at p.53.)

Section 1065 (a) of the Act sets out the general circumstances which would defeat a claim of sovereign immunity as follows: explicit and implied waivers by foreign states, commercial activities having a nexus with the United States, circumstances where 'rights in property taken in violation of international law are in issue', rights in real estate and in inherited and gift property located in the United States, all non-commercial tort actions for money damages. Section 1065 (b) further denies immunity to a foreign state where a suit in admiralty is brought to enforce a maritime lien against a vessel or cargo of that foreign state based on a commercial activity of that foreign state.

The conditions under which judgement, if not complied with, may be enforced against the property of the foreign state in the United States are set out specifically in Section 1610 (a) as those where immunity has been either explicitly or implicitly waived, where 'the property is or was used for the commercial activity upon which the claim is based' or where the execution is of a judgement establishing rights in property taken in violation of international law (or which has been exchanged for property taken in violation of international law). Section 1610 (b) allows execution, where judgement has been obtained against an agency or instrumentality of a foreign state engaged in commercial activity in the USA against all its property in the USA, where immunity has implicitly or explicitly been waived, or the judgement relates to a claim for which the entity is not otherwise immune from suit.

The Foreign Sovereign Immunities Act, while clarifying the law in a number of respects and being in both substance and procedure consistent with prevailing international practice (other than in the UK), does leave the ambit of 'commercial activity' sufficient to deprive a foreign state of sovereign immunity to be defined by a succession of judicial proceedings.

The passing into law of this Act left the United Kingdom as the only remaining important Western trading country with a tradition of absolute immunity, although events were already in motion in that country to break with that tradition. In 1975 in *Thai-Europe Tapioca Service Ltd.* v. *Government of Pakistan, Directorate of Agricultural Supplies* [1975] 1 W.L.R. it was once more confirmed by the Court of Appeal 'that ... except by consent the courts of this country will not issue their process so as to entertain a claim against a foreign sovereign' (*per* Lord Denning M.R. 1492).

Only in the next year, however, the Privy Council in *The Philippine Admiral* [1976] 2 W.L.R. 214 was able to find that, in an action *in rem* concerning a vessel owned by a foreign sovereign, immunity did not lie where that vessel was used for purely commercial purposes, arguing as one of the grounds for that decision: 'In this country – and no doubt in most countries in the western world – the state can be sued in its own courts on commercial contracts into which it has entered and there is no apparent reason why foreign states should not be equally liable to be sued there in respect of such transactions' ([1976] 2 W.L.R. 232).

The Privy Council in this case confirmed that its decision had no impact at all on the law regarding actions *in personam* and said at p.233, 'It is open to the House of Lords to decide otherwise but it may fairly be said to be at the least unlikely that it would do so.'

While in fact the House will be having a chance to do so in the case of *Trendtex Trading Corporation Ltd.* v. *Central Bank of Nigeria* [1977] 2 W.L.R. 356, the Court of Appeal, at one stage short of the House of Lords, extended the *Philippine Admiral* rationale .to an *in personam* action. The circumstances from which the Trendtex action arose were that payment for cement and demurrage was guaranteed by irrevocable letters of credit issued by the Central Bank of Nigeria. Nigeria's ports were unable to cope with the congestion caused by 20 million tons of cement a year being delivered into ports only able to accept 2 million tons of cement a year. Consequently there were shortages of other vital imports of food and in the crisis resulting from this and other reasons a new military administration took over the reins of government. As one of its first moves the new administration suspended the import of cement and then set up a committee to negotiate fresh terms.

In the instant circumstances shipment had been made by the plaintiff but the Central Bank of Nigeria declined to make the payments claimed to be due for the price and demurrage. The Central Bank of Nigeria claimed that it could not be sued in the United Kingdom on the letters of credit because it was entitled to sovereign immunity. It was held by a Court of Appeal comprising Lord Denning M.R., Stephenson and Shaw L.JJ. that the bank was not an emanation arm, *alter ego* or department of the State of Nigeria and was, accordingly, not entitled to immunity from suit (*per* Lord Denning M.R. and Shaw L.J.) that even if the bank were part of the government, since international law now recognised no immunity from suit for a government department with respect to ordinary commercial transactions, it was not immune from suit on the plaintiff's claim, and that since the bank was not entitled to immunity from suit the injunction preserving funds within the jurisdiction to satisfy the plaintiff's claim should be continued.

It should be noted that this last point is consistent in general terms with Section 1610 of the US Foreign Sovereign Immunities Act which provides that, where there is no immunity from suit, there should also be no immunity from attachment or execution. The Court of Appeal's decision in the *Trendtex* case is consistent with the rules set forth in the European Convention on State Immunity which has been signed (although not ratified) by the United Kingdom.

In this area of sovereign risk, as the above discussion suggests, for banks involved in commercial transactions with sovereign governments, their instrumentalities or agents, the law in both the USA and the United Kingdom has been clarified recently and more certainty seems to have been provided in respect to the ability to gain execution as well as judgement. Of course, problems still remain concerning especially the nature of 'commercial activity' sufficient to deny a claim of sovereign immunity, but it does appear that with respect to loan agreements the same result may be achieved by embodying explicit waivers into these agreements.

Further Reading

Delaume, Georges R., 'Public Debt and Sovereign Immunity: The Foreign Sovereign Immunities Act of 1976', *American Journal of International Law*, vol.71, no.1 (January 1977)
, 'Public Debt and Sovereign Immunity Revisited: Some Considerations Pertinent to H.R. 113.5', *American Journal of International Law*, vol.70, no.1 (January 1976)

Harfield, Henry, 'Legal Aspects of International Lending' in F. John Mathis (ed.), *Offshore Lending by U.S. Commercial Banks* (Robert Morris Associates, 1977)

Higgins, Rosalyn, 'Recent Developments in the Law of Sovereign Immunity in the United Kingdom', *American Journal of International Law*, vol.71, no.1 (January 1977)

International Legal Materials (American Society of International Law, Washington, 1977 and 1978), vols.16 and 17

Lauterpacht, H., 'The Problem of Jurisdictional Immunities of Foreign States', *British Yearbook of International Law* (Oxford University Press, London, 1951), vol.28

Von Mehren, Robert B., 'The Foreign Sovereign Immunities Act of 1976', *Columbia Journal of Transnational Law*, vol.17, no.1 (1978)

White, Robin C. A., 'State Immunity and International Law in English Courts', *International and Comparative Law Quarterly*, vol.26 (July 1979)

10 INFORMATION FLOWS AND THE MANAGEMENT OF MULTINATIONAL BANKS

> 'A bank's financial statement is but the departure point for discussions which will lead to sound credit appraisal.' (P. Henry Mueller, 'Sighting in on International Lending', *Journal of Commercial Bank Lending*, November 1972, p.6.)

In discussing domestic banking it was noted earlier that the more information the bank is able to acquire about potential borrowers, the less risk, and, consequently, cost it will face in its business operations. In the case of a multinational bank, its overseas operations will have an information advantage over other banks concerning the financial conditions of domestic firms operating subsidiaries in those overseas countries and may be able to service their requirements more cheaply as a result. This economy arises from the use of existing knowledge at a particularly low marginal cost.

A second potential advantage relating to information flows accruing to a multinational banking operation may be derived from its participation in the inter-bank market. It is alleged that once a bank is established within that market it is regarded — as it regards its fellow participants — as an acceptable lender and borrower to the extent that almost no credit investigation is required for lending, the risk of default is considered minimal, and a very narrow spread may exist between the borrowing and lending rates.

Thirdly, with the greatly expanded range of services now available from many multinational banks, it is quite often the case that a multinational bank will provide the facilities of a house bank for clients. This will enable the bank to acquire a much more perfect knowledge of its clients' operations than a more traditional bank might obtain.

Fourth, the operation of a multinational bank within the main financial centres of the world will provide the bank as a whole with information about both the world economy and the international monetary system which may be used to advantage in the movement of funds. Unlike a purely domestic bank the bank will have a wider range of currencies in which to transact and more information about which may be most appropriate.

Finally, because the multinational bank will usually be of greater size than its domestic parent, it should more readily be able to employ experts in particular aspects of operation, such as forward exchange, the use of tax havens and the use of roll-over loans, which should ensure that all profitable opportunities are pursued.

There is, however, another side to the advantages in information flows in a multinational banking operation, for instance with regard to the advantage in dealing with overseas subsidiaries whose parent is based in the domestic bank's country. This advantage may be to some extent offset by the additional costs in having to acquire knowledge about the environments, legal, economic and social, within which the bank operates. There will also be the costs of providing the information necessary to a larger number of monetary authorities as well as more information to the domestic parent's monetary authority. It is not anticipated that many economies could be derived from these latter requirements.

Turning now to the second advantage, although this may be a correct view for some banks, the unexpected losses by a few banks in 1973 and 1974 were sufficient to make the inter-bank market re-evaluate its lending procedures and establish a tiered market in which only the very largest and well-known banks were able to borrow at the most favourable terms. To some extent this *ad hoc* procedure might be regarded as an admission that the information on which entrée to the advantages of the inter-bank market was allowed was not sufficiently detailed and that only a long tradition in the market and some size could be regarded as providing necessary and sufficient information on which to base preferred treatment.

The second advantage also has another side, perhaps best exemplified by the Fibgest case. Société Continentale de Gestion Financière SA or Fibgest was a company, based in Lausanne, in the business of acquiring mortgages and investing in real estate, a procedure financed by three to six-month loans in the Eurodollar market. The company was forced to refinance its debts when, following the sharp rise in Eurodollar interest rates in 1970, the cost of debt-servicing exceeded its income. In order to refinance these debts the company increased its short-term loans to the extent that by the middle of 1971 95 per cent of its borrowings were of under twelve months maturity. Although its paid-up capital was only 1.4 million dollars, the company was in debt for over 60 million. This had apparently not affected its ability to borrow, as all that was required as security was mention of its parent companies – Continental Grain Company of New York (44 per cent shareholding) and Banque de l'Indochine (39 per cent). When Fibgest's problems finally surfaced, the parent companies disavowed Fibgest, leaving its Eurodollar creditors with some 68 million dollars in loan losses.

Barron's, in reporting the Fibgest collapse, commented that in the market there was 'no security, no collateral, no mortgages, no explicit guarantees. There is scant consideration for underlying assets. There is only trust, based on names.'

The inter-bank market within the Euromarket reacted to Fibgest and certain later unexpected losses by a few banks in 1973 and 1974 by re-evaluating its lending procedures and establishing a tiered market in which only the very largest and well-known banks were able to borrow at the most favourable terms.

Most serious of the difficulties created for those inter-bank market participants not categorised within the first tier was that if they did require access to the market they would be forced to accept terms that would classify them as not first-rate risks. Owing to the blow to reputation which this might involve, a number of banks sought alternative sources of funds and some needed to have recourse to their domestic parent for funds during the period of crisis. In order to be able to use the second advantage without risk it would appear to be necessary for a bank to have ready access to alternative sources of funds.

With regard to the third advantage, the information flow gains are quite clear for the individual bank. In terms of the interests of the growth of enterprise it might be argued that smaller companies, which will not require this range of services for some time yet, may find themselves unable to gain much acceptance with multinational banks that may be necessary bankers if they wish to gain entry into Eurocurrency markets. This seems to be an enforcement of a dichotomy prevalent in many domestic markets, that only large companies have continuous ready access to funds. On the other side, no bank appears to be large enough to single-handedly provide all the requirements of very large companies and syndication of loans will be necessary.

The fifth advantage assumes that the bank concerned is able to process and analyse the vast array of information which will flow to it and ignores the cost of doing so. As was noted in the discussion of the domestic bank's operations the more information available about a particular type of lending, the less risk could be attached to it. However, at the international level, and more particularly within the Eurodollar market, the necessity for short-run decisions creates a trade-off between the time it takes to assemble and analyse information about a particular loan and the time during which Eurodollar deposits need to be turned over in order to make a profit.

Further Reading

Baltensperger, Ernst, 'Cost of Banking Activities: Interactions between Risks and Operating Costs', *Journal of Money, Credit and Banking*, vol.4, no.3 (August 1972)

— and Hellmuth Milde, 'Predictability of Reserve Demand Information Costs and Portfolio Behaviour of Commercial Banks', *Journal of Finance*, vol.31, no.3 (1976)

Mueller, P. Henry, 'Sighting in on International Lending', *Journal of Commercial Bank Lending* (November 1972)

11 DIAGRAMMATIC ILLUSTRATIONS OF MULTINATIONAL BANK OPERATIONS

Owing to the sheer complexity of multinational banking operations, it is an unreasonable expectation that they should be able to be described in any completeness in a simple diagrammatic illustration. In this chapter, while a model of certain multinational banking operations is provided in order to illuminate certain critical differences between these operations and those of a purely domestic bank, it is emphasised that it is difficult to provide by this means any more than an illustration, in simplified terms, of main decisions made within the context of one market and two currencies. As a means of simplification the results of the decisions illustrated are shown as affecting the proportion of funds to be held as reserves.

In earlier chapters the risks associated with the roll-over credit procedure of lending and with exchange rate movements have been analysed, and it is apparent that these risks incorporate the major quantifiable elements of uncertainty in a multinational bank's operations. A number of assumptions are necessary before it is possible to illustrate these decisions diagrammatically.

First, it is assumed that the bank whose decisions will be shown is regarded as a typical multinational bank in its market of operation, that is, it is of reasonable size, it has an adequate ratio of capital to deposits and its loan structure is not dominated by a single borrower or a few borrowers. Its normal source of funds is the inter-bank market and it is sufficiently well regarded within that market to be able to attract funds at the best rate offering.

Second, it is assumed that the bank's transactions occur in only one currency, referred to as domestic currency, but that at the end of each income period they must be translated into a second currency, referred to as foreign currency, in which its accounts are expressed. Third, the bank is able to hedge its commitments in a forward exchange market at the market price. Fourth, it is assumed that the bank, as is normal within the Eurocurrency markets, lends either medium or long-term on a roll-over basis and, as it acquires its funds in the short-term inter-bank market, it must renew these funds sources at, say, six-monthly intervals. Fifth, it is assumed that the medium or long-term loans are made at rates fixed for their maturity, and that the roll-over risk relates to the

price at which the short-run funds flow may be renewed and to the
quantity of funds available. Sixth, we assume that the bank is not
subject to any regulatory constraints in either currency, which implies
that because it has no formal lender of last resort facility to call upon,
it must therefore hold sufficient reserves to act as a prudent cover on
its transactions. Finally it is assumed that the bank has been in operation for some time and that it has a series of medium and long-term
loans which it continually refunds by accepting short-term deposits.

Figure 10

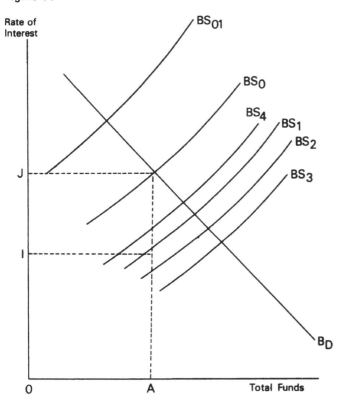

Let us begin with the bank's acquisition of funds from the inter-bank
market and its lending of these funds on a medium or long-term basis.
It is assumed that the bank has on the basis of earlier transactions lent
OA of funds on at least a medium-term basis at a rate of interest of OJ,
but that if possible it would wish to increase its lending if funds are
available at an acceptable cost.

At present, the bank must roll-over its short-term deposit funds in order to continue to finance the loan. It is assumed that the rate of interest on the loans already made is fixed for their maturity, which concentrates the bank's concern on the price at which it may renew its deposit funds. To illustrate this, the price of funds is depicted on the vertical axis and the quantity of funds is shown on the horizontal axis in Figure 10. The function of B_D represents the bank's demand function for funds to lend on at least a medium-term basis. At present, just prior to the renewal or roll-over of the short-term deposits, the bank has OA of funds lent at a return of OJ. For the last six-month period (assuming this to be the period of deposit) the bank paid OI to acquire these funds, allowing it a profit margin of IJ. BS_1, the supply function for short-run deposits, shows the supply of funds from the inter-bank market for the six-month period just ending. It is, of course, possible that the short-run supply function for the next six months may be quite different; for example, in 1974 short-run interest rates rose above long-term bond yields. At that extreme the bank could face a supply function such as BS_0 at which it just breaks even on the last amount of loan funds, or BS_{01} where all short-term funds are too expensive to be considered as available. More probably, however, the range of functions faced by a typical bank would be from BS_3 to BS_4, that is, representing at best an improvement in the bank's return and at worst a squeeze on that return.

For the moment it will be assumed that the bank's supply function does not change and that it is able to gain IJ in the current as well as in the immediate past period. It is further assumed that OJ of receipts which are in domestic currency must now be translated into a second currency, F, in which currency the books of the bank are written.

In Figure 11, market funds are expressed in terms of the currency of transaction converted to the currency in which the bank's balance sheet is denominated. Line F1 represents a 1:1 conversion, that is, no change on the current rate of exchange between the two currencies; line F2 represents a revaluation of the second currency in terms of the first currency, that is, OJ domestic currency will convert into less foreign currency than before; and line F3 represents a devaluation or depreciation of the second currency in relation to the first currency, that is, OJ of domestic currency will convert into more foreign currency than before. By using these lines to make the currency conversions we are able to look at the potential foreign exchange losses and profits and translate these (in a further diagram) into possible hedging commitments. Note that while it was often possible under the fixed exchange

rate system either to ignore foreign exchange risk, because signs of
impending change were available in sufficient time to move out of a
weakening currency, or to convert transactions into that comparatively
riskless international asset, the US dollar, under the managed floating
system it is now, more often than not, unrealistic to assume that a
constant rate of exchange would persist between the two currencies in
a six-month period.

Figure 11

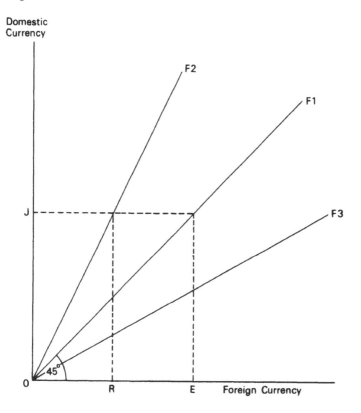

As illustrated above, if we assume that the domestic and foreign
currencies are convertible on a 1:1 basis, the bank's receipts and profit
will be the same in either currency, that is OE = OJ. In the current real
world environment, however, the position OE = OJ would be the mid-
point of a possible range of different exchange rates and, depending on
the direction in which the rate might most strongly be expected to
move, the bank may find it advantageous to hedge its position. That is,

just as the bank may foresee a range within which the short-run supply function for its funds may move and may, as we shall see shortly, hold reserves as an insurance against a shortfall or a too expensive supply, it may equally foresee a range of potential movement for the exchange rate between the two currencies against which it may wish to protect itself. It is assumed that the bank will wish to hedge against fluctuations in the foreign currency since it is not part of its own operations to take a net position or an exchange risk in that currency.

If we now put the above two diagrams together we may derive two additional schedules, one reflecting the hedging cost against possible foreign exchange rate fluctuations and the other summarising possible effects of exchange rate risk and roll-over risk on the bank's holding of reserves.

Figure 12

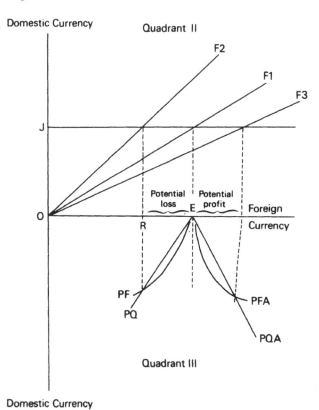

In Figure 12 we look at the possibility of the bank hedging or cover-ing its foreign exchange transactions given the information available from Figure 11. If OE in foreign currency is obtained from the transla-tion of OJ in domestic currency, the exchange rate between the two currencies will be constant and no need to protect against fluctuations in the exchange rate will arise. Under managed floating this will be too heroic an assumption to make, and let us instead assume that the bank is concerned that the foreign currency will revalue in terms of the domestic currency, that is, that OJ in domestic currency will convert into OR in foreign currency rather than into OE.

Rather than face the potential loss of ER, the bank may wish to take out a forward exchange contract which will protect it against this pos-sible loss. The schedule PF indicates the modification in the expected price of translation in the form of a forward exchange premium that the bank will wish to make to protect itself from the chance of loss. Purchasing a forward exchange contract to guarantee the rate of con-version between the two currencies will remove that chance.

Figure 13

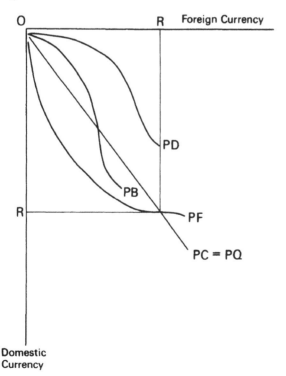

O   R   Foreign Currency

PD

PB

R

PF

PC = PQ

Domestic
Currency

While in Figure 12 we represent the bank's position as being concerned at an increasing rate over potential exchange rate changes as its
potential losses rise, this is not the only possible position the bank
might take. In Figure 13 we look at three other positions; the curve PD
represents a risk-lover's view of the increasing risk of loss, PC represents
the less usual case of risk changing at a constant rate with increasing
amounts of loss, while PB represents perhaps the most probable of
alternatives, where at low levels of potential loss the risk is regarded as
unimportant, at more average levels of potential loss the risk is regarded
as of consistent importance, and beyond average levels of potential loss
the risk is regarded as of increasing importance.

Of course it is not only the bank's view of risk as shown by its ability
to pay a higher or lower premium on forward exchange contracts that is
relevant here, but also it is the amount of forward exchange premium
that will be asked by the market for the level of protection sought. We
assume for simplicity that the line PQ represents the amount of forward
premium asked, expressed as a function of the amount of loss to be
protected against. In Figure 13, PQ is drawn so that only at a risk of loss
of OR will the bank undertake a forward contract. At a potential loss of
less than OR the bank will attempt to reduce its risk of loss by other
techniques, such as the early translation of accounts or by finding an
alternative means of matching the exposure to loss. Note that if the
bank's view of risk had been represented by PD it would hedge against
any risk of loss.

When we add this third quadrant into our four-sector diagram shown
in Figure 14, it will be noted that it is reduced in vertical scale since the
proportion of premiums paid to total funds will be quite small, and
because we wish to add the amount of reserves necessary to cover
premiums on forward exchange contracts to that amount necessary to
cope with roll-over risk. In fact the premiums asked and paid are
represented by the schedules PQ and PF respectively, while the total
forward contract commitment is represented by PF_1. That is, the
provision of OP in foreign currency from OJ in domestic currency is
achieved by paying PF to obtain PR to add to OR which would be
obtained if the exchange rate line was F2.

It remains for us to add the amount paid in forward exchange
premium to the amount necessary to take account of a rise in roll-over
price, in order to find the amount of reserves a bank would need to
hold entirely for the purposes of hedging against these two-price risks.
Of course the reserves committed to these purposes will be in addition
to the normal prudent proportion of deposits held as reserves by purely

Figure 14

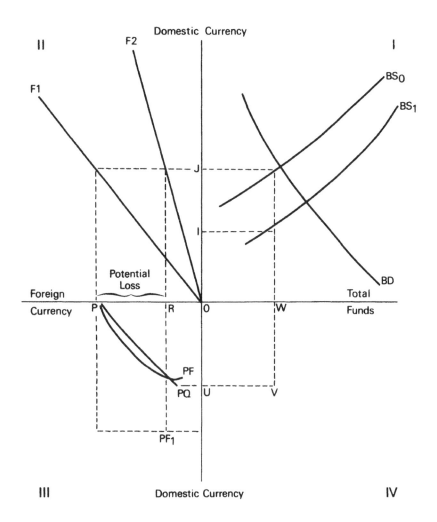

domestic banks. It is suggested that the additional reserves of an amount equal to the area OUVW will be held.

12 CONCLUSION

The main question that arises from the analysis of this Part is – what are the differences between these operations and those shown in our un-regulated and regulated domestic bank models? The essential difference appears to be that the multinational banks are most vulnerable to price risk and, owing to the spread of their operations and the number of markets they can tap, much less vulnerable to quantity risk than are regulated domestic banks. The unregulated domestic bank faces the problems of quantity risk in relation to its flows of funds and the level of liquidity of its voluntary reserves, but as it is itself the price-setter it does not face price risk.

For the regulated bank, the analyses of Parts 2 and 3 would support the view that the regulations of most impact on the bank's level of operations and profit are those which limit the quantity of its loans.

It might be argued on this basis that multinational banks do represent a diversification away from quantity risk, and an apparently successful one. Until the move in the 1970s to floating exchange rates it could also be argued that the volume of their operations and their spatial spread minimised roll-over risk as a serious problem. The move to managed floating has, however, increased the problem of foreign exchange risk, which is essentially a price risk, and has made it a prime concern not only of banks but of the various supervisory authorities.

The recent moves to place multinational banking in a number of countries within a domestic regulatory framework poses some diffi-culties, given the different nature of the important risk area. Quantity restrictions only turn these banks to other sources of funds, but price restrictions may impose losses, especially if they are varied unexpectedly. In terms of the model of our last chapter, the price of funds and of foreign exchange are the important determinants of profit. This may imply that regulatory constraints applied through the markets may be of much more importance for these banks than the more direct controls.

It is possible to make the interesting conclusion that the moving of multinational banks under domestic regulations may not be of serious disadvantage to these banks, unless combined with other requirements that change the structure of their operations. Before reasonable com-ment may be made on this point, it is necessary to investigate in Part 5 the moves towards regulating multinational banks.

Part 5

THE SUPERVISION AND REGULATION OF MULTINATIONAL BANKING

'A bank does not live and have its being moving from one crisis, or business triumph, to another. Once standing on its feet its life is for the most part spent pursuing the even tenor of its way.' (Geoffrey Tyson, *100 Years of Banking in Asia and Africa 1863-1963* (National and Grindlays Bank, London, 1963), p.213.)

1 INTRODUCTION

Three particular aspects of multinational banking operations have given rise to demands for some degree of controls to be implemented, whether by national or international monetary authorities. First, there is the off-shore location of consortium banks, or of subsidiaries of banks domiciled elsewhere in countries where regulatory control of banking does not meet the main European or American standards of control or their solvency and liquidity requirements.

The second aspect relates to certain features of multinational banking operations that have not been confined to, but which have been instanced by, banks operating in the Euromarkets. Here the issue is that of controlling the Euromarkets, or, as the Bank of England put it last year (March 1977), 'Should developments in the Euromarkets be a source of concern to regulatory authorities?' The features referred to are the foreign exchange losses incurred by a few banks which generated the 1974 crisis of confidence, the capital adequacy of the banks, the quality and country structure of lending, the risk of default in the Eurocurrency system due to the dealing in large unsecured loans, and the dangers inherent in the constant necessity to roll-over short-term deposits at satisfactory rates in order to finance loans of longer maturity than the deposits.

The third aspect relates to the operation of foreign banks alongside domestic banks when the latter are subject to regulatory controls from which the former are either partially or totally exempt.

All of these aspects raise a question about the kind of supervisory authorities that are appropriate for multinational banking – that is, should they be national central banks or some supranational agency or agencies? And a further question related to this is: should there be an international code of internal controls for these banks or should they rather be subject, as purely domestic commercial banks now are, to the whims and vagaries of the instruments used to implement monetary policy?

No universal panacea is proposed in this Part, but rather attention is given to the types of regulation which have been discussed both nationally and internationally, including the possibility of self-regulation.

In Part 4 the problems of the multinational banks in the Eurodollar market crisis of confidence of 1973-4 were discussed, and it is apparent that the regulatory authorities of some countries did take steps to ensure that a crisis of confidence in their own banks could not occur in the future — Germany with the 'Lex Herstatt' and the UK with the 'lifeboat' operation. Nevertheless *The Banker*, in a recent survey of City of London bankers published in March 1978, found that 49 per cent of those responding felt that current levels of spreads in the Eurocurrency markets were 'somewhat insufficient' to provide reserves against anticipated bad debts, 22 per cent felt the spreads were 'vastly insufficient', and only 2 per cent felt they were completely sufficient. Further, while pointing out that this was not an especially new or recently increased danger, 58 per cent believed that there was a danger of banks overtrading in the Eurocurrency markets. These results suggest that large-scale problems or non-payment of interest are still potentially of concern to the Eurocurrency markets, even allowing for the adjustments made to national regulations and certain international agreements to provide support.

Whether the current concern is justified or not and whether new regulatory controls are proposed or not, the debate on the need to regulate certain of these activities seems certain to recur whenever concern is expressed about any aspect of Eurocurrency operations.

The reasons for wishing to control multinational banking operations are, of course, the same reasons as are given as justification for the control of domestic banking operations, that is, the protection of depositors, the need to have control over the volume of money and credit, and the curbing of any tendency to monopoly power in banking at the same time as encouraging competition. The policy basis for control has two main sources; firstly the equity principle, which suggests that domestic banks operating abroad should be regulated in their foreign sphere of operations as if these operations comprised domestic operations. A rationale for this approach is that the domestic bank, wherever it sustains an unreasonable loss, would have ultimate recourse to the domestic central bank as a lender of last resort.

The second main source of a policy basis is the neutrality principle, which suggests that wherever domestic banks operate overseas, that part of their operations should be subject to the regulations of the country in which those operations occur. As the scope of national regulation of banking varies enormously across countries, it is improbable that pursuit of the neutrality principle could fail to breach the equity principle.

Discussion in these terms, however, follows the tendency still prevalent in much of the literature to confuse prudential supervision with regulatory constraint. In the chapters of this Part an attempt is made to separate these two areas. The first chapter examines prudential supervision in relation to multinational banking and suggests a scheme to cope with the difficult problem of providing a lender of last resort facility for consortium banks. In the remainder of this Part we are concerned with the regulatory constraints which vary with the implementation of changing monetary policies and to which domestic banks are normally subject.

There are four approaches to the regulation of foreign banks which are reflected in recent events; do nothing, adopt a restrictive approach to foreign banks, equalise regulatory treatment for foreign and domestic banks, and lessen some restrictions on domestic banks to enable them to compete more effectively with foreign banks.

In the United States it is alleged that the 'do nothing' approach has resulted in a major structural change in the banking system as foreign bank US assets have risen over the past five years by almost five times the rate of expansion of the assets of US domestic banks. The reaction to this was suggestions primarily for more restrictive legislation, but the International Banking Act of 1978 has tended to move towards equity between foreign and domestic banks and allows for subsequent moves to lessen certain restrictions on domestic banks. In contrast the Canadian Bank Act of 1978 has adopted a very restrictive approach to foreign banks.

The nationalistic Canadian approach and its gestation are examined in some detail, and its implications for the type of banking operations described in the last Part are discussed as an example of the restrictive approach to the control of foreign banks. All four approaches have either been followed or suggested in the USA, and for this reason some time is spent on the various arguments presented in the preliminary manoeuvres prior to the International Banking Act's implementation.

Finally, in this Part the potential impact of regulatory constraints on multinational banking is discussed and its implications for the genre of multinational banking are examined.

2 PRUDENTIAL SUPERVISION AND MULTINATIONAL BANKING

'No doubt all precautions may, in the end, be unavailing –
"On extraordinary occasions", says Ricardo, "a general panic
may seize the country, . . . – against such panic banks have no
security *on any system*." The bank or banks which hold the
reserve may last a little longer than the others, but if apprehension pass a certain bound, they must perish too.' (Walter
Bagehot, *Lombard Street*, 1873 (Irwin, Illinois, 1962), p.27.)

In modern economies the lender of last resort facility is the provision,
by an official authority, of credit under conditions of stress to the
financial system. The tradition that a central bank should provide the
lender of last resort function for banks only received unequivocal recognition following the publication of Walter Bagehot's *Lombard Street* in
1873. In this book Bagehot examined the nature of periods of internal
panic in England which put great strains on the banking system and
looked at possible remedies. He commented that the Bank of England,
which held the ultimate banking reserve of the country, had made very
large advances to the banks in the financial panics of 1847, 1857 and
1866 but 'it does not distinctly acknowledge that it is its duty' (p.30),
and even in 1866 it was at one time believed that the Bank of England
would not be making any advances on Consols. From the publication of
Lombard Street in 1873 the function of lender of last resort was recognised as a responsibility by the Bank of England and, subsequently, this
function came to be assumed by other central banks and to be automatically accepted by the twentieth century's new central banks.
Regulation A, Section 201.2(e) of the US Board of Governors of the
Federal Reserve System provides that 'Federal Reserves credit is available to assist member banks in unusual or emergency circumstances
such as may result from national, regional or local difficulties or from
exceptional circumstances involving only a particular member bank'.

Of course, all of the above cases refer to the acceptance of the lender
of last resort function by a central bank for the operations of banks
chartered in its own country and normally transacting in its own
currency. That is, the nationality of bank charter is the basis for the
protection offered by the central bank's provision of the lender of last
resort facility.

Multinational banking by its very definition comprehends jurisdictional overlap which may derive from the powers of the domestic country's central bank, the *lex debitoris* or regulations concerning both banking and exchange control regulations of economies in which its branches are domiciled, and the *lex monetae* or the currency laws of the economy whose currency is that of payment.

If a central bank acts as lender of last resort to those banks chartered in its country, that is, if the lender of last resort function is attached to the nationality of charter, this will be an inducement to hold this nationality of charter. Alternatively a central bank may accept a lender of last resort role on the basis of residence, usually requiring from branches of foreign banks in residence some 'endowment capital'. A central bank could base its lender of last resort role on currency in order to enhance its seigniorage return, providing an assurance to holders of external balances that they would be convertible into domestic assets which would encourage external banks to offer deposit accounts denominated in this currency.

The position taken by the Bank of England concerning branches of overseas deposit-taking institutions was stated in its paper 'The Licensing and Supervision of Deposit-Taking Institutions'[1] as follows:

> Branches of overseas deposit-taking institutions operating in the United Kingdom will, like deposit-takers incorporated in this country, need to hold a licence or be recognised as a bank in order to take deposits. The Bank will be concerned to ensure that they conform to appropriate standards in the conduct of their business, but the arrangements for their prudential supervision will remain primarily a matter for the supervisory authorities in the country of origin. Branches of overseas deposit-taking will not be required to have separate endowment capital in the U.K.

For the European Economic Community which is dedicated to the harmonisation of banking regulations and supervisory practices in common with the harmonisation of other aspects of economic activities, the Committee on Banking Regulations and Supervisory Practices was established in 1974 by the Governors of the Group of Ten to harmonise broad aspects of national banking. The Bank for International Settlements provides the secretariat for the Committee. Part of the Committee's work has been to attempt to set out guidelines for co-operation between national authorities in the supervision of the foreign branches of banks. While it was readily agreed that a major aim of co-operative efforts in this field ought to be to ensure that no foreign banking establishment is without supervision, gaps of coverage could still arise. For this reason the committee has sought to provide that the host country's main responsibility should be to supervise the liquidity position of foreign bank operations within its territory, while the home country's supervisory authority should assume responsibility for the other aspects of foreign bank operations.

Complications in providing for co-operation between the supervisory authorities of host and parent bank countries include the inability, often because of domestic legislative requirements, of the supervisory authorities to exchange confidential data provided by a bank to local supervisory authorities, and the inability of a parent bank's supervisory authority to obtain information directly from a foreign branch. If direct inspections of a foreign branch are not possible because of legal restrictions, the Committee urged that the host country's supervisory authorities ought to be able to undertake these on behalf of the supervisory authorities of the parent bank's country.

Differences in the accounting and auditing practices between countries are still sufficient to prevent, in a number of cases documented by the Committee, early recognition of signs of impending failure. To some extent the risks of default by borrowers may be reduced by a process of reporting all loans by financial institutions to a central agency, from which banks may discover the total indebtedness of individual countries, but this is much more difficult to achieve in the case of multinational companies which are able to borrow in many countries, both inside and outside the EEC.

A major approach of the Committee on Banking Regulations and Supervisory Practices (formerly known as the Blunden Committee, now as the Cooke Committee) has been in the area of increasing and improving information flows. The Committee comprises representatives of the banking authorities of the Group of Ten and Switzerland and Luxembourg. It has eschewed attempts to harmonise national banking systems, believing that to be the purpose of the EEC's committees, or to provide investigatory services for problem banks, and has turned its attention to much wider issues.

Its main endeavours have been to increase information flows and to attempt to set up international procedures which will prevent any foreign banking establishment from escaping supervision. Apart from its own publications through the Bank for International Settlements, all of the monetary authorities within the BIS reporting area have agreed to provide half-yearly surveys of the external positions of banks within their territories, and there are informal channels for the exchange of information. With regard to the supervision of foreign banking operations, the Committee has agreed that each country which is host to foreign banking enterprises has a responsibility to ensure that each of them is subject to some country's supervision. The case of consortium banks is more difficult but, in the Committee's first view, the only reasonable solution here is for the relevant authority to be the one for the area in which such a bank operates. It sees this approach as creating a problem in that a host country's monetary authority is unlikely to be able to judge the local subsidiary's liquidity, solvency or foreign exchange position in isolation from the parent enterprise's position.

A big step towards facilitating supervision at the international level will have been taken if the Committee's current co-operation with the International Accounting Standards Committee (the IASC) is successful in providing an accounting standard that will harmonise national bank accounting practices. The EEC is at present moving towards harmonising banks' accounts within its area.

George Blunden,[2] in a 1975 paper on the supervision of the UK banking system, discussed the position of the Bank with regard to overseas banks represented in London. Branches of foreign banks are integral parts of their parent bank, and ought to be the concern of that parent bank and its supervisory authorities with regard to support as well as supervision. 'Whilst – on practical grounds – we [the Bank of England] accept supervisory responsibility for banks registered here but owned overseas, such ownership entails responsibility for support, whether the bank concerned is wholly owned or is owned by a consortium' (p.192). In the case of British-owned banks, the Bank as their supervisory authority accepted supervisory responsibility for the overseas branches and subsidiaries of these banks and for their investments in overseas banks.

Blunden comments that the Bank of England had asked shareholders in those consortium banks operating in London and those banks owning subsidiaries in London to acknowledge their moral responsibility for their London operations. In the Bank's view, moral responsibility should be regarded as 'responsibility to support those investments beyond the narrow limits laid down by law of limited liability and, above all, as responsibility to protect depositors with those banks.' The Bank's belief was that in cases where a bank makes business from its association with a particular shareholding bank or banks, then the attachment of the reputation of the shareholding bank or banks to the operations of its branch, subsidiary or associate should ensure that it will support its affiliated operation, particularly with regard to the protection of its depositors.

In the United States the Federal Reserve System's Committee on Foreign Lending, having reviewed existing bank examination procedures for foreign credits in early 1977, recommended changes in Federal Reserve procedures to improve supervision of international banking, and the FRS, the office of the Comptroller of Currency, and the Federal Deposit Insurance Corporation agreed on a new supervisory approach to foreign lending. The Committee's Review had suggested that an effective approach to supervision would need to provide for the uniform measurement of a bank's country exposure, including a systematic approach to the identification of large or troublesome exposure, and to ensure that the banks use adequate internal systems to appraise, monitor and control country exposure which are separate from the normal risk classification systems. It was noted that although measures of country exposure should be uniformly applied throughout the Federal Reserve System there were great uncertainties in any assessment of country risk, and that loan diversification appeared to provide the best protection.

The new supervisory approach had three parts. First, the authorities initiated a common reporting system for international lending information, which attempts to measure international exposure on a consolidated bank basis and disaggregates the bank's claims for each country by both type of borrower and maturity. From this data bank examiners would be able to evaluate the volume, location, maturity and type of claims a bank has abroad, to evaluate these claims reallocated to the country of ultimate risk, and to compare the exposure levels thus identified with the bank's capital.

Second, research economists and country specialists would evaluate country conditions for examiners to use as a basis on which to analyse foreign loan portfolios on objective criteria. From this, examiners will comment on those country exposures which appear excessive either in the light of the country's conditions or the bank's ability to absorb risk. Third, bank examiners would evaluate the risk management system of banks to ensure that it is comprehensive and takes into account all aspects of the bank's foreign operations.

Sir Jeremy Morse,[3] the chairman of Lloyds Bank, in an address to the Institut International d'Etudes Bancaires in 1977, argued that the multinational banks have four lines of defence in the matter of prudential control. First they need to set up good internal systems of control in order to ensure the observance of adequate liquidity and capital ratios and to avoid serious mismatching in maturity, interest rates or exchange rates. It could be argued that if this first line of defence was completely mounted, there would be no need and in fact no case for any regulation to be considered appropriate. However, the three remaining lines of defence advanced in the address suggest that this first line has not been at all well developed by the banks.

The second line of defence is to obtain the benefit of the experience of other banks, not only in reference to the components of the first line of defence but also in providing information exchanges and risk central-isation systems. A vital clue to the increased lack of acceptance by national monetary authorities of the multinational banks' ability for self-regulation is contained here, and that is, the absence (at least for those multinational banking operations within the Eurocurrency markets) of sufficient information on which to make the normal domestic bank assessments of risk. The reliance on reputation and the procedures of loan syndication create at least the inference that each individual loan application is not assessed by each party to a syndication to the extent that each would normally do within its own domestic sphere of operations. The lack of information creates doubt about the validity of risk estimates and tends to make national monetary authorities reflect on the possibilities of losses sufficient to threaten the viability of the operation should such apparently imperfectly informed estimates of risk prove to be wrong.

As the third line of defence, Sir Jeremy Morse suggested that the banks ought to welcome the regulatory reinforcement by authorities, presumably national monetary authorities, of 'good prudential practices', at the same time complaining if the authorities seem to confuse pru-dential requirements with monetary policy regulatory controls. One of the problems here is the vast difference even in prudential requirements of the various national monetary authorities, and these differences very often arise from the different nature of commercial banking operations in various countries. A strong case could be made here for a supra-national code of minimal prudential requirements and, within the limits of their membership, this appears to be capable of achievement through the Basle scheme of supervision.

It is more likely, however, to be the final line of defence advanced which has most hope of creating a bulwark against the encroachment of regulation into this area, and this is the agreement by the banks to submit their affairs to outside auditors and consultants and to make disclosures of information about their operations. If this occurred, the case argued by the banks – that their operations have a high degree of security and that the risks of loss are in fact more apparent than they are real – could be tested in the public area. At present, apart from the US and BIS efforts, the only detailed public information widely diffused in this area relates to those few banks which have suffered serious losses, mostly in the area of foreign exchange. The case for wider knowledge of the multinational banking operations ought to be supported by the banks themselves as a means, for example, of eliminating the need for 'tiering' of interest rates on funds which was often based, for instance in 1973-4, on lack of information. For example, while David Montagu of Orion Bank was able to talk about the strength of his bank, certain market operators, lacking experience in dealing with this and other consortium banks and not having access to sufficient information about Orion to compensate for this lack of experience, classified that bank in an 'unknown risk' category. While it can be argued that information does not necessarily provide a complete substitute for lending experience, its acquisition is surely a crucial part of that experience.

More complete information would also, it is hoped, convince the relevant authorities that regulatory rather than prudential controls of the type used in many countries would threaten the viability of the multinational banking system. We have seen in the last Part that various price risks are the critical area of multinational operations and that attempts to use regulatory controls that affect the pricing mechanism may seriously increase the risk of losses. This is, of course, the contrary conclusion to that which may be made about purely domestic operators who are able to cope with regulations impinging on pricing but find their businesses limited by controls on quantity.

The most serious problem that arises for prudential supervision remains that of attaching responsibility in the case of consortium banks. It is proposed in the remainder of this chapter to examine the nature of this problem and to suggest a solution that may have appeal for both multinational banks and supervisory authorities.

The problem of attaching responsibility is not always a simple one to solve. To illustrate this we shall use an example provided by Allen Frankel[4] and then extend it to a more complex situation. Let us first of all consider the setting up of a Luxembourg branch of a bank chartered in the USA and offering deposit accounts denominated in Deutsche marks. Setting up the branch in Luxembourg necessitates the obtaining of concurrent approvals of the Board of Governors of the Federal Reserve System (in the case of a national bank, also the approval of the state bank supervisory agency if it is a state member bank) and of Luxembourg's Bank Control Commission. It is the prerogative of the US Board to define the widest extent of the banking powers of the Luxembourg branch, which may then be narrowed by the Bank Control Commission of Luxembourg. With regard to its Deutsche mark denominated deposit accounts, the Luxembourg branch will inform its depositors that it will be able to meet its Deutsche mark obligations subject to all of the regulations of Germany being applicable to the customer accounts with the bank, in particular restrictions on the availability of holdings in that currency.

Because the regulatory jurisdiction of the Board of Governors of the Federal Reserve System is based on nationality rather than on residence, the Luxembourg branch will be within the Federal Reserve System's jurisdiction. By operating Deutsche mark denominated deposit accounts in Luxembourg rather than in Germany, the branch is able to avoid holding the reserves required by German authorities against Deutsche mark denominated liabilities. Of course, it is possible for the Bank Control Commission of Luxembourg to place reserve requirements on Deutsche mark deposit accounts, if they wish to do so.

Let us now consider a more complex case of a consortium bank, in which six large banks, each domiciled in a separate country, hold a 16.5 per cent shareholding each. This bank is established in Bermuda which we assume does not offer the usual services of a supervisory authority to the extent of providing lender of last resort facilities. This consortium bank has as its main aim of operation the acceptance of Eurocurrency deposits to provide a base for lending and relending, primarily within the European inter-bank market. To accomplish this aim it sets up branches in London, Paris, Brussels, Amsterdam and other European cities, and each of these offers accounts denominated in a range of currencies. In these circumstances what supervisory authority exists for the protection of depositors? Two answers most readily suggest themselves. First, the supervisory authorities of the countries in which the consortium bank's branches operate might be considered to protect the interests of the depositors of each of these branches. However, as has already been noted above, the solvency of individual foreign branches is incorporated with that of its parent, and without knowledge of the complete operation, which is information unlikely to be available to the supervisory authorities of the branches, adequate supervision becomes very hard. It is of course possible for the supervisory authorities of the branches to require, as the Bank of England has done, a letter of support from the six shareholders in the consortium bank. There is some question about the legal status of these letters and the validity and enforceability of any guarantees contained therein, not to mention the additional complexity of having to enforce any responsibility in six separate cases.

The second answer is that the six shareholders of the consortium bank could provide explicit guarantees to depositors of the consortium bank *de novo* on the grounds that, as the Bank of England quite reasonably points out, the consortium bank's branches trade to some extent on the consortium's associations with its shareholding banks. In the case of consortium banks which have a myriad of shareholders with 2, 3 or 4 per cent each, some of whom are very small banks, the size of the potential debts may appear too great to be accepted by these shareholders. However, it is curious that such guarantees are not provided in cases where a consortium is set up by a small number of very large banks.

In the case of the Western American Bank, when it had liquidity problems because it was either too difficult or too expensive for it to fund some of its loans, the shareholding banks moved to fund their consortium bank's loans. Similar backing on a domestic scale has of course been provided within the USA by banks associated with a number of Real Estate Investment Trusts whose potential has shown no signs of becoming translated into profitable performance but whose names have been associated in the public mind with their backing bank or banks.

Apart from the provision of explicit guarantees by shareholding banks, one further possibility of providing a lender of last resort facility for consortium banks would be to provide a type of reinsurance arrangement on the occasion of the establishment of the consortium bank. In essence, a reinsurance contract commits an insurer to accept part of a future liability underwritten by another insurer at a rate of compensation which may be determined *ex ante*, *ex post* or both. In normal circumstances the amount of the losses to be assumed by the reinsurer will not be known for a considerable time. Reinsurance contracts may be used to provide insurers with short-term finance, with general or specific catastrophe cover, or with the ability to underwrite larger amounts.

In the present context, it would appear to be feasible for each of the shareholder banks to agree on the formation of a consortium bank to accept part of the future liability of the consortium bank by agreeing to insure the same proportion of the consortium's deposits as it has shareholding in that bank, or to accept a stated proportion of any foreign exchange losses incurred by the consortium bank in the future. The consortium bank would pay to its parent shareholders the equivalent of a premium for deposit insurance and the parent shareholders would note the contingent liability on their own balance sheets. Because the nature of the risk insured by the parent shareholders would be part of the memorandum and articles of association of the consortium bank, the markets within which the consortium bank dealt would not have to hypothesise about the extent of parent bank backing or their acceptance of moral responsibility for their offspring. The risk of loss which may be very large for the individual consortium bank becomes much less when divided up amongst its shareholders and, even in the case of a consortium bank with a number of very small banks as shareholders, the premium paid could be regarded as reasonable compensation for acceptance of part of the risk.

Unlike reinsurance contracts, it is quite possible that no future liability may eventuate and, in fact, incorporation of the above provisions in the originating documents of a consortium bank should go a long way towards preventing the bank from being charged more on its borrowings or from being the recipient of some uncertainty in the market because of doubts about its access to a lender of last resort facility.

By placing the shareholding banks' portions of risk on their own balance sheets as a contingent liability, the shareholding banks' recourse to their own supervisory authorities as lenders of last resort (should the losses in fact be catastrophic) should be more assured than under present conditions. The main source of risk in multinational banking in general, and consortium banking in particular, is that the market may become uncertain of the viability of the enterprise and either deny it funds or seek to charge it a premium for funds. By the use of the form of reinsurance-type guarantee suggested here, this risk may not only be removed, but the consortium bank may be accorded much more closely the status which its parent banks hold in the market.

Of course, a third alternative which has not been canvassed here would be the establishment of a supranational monetary authority charged with the provision of supervision, including the provision of lender of last resort facilities to multinational banks. It would appear, however, that the diversity of legislative backgrounds, banking systems and even political structures which exist will prevent this solution from occurring, even more than those problems currently inhibit the creation of monetary union within the EEC.

Notes

1. *The Licensing and Supervision of Deposit-Taking Institutions*, Cmnd. 6584 (HMSO, London, 1976).

2. George Blunden, 'International Co-operation in Banking Supervision', *Bank of England Quarterly Bulletin* (September 1977).

3. Sir Jeremy Morse, 'Control of Multinational Banking Operations', *The Banker* (August 1977).

4. Allen Frankel, 'The Lender of Last Resort Facility in the Context of Multi-national Banking', *Columbia Journal of World Business* (Winter 1975).

Further Reading

Bagehot, Walter, *Lombard Street*, 1st edn 1873 (Irwin, Illinois, 1962)
Blunden, George, 'International Co-operation in Banking Supervision', *Bank of England Quarterly Bulletin* (September 1977)
Federal Reserve Bank of New York, 'A New Supervisory Approach to Foreign Lending', *Federal Reserve Bank of New York Quarterly Review* (Spring 1978)
'Supervising the Euromarket Dinosaur', *The Banker* (August 1978)
Taylor, Martin, 'The EEC Moves towards Harmonising Banks' Accounts', *The Banker* (November 1978)

3 A NATIONALISTIC APPROACH: THE CONTROL OF FOREIGN BANKS IN CANADA

'... unless action is taken soon, control of foreign activities in key sectors of our financial markets will be lost.' (*Study of Foreign Banking in Canada* (Bank of Nova Scotia, 1974).)

Prior to the recent review of the Canadian Bank Act, there had been a considerable history of debate on the thorny issue of foreign banks in Canada. Quite apart from disagreement even within the Canadian banking industry itself about the extent of the problem, there was the problem documented in several studies[1] that Canadian multinational banking expansion was centred in a few countries, in a number of which the regulatory framework was under review. It was feared that if a tight system of controls over foreign bank activity in Canada was implemented it could attract retaliation, but that an open system would pose domestic competitive difficulties.

In 1976, however, the Canadian Bankers Association made four requests in relation to foreign bank regulation in Canada; first, that foreign bank operations be licensed and brought under Federal jurisdiction, second that foreign banks be subject to the Bank of Canada's reserve requirements and to Canadian banking law, third that the operation of any foreign bank within Canada would require that reciprocal facilities are available in its country of origin, and fourth, that foreign banks be restricted to one office per bank.

The large US banks had been the most feared of the foreign entrants, particularly since the 1963 purchase of Mercantile Bank in Canada by Citibank, although Citibank was forced to reduce its holding by 75 per cent.

Following this episode, the Bank Act of 1967 had restricted the foreign ownership interests in chartered banks, to which the term 'bank' was restricted. Allowing the Mercantile holding of Citibank as an exception, no resident or non-resident shareholder was allowed to own over 10 per cent of the voting shares of a bank; non-resident shareholding in total was not to exceed 25 per cent; and the growth of any bank was to be restricted if any individual shareholder or group of associated shareholders owned over 25 per cent of the shares of the bank. In fact, despite the apparent scope of these restrictions there were no limitations on the setting up of foreign bank subsidiaries provided they were not described as banks, and they became competitors of domestic financial institutions in leasing and foreign exchange operations, among other areas, without being subject to control by the Bank of Canada. The establishment in 1973 of the Foreign Investment Review Agency with the aim of screening foreign direct investment in Canada was restricted to new investment, and the Agency had no authority to prevent the extension of services by foreign banks in their existing business.

Two public policy documents relating to the revision of the Bank Act made by the Banks and Banking Law Revision Act, 1978, which consider the problem of foreign banks are the Economic Council of Canada's 1976 study *Efficiency and Regulation: A Study of Deposit Institutions*[1] and the White Paper, *Canadian Banking Legislation*.[2]

In its discussion of foreign bank entry, the Economic Council study noted the conflict inherent in the principles of efficient international specialisation and of adequate domestic control. In its view the foreign bank entry into the domestic wholesale banking area had probably 'lessened the transaction, search and credit rating costs of doing business' (p.92) in Canada. The disadvantages suffered by domestic banks, that they were prevented from entering leasing or the trust and loan area were removable in the Council's view, by widening the powers of chartered banks in some areas as well as by limiting the foreign banks' range of operations.

The approach to regulation put forward in the Council's study has its basis in the principle of non-discrimination which requires that all banks, whether domestic or foreign, be treated equally. It proposed that a separate Foreign-Owned Banks Act accompany the revised Bank Act. The Foreign-Owned Banks Act would require that foreign-owned institutions accepting deposits in Canada meet certain conditions which would involve providing stages for foreign bank entry into domestic retail banking. For no longer than ten years after the Act came into force, each foreign bank entering Canadian banking would be allowed to control only one Canadian banking operation, with its activities limited to those allowed to domestic banks under the Bank Act. The Council believed that this restriction ought to be sufficient to allow existing domestic near-bank institutions to enter the field if they wished to do so.

After this initial stage, a foreign bank might either operate as in this first stage, or obtain the same branching powers as domestic banks provided that it sold a stipulated proportion (possibly up to 50 per cent) of its equity to Canadian shareholders, and that the parent foreign bank held no more than 25 per cent of the equity, with other shareholders restricted to holdings of 10 per cent. In this second stage a foreign bank could buy into an existing Canadian institution with regulatory approval.

In order to accept deposits within Canada it would be necessary for any foreign-owned corporation to obain a licence from the Supervisor of Deposit Institutions (or the equivalent provincial authority) which would be available only where the parent bank was a financial institution subject to regulatory control within its own country, the regulatory authorities of which were willing to exchange information and communicate the results of their regulatory inspections of the parent bank. Should this co-operation by other banking authorities not be possible, the federal government could use its exclusive power under Section 91 (15) of the British North America Act to acquire jurisdiction of any bank. However, the operation of foreign banks in non-banking areas appears to be outside the scope of this authority. A further sub-section of the same Act, Section 91 (25), however, provides the federal government with exclusive jurisdiction over all matters concerning aliens which could be used to achieve control.

The White Paper, the second document, also proposed to place foreign bank operations in Canada within the legislative framework of domestic banking. While the maintenance of Canadian control of the domestic banking industry was a major aim, the White Paper supported a balance between this aim and the gains from additional competition which it was thought foreign banks would bring to the industry.

Apart from purely domestic considerations, the White Paper was also concerned with using its proposals for foreign branches as a basis for reciprocal treatment for Canadian banks and financial institutions operating multinationally.

The White Paper proposed that the Bank Act allow for the incorporation of subsidiaries of foreign banks as banks under that Act, subject to certain restrictions. Those foreign bank affiliates that both made loans and accepted transferable deposits were to be required to incorporate as banks under the Act if they wished to continue these activities. Further, foreign banks interested in limited operations in Canada would be allowed to invest in the equity of non-bank affiliates or to continue their existing investment. Except where the equity was less than 10 per cent of the voting stock, affiliates would be required to file reports on their activities. Foreign bank affiliates would normally not be permitted to borrow in the Canadian market with the guarantee of their foreign parents or associates. Those foreign banks which had, or wished to establish, representative offices in Canada, would have to register these with the Inspector General of Banks.

It was intended that these forms of organisation be the only forms permitted for foreign banks and that branches or agencies of foreign banks be prohibited. The effect of this restriction would be to limit foreign interests to forms of organisation which would be Canadian legal persons subject entirely to Canadian laws. Subsidiaries thus incorporated would be accorded the general powers accorded to Canadian chartered banks.

The existing Canadian requirements that any shareholder or associated shareholders be denied a controlling interest in a bank in order to avoid potential conflicts of interest would be extended, in the case of foreign bank subsidiaries, to prohibit parent banks of any foreign bank subsidiary from establishing or retaining any other Canadian affiliates.

Special conditions for the incorporation of a foreign bank subsidiary in addition to those applied to domestic banks were recommended in the White Paper. It was proposed that the minimum authorised capital be 5 million dollars, 2.5 million dollars of which was to be fully paid, while the maximum size of a foreign bank subsidiary was to be limited to twenty times its authorised capital. With approved increases in authorised capital to a maximum 25 million dollars, it would be possible for a bank subsidiary to have 500 million dollars of assets. The total operations of foreign banks within Canada would be restricted to 15 per cent of total Canadian commercial lending, although at this point a foreign bank subsidiary could 'Canadianise' itself by reducing its foreign equity holding to 25 per cent in total and 10 per cent for each holder or group of associated holders, and then continue to grow.

The ceiling on authorised capital would be subject to increase by regulation of the Governor in Council in the light of experience.

Foreign bank affiliates would be limited to one place of business, except with the Minister of Finance's approval which would allow them a maximum of five branches, and would have to maintain assets within Canada at least equal to Canadian liabilities.

Incorporation of a foreign bank subsidiary under the Bank Act would be permitted where Canadian banks are as favourably treated within the jurisdiction of the parent bank.

The 1978 Bank Act accepted the White Paper proposals on foreign banks, except for certain modifications in the conditions of incorporation. The new Bank Act adopted size limits on the total assets of foreign bank subsidiaries of 15 per cent of the total bank commercial financing market and provided a mechanism to apply the 500 million dollars limitation on assets of individual foreign bank subsidiaries. While it was provided that the overall size limit would be raised with the growth of the banking system, the individual size limit was to be more flexible and subject to review and the only requirements of the Act were for minimum capital, with increases in that minimum to be subject to approval.

In addition to the White Paper requirement that foreign bank subsidiaries were to have only five branches, the Act further provided that none of the five branches could be located outside Canada and that a foreign bank subsidiary could not itself have a foreign subsidiary.

As a result of the provisions of the 1978 Bank Act the future growth of foreign banks in Canada appears to be limited, unless they are prepared to 'Canadianise' themselves. The Bank Act prohibits foreign banks from having branches or agencies within Canada, as part of a general move within the Act to ensure that foreign interests within the Canadian banking industry are confined to forms of organisation subject entirely to Canadian law. The denial of branching facilities to foreign banks eliminates one of the main advantages that US banks in particular have derived from overseas operations. Alexander Wolfe jun., President of the US Bankers' Association for Foreign Trade, in his statement before the FINE subcommittee, said — 'Depositors of U.S. banks operating abroad derive greater confidence from dealing with a branch of a U.S. bank as opposed to a subsidiary with a legally specified but limited capital.' This advantage has been even further diminished by the provision that a foreign bank affiliate would be unable to borrow in Canada with the guarantee of its parent.

In essence, the foreign banks' operations within Canada are to be limited to a lower level of activity than purely domestic banks, while being subject to the legislative requirements as if they were domestic banks. The best result which could now be achieved by a foreign bank in this environment appears to be to become a domestic bank with minimal foreign equity. The multinational operations of such a bank are seriously limited by the Bank Act provisions and there seems little doubt that intending foreign bank entrants would be deterred.

Notes

1. Economic Council of Canada, *Efficiency and Regulation: A Study of Deposit Institutions* (Ottawa, 1976).
2. Minister of Finance, *Summary of Banking Legislation* (Department of Finance, Ottawa, 1978).

Further Reading

Bank of Nova Scotia, *Study of Foreign Banking in Canada* (1974)
Canada, Bill C-57, Bank Act, 1978

4 MULTINATIONAL BANK REGULATION IN THE UNITED STATES

'The argument boils down to the question — what are fair competitive conditions?' ('The Regulatory Environment: Killing the Golden Goose?', *Euromoney*, June 1977, p.52.)

It may be argued that within the past decade in the United States all four approaches to the regulation of foreign banks have been suggested, analysed and discussed. Without examining the historical pattern in detail, in this chapter we approach the US multinational bank regulations by considering them in relation to the FINE study. First, we outline the provisions relevant prior to the FINE Commission for US banks abroad and for foreign banks in the USA. Next we look at the Brimmer proposals for the first type of bank and at the Bankers' Association for Foreign Trade proposals for the second type. These may be considered the premisses for future action. The FINE study's recommendations, which are briefly discussed, and the Federal Reserve's proposed Foreign Bank Bill are the promises, while the much less sweeping International Banking Act is the performance.

Pre-FINE Provisions

1. US Banks with Overseas Operations

The legislative enactments which facilitated the early twentieth century international moves of US banks have already been discussed in Part 4 in the chapter 'From International to Multinational Banking'. Briefly the 1913 Federal Reserve Act enabled national banks and state member banks to establish branches outside the USA, the 1916 amendment to Section 25 of that Act allowed national banks to invest in corporations engaged in international or foreign banking and the 1919 Edge Act (Section 25(a) of the Federal Reserve Act) provided for national bank investment in, and the formation of, federally-chartered corporations organised for the purpose of international or foreign banking or financial operations. A 1962 amendment to the Federal Reserve Act was intended to allow US banks to compete more effectively in foreign markets by allowing prescription of additional powers for the foreign branches of national banks. A further amendment to Section 25 in 1966 enabled national banks to invest directly in the stock of foreign banks, while in

1970 the Bank Holding Company Act of 1956 was amended to provide a regulatory framework to govern the international activities of US bank holding companies.

As noted in the chapter on prudential supervision, the Federal Reserve has recently moved to improve the information flow concerning these operations and to improve its bank examination methods on the basis of this information.

2. The US Operations of Foreign Banks

Owing to the absence of Federal regulation of foreign banks, these enterprises have been almost entirely subject to state laws, which vary widely in their requirements. The usual beginning for a foreign bank's US operations is a representative office, requiring neither licensing nor state regulation, although it may not accept deposits or approve loans. From that beginning foreign banks may move to agencies, subsidiaries or branches. The main limitation of agencies is that they are unable to accept domestic deposits. However, they are able to lend money, generally for international transactions, and they may hold credit balances related to these transactions and may borrow money.

Subsidiary banks which are foreign-owned are chartered in the USA under either federal or state law and through that procedure become subject to the federal or state regulations. Branches, which are licensed by the states, are subject to state laws and regulations. Foreign banks have also been able to establish broker-dealer security affiliates to operate on US stock markets both as principals, underwriters and investment advisers.

Foreign banks have not been obliged to restrict their operations within state boundaries and they have faced few restrictions in taking over other banks in the USA.

The Brimmer Proposals

Andrew Brimmer,[1] in a series of papers published during and after his term as a member of the Board of Governors of the US Federal Reserve System (1966-74) and subsequently in evidence to the FINE Committee, considered the impact of the activities of US multinational banks on the management of monetary policy and argued for additional weapons to be added to the Federal Reserve System's arsenal to check the extent to which US banks operating multinationally were able to use their overseas resources to reduce the impact of US monetary policy.

Brimmer describes the legal structure which directs banks' ability to operate internationally as built up by six legislative provisions. First, the

Federal Reserve Act of 1913 which initially permitted national banks to establish branches outside the United States; second, the 1916 amendment to the Federal Reserve Act, allowing national banks to invest in corporations operating in international or foreign banking; third, the Edge Act of 1919 which added Section 25(a) to the Federal Reserve Act and authorised the Federal Reserve Board to charter corporations 'for the purpose of engaging in international and foreign banking – either directly or through the agency, ownership or control of local institutions in foreign countries'; fourth, an amendment in 1962 which allowed the foreign branches of national banks to compete more efficiently in overseas markets; fifth, a 1966 provision which allowed national banks to invest directly in the equity of foreign banks; and sixth, the 1970 amendments to the Bank Holding Company Act which established a regulatory framework for the overseas activities of US bank holding companies.

Brimmer characterises these legislative enactments as enabling or permissive, allowing significant discretionary authority to the Federal Reserve which has been used largely with permissive intent. US national banks have been permitted to provide a wider range of services in foreign countries than they are able to do within the US domestic environment.

To the extent that the motive for allowing this overseas expansion has been to improve the effectiveness of US banks overseas in order to promote the foreign commerce of the United States, it is not surprising that the banks' external operations have been limited to the financial area by the authorities.

Brimmer investigated the reactions to monetary policy in the late sixties of twenty large US multinational banks as shown in their sources and uses of funds. During 1969 and early 1970 a main intent of monetary policy was to restrict bank lending to the business sector and this policy was in part implemented by holding interest rate ceilings on time deposits below market rates. In consequence of this policy the large denomination CDs outstanding more than halved between the last quarter of 1968 and the first quarter of 1970 for all of the System's weekly reporting banks (330 in total), with the outstanding CDs of the top twenty multinational banks among that group declining by almost three-fifths. Brimmer suggests that the reporting banks replaced the lost CD funds with a Eurodollar inflow which more than doubled between the last quarter of 1968 and the third quarter of 1969.

In this latter quarter marginal reserve requirements were imposed on Eurodollar borrowings, and the banks' use of this source of funds immediately began to fall as the multinational banks repaid almost one-third of their peak volume of Eurodollar loans between late 1969 and the third quarter of 1970. Because of the size of this repayment the Federal Reserve Board modified the Eurodollar regulation in what proved to be an unsuccessful attempt to stem the flow.

Brimmer examines the changes in the average level of large CDs, Eurodollar borrowings, US Treasury securities, and total borrowings (less Eurodollar borrowing) for all reporting banks, and multinational, regional and local banks within the first group over the quarters from the beginning of 1968 to the second quarter of 1972. From this study he suggests that the rise in Eurodollar borrowings made up about four-fifths of the loss of CD funds for all reporting banks between the last quarter of 1968 and the third quarter of 1969, and 108 per cent of the loss for the multinational banks.

In 1969 and early 1970, a period of severe credit restraint, all of the reporting banks provided more funds to the business sector at the expense of the household and government sectors. Brimmer argues that the multinational banks 'in effect, liquidated loans to households and re-employed the funds elsewhere' (p.451).

From his consideration of these factors, Brimmer concludes that the ability of the multinational banks to acquire Eurodollar inflows enabled them to at least postpone their recourse to more costly domestic sources of finance in order to compensate for the reduction in deposit flow. He argues, on the basis of this conclusion, that additional weapons ought to be added to the Federal Reserve arsenal to control this ability of banks with multinational connections to reduce the impact of monetary policy. The two measures he discusses are an extension of the range of reserve requirements and a variable investment tax credit.

He wished to see the reserve requirements extended to apply to loans to foreign borrowers in the form of either a reserve requirement applicable only to the amount of lending above some determined level, or a requirement applied only against new loans extent. The size of the reserve requirement in either case would be determined by the Federal Reserve's intentions with regard to stabilisation. The groups of loans to be subject to this supplemental reserve requirement should be varied according to policy priorities.

The second instrument suggested was the variable investment tax credit as a means by which the business sector could be required to bear a reasonable proportion of the burden of monetary restraint and to stabilise business demands for external financing. That is, rather than influence bank ability to meet the demand for credit, the authorities could enforce a restriction on that demand at its source.

Both of these suggested instruments are representative of the argument that differential treatment of various sectors of the economy ought to be an available strategy for every instrument of policy, an argument which has not found much support among economists or financial institutions. However, the real burden of Brimmer's argument on closer examination is not access to the external sources of funds but the priority given by multinational banks to lending to business. In several respects this argument is a description of the main rationale for multinational banking rather than an antisocial characteristic of it. As we have already shown in Part 4, the motive for the multinational expansion of banks has been to provide the international services required by the international expansion of business, especially of manufacturing. That is, the banks that have become multinational have been those which already served business as their major clients, and giving preference to them domestically is of course a prerequisite to servicing their financial needs internationally. Lending to the household sector is likely to be peripheral for these multinational banks as also will be lending to government.

Access to Eurocurrency markets has been used by the US multinational banks as a means of both investing funds and acquiring funds, and owing to the business which multinational banks primarily serve (that is, large companies with operations in several states and various foreign countries) it is necessary that within their base economy they provide a full line of services. To restrict access to funds and to limit the line of services able to be provided by these banks could have the consequence that companies will shift their entire allegiance to a foreign-based bank.

The Bankers' Association for Foreign Trade Proposals

In evidence before the FINE subcommittee hearings, Alexander Wolfe jun., President of the Bankers' Association for Foreign Trade, succinctly put the foreign banks' position concerning the regulation of their operations in the USA. The Association (hereafter BAFT) dates from 1921 and includes almost all US banks with significant international operations as voting members, and sixty-eight foreign banks with US operations as non-voting members.

Wolfe, in his evidence, noted that foreign banks were subject almost entirely to state regulation, a practice which resulted in uneven treatment of the same operations between states, and suggested that the best approach would be to allow a foreign bank to select its base state of operation and to elect to operate under either Federal or state charter.

Of prime concern to BAFT was the suggestion in the FINE Discussion

Principles that foreign bank branches should be barred from accepting deposits from domestic entities. It was pointed out in Wolfe's evidence that depositors in US banks overseas derived more confidence in dealing with a US bank branch than with a subsidiary which had legally specified but limited capital, and that depositors in foreign banks in the USA would feel the same way. Further, the protection of deposit insurance was thought to be necessary only for retail banking, whereas for these and other foreign bank operations a more appropriate alternative might be to regulate the proportion of branch assets which must be domiciled in the USA.

The basic premiss behind all of the BAFT suggestions was that foreign banks ought to have equal rights and privileges with domestic US banks, and this involved supporting the extension of the Bank Holding Company Act (1970) provisions to foreign bank operations, and providing them with the same range of activities and reserve requirements as domestic banks.

Of special concern to BAFT were the non-conforming activities of foreign banks, but here their even-handed approach was less evident. Non-conforming activities may be defined as those activities carried on by foreign banks in the USA that went beyond those permitted to US domestic banks. Here BAFT is concerned with the problems of changing the rules for investment after the fact, and it argues that consistency requires that existing non-conforming activities already established be permitted to continue, and also alleges that this 'grandfathering' principle should be applied to existing multistate banking operations and to bank-owned security affiliates. In BAFT's view this applies to an insignificant part of the US commercial banking and securities markets.

The FINE Study – Financial Institutions and the Nation's Economy

The FINE study considered the rapid growth of foreign banks in the United States and of US banks abroad over the preceding decade in some detail and offered certain recommendations in both areas without, however, providing any framework within which its proposals for regulation could be set.

Within the United States foreign banks operated in three main forms – agencies, branches and subsidiaries. Agencies, which are unable to accept domestic deposits other than credit balances generated from their lending activities, are the least regulated. Branches may be considered as analogous to non-member domestic banks in their reserve requirements and the Regulation Q restrictions on their deposits from US non-bank intermediaries. State regulations cope with capital requirements – for example New York State, within which a majority of foreign branches are located, requires 108 per cent of liabilities obtained within the state to be held in specific assets within the state. Branches may make commercial and industrial loans, subject to the limitation that loans to one borrower are restricted in relation to the size of capital of the parent bank. There are also representative offices of many foreign banks in the United States which solicit deposits from US residents and make loans to US residents for their parent banks overseas.

In its 1975 'Discussion Principles', the Committee on Banking, Currency and Housing of the US House of Representatives noted five advantages which foreign banks operating within the United States have over US domestic banks. First, while the domestic banks have been denied access to full-scale operations in more than one state since the McFadden Act of 1927, foreign banks may engage in full-service banking operations in more than one state. Second, the underwriting of and dealing in corporate securities is prohibited for domestic banks by the Glass-Steagall Act but foreign banks may provide these services through subsidiaries and affiliation. A third advantage is the ability, denied to US banks and bank holding companies but allowed to foreign banks, to hold equity investment in US businesses or US subsidiaries of foreign businesses. A fourth advantage is that foreign banks are not subject to the 'closely related to banking' restriction of the Bank Holding Act of 1970, and a fifth is that foreign bank branches and agencies are not subject to the restrictions of member bank reserve requirements.

It was the intention of the FINE proposals to shift the foreign bank operations from their primarily state regulation to federal control. In its examination of the operations of foreign banks within the USA, the study revealed that both agencies and branches transacted quite substantially with their parent or affiliated banks and were more heavily involved in commercial and industrial loans than domestic banks.

The most controversial of the FINE proposals would prohibit branches of foreign banks from accepting deposits in the USA from individuals, partnerships, corporations, states and local government. It was also proposed that branches should be subject to reserve requirements, not only on their borrowings from US depository institutions but also on their Eurodollar borrowings. Other than these proposals, FINE intended that the privileges foreign banks had over domestic banks be withdrawn. Most significant of these privileges were their ability to operate in more than the one state permitted to domestic banks and the ability of their agencies and subsidiaries to underwrite while the Glass-Steagall Act prohibited domestic banks from entering this field.

With regard to the activities of US banks in other countries, the FINE study focused on three elements of risk in these operations — loans to non-banks, inter-bank deposits, and foreign exchange transactions and their potential influence on the stability, competitiveness and response to monetary policy of the US banking system. The solution proposed was essentially to increase the federal US control of the operations by providing that the monetary authorities could impose capital requirements on banks with foreign operations; by restricting the branching of US banks to those countries that allow examination of the branch and its records by US authorities; and by requiring the advance approval of the US authorities for US banks to enter into a joint banking venture abroad to set up a foreign subsidiary or to buy an interest in an overseas bank. One of the difficulties in making recommendations in this area was the paucity of data which justified suggestions for increased data collection on the foreign operations of the banks, subsequently implemented by the Federal Reserve Board of Governors.

The Foreign Bank Bill, Proposed by the Federal Reserve System

This Bill was one of the more moderate proposals for enactment. With regard to those foreign banks operating in the USA entirely through branches and agencies, the Bill proposed an amendment to the Bank Holding Company Act to redefine 'bank' to include these forms of operation. New York State Investment Companies and joint ventures were excluded from this provision. Equality of treatment for foreign banks was further provided for by enlarging entry alternatives by enabling ownership of national banks and by allowing the establishment of a federally licensed branch and of foreign-owned Edge Corporations. The proposed legislation also required Federal Reserve membership for those foreign banking operations with world-wide assets in excess of 500 million dollars. It was proposed that branches and agencies of foreign banks should join subsidiaries in being required to carry Federal Deposit Insurance.

A federal banking licence was to be obtained for all banking facilities of foreign banks, whether they operated under state or federal law. The Secretary of the Treasury was to approve the issuing of a licence by the Comptroller of Currency, after consulting with the Secretary of State and the Federal Reserve Board of Governors. The federal supervisory authorities were to be empowered to enter into mutual arrangements with their foreign equivalents for the interchange of information.

On the contentious issue of foreign banks being able to conduct operations in more than one state, it was proposed that future multistate banking operations and ownership interests in securities and other non-banking enterprises be limited to the same extent as they were for domestic banks. However, it was proposed to grant permanent grandfather status to those non-conforming activities already in existence. That is, in the case of multistate banking operations, a foreign bank would be permitted to retain its operations in the states in which it already operated and could expand within those states in accordance with state law. Foreign banks with grandfathered securities affiliates would not be allowed to acquire or to establish additional securities affiliates.

The International Banking Act 1978

This Act marked the end of an extensive debate within the banking community as well as among the regulators, and, because of that debate, a number of provisions must be regarded as compromises. At the beginning of this chapter two aspects were described, American banking abroad and foreign banking in the USA. A serious problem involved in any proposals to limit the latter severely was the possibility that reciprocal limitations might be placed on US banks abroad. This problem was counterbalanced to some extent by concern that foreign banks had a significant competitive advantage over US banks. The compromise between these is seen in many sections of the Act.

For example, the permission for foreign banks to maintain offices in more than one state, provided that they restrict their soliciting of deposits to their home state, has some counterbalance in the provision for a Presidential review of the McFadden Act which limits US banks to a single state.

The provision allowing foreign banks the option of establishing their US offices under federal or state law is comparable to the alternatives available to domestic US banks. Foreign banks may open branches or agencies under the administration of the Comptroller of Currency with the same requirements and advantages that would apply to a national bank under the National Banking Act. Foreign banks are permitted to operate on a fully competitive basis with domestic banks in their 'home state' but, like domestic banks, only under the rules of the Edge Act are they able to establish branch offices in other states. This limits their out-of-state deposits to foreign sources or to those related to international trade, but they are able to take credit balances (although this latter term is not clearly defined). Offices established on or before 27 July 1978 will not face these restrictions and are allowed unlimited lending powers.

Primary responsibility for bank examinations is given to the Comptroller of Currency for federally chartered foreign bank offices, with state authorities remaining responsible for examining state chartered offices. Foreign offices that accept deposit balances of less than 100,000 dollars (known as 'retail' accounts) are required to be insured by the FDIC and to be subject to its examination, where they are not under the Comptroller's supervision. The Federal Reserve was given a residual authority over all foreign banks, including the power to conduct 'special examinations' with other regulatory agencies. Further, the Federal Reserve was given authority to set reserve requirements for those federally chartered offices of foreign banks with assets of at least 1 billion dollars, and to establish comparable requirements in conjunction with the state regulatory authorities for state chartered offices. In exchange for this reserve requirement which is to be comparable to that for US banks, the foreign banks will be allowed the advantages of Federal Reserve discount, borrowing and clearing facilities.

Considerable controversy had resulted from earlier proposals bringing foreign banks under the provisions of the Bank Holding Company Act in view of their existing non-conforming activities. The Act grandfathers all these activities in the USA from 26 July 1978 and exempts all business external to the USA conducted by a foreign bank from the provisions of the Bank Holding Company Act.

Conclusion

From the above scenario the foreign and domestic banks appear to survive very well. The eventual impact of the Act and the reviews foreshadowed in it seem likely to result in a more competitive, if perhaps more concentrated, industry. Notice that a main advantage claimed for foreign banks in the USA has been their lower prices for loans, which were a consequence (at least partly) of the minimal regulation to which they had been subject. Although this advantage may be removed by reserve requirements, cheap funds may still be available from elsewhere in the multinational banks' operations, perhaps quite reasonably at times from the Federal Reserve. Owing to the nature of US domestic banking regulation, the quantity risk may be minimised still further for multinational banks, without here restricting these banks to only US funds and hence to price risks that may derive from open-market operations.

Notes

1. Andrew F. Brimmer, 'Foreign Banking Institutions in the U.S. Money Market', *Review of Economics and Statistics* (February 1962).

Further Reading

Brimmer, Andrew F., 'Eurodollar Flows and the Efficiency of U.S. Monetary Policy', *The Banker* (April 1969)

—, 'Multinational Banks and the Management of Monetary Policy in the United States', *Journal of Finance*, vol. 28, no. 2 (May 1973)

—, 'How to Control the U.S. Multi-national Banks', *Euromoney* (February 1973)

—, Statement before the Subcommittee on Financial Institutions of the Committee on Banking, Housing and Urban Affairs, U.S. Senate, April 7, 1971, reprinted in the *Federal Reserve Bulletin* (April 1971)

Brown, Marilyn V., 'The Prospects for Banking Reform', *Financial Analysts Journal* (March/April 1976)

Chandler, Lester V. and Dwight M. Jaffee, 'Regulating the Regulators: A Review of the FINE Regulatory Reforms', *Journal of Money Credit and Banking* (1977)

Edwards, Franklin R. and Jack Zwick, 'Activities and Regulatory Issues: Foreign Banks in the United States', *Columbia Journal of World Business* (Spring 1975)

International Banking Act of 1978, Pub. Law 369, 95th Congress, 2nd Session

Peat, Marwick, Mitchell and Co., *Establishing an Office of a Foreign Bank in the United States: A Guide for Foreign Banks*, 2nd edn (New York, 1977)

Pierce, James L., 'The FINE Study', *Journal of Money Credit and Banking* (November 1977)

Schmidt, C. E., 'U.S. Banking – The Regulators Attack', *Euromoney* (July 1978)

Scott, Kenneth E., 'The Dual Banking System: A Model of Competition in Regulation', *Stanford Law Review* (November 1977)

Subcommittee on Financial Institutions Supervision, Regulation and Insurance, of the Committee on Banking, Currency and Housing, *Financial Institutions and the Nation's Economy*, Discussion Principles Hearings and Report, 94th Congress, 1975 and 1976.

5 CONCLUSION

It has been the intention of this study to take a modern view of the form and scope of banking. We began with the problem of identifying the nature of banking and considered that this was appropriately described as the retailing of services. In order to consider the effects of regulation, we began with a model of a bank operating in an unregulated environment, which provided a simplified description of the operations of a bank. Next, we investigated the main regulatory constraints imposed in nineteen countries, and derived from this the main forms used and certain combinations preferred by monetary authorities. It was seen that the quantity restrictions were the most critical for domestic banks when placed in our model (as well as empirically) and this was seen to offer some impetus to diversification both domestically and internationally.

The multinational spread of banks may be described as a diversification away from the influence of domestic regulation, so that a multinational bank is more able than is a domestic bank to maintain stable flows of funds over time, with a favourable effect on profit levels.

More recently, there have been moves internationally and nationally to regulate or constrain multinational bank operations. It is argued that some form of prudential supervision or equivalent voluntary scheme would remove doubts about the continued viability of certain multinational enterprises to the benefit of multinational banks as a group.

Of more serious concern still are certain moves to 'domesticate' multinational banks. The nationalistic provisions of the recent Canadian Bank Act go a fair distance towards forcing foreign banks in Canada to accept domestic fluctuations without allowing them much room to diversify away from these externally. The ultimate result of this approach if taken much further is that foreign banks will be merely domestic banks with a small foreign equity, and funds flows determined largely by Canadian monetary policy.

The US approach, predicated as it is on the principle of reciprocity, does appear to allow the survival of multinational banks as a non-domestic form of banking.

The danger of the Canadian type of approach is that multinational banks will lose their distinctive characteristics by being unable to spread their operations over a number of countries and by being forced to operate as domestic banks within each economy. On the other hand, the US type of approach, as reflected in the International Banking Act, allows the multinational banks to maintain many of their advantages, while subjecting them to regulation which assists rather than deters their operations.

It is apparent that a more serious risk for multinational bank operations would be provided if supervisory authorities elected to use price constraints, rather than quantity constraints, as their prime regulatory mechanism. In the absence of such a move the survival of multinational banking appears assured.

EPILOGUE

In this book a blend of theory and empirical analysis has been used to examine the progressive development of commercial banking from the completely unregulated bank to the regulated domestic bank, and then to international and multinational banking and the proposals for regulating the multinational banks. To escape from the nationalistic bias with which most of the literature examines the forms of regulation and the effects of policy on banks, Part 1 was concerned with the development of a model of a bank as a retailer of banking services that is independent of country. Because banking has within our lifetimes virtually always been the subject of regulation, it is conceivable that a number of banking practices may have arisen in response to regulation and might not have come into existence if banking had not been regulated.

By offering a model of a bank as a retailer of banking services, which is preferred to the alternative models of banks as pure portfolio managers or as producers, it is not intended to exclude entirely the use of portfolio theory or production theory in the analysis of banking operations. Rather it is suggested that more of the characteristics of more commercial banks are explicable by the use of the retailing paradigm than by either of the other two theories. Where the right environmental conditions exist, a bank may only offer the services of a portfolio manager, but, while these may be of some importance within a large and integrated financial sector such as exists in the United States, it is a much less appropriate paradigm for the banks operating in the other countries considered in this study. The retailing of services paradigm allows us to consider all of the various forms of speciality and also of universal banking that may be identified within these countries.

Within the development of the model of the unregulated bank, which is a modification of Fischer Black's world of uncontrolled banking, the effective limits of market structure are identified as taking the form of two constraints on the scale of operations. One of the difficult elements in specifying these limits to market structure is to take account of evidence supporting economies of scale in financial intermediation and in banking. There is sufficient evidence, it seems, to justify the case made that the economies of scale gained by being large are a strong barrier to the entry of new, smaller banks. This also explains why, if banks of sufficient size to gain those economies elect to provide all financial services, there would be no way that other firms could enter and provide the same services, unless they were instantaneously able to operate at the same scale, which they cannot do if the existing banks are satisfying their customers. The tendency to oligopoly will be reinforced by these considerations.

As it is intended in introducing regulation into the model to draw on features of banking regulation in many countries without being tied to any one country's package, a necessary prelude to this introduction is provided in Part 2's survey of the impact of regulation on the domestic banks of nineteen countries and within a united Europe. From this survey we are able to identify the main individual types of banking constraints used and a number of the most frequently used combinations of regulations.

For each of the countries surveyed an outline of the institutional framework within which the banks operate is provided, a description of the instruments of regulation used, a discussion of the recent experience of controls and a brief commentary on the effects of recent changes on the operation of individual banks. It is evident from this survey that there has been no consistent pattern along which domestic banking regulations in these countries have moved in the present decade. The failure of a pattern to develop is partly accounted for by the varying levels of development of money and finance markets in these economies. For many of the European economies their experience with 'hot' money flows has left them relatively unimpressed with the efficiency of indirect controls and has persuaded them to return to more direct controls. Credit ceilings have proved quite efficient in some small open economies and of minimal use in others. Some interesting contrasts are revealed. For example Australia has moved to increase its indirect controls, especially open-market operations, and New Zealand has moved from a rather restrictive regulatory system to permitting its banks wide scope in their liquidity management, while virtually at the same time West Germany has all but eliminated the ability of its banks to manage their liquidity.

A further reason for the lack of a consistent pattern is that not only does the environment in which banking operates differ among countries, but the services provided and the sectors in which most business is done are sharply contrasting in a number of countries. The West German 'universal bank' provides perhaps the widest range of services, but in several countries banks have been active in much broader activities than merely accepting deposits and providing loans. It is this variety which justifies further the defining of banks as retailers of services. The pattern of services provided depends on the environment within which the banks operate, which accords with the retail paradigm that the products or services marketed should be those that the retailer believes will be demanded by the market, subject to regulations restricting his right to supply certain services or to satisfy certain needs completely at various times.

In Part 3 we introduced the main types and combinations of regulatory constraints, which were found to be in use from the survey undertaken in Part 2, into the model developed in Part 1. Comparing the operations of a bank in the unregulated and regulated states, we are able to see some of the effects of regulation. An unregulated bank's main difficulties were seen to be uncertainty about its funds flows, the assessment of risk on loans and the maintenance of a prudent level of liquid reserves. Positive effects of regulation are: reducing the risk of bankruptcy and, where there are maximum interest rate ceilings, allowing the bank to limit its loans to the level for which the ceiling rate is equal to the rate it would have charged under unregulated conditions.

The main impacts of regulation are shown to be reducing the bank's potential for maximising profit and reducing the possibility of price competition between the banks. As a consequence of regulation banks are likely to decline to service the demands of the riskier classes of borrower, which allows the introduction of non-bank financial intermediaries to satisfy those needs. The presence of new intermediaries will provide competition for bank deposits and encourage the banks to expand their range of services to retain their depositors. This strategy is further encouraged because a relatively higher level of deposits and loans must be reached under regulatory conditions to overcome the take-over constraint.

The case for non-price competition and product augmentation is strengthened with the reduction of the possibility of price competition, and this switch in strategy raises the costs of banking services because of the 'lock-in' effect of non-price competition. To that point it was assumed that regulation of banks was effective, but it is necessary to examine whether the banks may avoid the intended impact of regulation in the light of Fischer Black's allegation that 'it is relatively easy to get around most of the regulations that are applied to banks'.

It is argued that in general terms the wholesale evasion by banks of regulatory constraints where possible offers, at best, very short-run advantages, and these gains are more easily achieved and persist longer if they are achieved by diversification rather than by evasion. Of the range of constraints, the restriction of the credit base is the most effective weapon. However, it must be noted that the stated purpose of most bank regulation is to influence rather than to formally control bank operations, and in many countries public knowledge of the imminent or actual variation of constraints is sufficient to modify public demand for credit. Further, even if individual constraints may be evaded or their effects minimised, the business of a bank is likely to be reduced by a domestic contraction.

While a bank, like other businesses, may have a plethora of justifications for diversification, the impact of regulation on domestic banks may most commonly be seen in a diversification domestically away from pure banking overseas and away from regulation.

Consistent with our earlier discussion of banking as the retailing of services, it can be seen that both domestic and multinational diversification involves the provision of additional services in response to demand. It is quite inadequate to regard multinational banks as merely the original domestic bank operating similarly in more countries, and, accordingly, in Part 4 we examined the nature and practice of multinational banking. The foreign expansion of a country's banks has normally occurred in order to service the increasing demand for overseas services by their domestic customers, but the type of overseas operation preferred by particular domestic banks has depended on their own experience in international transactions, and the timing of the move and the extent of the overseas spread have been mainly influenced by domestic restrictions.

Domestic banks with little previous international exposure have often used the consortium bank as a means of participating in multinational operations. The nature of multinational banking operations, whether conducted by a consortium or other forms of banks, involves risks that are different to those of purely domestic banks and a detailed examination was therefore made of these risks, which are instanced most clearly by bank operations within the Euromarkets. As activities within the Euromarkets are the focus of present moves towards prudential regulation, to which purely domestic banks are already subject, it was thought that examining the main aspects of these operations would provide a useful base from which to consider, in Part 5, the prudential regulation of multinational banks.

From the discussion of roll-over risk and mismatching we concluded that neither of these elements appears to be of critical concern to those banks which are the core of the market, but may be of importance to those on the periphery. Of more importance for all multinational banks, not only those operating within the Euromarkets, are the several aspects of foreign exchange risk – banking risk, currency risk, country risk and sovereign risk. In a brief diagrammatic illustration of multinational bank operations we examined the relative importance of roll-over and interest rate risk, and foreign exchange risk within the context of one market and two currencies. We conclude from this survey of the nature of multinational banking that regulations which affect the quantity of deposits and/or loans may be used on multinational banks with much the same result as on domestic banks, that is, to limit the extent to which they are able to satisfy demand, but, in contrast, the implementation of controls affecting the cost and pricing of loans may have much more serious consequences for the banks and threaten the now only occasionally precarious stability of the multinational banking system.

With this background, we examined in Part 5 the supervision and regulation of multinational banking. Three separate aspects of the operations of multinational banks have given rise to demands for their control: the offshore location of consortium banks or of subsidiaries of banks domiciled elsewhere in countries where regulatory control of banking does not meet the main European or American standards of control or solvency and liquidity requirements; those features particularly instanced by but not confined to banks operating in the Euromarkets, that is, foreign exchange losses, capital adequacy, the quality and country structure of lending, among others; and the operation of foreign banks alongside domestic banks when the latter are subject to regulatory controls from which the former are either partially or wholly exempt.

Most discussion of these issues has tended to confuse prudential supervision with regulatory constraint, and care has been taken therefore to distinguish between them in this Part. Clearly some form of prudential supervision or equivalent voluntary scheme would remove doubts about the risk of inadequate flows of funds, often regarded as a major source of risk in multinational banking. In the chapter on prudential supervision a form of reinsurance type guarantee is proposed as a means by which the banks themselves could voluntarily achieve this result, and official moves to prudential supervision in the UK, US and EEC are discussed. Universal prudential supervisory controls appear to be unlikely and it is suggested that in its own interests the multinational banking community ought to introduce a scheme such as the one outlined here to remove doubts about the continued viability of certain multinational banks.

In the remainder of Part 5 we discussed recent moves to impose regulatory controls on multinational banks. Four approaches have been used: do nothing; adopt a restrictive approach to foreign banks; equalise regulatory treatment for foreign and domestic banks; and lessen some restrictions on domestic banks to enable them to compete more effectively with foreign banks.

The Canadian Bank Act is a move to 'domesticate' multinational banks that operate within its borders and goes a fair distance towards forcing foreign banks operating in Canada to accept domestic Canadian fluctuations, without allowing them much room to diversify away from these externally. A danger of this restrictive approach taken to its logical conclusion is that foreign banks will become simply domestic banks with a small foreign equity and with funds flows determined almost entirely by Canadian monetary policy.

Within the United States all four approaches to the regulation of multinational banks have been suggested, analysed and discussed. The 'do nothing' approach, which was reflected in US policy until quite recently, was alleged to have caused a major structural change within the US banking system as foreign bank US assets grew at almost five times the rate of assets of US domestic banks. An obvious reaction to this was seen in the proposals for legislation to restrict the operations of foreign banks within the United States. However, it was equally clear that very restrictive limits imposed on foreign banking operations within the US would be likely to result in similar restrictions being imposed on US banks operating abroad.

The International Banking Act 1978 was essentially a compromise between these two views, with the influence of the reciprocity principle being sufficiently strong for the Act to allow the survival of multinational banks as a non-domestic form of banking. It has the benefit of allowing them to maintain many of their advantages while subjecting them to regulation which assists rather than deters their operations. The US approach allows the survival of multinational banks as a non-domestic form of banking, while by comparison the Canadian approach prejudices that survival.

Nevertheless, a more serious danger remains apparent from Part 4's analysis which is not approached in any of the regulatory proposals and enactments advanced thus far, and that is whether the supervisory authorities will elect to use price or quantity constraints as their prime regulatory mechanism. In the light of our earlier analysis, which suggests that price constraints pose a serious risk to the continued viability of multinational banks in their present form but that quantity constraints do not pose a similar threat, care should be taken in the application of regulation to ensure that it assists rather than diminishes the viability of these enterprises. One of the advantages of multinational banks has been their ability to maintain stable flows of funds over time. It would be unfortunate if regulation was able to eliminate that advantage altogether.

For order to be attained in the supervision of multinational banking, it is important that a consistent system of prudential control be devised (whether voluntary or imposed) and that discretionary regulations consistent with the survival of multinational banks in their non-domestic form be applied. A failure to achieve these ends may create much more instability in the multinational banking sector than has occurred while they have been comparatively unregulated.

INDEX

For Product Safety Concerns and Information please contact our EU
representative GPSR@taylorandfrancis.com Taylor & Francis Verlag GmbH,
Kaufingerstraße 24, 80331 München, Germany

Printed and bound by CPI Group (UK) Ltd, Croydon, CR0 4YY
08/05/2025
01864504-0001